# Vocational Education and Training Reform

*Matching Skills to Markets and Budgets*

A Joint Study of
THE WORLD BANK
and
THE INTERNATIONAL LABOUR OFFICE

# Vocational Education and Training Reform

## Matching Skills to Markets and Budgets

*Edited by*

Indermit S. Gill

Fred Fluitman

*and*

Amit Dar

Published for the World Bank

OXFORD UNIVERSITY PRESS

*Oxford University Press*

Oxford  New York  Athens  Auckland  Bangkok  Bogota  Buenos Aires
Calcutta  Cape Town  Chennai  Dar es Salaam  Delhi  Florence  Hong Kong
Istanbul  Karachi  Kuala Lumpur  Madrid  Melbourne  Mexico City  Mumbai
Nairobi  Paris  São Paulo  Singapore  Taipei  Tokyo  Toronto  Warsaw

and associated companies in

Berlin  Ibadan

Published by Oxford University Press, Inc.
198 Madison Avenue, New York, N.Y. 10016

Manufactured in the United States of America
First printing March 2000

1 2 3 4 5 03 02 01 00

**Library of Congress Cataloging-in-Publication Data**

Vocational education and training reform : matching skills to markets and budgets /
    edited by Indermit S. Gill, Fred Fluitman, Amit Dar.
        p. cm.
    Includes bibliographical references.
    ISBN 0-19-521590-7
    1. Vocational education—Economic aspects. 2. Occupational training—Economic
aspects. I. Gill, Indermit Singh, 1961– II. Fluitman, Fred. III. Dar, Amit.

LC1044 .V62 2000
331.25′92—dc21

99-044096

# Contents

v

# Tables, Figures, and Boxes

## Tables

## Chapter 2 Poland

## Chapter 3 Czech Republic

## Chapter 4 Russian Federation

## Chapter 5 Kazakhstan

## Chapter 6 China

*Chapter 9 Republic of Korea*

*Chapter 10 Chile*

*Chapter 11 Mexico*

*Chapter 12 South Africa*

*Chapter 13 Tanzania*

## Chapter 14 Zambia

## Chapter 15 Arab Republic of Egypt

## Chapter 16 Jordan

## Figures

## Boxes

# Foreword

In 1991 THE World Bank, with International Labour Office (ILO) contributions, published its policy paper on Vocational Education and Training (VET). Since that time, the experience of reform of VET in both poor and rapidly growing countries has pointed to new directions in making skills more relevant for economies in which private sector employment has grown increasingly dominant. In addition, the problems of VET in transition countries in Eastern Europe and Central Asia have come to occupy the attention of the World Bank. Both the ILO and World Bank have been monitoring VET reform in recent years, including in transition economies, where the World Bank is a relative newcomer while the ILO has longstanding expertise.

This book builds on the fruitful cooperation between the two institutions at the policy as well as the operations level. VET policy experts at both the World Bank and ILO participated equally in every aspect of this study. *Vocational Education and Training Reform: Matching Skills to Markets and Budgets* perhaps has the distinction of being the first joint study of the two institutions at the global level.

For years vocational education and training policy has been hotly debated, and it continues to stimulate impassioned discussions in all parts of the world. The debate concerns both costs and relevance and this book, aptly subtitled *Matching Skills to Markets and Budgets*, gets to the heart of these issues. It does so in an analytic rather than prescriptive manner, it eschews broad generalizations in favor of insightful country-specific analysis, but it still draws lessons that most countries would do well to heed. We hope that the information presented here stimulates further research and that the policy lessons engender useful change.

Robert Holzmann
Director, Social Protection
Human Development Network
The World Bank
Washington, DC

Maria Angélica Ducci
Director, Bureau for
External Relations and Partnerships
The International Labour Office
Geneva

# Acknowledgments

WE ARE GRATEFUL TO MANY PERSONS in the World Bank and the International Labour Office for making this book a reality. In particular we would like to thank Jane Armitage and Maria Angélica Ducci, without whose encouragement this project would never have gotten off the ground, and Robert Holzmann and Steen Lau Jorgenson, without whose guidance the project would never have been completed. For their help we are also grateful to Arvil Van Adams, K. Y. Amoako, Joseph Bredie, Nat Colletta, Peter Fallon, David Fretwell, Ishrat Husain, John Middleton, Peter Moock, and others at the World Bank and the ILO. Estela Kinyon cheerfully tolerated our emergency requests on budget-related matters. Cristina Perez quickly put the book into shape for an editorial committee review. David Lakshmanan provided assistance in responding to the helpful reviews by three anonymous referees. Alice Dowsett and Jenepher Moseley provided excellent editorial support in the initial stages, and Barbara de Boinville expertly edited the entire volume in an efficient manner. Cynthia Stock designed the book, and Mark Ingebretsen and Thaisa Tiglao assisted with production. Finally, we are thankful to Donald Reisman and Nicola Marrian of the World Bank's Publications Department for giving us balanced and wise advice that prompted a final effort to improve the substance and form of the book.

# Abbreviations
# and Acronyms

| | |
|---|---|
| ANTA | Australian National Training Authority |
| BIBB | Federal Institute for Vocational Training (Germany) |
| CECATI | Industrial training center (Mexico) |
| CIMO | Total Quality and Modernization Program |
| CONALEP | National College of Professional Technical Education (Mexico) |
| DDIT | Double Deduction Incentive for Training (Malaysia) |
| DTEVT | Department of Technical Education and Vocational Training (Zambia) |
| EF | Employment Fund (Hungary) |
| FES | Federal Employment Service (Russian Federation) |
| GDP | Gross domestic product |
| GNP | Gross national product |
| HRDF | Human Resource Development Fund (Malaysia) |
| IKK | Army training center (Malaysia) |
| IKM | Institute Kemahiran Mara (Malaysia) |
| ILO | International Labour Office |
| ITB | Industrial training boards (South Africa) |
| ITI | Industrial training institute (Malaysia) |

| | |
|---|---|
| KOMA | Korea Manpower Agency |
| MIDA | Malaysian Industrial Development Authority |
| MITP Survey | Malaysia Industrial Training and Productivity Survey |
| NEDLAC | National Economic Development and Labour Council (South Africa) |
| NTB | National Training Board (South Africa) |
| NVTC | National Vocational Training Council (Malaysia) |
| OECD | Organization for Economic Cooperation and Development |
| PROBECAT | Labor Retraining Program for Unemployed Workers (Mexico) |
| PVTD | Productivity and Vocational Training Department (Arab Republic of Egypt) |
| R&D | Research and development |
| RTC | Regional Training Center (Hungary) |
| RTCs | Regional training centers (South Africa) |
| SIDA | Swedish International Development Authority |
| SOE | State-owned enterprise |
| STS | Secondary technical school |
| SVS | Secondary vocational school |
| SWS | Skilled workers' school |
| TAFE | Technical and further education |
| TOMOHAR | Training Organization of the Ministry of Housing and Reconstruction (Arab Republic of Egypt) |
| VET | Vocational education and training |
| VETA | Vocational Education and Training Authority (Tanzania) |
| VTC | Vocational Training Corporation (Jordan) |
| VTE | Vocational and technical education |
| VTF | Vocational Training Fund (Hungary) |
| VTS | Vocational/technical school |
| YTC | Youth training center (Malaysia) |

# Introduction

INDERMIT S. GILL, AMIT DAR,
AND FRED FLUITMAN

GOVERNMENTS OFTEN EXPECT their vocational education and training (VET) systems to perform feats that they would not expect from other systems such as general education. Governments have perceived an increased demand for training if the labor supply shows rapid growth, if employment grows quickly, or if unemployment increases significantly. They have called upon VET systems to help unemployed young people and older workers get jobs, to reduce the burden on higher education, to attract foreign investment, to ensure rapid growth of earnings and employment, to reduce the inequality of earnings between the rich and the poor, and so on. The list is disconcertingly long. These high expectations have resulted in heavy government involvement in VET, but the record has been disappointing. Both factors—exaggerated expectations and overly involved governments—are probably responsible for the disappointments that have plagued VET in many countries. Some countries now recognize that the government's role as a VET provider has been overemphasized. Others are slowly realizing that expectations of VET, even when the private sector and nongovernmental organizations have fully participated in provision, have been unreasonably high. This chapter traces the experience of countries in reforming their VET policies and summarizes the lessons learned.

## Previous Research by the World Bank

A research effort led by the World Bank that culminated in a policy paper (Middleton, Ziderman, and Adams 1993; World Bank 1991) emphasized that the dual goals of VET policies should be to encourage private provision and financing and to improve the efficiency of publicly provided VET. The basic approach the policy paper proposed was a two-step strategy. The first step involves addressing important non-VET problems—in particular, improving access to and the quality of general, especially basic, education; creating a regulatory framework that encourages investment in physical and human capital; and instituting macroeconomic policies that foster sustained output and employment growth. The second step entails the reform of VET by assessing VET policies and evaluating the supply of VET in relation to changing labor market demands, tailoring actions to country-specific situations, and building commitment and maintaining support for the implementation of policy reform.

In operationalizing this approach, countries face a number of constraints. Middleton, Ziderman, and Adams (1993) list the most important obstacles as inadequate financing of public VET systems, incomplete information on private training supply, fragmentation of VET systems, weak information links between training providers and employers, and weak institutional capacity. While spelling out the constraints to improving the efficiency and relevance of VET systems, they stop short of proposing strategies to overcome these obstacles. The timing of their research effort also precluded systematic analysis of the problems of formerly communist countries, whose transition gathered momentum during the 1990s.

## Scope and Sample

Based on the experiences of countries worldwide, this study examines the constraints they face in implementing VET and related policies; analyzes how some countries have successfully implemented reforms; and evaluates VET reforms in central and eastern Europe, the former Soviet Union, and other countries in transition to a market economy, such as China.

This chapter focuses on the obstacles to implementing change in response to changing labor markets as well as innovative approaches to overcoming these constraints. It introduces in summary fashion the results of studies of 16 countries and 2 territories: Hungary, Poland, the Czech Republic, the Russian Federation, Kazakhstan, China, Indonesia, Malaysia, the Republic of Korea, Chile, Mexico, South Africa, Tanzania, Zambia, Egypt, Jordan, and the West Bank and Gaza. They were selected to obtain a regional balance and to present a broad range of economic and labor market conditions (table 1). Moreover, these are places where the World

TABLE 1
General Characteristics of Sample Countries

| Country | Population (1995, millions) | Per capita income (1995, US$) | GDP growth rate (1990–95, percent) |
|---|---|---|---|
| Hungary | 10 | 4,120 | (1.0) |
| Poland | 39 | 2,790 | 2.4 |
| Czech Republic | 10 | 3,870 | (2.6) |
| Russian Federation | 148 | 2,240 | (9.8) |
| Kazakhstan | 17 | 1,330 | (11.9) |
| China | 1,200 | 620 | 12.8 |
| Indonesia | 193 | 980 | 7.6 |
| Malaysia | 20 | 3,890 | 8.7 |
| Korea, Rep. of | 45 | 9,700 | 7.2 |
| Chile | 14 | 4,160 | 7.3 |
| Mexico | 92 | 3,320 | 1.1 |
| South Africa | 41 | 3,160 | 0.6 |
| Tanzania | 30 | 120 | 3.2 |
| Zambia | 9 | 400 | (0.2) |
| Jordan | 4 | 1,510 | 8.2 |
| Egypt, Arab Rep. of | 58 | 790 | 1.3 |
| West Bank and Gaza | 2 | 1,750 | 0.0 |

*Note:* Numbers in parentheses are negative.
*Source:* World Bank (1997); for West Bank and Gaza: World Bank data.

Bank and the International Labour Office (ILO) have recently completed economic and sector studies. The results of two special papers—on the lessons of Australia's comprehensive VET reforms for and the applicability of Germany's dual system to low- and middle-income countries—are also discussed. Australia and Germany were chosen because their reforms have not been adequately analyzed, these countries are relatively new entrants to the role of international advocacy, and there are unresolved issues regarding the applicability of their training systems to developing countries.

Each of the 17 studies examined the labor market developments that determine the demand for VET, the supply response of the VET system, the problems that arise in matching demand and supply, and the major innovations in resolving these problems. Labor market analysis was restricted to labor regulations and indicators (labor supply, employment, unemployment, and wages) that are relevant to the demand for skilled and technical workers. VET supply responses were categorized into secondary and postsecondary vocational and technical education, pre-employment vocational training, and in-service or on-the-job training. The treatment of VET issues emphasizes the distinction between public and private management, financing, and provision. Innovations, defined as policies that efficiently or equitably match the supply of VET with labor market demands, are country specific, although some general lessons are drawn.

This chapter investigates both the demand-side pressures on VET systems, which can be viewed as the roots of reform, and the supply responses or the nature of reform. It also examines special issues that arise in the course of VET reform and draws some general conclusions based on the experience of the countries included in the World Bank–ILO study. Boxes provide country-specific examples. Note that while this chapter seeks to draw general conclusions, it does so only on the basis of the experience of the countries included in the World Bank–ILO study.

Given the complexity of this subject, the experience of particular countries may qualify, or even contradict, some of the general conclusions. Therefore, this chapter may be best viewed as an introduction to the country studies, which illustrate the uniqueness of experience in each country. We are confident, however, that careful interpretation of the experience of our sample countries will provide lessons that are applicable to most low- and middle-income countries.

## Demand-Side Pressures: The Roots of Reform

The sample countries can be classified into three groups according to their labor market characteristics. The first group has high labor-force growth, low employment growth, and consequently high unemployment and underemployment rates. These are relatively low-growth developing countries in Africa and the Middle East, represented here by South Africa, Tanzania, Zambia, Egypt, Jordan, and the West Bank and Gaza. The second group has high labor-force and employment growth and low unemployment rates. These are the emerging market countries of East Asia and Latin America, represented here by China, Indonesia, Malaysia, Korea, Chile, and Mexico.[1] The third group consists of those countries with low labor-force growth, low employment growth, and high unemployment rates. These are countries that are in transition to a market economy, represented here by Hungary, Poland, the Czech Republic, the Russian Federation, and Kazakhstan (table 2 and figure 1).[2]

## FIGURE 1
### Labor Market Characteristics of Sample Countries

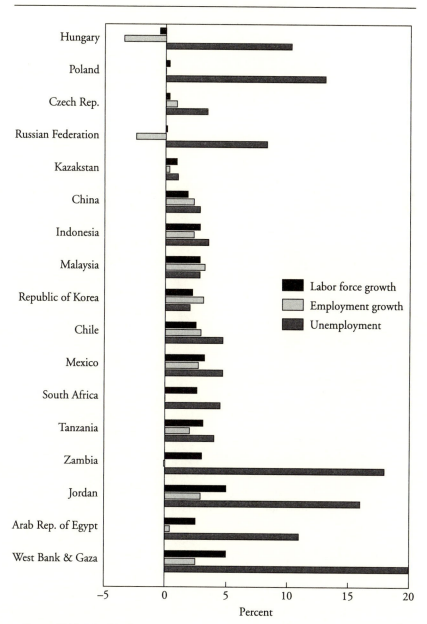

*Source:* Table 2 in this chapter.

TABLE 2
Growth in the Labor Supply, Employment,
and Unemployment, Selected Years
(percent)

| Country | Labor force (1980–95) | Employment (1986–95) | Unemployment (1995) |
|---|---|---|---|
| Hungary | (0.5) | (3.4) | 10.3 |
| Poland | 0.3 | 0.0 | 13.1 |
| Czech Republic | 0.3 | 0.9 | 3.4 |
| Russian Federation | 0.1 | (2.4) | 8.3 |
| Kazakhstan | 0.9 | 0.3 | 1.0 |
| China | 1.8 | 2.3 | 2.8 |
| Indonesia | 2.8 | 2.3 | 3.5 |
| Malaysia | 2.8 | 3.2 | 2.8 |
| Korea, Rep. of | 2.2 | 3.1 | 2.0 |
| Chile | 2.5 | 2.9 | 4.7 |
| Mexico | 3.2 | 2.7 | 4.7 |
| South Africa | 2.6 | 0.0 | 4.5 |
| Tanzania | 3.1 | 2.0[a] | 4.0 |
| Zambia | 3.0 | (0.1) | 18.0 |
| Jordan | 5.0 | 2.9 | 16.0 |
| Egypt | 2.5 | 0.4 | 11.0 |
| West Bank and Gaza | 5.0 | 2.5[a] | 20.0 |

a. Estimate.
*Note:* Numbers in parentheses are negative.
*Source:* ILO (1996).

An examination of the main labor market indicators—especially labor force growth, employment and wage growth, and unemployment rates—reveals the demand-side pressures on VET systems to change. The studies show that there are common patterns in the manner in which countries react to these pressures, but some countries have resorted to more innovative measures.

## Pressures Caused by High Labor-Force Growth

Large numbers of labor force entrants pose a problem for policymakers when public employment growth is no longer feasible and private employment growth is sluggish. Countries such as Egypt, Tanzania, and Zambia have responded to labor supply pressures by expanding formal public education and training systems and absorbing their graduates into government employment. With the reduction in government employment and the growth of the informal sector, the demand for and supply of skills are mismatched.[3] This results in the VET system, which is largely formal, and irrelevant in the increasingly informal world of work. For example, formally trained workers constituted between 50 and 80 percent of entrants into Egypt's construction sector in the 1970s and 1980s, but they accounted for only 5 percent of employment in the 1990s. In Tanzania, where less than 10 percent of employment is in the formal sector, graduates of public training institutions have found only informal employment since government employment began to decline in the late 1980s.

Because secondary school graduates face poor employment prospects in countries where education systems are government run and financed, demand for higher education can become bloated. Some countries have responded by rationing places in colleges and universities. The secondary vocational track is usually the main instrument for this rationing. In Egypt, for example, only general secondary school graduates are eligible for admission to fully subsidized universities, and the vocational track has swelled to include almost 70 percent of secondary enrollment. Of course, this has done nothing to rectify labor market imbalances: the Egyptian VET system supplies five to seven times the required number of skilled workers. However, the unsustainable financial burden of maintaining a large public VET system has resulted in a deterioration of quality to the point where it supplies at best semiskilled workers.

More effective responses to these pressures involve non-VET measures. Countries that introduced cost sharing in higher education have kept enrollments down, while not expanding vocational enrollments unnecessarily. Jordan, for example, expects university students to pay about one-third of the costs in the form of fees, a level closer to that in countries such as Chile and Korea. By contrast, Egypt, Tanzania, and Zambia recover less than 5 percent of costs from college students. Obviously, the pressures to absorb a growing number of young job seekers are most effectively met by improving their employment prospects. With a rapidly growing labor force and poor employment growth, Malaysia faced a similar situation in the early 1980s. It emphasized primary and general secondary education (only 11 percent of secondary school enrollment is in vocational education) and growth-oriented economic policies. As a result, employment growth outstripped the growth of the labor supply in the late 1980s and 1990s.

## Pressures Caused by High Employment Growth

Rapid employment growth can create problems, too. In the export-oriented East Asian and Latin American economies, the supply of skilled workers and technicians has occasionally fallen short of demand despite increasing wages. In Malaysia during 1986–94, only a small fraction of the rising wage gap between skilled and unskilled workers was attributable to differential demand elasticity; technical and skilled workers had smaller supply elasticities than did semiskilled and unskilled workers. In Korea unfilled vacancies for skilled workers as a share of employment grew from 2 to 7 percent between 1980 and 1991. In China shortages of skilled workers emerged following rapid growth over the past decade as a result of the pressures to improve competitiveness and adopt modern technologies. The demand for professionals and technically and manually skilled workers is growing faster than supply. This imbalance may be exacerbated because some state enterprises continue to hoard such workers. Since trade liberalization in the 1980s, Chile has becoming increasingly concerned about increased inequality in labor earnings between skilled and unskilled workers because of a relative scarcity of the former.

Improving the supply responses for these skill categories requires reforms in the VET system. Korea's VET system appears to have responded well to high growth in demand. While all workers experienced increases in real wages between 1975 and 1993, the ratio of wages of professionals and technicians to those of semiskilled and unskilled workers fell from 2.5 to 1.5. The expansion of private pre-employment education and training in Indonesia led to a significant narrowing of wage differentials between unskilled and skilled workers before the current crisis. Chile's success in expanding access to secondary and postsecondary vocational education may partially explain the decline in earnings inequality between 1987 and 1996.

Upgrading workers' skills is an important concern in these countries. With rapidly changing demands for ever more sophisticated skills, enterprises are increasingly expected to supply their own training. Although this avenue is largely free of the problems of mismatch between the demand for and the supply of training, governments feel pressured to intervene because of longer-term growth and equity considerations. The most important question here is whether firms should be coerced or encouraged to provide even more in-service training to workers. Firm-level data from Indonesia, Malaysia (box 1), and Mexico show that firms are more likely to train workers when these firms are large, employ an educated work force, and invest in technological change (Tan and Batra 1995).

## BOX 1
### Determinants of Enterprise Training in Malaysia

Malaysia's manufacturing sector has experienced rapid employment and productivity growth. A 1994 survey of 2,200 firms indicates that formal training is not widespread: 33 percent of firms provide no training, 50 percent rely on informal training, and only 17 percent provide formal training. The likelihood of formal training rises with firm size but is not universal, even in large firms. Employers are more likely to train more educated workers. The survey cites the following reasons for not training: mature technology, high training costs, lack of information about training sources, and the availability of skilled workers from schools and other firms.

A scheme allowing a double deduction for investments in training has not succeeded in increasing training and has now been reduced in scope. The main beneficiaries have been large multinationals, which would have provided training anyway, and smaller firms were often unaware of the scheme. A new levy-rebate scheme appears to be more successful in increasing training, but it is too recent to be evaluated. Although the scheme is efficiently managed, small firms exhibit significant noncompliance.

The most common external sources for employer-sponsored training are private providers: 35 percent of firms that train use private training institutes, 25 percent use joint-venture skill development centers, and 20 percent use advanced public institutes. The least popular sources are public youth training centers and vocational and technical schools.

*Source*: Malaysia chapter in this volume.

## Pressures Caused by High Open Unemployment

As a legacy of their communist past, many transitional countries were handicapped by narrow wage differentials across skill levels. The move to a market economy has resulted in increasing returns to schooling. In Hungary the rate of return to general secondary education increased 12 to 19 percent. In Poland and the Czech Republic wage differentials across skill levels have also widened, which is a welcome development in these countries, because it improves private incentives to acquire and pay for education and training.

Rising unemployment and falling real wages are the most visible and costly aspects of transition. Long-term unemployment is particularly pernicious, and governments are using active labor programs, especially retraining, to address this problem. Little reliable information about the effectiveness of these programs is available, since they have not been rigorously evaluated, even in most countries of the Organization for Economic Cooperation and Development (OECD) except the United States (Dar and Gill 1998). In large part the problem is a fall in labor demand in the formal sector. In Poland, for example, the number of unemployed for each vacancy increased from 13 in 1990 to 87 in 1993. However, as the skill mix required has changed, mismatches between workers and jobs arise. For instance, Russian industry has shed clerical and professional staff, but job growth has been mainly for manual and production work. Evaluations of retraining programs in Hungary reveal that some workers do benefit from training, and curriculum reform in schools has resulted in better worker-firm matches, but not all mismatches can be rectified through VET. In Russia, for example, most vacancies have been for manual and physically demanding jobs, but unemployment is worse for women than for men. Training may not result in reduced unemployment of women until industry has restructured sufficiently, which may take many years.

The Czech Republic has dealt with the problem of a fall in formal sector activity during the transition to a market economy in a relatively innovative manner. A large component of the reduction in employment between 1990 and 1995 was countered by pushing or keeping people out of the labor force, and reducing the incentives to stay unemployed. The Czech Republic relied more on early retirement schemes and reduced levels and stricter eligibility rules for unemployment benefits. Training programs have been kept small. The number of new job seekers was kept temporarily low by increasing enrollments in and the length of vocational education programs. Poland and Russia have also expanded vocational education in schools. However, the success of this approach depends critically on the success of policies to encourage employment growth: the Czech Republic appears to be alone in both encouraging private sector job creation and increasing the incentives for job seekers to accept employment at relatively modest wage levels (box 2).

All the transitional countries have experienced large increases in the share of private employment despite labor hoarding in public enterprises. In Poland, while total employment fell by 2.6 million between 1989 and 1995, private employment grew by 2 million. During the same period in the Czech Republic, private employment as a share of the total rose from 1 percent to 64 percent. By 1994 more than 60 percent of Russia's industrial

## BOX 2
### Reform of Unemployment Benefit Legislation and Outflows to Jobs in Transition Economies

Reform of labor laws can have immediate effects on employment and unemployment rates. Shown below are outflows from registered unemployment in four transitional countries following the tightening of eligibility for unemployment benefits and reductions in their size and duration. In all countries this resulted in increased outflows from unemployment and (except in Poland) increases in wage employment in registered jobs. Although some of the outflows reflect exit from the labor force, many workers are going into informal unregistered employment.

| Country | Reform period | Outflow from unemployment | | Filled vacancies | |
|---|---|---|---|---|---|
| | | Before | After | Before | After |
| Czech Republic | 1/91–5/93 | 7.0 | 23.4 | 11.0 | 16.5 |
| Slovak Republic | 12/90–6/93 | 5.1 | 9.4 | 3.5 | 4.7 |
| Hungary | 4/91–4/92 | 6.2 | 8.0 | 3.4 | 3.8 |
| Poland | 1/92–3/93 | — | 4.3 | 2.5 | 2.2 |

— Not available.

*Note:* In all four countries, the main changes in regulations were announced in January 1992. Outflows from unemployment and vacancies are monthly flows as a ratio of unemployed stock.

*Source:* Gill and Dar (1995).

The Czech Republic had the sharpest change in legislation and experienced the most favorable changes in unemployment and employment. After February 1991 unemployed workers were ineligible for benefits and severance pay if they became redundant because of organizational change, double payments of severance pay and unemployment benefits were stopped in 1992, and the amount of income allowed while receiving unemployment benefits was reduced. Low open unemployment (that is, registered unemployment) has allowed the Czech Republic to keep the size of public training programs, which are expensive and at best modestly effective, small.

*Source:* Country studies in this volume.

work force was employed in privatized enterprises, and in Kazakhstan the private sector had grown to more than one-third of employment. Even in China the share of urban private employment has doubled since 1990 to 14 percent.

This change in the clientele of the VET system has spelled trouble for vocational schools, many of which were traditionally attached to enterprises. In Russia, faced with declining overall employment, these institutions have become less specialized. They now offer training in 10 to 15 occupations instead of 3 to 5 as in the past and have shifted from technical disciplines such as instrument making and machining to service sector–oriented training such as law and economics. In areas of high employment growth, similar institutions in China have diversified their clientele to include programs catering to the specific skill demands of private enterprises.

## Supply-Side Responses: The Nature of Reform

Drawing the sectoral boundaries of VET is difficult. Within each country, VET is managed by a number of public agencies. It is financed both by the government and by the private sector and provided by schools, training institutions, and on the job. While this multiplicity of financiers and providers can be beneficial, the government has traditionally dominated the sector. Therefore, VET supply in many countries is not characterized by competition but by fragmentation. Several ministries often manage similar training programs, leading to duplication of public provision and to the crowding out of private supply that would be forthcoming.

Because skills can be provided in a wide range of settings, and because of the multiplicity of providers, dividing VET supply into subsectors is not easy.[4] Nevertheless, it is useful to think of it as consisting of three parts: vocational and technical education that is part of the formal schooling cycle; pre-employment vocational training, which is usually outside the schooling cycle; and in-service training for workers provided in or outside the workplace. This distinction is used throughout this chapter and in all the country studies.

### Organization and Management of the VET Sector

The main government agencies involved in the management of VET are the ministries of education and labor, although other ministries usually play an important role. In our sample countries, ministries of education invariably managed vocational and technical education with the exception of Zambia (table 3). In general, multiplicity of management is not a problem for this subsector, but in a few cases—generally countries where large public enterprises managed the vocational schools that supplied them with workers—ministries of labor and industry were also involved. Egypt, where more than eight ministries manage their own vocational and technical schools, is the extreme case in this regard. In some countries the nongovernmental organization (NGO) sector is also becoming a significant player in the management and delivery of vocational education. In Hungary, for example, about 90 foundations deliver secondary vocational school education.

Ministries of labor usually oversee vocational training outside the formal school cycle. The exceptions are Jordan, where it is under the purview of the ministry of education, and Kazakhstan and Zambia, where the responsibility lies with other ministries. Responsibility for pre-employment training, compared with school-based vocational education, is somewhat more dispersed. An increasing recent trend is the involvement of tripartite bodies of employers, government representatives, and individuals in the management and provision of vocational training.

The responsibility for in-service training is considerably more dispersed across ministries. In about half of the sample countries, this responsibility lies with the ministry of labor, and in about half other ministries are responsible. The ministry of education rarely plays a role in managing in-service training: only in the Czech Republic is the ministry of education responsible for accrediting training providers if they wish to award recognized certificates. The management of these subsystems determines how they are used. Ministries of education may use vocational education in schools to keep students out of higher education, for which they are also responsible. Ministries of labor often provide training courses to unemployed workers who are eligible for unemployment benefits. Ministries of planning or finance sometimes view in-service training as a way to increase investment and growth.

## Vocational and Technical Education

Vocational education is distinguished from general education by its higher cost of delivery, especially at the secondary level, and by the options it opens or closes at the secondary and postsecondary levels. In Tanzania, for example, the unit costs of vocational education are twice those of general secondary education. To meet these higher costs, Chile's per student subsi-

TABLE 3
Management of VET Systems

| Subsector | Ministry of Education[a] | Ministry of Labor | Other agencies[b] |
|---|---|---|---|
| Vocational and technical education | Czech Republic, Hungary, Poland, Russian Federation, Kazakhstan, China, Rep. of Korea, Indonesia, Malaysia, Chile, Mexico, South Africa, Tanzania, Egypt, Jordan, West Bank and Gaza | Hungary, Mexico | Czech Republic, Kazakhstan, Zambia, Egypt |
| Pre-employment training and retraining | Indonesia, Mexico, Jordan | Czech Republic, Hungary, Poland,[c] Russian Federation, China, Rep. of Korea, Indonesia, Malaysia, Chile, Mexico, South Africa, Tanzania, Egypt, West Bank and Gaza | Hungary,[c] Kazakhstan, Malaysia,[c] Zambia,[c] Egypt |
| In-plant training | Czech Republic | Czech Republic, Poland,[c] Russian Federation, Kazakhstan, Rep. of Korea, Indonesia, Chile, Mexico, Tanzania, Jordan, West Bank and Gaza | Hungary,[c] Kazakhstan, China, Indonesia, Malaysia,[c] South Africa, Tanzania, Zambia,[c] Egypt |

a. Includes ministries of education and of higher education.

b. Includes individual ministries, other government bodies, and multiagency organizations such as training boards.

c. Training governed by tripartite training boards of employers, individuals, and the government.

*Source*: Country studies.

dies for secondary industrial and commercial schools are 25 to 100 percent greater than those for general education. In Egypt secondary technical education costs two-and-a-half times more than general education at the same level. In these and many other countries, students who enter the vocational stream cannot go on to a university education. In some places, such as the West Bank and Gaza, the only avenue for further study for vocational students is enrollment in community colleges or polytechnics. In other countries, such as Korea, the barrier is curriculum-related: entrance examinations for universities are based more on the curriculum of general secondary schools, so vocational school students face an uphill task competing with their general secondary counterparts. As a result, parents have pressured vocational schools to make their curriculum more general.

The effectiveness of school-based vocational education programs appears to depend on their objectives. The most common objectives are, first, to keep less gifted students out of higher education and off the streets; second, to keep people temporarily out of the labor market; and third, to provide employers with skilled workers and technicians. Other objectives include providing students with general vocational skills to prepare them for lifelong learning or for postsecondary specialized training.

Experience shows that vocational education does not seem to be a cost-effective way to keep less able students out of subsidized higher education. For example, even a well-organized and powerful government has not had much success in using vocational secondary education to curb the voracious appetite of Koreans for higher education. Despite several measures to increase vocational school enrollment—secondary school entrance examinations for Korean primary school leavers are sequenced so that vocational schools are favored, these schools receive an increasing share of the budget, and parents are exhorted to send their children to vocational programs— the government has not been able to attain its target of a 50-50 distribution of secondary school students in vocational and general streams. In Egypt attempts to maintain a heavily subsidized higher education system have resulted in more secondary students being channeled into the vocational-technical track (table 4). Because of budgetary pressures and because good technical education is more expensive than general education, the quality of instruction has fallen to abysmal levels. Since Tanzania's secondary enrollment rate is low, the high proportion in vocational-technical streams does not pose a major budgetary problem. However, the high costs of vocational education may thwart future attempts to raise secondary enrollment ratios.

TABLE 4
Size of Vocational-Technical Secondary Education Track

| Country | Secondary enrollment ratio | Number of students (thousands)[a] | Vocational technical share[a] |
|---|---|---|---|
| Hungary | 81 | 135 | 73 |
| Poland | 84 | 2,206 | 67 |
| Czech Republic | 86 | — | 84 |
| Russian Federation | 88 | 6,277 | 60 |
| Kazakhstan | 90 | 1,750 | 33 |
| China | 52 | 15,300 | 55 |
| Indonesia | 43 | 4,109 | 33 |
| Malaysia | 59 | 533 | 11 |
| Korea, Republic of | 93 | 2,060 | 39 |
| Chile | 70 | 652 | 40 |
| Mexico | 58 | — | 12 |
| South Africa | 77 | — | 1 |
| Tanzania | 5 | 23 | 65 |
| Zambia | 20 | — | 2 |
| Jordan | 53 | — | — |
| Egypt | 76 | 2,788 | 68 |
| West Bank and Gaza | — | 53 | 4 |

— Not available.

a. For levels of secondary education at which students are streamed into general and vocational-technical programs.

Source: Enrollment ratios: World Bank (1997); other data: individual country studies in this volume.

Formerly communist countries traditionally had a high proportion of secondary students (between 60 and 85 percent in many cases) in vocational-technical streams. These countries now face both severe budgetary pressures and a rapidly changing skill mix. The experience of the Czech Republic during its transition to a market economy shows that vocational education can be a cost-effective instrument for keeping people temporarily out of a labor market that is undergoing large-scale restructuring. The Czech Republic's experience also reveals that several conditions are critical for the success of this strategy. First, the government tackled non-VET measures, such as macroeconomic and labor market reforms, simultaneously. This encouraged rapid private employment growth. Second, it made vocational programs more general, so that graduates entered the uncertain labor market with appropriately general skills. Third, the government financed expansion of vocational-technical education not by borrowing, but by limiting public funding of universities. Finally, it made vocational programs less terminal so that they remained attractive. While in 1989 only 45 percent of Czech secondary students were eligible to apply for higher studies, by 1995 this figure had increased to 60 percent.

The experience of rapidly growing countries suggests that vocational education is most effective when used to meet current demand for skilled workers and technicians. Making schools responsive to the changing demands of employers is difficult, but in Chile a mix of financial incentives and decentralization appears to have helped some of the agricultural and industrial schools do just that. Per student subsidies for agricultural schools in Chile are twice as large as those for humanistic-scientific schools, and for industrial schools they are 50 percent higher. Assisted by these subsidies, a private corporation for rural development has successfully responded to employers' demands. Although rigorous evaluations are not available, placement rates that range between 60 and 75 percent indicate that Chile's model is quite successful. Left to their own devices, China's secondary vocational and technical schools, which were each traditionally attached to a single public enterprise, have diversified programs to better suit local industries' demands. The State Education Commission's schools and other institutions provide tailored technical programs to 50 million adults, many of whom are already employed. This has sometimes blurred the distinction between vocational education in China's schools and vocational training programs, which are shorter and more specific.

## Vocational Training Programs

Unlike vocational education, vocational training usually falls outside the formal schooling cycle. Thus, it varies more in terms of training duration and entry requirements. Unlike in-service training, vocational training is outside the workplace and is generally not intended for currently employed workers, but for those outside the schooling cycle who are seeking work. The proportion of practical to theoretical instruction in vocational training programs is higher than in vocational education, but lower than in in-service training. Although secondary vocational education lasts two to three years in Korea, vocational training programs take from one month to three years. The curriculum for school-based vocational education in Korea is 70 percent theoretical and 30 percent practical, but the ratios are reversed in training institutes. As in many countries, Indonesia's public vocational training institutions target school dropouts, school and university graduates, and homemakers; vocational schools only admit recent primary school leavers.

Again, the success of these programs appears to depend more on their objectives than on how they are designed and delivered. The main objectives of the vocational training programs in our sample countries have been to help unemployed workers find jobs, to prepare school leavers to enter the labor market, and to upgrade the skills of employed workers.

Public training programs are usually not a cost-effective way to help the unemployed find jobs. The experience of our sample countries is similar to that of OECD countries (Dar and Gill 1998). However, these programs have rarely been rigorously evaluated in developing countries, and their costs have not been monitored. In Eastern Europe, where scientific evaluations do exist, the findings suggest that while the impact of untargeted public training programs is low, they have been somewhat more effective for selected subgroups among the unemployed, for instance, for older, less educated, unemployed workers in remote areas (box 3). Evaluations in industrial, transitional, and developing countries suggest that if public training programs are even moderately effective for job seekers who can be classified as the poorest members of society, tightly targeted programs for these groups can be justified on equity grounds. The training scholarship program of the Chilean Ministry of Labor's National Training and Employment Service has not been carefully evaluated, but it appears to have helped relatively disadvantaged workers such as women and former convicts. However, whether the participants are the worst-off among those seeking employment is not clear.

Vocational training can be effective in preparing school leavers for jobs if the delivery is competitive and the economy is buoyant. The experience of Chile and Indonesia shows that when these conditions are met, effective training programs can be delivered in different ways. Through the Ministry of Labor's National Training and Employment Service program, Chile has used public subsidies to encourage relevant training for young people. The program invited bids from private and public providers to deliver training programs for narrowly specified groups in specific locations; for full payment to the provider, the program required a minimum fraction of trainees to be placed in jobs on completion of training. Indonesia has chosen a different route by encouraging unsubsidized, competitive, private provision of training. Although public training centers enroll fewer than

BOX 3
Retraining Programs in Eastern Europe:
Efficiency and Equity Considerations

In response to rising unemployment and falling real wages, governments in the Czech Republic, Hungary, Poland, and Turkey instituted retraining programs in the early 1990s. A recently completed study carried out jointly by the governments of these four countries and the World Bank examined the effectiveness of retraining and other active labor market programs in these countries. The findings provide valuable lessons for other developing economies in designing, administering, and monitoring their training programs. The following are the main VET-related findings of this study:

- Shorter training courses are more effective than longer courses in raising employment probabilities and earnings.
- Training by private providers is more effective than training by public providers.
- Training does not benefit all groups. Retraining is a substitute for attributes that lead to higher re-employment probabilities in the absence of any intervention (for example, being younger, more educated, and from more dynamic regions). In other words, the program's value added in improving labor market outcomes is greater for relatively disadvantaged job seekers.

Before the results of these evaluations were incorporated into the design of labor market programs, public training schemes in these countries were more likely to have young, educated job seekers from relatively dynamic regions. The results of rigorous evaluations show that targeting job seekers who are disadvantaged in terms of age or education or come from backward regions appears to better serve both equity and efficiency objectives.

*Source*: Fretwell, Benus, and O'Leary (1998).

100,000 trainees, more than 1.5 million people are enrolled in private centers. Note that both Chile and Indonesia have had sustained output and employment growth during the past decade.

Vocational training programs appear to be most effective when aimed at helping employed workers upgrade their skills. Firms can send workers to

TABLE 5
Government In-Service Training Initiatives

| Country | Levy-grant system | | Other incentives | |
|---|---|---|---|---|
| | Rate[a] | Used to finance | Tax credit | Subsidy |
| Hungary | 1.5 | Employment fund | n.a. | n.a. |
| Poland | 2.0 | Employment fund | n.a. | Trainee wages |
| Czech Republic | | | | |
| Russian Federation | 1.5 | Employment fund | 1.5% of profits | n.a. |
| Kazakhstan | 2.0 | Employment fund | n.a. | n.a. |
| China | n.a. | n.a. | n.a. | n.a. |
| Indonesia | n.a. | n.a. | n.a. | n.a. |
| Malaysia | 1.0 | Training fund | Double deduction | n.a. |
| Korea, Rep. of | 0.5 | Public centers | n.a. | n.a. |
| Chile | n.a. | n.a. | 1% of payroll | Trainee wages |
| Mexico | n.a. | n.a. | n.a. | Trainee wages |
| South Africa | 0.5–2.0[b] | Industry funds | n.a. | n.a. |
| Tanzania | 2.0 | Public centers | n.a. | n.a. |
| Zambia | n.a. | n.a. | n.a. | n.a. |
| Jordan | n.a. | n.a. | n.a. | Trainee wages |
| Egypt | n.a. | n.a. | n.a. | n.a. |
| West Bank & Gaza | n.a. | n.a. | n.a. | n.a. |

n.a. Not applicable.
a. Percentage of payroll.
b. Taxes levied by industrial training boards are either a share of payroll costs or per employee.
Source: ILO (1996).

training institutions for skill upgrading, rely on formal in-house programs, or simply encourage on-the-job learning. Malaysia's enterprise survey (box 1) shows that of the firms that train their workers formally, more than half rely on external training providers, most commonly private training institutes and joint-venture skill development centers. Training provided in public institutes, such as youth training centers and vocational schools, which focus on training for first-time job seekers, is not popular with employers. Malaysia's experience suggests that for public expenditures on training programs to yield the highest payoff, targeting the "correct" clientele may be at least as important as ensuring competition in delivery.

## In-Service Training Initiatives

In-service training differs from vocational education and pre-employment training by taking place in the workplace, that is, on the job; by being job specific; and often by being relatively informal, even in the formal sector. However, as noted earlier, the distinction between vocational training and in-service training is sometimes blurred. All the sample countries had government initiatives to increase in-service training, which generally take the form of levy-grant schemes, tax credits, and training subsidies (table 5). The objectives of these initiatives are to encourage firms to pay for investments in their workers' general skills; to help school-to-work transitions (for instance, through apprenticeships); and to help workers acquire job-specific skills that are currently needed. Governments have used various forms of coercion and financial incentives, with varying degrees of success, to attain these objectives.

Few rigorous evaluations of the effectiveness of these initiatives exist. The scattered evidence suggests that mandatory requirements, levy-rebate schemes, and tax incentives have at best a mixed record in increasing in-service training. Despite simplifying the application process, Malaysia's double deduction incentive for training has had little success in encouraging training by firms (namely, small domestic enterprises) that otherwise would not have trained their workers. The case of Korea, which has used all these measures at one stage or another since the late 1960s, best illustrates their effectiveness. In 1974 the government made in-plant training compulsory for firms with more than 500 employees, and the number of trainees rose. In 1976 the government expanded this to include firms with 300 to 500 employees, but it gave firms the option to pay a levy instead of providing the training. The number of trainees declined, and despite an eightfold increase in the levy between 1977 and 1985, about one-third of the covered firms opted not to provide training. Recent evaluations have indicated that the levy-rebate system has been ineffective in increasing in-service training, and the levy-rebate scheme is being phased out. Chile discontinued its program in 1980, opting to subsidize training instead through a tax credit scheme.

Extremely efficiently run levy-rebate schemes (for instance, with quick processing of claims and simple administrative procedures) may lead to increased in-service training by some firms. Malaysia's Human Resource Development Fund, a levy-rebate scheme initiated in 1992, appears to have increased the incidence of training modestly. Surveys find that about 50 percent of covered firms have increased their training since the scheme began compared with about 30 percent of firms that are eligible but have not registered. Despite being efficiently and transparently run, the scheme still faces considerable noncompliance problems and uneven implementation across sectors. South Africa is the only sample country with a levy-rebate scheme administered by industrial training boards. The evidence does not appear encouraging: compliance is low despite the decentralization of control, and the effectiveness in increasing training is doubtful.

Schemes that provide earmarked subsidies appear to have been more successful in encouraging in-service training. In Chile the Ministry of Labor's National Training and Employment Service uses a tax credit scheme to encourage firms to send workers for training programs, and in Korea the number of trainees rose sharply when the government subsidized in-plant training between 1968 and 1971. However, these schemes have not been evaluated carefully. Even if found to be effective, straight subsidies pose obvious budgetary questions. Levy-rebate schemes have the advantage that they are self-financing, but they may discourage employment because the tax is levied on payrolls.

## Critical Issues, Constraints, and Innovations

This section summarizes three important reform issues relating, respectively, to the organization, provision, and financing and content of VET. It is not intended as a comprehensive treatment of these aspects of VET. Instead, it focuses on aspects that are of interest worldwide, have received in-depth treatment in the case studies, and have not been satisfactorily covered in the last two sections. In particular, we discuss the main messages gleaned from studies on Australia's reforms since 1985 and the applicability of the German dual system to low- and middle-income countries.

## Reorganizing to Facilitate Continual Reform

Fragmentation because of the involvement of multiple government agencies and the difficulty of obtaining timely inputs from employers and trainees make it hard to ensure efficient and accurate feedback to VET suppliers and quick reforms in response to this feedback. Sometimes the sluggish responses prompt interventions by officials in higher levels of government. Korea's Presidential Commission on Education Reform has helped to resolve contradictions between general and vocational secondary education and higher education. Malaysia's Economic Planning Unit helps to monitor whether labor market demands are being efficiently met and the changes required to ensure that VET supply keeps pace with other efforts to reach industrial country status by 2020. Chile's Planning Office played a crucial role in the 1980s in designing VET policies and in determining the pattern of government subsidies for general and vocational education. However, the case of Australia, which launched reforms to ensure that its VET system would be sustainable and self-adjusting as circumstances change, is perhaps the most innovative.

Despite the expansion of Australia's VET system up to the mid-1980s, it remained subject to criticism. Critics charged that the system was too inflexible to respond quickly to skill shortages or new labor market demands and that it operated with procedures and standards that were out of date and no longer cost effective. Australia's efforts to facilitate smooth and cost-effective VET system responses to changing labor market conditions can be classified into four sets of measures as follows:

• *Combining the relevant government agencies into one body at the federal level for more coherent policymaking and allocation of public funds.* Between 1975 and 1985 the federal government's actions had distinctly changed the relationship between the ministries of employment and education. The government had increased the Ministry of Employment's responsibilities for developing traineeships, interacting with employers to determine the types of training required, and implementing programs for the unemployed. However, VET, which fell under the purview of state education ministries, remained the country's major vehicle for the system's formal training component. The federal government became unwilling to tolerate the division and combined the employment and education ministries into the Department of Education, Employment, and Training. Bearing in mind that its role in education was mainly as financier rather than administrator, the federal government was able to take major initiatives in setting policy. Its actions eventually led some states to combine their education and labor ministries.

•  *Ensuring employers' and workers' participation in policy setting at the federal and state levels.* The second major reform was the establishment of the Australian National Training Authority by the federal and state governments. The authority was established as a company, with the federal and state governments being equal shareholders. These governments recognized that their role in managing VET reform could not supersede the role of employers and workers, so they were included, making the authority a tripartite body. The Australian National Training Authority embarked on an ambitious plan to develop a nationwide assessment and certification system and to encourage private training providers. The task was approached on the understanding that the major responsibilities should not simply be vested in government bureaucracies. The intent was to pass control of training from the supply side to the demand side.

•  *Shifting some of the financial burden of VET investments onto the beneficiaries.* The financing of VET is as big an issue in Australia as in developing countries. As in other countries, employers look critically at the costs and benefits of training. State and federal governments are increasingly interested in having a more cost-effective system. Trainees and students, however, have probably been less concerned; when the reforms began, they bore few direct costs for training. By the mid-1980s the federal government, with its sole management responsibilities for higher education, was finding it difficult to sustain its decision, made a decade earlier, to abolish higher education fees. Consequently, it introduced a higher education contribution, which initially covered 20 percent of the cost of higher education. However, the federal government left it to the states to consider introducing student fees for VET, which many of them did. To relieve the burden on employers, the government in 1996 instituted a training wage, which is below union wage levels. Trainees are thus being asked to bear a greater share of the cost of training. Recognizing that the training wage could fall below acceptable standards, the government proposed in 1996 to top up the wage.

•  *Ensuring competition in provision so that the supply is cost effective and relevant.* The Department of Education, Employment, and Training introduced competitive bidding among training providers. Training courses were put out for bids, and although the government system maintained its position as the major supplier, others, including private providers, were allowed to bid to become suppliers. The federal and state governments concluded that employers should be allowed to use nongovernmental training providers (for apprenticeship training as well), even though in many cases such providers did not yet exist. Through a system of financing, employers could buy training from any supplier rather than direct funds automatically to the government system or to other government-funded providers.

Australia's reforms contain these important lessons for developing and transitional countries:

• *Expansion of VET without institutional change is rarely an answer in itself.* The Australian experience shows the importance of basing reform on sound institutions, without which investments run the risk of turning bad systems into expensive bad systems. One particular problem concerns the relations among the industrial partners, employers, and unions, and between each of them and the VET system. In this respect, a great deal depends on the broader relationship between the industrial partners and the government. Such an approach is difficult to adopt in countries that have depended on the public sector for their development. In the end, however, this is the only way for these countries to get full value for their investments.

• *Links with the labor market must be predominant.* To keep links between the VET system and the labor market strong, the government must examine its own internal structures and operations. Many countries have experienced tensions between achieving educational and labor market objectives. Resolving these is not easy in industrial countries and may be even more difficult in countries with well-entrenched public sectors where interagency discussions are weak. Australia's solution was to amalgamate the players into one portfolio. With the establishment of a single national ministry encompassing employment, education, and training, competing priorities could be resolved closer to the operating level.

• *Financing of VET should reinforce, not contradict, market forces.* Allowing market forces to work does not only depend on setting up institutions that encourage industry to determine its own training needs. This can be achieved by ensuring that costs are shared, but this is not the entire answer: costs are best apportioned in a way that enables buyers to exercise judgment. Again, this implies a shift in control away from the public sector and toward employers and trainees. Industry should become the main force behind the development of VET training standards, assessment procedures, and accreditation.

## Encouraging Private Providers

The domination of VET by developing-country governments since the 1950s has often shut out private providers (private suppliers of training, NGOs, and public-private partnerships) from the market for formal training. Private sector firms that sought external training for their workers were generally steered toward public providers. Recognizing that a healthy private supply of vocational training is good both for labor market efficiency and for budgetary reasons, many governments are trying to encourage private provision while at the same time "protecting" consumers from high prices and malpractice. The requirements for success, as demonstrated by some of our sample countries, appear to be as follows:

• *Clear and lenient laws are necessary.* Removing ambiguity about the setting up of training firms results in a vigorous response, especially for postsecondary training programs. The most striking case is that of Chile, where streamlining the legal requirements for starting training firms in 1989 was accompanied by a rapid growth of unsubsidized private training (box 4). With clear and balanced legislation, government financing may not be necessary to bolster the demand for short training programs that are expected to be followed by employment (and not further study). Legislation in Hungary that has permitted NGOs and public-private partnerships to participate in the delivery of VET at all levels has also had a positive impact. In many cases these partnerships are formed on a tripartite basis— that is, they consist of government, employer, and union representatives. For example, all Regional Human Resource Development Training Centers in Hungary are governed by tripartite boards and obtain equal portions of funding from employers, individuals, and the government. Malaysian training centers and many postcompulsory training centers in Poland are now allowed to operate on a similar basis. NGOs are also entering the postcompulsory vocational training field, as they already have in secondary-level schooling. In Hungary about 90 foundations deliver secondary school vocational education.

• *Balanced funding formulas are essential.* Public funding can be used to encourage private provision of longer, for instance, secondary, technical-

BOX 4
Private Provision of Postsecondary Education in Chile:
The Importance of Transparent Legislation

Since the early 1980s, Chile has reformed the financing and regulatory mechanisms for its postsecondary education and training institutions. Before the reforms,
all postsecondary education was provided by eight universities that were allocated
one-third of the government education budget. Private training institutes were prohibited from offering postsecondary technical programs. A 1980 law established
minimum requirements for setting up postsecondary institutions, but proposals
were dealt with on a case-by-case basis until 1988. In the first nine years after the
reforms, the number of universities grew from 8 to 34, the number of professional
institutes from 0 to 41, and the number of technical training centers from 0 to 133.

In 1989 the government clarified the requirements for establishing postsecondary
institutions and began treating proposals quickly and uniformly. Within a year the
number of universities and professional institutes had doubled, and the number of
technical training centers had increased by 25 percent. The table shows the percentage of these that relied on public subsidies. Note that much of the expansion in
supply since 1989 is in the private unsubsidized sector, which indicates that government support for these institutions through clear and balanced legislation is
more important than public subsidies.

*Number of Postsecondary Institutions, Selected Years, 1980–90*

| Institutions | 1980 | 1986 | 1989 | 1990 |
|---|---|---|---|---|
| Universities | 8 | 20 | 34 | 60 |
| Percentage without public funds | 0 | 15 | 41 | 66 |
| Professional institutes | 0 | 24 | 41 | 82 |
| Percentage without public funds | 0 | 70 | 93 | 97 |
| Training centers | 0 | 86 | 133 | 168 |
| Percentage without public funds | 0 | 100 | 100 | 100 |

*Source*: Chile chapter in this volume.

vocational programs. In Chile only 28 percent of secondary vocational school enrollment was private in 1980. By 1993 this ratio had more than doubled, thanks to a new funding formula that did not discriminate between public and private providers. In Hungary, by contrast, special funding for public training institutions has discouraged private providers.

• *Growth of relevant employment is a critical prerequisite.* People often assert that supplying technical training requires large set-up costs and that private entrepreneurs would shy away from these investments. They argue that training for commercial fields, such as in languages and secretarial skills, is cheaper to provide and hence private providers would be more willing to supply it. They cite this as the rationale for government provision of technical training, even where it is accepted that the government's role in provision should be curtailed or reduced. The experience of our sample countries shows that when private providers are not discouraged by stringent laws, rapid industrial growth can lead to a strong private supply of technical training. In the Czech Republic, where manufacturing employment has grown rapidly since 1993, all new technical training programs are privately provided.

• *Universal accreditation schemes are not necessary for a healthy private supply.* Little empirical support is available for the popular belief that low quality training at exorbitant prices will result unless private providers are tightly regulated (for instance, by requiring that all providers meet standards set by the government). In Indonesia, which does not have an accreditation scheme, two-thirds of secondary and postsecondary technical-vocational enrollment is in private institutes. Regulations in Chile and the Czech Republic stipulate that private providers must be accredited if they intend to apply for public subsidies but not otherwise. In Russia accreditation is necessary only if providers wish to award certificates recognized by the government. The experience of these countries—which span a broad economic and institutional spectrum—shows that a government-organized system of accreditation is neither necessary nor sufficient for a balanced private system of training. The experience of other countries shows that government-run accreditation systems, which are intended to inform people of quality levels, can easily degenerate into licensing regimes that rule out the existence of nonconforming firms. This discourages the development of a vigorous private sector.

• *Unplanned public provision crowds out private supply.* Many countries make VET policy decisions based on a poor or incomplete picture of private supply. Indeed, relying on government sources of information, we found it difficult to compile a table on the share of the private sector in providing VET. The case of Indonesia, which has experienced rapid growth of private VET supply, best illustrates the dangers of an unplanned expansion of public training. Originally, the government was to provide only high-cost training programs (for example, for technicians and mechanical operators), but erratic and declining external funding forced public centers into lower-cost areas, such as commercial programs, for which trainees were willing and able to pay. However, this area was already well catered to by fee-charging private centers. Rather than helping private suppliers, subsidized government centers ended up crowding out some private providers.

When VET policies are well designed, a vigorous private supply response can be forthcoming. In Chile funding mechanisms require public providers to compete on equal terms with private firms. As a result, private firms now supply a healthy portion of commercial, industrial, and agricultural secondary education. For shorter courses that lead trainees directly to jobs, Chile's experience shows that clear and balanced legislation may be even more important than government subsidies. Although these conditions are necessary, they are not sufficient. For a vigorous private supply of training, the demand for the skills that these programs provide must also exhibit growth. Generally, the willingness to pay for skills that are relatively general, such as English language proficiency and computer-related and secretarial skills, arises sooner than for comparatively specific skills, such as those required to obtain work as a technician or machinery operator. As a result, when regulations are favorable, the private supply of commercial training emerges first. The Czech Republic's experience shows that with the growth of demand for technical skills, brought about by growth in the modern manufacturing sector, the private supply response for technical training can be equally vigorous. In light of these findings, two popular beliefs should be reconsidered: government provision of technical training is necessary because the private sector is "reluctant" to enter this field because of risks or costs, and universal (government) accreditation schemes are necessary to ensure that the "poor are not taken advantage of" by profit-seeking training firms.

## Implementing the Dual VET System

The problem of strengthening the links between education and employment preoccupies policymakers in all countries. In countries that are growing rapidly, this preoccupation stems from the concern that the economy's demand for skilled workers will outstrip its supply. In countries where economic growth is slow, the concern may arise as a result of growing unemployment among young people. In both cases this attention often turns into efforts to make curricula more vocational, to involve employers in schooling decisions, to increase pre-employment training, or to create incentives for employers to participate in apprenticeship training. These attributes are all associated with the current German approach to VET, commonly referred to as the dual system. The dual system is attractive for countries at all stages of development. In our sample countries, the Czech Republic, Egypt, Indonesia, Jordan, Korea, and Poland all have some form of this system, and other countries, such as Kazakhstan, Tanzania, and Zambia, are considering adopting this approach.

The system is referred to as dual, because schools and employers respectively provide vocational education and occupational training simultaneously, that is, during a single program of work and study. Theoretical aspects of training are provided in publicly run and publicly financed vocational secondary schools, and practical aspects in firms that provide and finance apprenticeships. Apprentices spend one or two days each week in vocational schools, and the remainder in firms. In small firms apprentices usually acquire skills through learning by doing; in larger firms training is often in specialized centers. In Germany the formal vocational education component was introduced many years after the vocational training part had been refined, but this sequence is ordinarily reversed in developing countries trying to adopt the dual system. In these countries a public vocational education system usually exists, and governments attempt to tack on an apprenticeship program to make the system a dual one.

A pertinent question to ask is whether the following employment structures and institutions of countries that are trying to import the system are similar to Germany's:

- *Sectoral and size distribution of firms.* Almost 90 percent of employment in Germany is in manufacturing and services, sectors where most apprenticeships are provided. This ratio is considerably lower in low-income countries; for instance, it is about 45 percent in Egypt and Indonesia. Even in the relatively modern manufacturing and services sectors in developing countries, employment is concentrated in microenterprises and small-scale enterprises. Germany's experience with the dual system shows that extremely small firms generally do not provide apprenticeships; when they do, they often do not retain trainees who complete their apprenticeships. In developing countries where small firms dominate even the regulated formal private sector, this would imply low participation in such a system.

- *Regulation and union coverage.* Firms in developing countries are more likely than German firms to be unregulated and to have weak union representation. Therefore, it may be difficult for the government or unions to ensure that employers conduct apprenticeships in conformity with established standards and regulations. In the German *handwerk* sector, which most resembles manufacturing and services sectors in developing countries, many German firms use trainees as cheap, flexible labor. In most developing countries the absence or nonenforcement of minimum wage legislation reduces the need for firms to use apprenticeship wage laws to avoid hiring untested workers at high entry wages.

- *Capacity to bear high costs.* Because of both tradition and pragmatism, firms in Germany bear the high costs of the vocational training component of the dual system, but in our sample countries firms tend to be reluctant to bear the costs of apprenticeships. Faced with private firms' reluctance to finance the vocational training component of the dual system, developing-country governments may be tempted to bear the entire burden, but they should weigh this decision carefully. It appears that the poorer the country, the greater the real burden of implementing a German-style dual system. Although the annual unit cost of the dual system in Germany is about the same as its per capita gross national product, simulations show that this ratio is greater than two in Korea, more than three in Indonesia, and more than four in Egypt (box 5).

Although the German system is not directly importable, the following principles underlying it provide valuable lessons that are relevant across a broad socioeconomic spectrum:

- *Participation in the dual system is voluntary.* Even some firms that are qualified to offer apprenticeships do not do so. In addition, employers are under no obligation to retain trainees upon their completion of the dual program, and less than half do. Developing-country governments trying to adopt the dual system while using coercive measures, such as mandated training requirements or forcible retention of apprentices, should be informed that this is inconsistent with the German system.

- *The organization and control of vocational education and training are left to the body that pays for the instruction.* State and local governments pay

BOX 5

Costs of the Dual System in Low- and Middle-Income Countries

In Germany the government pays for and controls vocational education in schools, and employers finance and manage apprenticeship training. Using a simple methodology, we impute the annual unit costs of a dual system participant to equal US$17,200 in Korea, US$2,750 in Egypt, and $2,250 in Indonesia. For example, the imputed cost of putting an Indonesian trainee through the dual system is about US$7,000. This imputed measure is almost identical to the actual cost of a dual system pilot program in Indonesia reported in independent surveys.

*Unit Cost of Dual System Components, 1991*
(1991 U.S. dollars)

| Country | Actual or imputed cost | | | Ratio of total to GNP/capita |
| | Training | Vocational education | Total | |
| --- | --- | --- | --- | --- |
| Germany | 17,700 | 3,300 | 21,000 | 0.9 |
| Korea, Rep. of | 14,500 | 2,700 | 17,200 | 2.3 |
| Indonesia | 1,900 | 350 | 2,250 | 3.1 |
| Egypt | 2,350 | 400 | 2,750 | 4.2 |

*Source:* Country studies in this volume.

for and control the relatively general skills that are acquired in school, and employers pay for and determine the job-specific training acquired in the workplace. Efforts by developing countries to adopt the German dual system often violate this principle and allow governments, not employers, to take the lead in organizing and financing vocational training.

• *Education and the dual system appear to be complements.* Germany does not use the dual system to keep high school graduates from pursuing higher education. In fact, the education level of Germany's dual system entrants has risen significantly over time, as the pace of technological change has increased the importance of general education relative to specific skills. Poorer countries may be better served by government efforts to improve general education levels rather than allocate scarce resources to public vocational education programs or government-led apprenticeship schemes.

## Summary and Lessons Learned

As stated earlier, given the complexity of this subject and the large variations in the characteristics of the countries studied, the following summary may not adequately represent the experience of some of the sample countries. A full appreciation of VET reforms can perhaps only be obtained by reading the individual country studies. However, some general lessons can be drawn from these disparate experiences.

At the risk of oversimplifying the complex changes in the countries studied, we can summarize the ingredients of success in VET reforms as follows:

• Successful reforms make school-based vocational education more like general education in two ways: the content is made more general, and the vocational-technical track is made less of a dead-end.

• Successful reforms combine public financing of pre-employment training with rigorous evaluation of program impact and ensure competition between providers in delivery.

• Successful initiatives to encourage in-service training recognize that formal training is not widespread, even in formal sector enterprises; that mandatory training targets and levy-rebate schemes do not increase training significantly; that tax incentives work only where tax coverage is comprehensive; and that while subsidies may increase training, they will also increase expenditures.

The main messages gleaned are as follows:

• *Matching instrument to target group is as important as picking the best delivery mode.* Regardless of the mechanisms through which VET is supplied (public or private, subsidized or unsubsidized private), it is critical that these programs target groups that will most benefit from them. This is because VET is more effective when used for some purposes (for instance, to meet clearly observed, current labor market demands), than for others (such as keeping less gifted students out of higher education or helping the unemployed find jobs). In most cases VET programs are more expensive than alternatives, such as general education and job search assistance. In matching instruments to objectives, most developing countries are only now appreciating the importance of scientific evaluations.

• *Preoccupied with providing or financing VET, many governments have neglected their roles as providers of information about the availability and effectiveness of vocational programs.* An expansion of this role may be one of the most effective ways for governments to foster a relevant and cost-effective VET system. Better information about VET programs helps policymakers redesign their VET policies and interventions so that private providers are not crowded out of the market. Wider access to information on the availability and quality of training supply can protect prospective trainees from unfair trade practices better than can government-run accreditation schemes and stringent licensing practices in countries where institutional factors circumscribe the regulatory powers of government. In general, this role has been overlooked or underemphasized. The lack of reliable information about public training programs and privately provided VET programs in most of our sample countries is striking evidence of this neglect.

• *A vigorous private response has refuted claims of the reluctance of private providers to enter the field.* The experience of our sample countries indicates that when VET policies are designed to encourage rather than replace the private sector (either private training providers, NGOs, or public-private partnerships), a vigorous private supply response can be forthcoming. Thus, for example, public funding mechanisms that require public providers to compete on approximately equal terms with private trainers can result in the latter acquiring a healthy portion of the market for longer vocational education programs. Experience also shows that for shorter courses that lead trainees directly to jobs, clear and balanced legislation seems to be even more important than government subsidies. However, while these conditions are necessary, they are not by themselves sufficient. For a vigorous private supply of training, there must also be growth in the demand for skills that these programs help workers acquire. Generally, people's willingness to pay for skills that are relatively general (for instance, language proficiency and computer skills) arises sooner than that for occupation-specific skills (for example, as technicians or operators). As a result, with balanced regulations, the private market for commercial training emerges before that for technical programs. Where the demand for technical skills has grown because of the growth of modern manufacturing, and the regulatory conditions are favorable, private supply responses for technical training have been equally vigorous. In light of these findings, the private sector should not be viewed as reluctant to enter this field.

• *Political will, not institutional capacity, is the main obstacle to comprehensive reform of VET systems.* This message is based on the experience of countries worldwide (for example, Australia in the OECD, Chile in Latin America, the Czech Republic in Eastern Europe, and Korea in East Asia).

Resistance to the reallocation of responsibilities and government funds in response to changing labor market conditions may be overcome (as in Australia) by comprehensive reforms that consolidate responsibility for policymaking and oversee public spending on education, training, and employment under one umbrella; implement institutional measures to involve employers and workers in determining VET policy; and reduce significantly the role of government in supplying VET by restructuring financing rules to encourage rather than crowd out private provision. This is a tall order for any country, but the most important prerequisite is the political will to reform, which is perhaps neither dependent on a country's wealth, nor on its level of institutional advancement.

## Notes

1. The financial crisis in Indonesia, Malaysia, and Korea has dampened employment growth and led to an increase in unemployment since late 1997.

2. Countries may fit into more than one group. For example, China is in transition and has high employment growth, and Mexico has experienced both high growth and high unemployment episodes.

3. In South Asia the share of the urban informal sector in nonagricultural employment is about 60 percent. In Africa the share of wage employment in the labor force declined from 12 percent in the 1980s to 9 percent in the 1990s. In Latin America, by contrast, urban formal employment grew faster than the informal sector during the 1980s and 1990s.

4. One of the emerging trends in education and training is lifelong learning, which incorporates three interrelated topics: civics and consumer education, literacy and foundation skills, and occupational skills. A few of the countries in the sample have recently been attempting to develop a lifelong credit system for skills training that will allow individuals to accumulate skills and qualifications throughout their working lives. However, this study does not examine the issue of lifelong learning in detail.

## References

Dar, Amit, and Indermit Gill. 1998. "Evaluations of Retraining Programs in OECD Countries: Lessons Learned." *World Bank Research Observer* 13(1): 79–101.

Fretwell, D., J. Benus, and C. O'Leary. 1998. "Evaluating the Impact of Active Labor Programs: Results of Cross-Country Studies in Europe and Central Asia." Social Protection Discussion Paper. World Bank, Washington, D.C.

Gill, Indermit, and Amit Dar. 1995. "Labor Market Policies, Institutions, and Interventions." World Bank, Washington, D.C.

ILO (International Labour Office). 1996. *Yearbook of Labour Statistics*. Geneva.

Middleton, John, Adrian Ziderman, and Arvil Van Adams. 1993. *Skills for Productivity: Vocational Education and Training in Developing Countries*. New York: Oxford University Press.

Tan, Hong, and Geeta Batra. 1995. "Enterprise Training in Developing Countries: Overview of Incidence, Determinants, and Productivity Outcomes." Occasional Paper 9. World Bank, Private Sector Development Department, Washington, D.C.

World Bank. 1991. *Vocational and Technical Education and Training: A Policy Paper*. Washington, D.C.

———. 1997. *World Development Indicators*. Washington, D.C.

# I Transition Economies

VOCATIONAL EDUCATION and training systems in countries in transition to a market economy face a double challenge. First, they must transform themselves: developed to serve a centrally planned economy and geared toward technologically backward industrial production, they must become compatible with an economy based on market principles that incorporates a greater variety of industrial production and services. Second, they must contribute to the health of that market-based economy. Part I analyzes how the countries of Central and Eastern Europe (CEE) and the former Soviet Union (FSU) are coping with these two challenges.

In Hungary, the first of the reformers, the duration of primary education has increased, and the age of entry to vocational education has been postponed. Moreover, the relative roles of the state and the private sector in providing training outside the school system have changed. Many state training centers, which once were important, have been closed or privatized, and many must compete with private training institutions for publicly financed contracts to retrain the unemployed.

In Poland, however, the amount of public funds spent for training has remained low, and the people involved in labor market training are still few in number. The main reason is that few vacancies can be filled on the basis of retraining. Vocational education has traditionally been organized along sectoral lines, with schools focusing on a single sector and switching from one vocation to another only with difficulty. The industrial and vocational education structures have proven to be a major barrier to industrial and regional development during the transition. But Poland is the only formerly socialist country that has maintained a successful traditional apprenticeship system in the handicraft sector.

Vocational and technical education in the Czech Republic has been made more general. No longer is it a dead-end. Financing rules and regulations have been changed so that private and public schools benefit from the same financial arrangements and face the same incentives for cost sharing with students and firms. Most private schools are in the secondary technical sector, a development unique to the Czech Republic. (Private schools in other CEE countries are mostly primary or general secondary.) A lenient law for setting up training centers has encouraged the private provision of education in the Czech Republic; accreditation requirements are more stringent, but accreditation is needed only if certificates are to be issued or public funds are sought. Unlike other CEE countries, the Czech Republic has relied more on restricting labor supply (by delaying the entry of youth into the labor market and by expanding the secondary education system) and less on propping up labor demand through interventions.

The countries of the former Soviet Union face these challenges under more uncertain political and economic conditions, and under more acute financial constraints. Most educational institutions in the Russian Federation continue to cling to the old ways. One major change has been to allow private institutions. But private training provision has been slow to grow, in part because of the attitude of accrediting authorities toward private schools, which they view as a threat to the public system. Many vocational schools continue to be aligned with specific enterprises, but apart from this there is little involvement by employers. The curriculum is developed at the center, either in ministries or methodological institutes. The main issue facing policymakers is how to make the system more responsive to changes in the labor market. Financial constraints mean that new alternatives must be found to finance the needed improvements. However, efforts to share the costs of vocational training with the beneficiaries, particularly the trainees themselves, are limited by legislation: initial vocational training is by law free to the participants. Russia has not yet begun to address the fundamental question of how to reform its VET system.

In other FSU countries, such as Kazakhstan, the VET system continues to operate in ways suited to a command economy. For example, it churns out trainees for manufacturing and agriculture even though these sectors are declining relative to trade and services. The VET system is in dire financial straits, but it is not alone in that. Kazakhstan presents the classic dilemma in vocational education and training, best summarized in the phrase "training for what?" The government appears to have been unable to answer this question and has given VET a low priority. Despite the problems that VET is facing, the government of Kazakhstan has been correct in its decision not to accord vocational education and training a high priority. Economic development has been slow and uncertain, giving rise to a poor labor market and slowing any investments in VET by employers. The relevant government agencies have been unable to define a role for themselves. But the low priority accorded to vocational education and training while the economy takes the path of transition to market should not lead to its desertion by government: even decisions not to reform should be taken deliberately.

# 1 Hungary

Martin Godfrey

Hungary began its transition to a market economy earlier than its neighbors, taking significant steps during the 1980s toward enterprise reform and decontrol of prices and wages. The process gathered speed after 1989 with the change in the political system and the democratic election of a government committed to full liberalization of the economy.

At the outset of the transition Hungary had many advantages in addition to its early start. In particular, its population, though small, is well educated. With an adult literacy rate estimated at 99 percent, the country is placed in the top category for human development by the Human Development Report (UNDP 1995). The 1990 census showed that 78 percent of the adult population (ages 15 or older) had at least eight years of primary education. The 1992 round of the Household Panel Survey found that 33 percent of unskilled workers and 81 percent of skilled workers had a postprimary qualification, and that 64 percent of managers had a tertiary qualification. Moreover, education is of high quality: in 1991 tests placed Hungary second only to Japan in achievement in science among 13-year-olds (OECD/CCET 1995).

As table 1-1 shows, Hungary's population continued to fall during the 1990s. By 1994 it was 4 percent below its level of 14 years earlier. The economy collapsed in the early 1990s, partly because of the process of transformation, partly because of the disintegration of the Council for Mutual Economic Assistance trading system and of the Soviet Union, and partly because of difficulties in gaining access to new markets. Industries

TABLE 1-1
Trends in Population, Output, and Income, 1989–94
(percent)

| Indicator | 1989 | 1990 | 1991 | 1992 | 1993 | 1994 |
|---|---|---|---|---|---|---|
| Population (thousands) | 10,578 | 10,365 | 10,346 | 10,324 | 10,294 | 10,261 |
| Rate of change in real GDP | 0.4 | –3.3 | –11.9 | –3.0 | –0.8 | 2.0 |
| Share of industry in GDP | 30.0 | 27.0 | 27.0 | 24.0 | 24.0 | — |
| Share of services in GDP | 37.0 | 41.0 | 53.0 | 53.0 | 55.0 | — |
| Rate of change in real GDP per head | 0.4 | –2.1 | –11.7 | –0.2 | –0.3 | 2.3 |
| Rate of change in real wages | 0.9 | –3.7 | –4.0 | 1.4 | –0.8 | 3.1 |

— Not available.
*Source:* UNICEF (1995); World Bank (1995a).

linked to old structures and trading systems, such as metallurgy and engineering, were hit particularly badly. Structural change has consisted mainly of fast growth in the services sector, and the shrinking of agriculture from about a third of gross domestic product (GDP) in 1989 to about a fifth in 1993. Real GDP per head and real wages have fallen substantially and, as unemployment and inequality in income distribution have increased, so has the incidence of poverty (World Bank 1995b). Hungary's GDP per head, equivalent to US$3,981 in 1994, remains the highest among Central and Eastern European countries. While the upturn in economic activity during the past few years is welcome, some doubt its sustainability.

Hungary failed to achieve as smooth a transition as many had expected. One of the most important reasons was the fall in export earnings by almost 30 percent since 1989 because of a combination of labor cost and exchange rate factors (Godfrey 1994). As a result, the current account has gone into substantial deficit, and the debt-service ratio, which had begun to fall during the early 1990s, has risen again to an alarming extent. Since the government budget deficit in 1994 was equivalent to 7.5 percent of GDP—one of the highest such ratios in Central and Eastern Europe—fiscal and monetary policy has had limited room for maneuver. The need to restore external and internal balance has forced the government to concentrate on stabilization rather than on transformation and revival.

Nevertheless, the economy is being transformed in many respects (table 1-2). The private sector's share of GDP has grown dramatically. As far as employment is concerned, the public administration resisted attempts to

TABLE 1-2
Estimated Private and Public Sector Share in GDP
and Employment, 1990–94
(percent)

| Enterprise share | 1990 | 1991 | 1992 | 1993 | 1994 |
|---|---|---|---|---|---|
| Private sector share in GDP | 16 | 18 | 25 | 65 | 70 |
| *Share in total employment of* | | | | | |
| Public administration | — | — | 16 | 17 | 21 |
| State-owned firms | — | — | 39 | 34 | 24 |
| Local-government-owned enterprises | — | — | 5 | 5 | 4 |
| Cooperatives | — | — | 7 | 6 | 5 |
| Joint ventures | — | — | 9 | 11 | 13 |
| Private enterprises | — | — | 14 | 17 | 21 |
| Sole proprietors | — | — | 10 | 10 | 12 |
| Total | — | — | 100 | 100 | 100 |

— Not available.
*Source*: Labor Research Institute (1995).

reduce its size (at least until 1995–96). Yet the fall in employment in state enterprises in particular has been reflected in an increase in private sector employment from 33 percent of total employment in 1991 to 46 percent in 1994.

Although employment in the private sector has been rising, this has not prevented total employment from falling from around 5.0 million in 1991 to 3.5 million in 1995. This reflects partly an exodus from the labor force and partly the painful emergence of mass unemployment. The level and rate of unemployment reached their peaks in 1993, but the rate is still above 10 percent, and as the number of unemployed has fallen, the proportion out of work for more than a year has risen disturbingly from 21 percent in 1992 to 46 percent in 1995.

## The Labor Market

Almost as worrying as the growth of unemployment has been the exodus from the labor force. Participation rates fell sharply from 84 percent in 1991 to less than 70 percent by 1995. Some of the newly inactive of working age are students prolonging their studies, but a much greater proportion are home workers and the prematurely retired. In February 1994, 27 percent of those receiving pensions were below the age of 60, and 58 percent of these younger pensioners received disability pensions. This reflects not increased morbidity, but "'soft layoffs' and collusion between employers and employees" (World Bank 1995a, p. 34). The consequences for government expenditure and for payroll taxes have been disastrous. Public expenditure on pensions accounted for more than 10 percent of GDP in 1993, and employers' contributions to pensions, health insurance, and unemployment compensation represented nearly 50 percent of their payroll costs in 1994 (compared with 32 percent in Poland, about 31 percent in Western Europe, and 26 percent in the Czech Republic).

Employment has also fallen sharply. As table 1-3 shows, total employment fell by 18 percent between 1989 and 1994. Since GDP fell by 16 percent during the same period, this implies a slight reduction in labor hoarding by employers and a consequent increase in productivity. With the growth of employment in the services sector, the relative importance of self-employment has grown, but, as can be seen, the vast majority of workers are still wage employees. The share of women in total employment has also increased slightly.

An increasing proportion of the labor force works in the so-called hidden or unregistered economy, which includes those working for employers attempting to evade taxes and the self-employed. Sik (1995) reports that Hungary's hidden economy (excluding domestic production) accounts for a 27 percent larger share of the GDP than in the United States, implying a share of around 13 percent. His study supports the view that the unregistered economy is becoming increasingly important. He finds that only 61 percent of the total working hours of the adult population (excluding domestic work) in 1994 was spent on a first job, with the remainder being devoted to informal wage labor (5 percent), subsistence agriculture (36 percent), and interhousehold barter (2 percent). Árvay and Vértes (1994) arrive at an even higher estimate of the size of the hidden sector in 1992: 26.5 percent of GDP.

The growth of the hidden economy may have moderated the growth of unemployment to some extent, but in 1994 the unemployment rate still exceeded 10 percent. A striking aspect is the significantly lower unemployment rate among women: 8.4 percent compared with 11.8 percent for men. Those under 25 are the most severely affected, with a rate of around 20 percent. Rates for older groups are also high and have been rising. In

TABLE 1-3
Employment by Sector, 1989–94
(percent)

| Sector | 1989 | 1990 | 1991 | 1992 | 1993 | 1994 |
|---|---|---|---|---|---|---|
| Agriculture share | 19 | 18 | 16 | 14 | 9 | 9 |
| Industry share | 37 | 37 | 37 | 35 | 34 | 33 |
| Services share | 44 | 45 | 47 | 51 | 57 | 58 |
| Annual rate of change in employment | −0.5 | −0.6 | −3.2 | −10.6 | −1.2 | −3.6 |
| Wage employees as percentage of total employment | — | — | — | 92 | 91 | 90 |

— Not available.

Source: CSO (various years); World Bank (1995a).

general, unemployment rates decline with education level. They are close to 30 percent for those with less than primary education, 20 percent for those with primary education, and just 2 percent for university graduates.

Long-term unemployment is a growing problem. This category included only 6 percent of the unemployed in 1991, but by the middle of the decade more than 40 percent of the unemployed were long-term unemployed. A significant proportion of these have low skill and education levels: 43 percent were classified as unskilled and semiskilled, and 79 percent of the long-term unemployed had at most primary schooling (Labor Research Institute 1995). Long-term unemployment is also disproportionately concentrated in those regions that depend on heavy industry and agriculture, with little potential for trade and tourism and less developed entrepreneurial capacity than elsewhere in the country (Galasi and Kertesi 1996).

As the labor market has developed in the past few years, wage differentials have tended to increase. Kertesi and Köll (1995) analyzed Hungarian labor market data between 1986 and 1994. Their analysis shows that education is an increasingly important determinant of differences in earnings. The impact, all other things being equal, on wage earnings of higher education (compared with completed primary schooling) increased from 34 percent in 1986 to 46 percent by 1994. The impact of secondary education (both vocational and general) increased by even more, from 12 to 19 percent. By contrast, the impact of apprentice schooling remained unchanged during this period. In line with the increasing influence of market forces are other interesting developments: a reduction in the impact of gender on wages; an increase in the impact of age and experience on wages; and a widening of differentials between managers and nonmanual workers on the one hand, and manual workers on the other.

## The Vocational Education and Training System

In the current education system, eight years of primary schooling open the way for access to various alternatives: four years of grammar school (although some grammar schools have presecondary classes that enable them to take pupils from primary school at an earlier stage); four years of vocational secondary school; three years of vocational training, for the most part in an apprentice school; or two years in another vocational training school, for example, for typist training. Graduates of secondary grammar and vocational schools can gain access to postsecondary education in universities, colleges, vocational training institutions, or in the additional class of a vocational secondary school. The main reforms, presaged by the 1993 Public Education and Vocational Education Acts now being implemented, are an increase in the duration of primary education from 8 to 10 years and postponement of the age of entry to vocational education from 14 to 16. However, the whole system is in a state of flux as schools respond in different ways to the pressing problems they face.

The trauma of transition has not caused any reduction in educational enrollment ratios. Indeed, for all except apprentice schools, such ratios increased substantially during the 1990s. Table 1-4 shows the continuation rates in the educational system in 1990 and 1994. As can be seen, almost all primary school graduates now go on to postprimary education, most of them into some form of vocational education or training (VET). The proportion of vocational secondary school graduates going on to higher education is much lower than in the case of grammar school graduates. The proportion of primary school leavers who eventually enter higher education is more than 11 percent and rising.

Those who do not continue their studies join the labor market from the various levels of the education system. Few new entrants to the labor force are primary school dropouts—less than 4 percent in 1994—but they are overrepresented among the unemployed. Even though their importance is diminishing, graduates from apprentice schools still account for a third of new entrants. Only 15 percent of those who had just graduated from secondary school who joined the labor market in 1994 were from grammar schools, which illustrates the dominance of VET.

TABLE 1-4

Continuation Rates from Primary to Secondary Schools and from
Secondary Schools to Higher Education, 1990 and 1994

(percent unless otherwise indicated)

| School continuation rate | 1990 | 1994 |
|---|---|---|
| Completed primary school (number) | 164,616 | 136,864 |
| Entering secondary schools | 93.8 | 98.8 |
| Entering grammar schools | 21.1 | 25.7 |
| Entering vocational secondary schools | 27.5 | 32.6 |
| Entering apprentice schools | 42.0 | 35.2 |
| Entering other vocational training schemes | 3.2 | 5.3 |
| Completed grammar school (number) | 24,053 | 30,829 |
| Entering higher education | 30.1 | 40.9 |
| Completed vocational secondary school (number) | 28,382 | 36,580 |
| Entering higher education | 11.9 | 16.9 |

*Source:* Benedek (1995); CSO (various years).

## Vocational Education

Vocational education has expanded at a slower rate than has general education. Growth between 1985–86 and 1994–95, however, was fast (table 1-
5). Enrollment in vocational secondary schools overtook that in the declining
apprentice schools in 1993–94, and enrollment in other vocational schools
(including health and typing) stabilized at around 30,000.

As table 1-6 shows, by far the largest category of vocational secondary
schools is the industrial/technical. The fastest expansion has been in the
small "other" category, followed by commercial, art, agricultural, and economic vocational secondary schools. Some gender stereotyping is evident,
with women overrepresented in kindergarten teaching, health, postal, economic, commercial, and art schools and underrepresented in industrial/
technical and agricultural schools.

In apprentice schools the largest categories are machine production,
maintenance and repair, construction, clothing, and trade, although enrollment in all these fields contracted during the 1990s (table 1-7). Miscellaneous services and the wood industry are the only major categories that
expanded. Evidence of some lumpiness in the system is the increase in
third-year enrollment in some categories for which total enrollment has
fallen, such as metallurgy, clothing, construction, and transportation.

TABLE 1-5
Full-time Enrollment in Secondary Vocational Education,
1990–91 to 1994–95
(thousands of students)

| Year | Vocational secondary schools | Apprentice schools | Other vocational training schools | Total |
|---|---|---|---|---|
| 1990–91 | 168 | 209 | 16 | 393 |
| 1991–92 | 179 | 205 | 21 | 405 |
| 1992–93 | 186 | 189 | 28 | 403 |
| 1993–94 | 192 | 174 | 30 | 396 |
| 1994–95 | 196 | 163 | 28 | 387 |
| Percentage change, 1985–86 to 1994–95 | 85 | −7 | 115 | 21 |

Source: Benedek (1995).

TABLE 1-6
Enrollment in Vocational Secondary Schools,
by Type of School and Gender, 1990–91 and 1994–95

| Type of school | Total enrollment 1994–95 | Percentage change from 1990–91 | Full-time enrollment 1994–95 | Percentage of women enrolled full time |
|---|---|---|---|---|
| Industrial/technical | 120,803 | 17 | 84,626 | 23 |
| Agricultural | 20,472 | 22 | 19,792 | 38 |
| Economic | 51,138 | 21 | 39,546 | 75 |
| Commercial | 20,126 | 30 | 15,402 | 74 |
| Catering | 10,799 | 17 | 7,255 | 53 |
| Transport | 792 | −17 | 631 | 45 |
| Postal | 4,265 | −5 | 3,675 | 83 |
| Health | 16,166 | −6 | 16,002 | 94 |
| Kindergarten teachers | 1,306 | −71 | 1,306 | 98 |
| Art | 3,345 | 26 | 3,345 | 62 |
| Other | 5,466 | 500 | 5,385 | 81 |
| Total | 254,678 | 17 | 196,965 | 50 |

Source: CSO (various years).

TABLE 1-7
Apprentice School Trainees, by Field, 1990–91 and 1993–94

| Field | Total trainees, 1993–94 | Percentage change from 1990–91 | Third-year trainees, 1993–94 | Percentage change from 1990–91 |
|---|---|---|---|---|
| Machine production, maintenance | 50,911 | −11 | 14,943 | −3 |
| Clothing | 18,544 | −2 | 5,943 | 13 |
| Construction | 19,737 | −17 | 6,318 | 4 |
| Trade | 16,109 | −37 | 6,738 | −13 |
| Catering | 9,694 | −6 | 2,985 | −5 |
| Transportation | 928 | −29 | 361 | 52 |
| Wood industry | 10,360 | 10 | 3,164 | 20 |
| Miscellaneous services | 12,023 | 34 | 2,515 | 33 |
| Others | 39,500 | −15 | 15,500 | −5 |
| Total | 174,418 | −17 | 54,867 | −2 |

Source: Fejes (1994).

Total enrollment in higher education is more than 150,000, with engineering being the largest single specialization (close to 35,000 students), while the various kinds of teacher training account for almost a quarter of total enrollment. Universities account for 43 percent of total enrollment in higher education, and foreign students for 4 percent of university students.

As table 1-8 shows, the differences between current expenditure per student in various levels of education are relatively small, with the exception of tertiary education, which is three to four times as expensive as other levels. In real terms, unit costs at all levels except primary and apprentice schools fell during the 1990s.

Most of the recurrent expenditure incurred by schools consists of salaries. Different types of schools vary little in this respect (65 percent for grammar schools, 63 percent for vocational secondary schools, and 61 percent for apprentice schools), which is perhaps a sign of inadequate expenditure on materials by vocational schools.

Most funding for education comes in the form of a subsidy from the central government (the so-called "normative" contribution per pupil). It is channeled through local governments. This subsidy is estimated to account for 59 percent of total current costs in the case of grammar schools,

TABLE 1-8
Recurrent Expenditure Per Full-Time Student,
by Level and Type of School, 1990–91 and 1994–95
(Hungarian forints)

| School | 1994–95 | Nominal percentage change from 1990–91 | Real percentage change from 1990–91 |
|---|---|---|---|
| Kindergartens | 93,417 | 136 | –2 |
| Primary schools | 99,332 | 167 | 10 |
| Apprentice schools | 121,503 | 155 | 6 |
| Secondary grammar schools | 106,034 | 116 | –11 |
| Vocational secondary schools | 113,469 | 92 | –21 |
| Third-level education | 377,474 | 89 | –22 |

*Source:* CSO (various years); National Bank of Hungary data.

61 percent for vocational secondary schools, and 85 percent for apprentice schools (Lannert 1994). There is some dispute about the figures for apprentice schools. In 1992 an official survey found that 70 to 80 percent of their costs were financed by the central government grant, 7 to 8 percent by local governments, 2 to 13 percent by direct contributions from companies, up to 2 percent by the Vocational Training Fund (VTF) and other foundations, and 4 to 13 percent by the schools' own income and other sources. However, representatives of the Budapest and Debrecen local governments have stated that they had to find 30 to 40 percent of funding from noncentral government sources.

The VTF, a central budgetary subfund estimated to be worth about 10,000 million Hungarian forints (HUF) in 1995, is financed by contributions from employers (1.5 percent of the wage bill, or 1 percent in the case of agriculture). It operates as a levy-grant fund and is of significant importance to vocational education. If an enterprise engages in training, its contribution to the VTF is commensurately reduced, to the extent that it can claim back a surplus of expenditures over contributions. Training for this purpose can consist of providing training within the enterprise, including the purchase of equipment for group training. Supporting workshop-based practical training in a vocational secondary school or apprentice school or making direct, voluntary payments to schools also count as training.

Few nongovernment schools exist: 91.6 percent of secondary schools are funded by local governments, 2.6 percent directly from the central government budget, 2.1 percent by foundations or private owners, 3.1 percent by churches, and fewer than 0.7 percent by other organizations. However, the number of private foundations is growing. There are 3,000 of them concerned with education, of which 600 are concerned with VET (Benedek 1995).

The framework for managing and regulating Hungary's vocational education system is complex, since many actors are involved. The Ministry of Labor is responsible for vocational education, though other ministries have a say in the content of training relevant to them. The Ministry of Education is responsible for general education, including the teaching provided in the vocational schools, and for the transfer of the funds from the central government to local governments. Local governments are responsible for almost all schools and make decisions about establishing schools or closing them down and on appointments of principals. The National Training Council, a subcommittee of the National Council for Reconciliation of Interests, which includes representatives of employers' and employees' organizations, has authority over the distribution of the VTF.

The Vocational Training Act, which became law in 1993, defines a new division of labor between schools (which are responsible for teaching theory) and enterprises (which are responsible for practical training of formally contracted apprentices). The act sets out the conditions for the provision of vocational training by institutions outside the school system.

## Vocational Training Institutes and Retraining Programs

The relative roles of the state and the private sector in providing training outside the school system changed a great deal during the 1990s. State training centers used to be extremely important. (More than 306,000 people completed some training in them in 1989.) No reliable data on current enrollment are available, however. Many state training centers have been closed or privatized. Of those currently operating, the most important are the new regional training centers (RTCs), partially financed from a World Bank loan. Eight are now up and running. They compete with the growing number of private training institutions for contracts for retraining the unemployed; the contracts are financed from the VTF and from a second central budgetary subfund known as the Employment Fund (EF).

TABLE 1-9
Participants in State-Subsidized Retraining Courses, 1992–94
(thousands)

| Participants | 1992 | 1993 | 1994 |
|---|---|---|---|
| Total number of participants | 58 | 90 | 94 |
| Number in courses offering a training certificate | 57 | 78 | 81 |
| Number in semiskilled courses | 7 | 12 | 13 |

Source: Benedek (1995).

The EF finances all types of active labor market programs. The tripartite National Labor Market Committee has determined the principles on which the EF is to be used. The committee distributes approximately 60 percent of the EF, based on set criteria, to county labor councils that can spend the funds as they deem fit. The remainder of the EF that is earmarked for training is then distributed by the National Training Council on the basis of competitive bidding. Table 1-9 shows the growth in the number of participants in training courses funded by the EF. Of the 1994 participants, only 4 percent were currently employed; 36 percent were unemployed school leavers, and 60 percent were other unemployed. Half of the participants were below the age of 25; two-thirds, below the age of 35. Eighty-five percent had secondary school or higher qualifications and/or a vocational certificate. Seventy-four percent were trained in groups; the remainder, as individuals.

Established in October 1991, the first RTC serves three counties in northern Hungary with high unemployment rates. During its first two years more than 5,000 students completed courses in a wide range of trades. By 1994 three centers were operating; they launched a total of 810 courses involving 14,000 students. The dropout rate was estimated at 12 percent. Most of those who dropped out left to take up employment. The centers are owned by local governments and the Ministry of Labor, but only 30 to 40 percent of their income comes from a state subsidy (Benedek 1995); the rest comes from income from training contracts.

For those contracts the RTCs compete on equal terms with nongovernment training institutions of various types. Some are the privatized training departments of state enterprises such as the Csepel power station (Lannert 1994). Some in urban areas belong to foundations and have specializations similar to the RTCs. Some are new private companies aimed at

TABLE 1-10
Training Providers for Labor Market Courses, 1995
(number)

| Ownership | Institutions | Courses | Participants |
|---|---|---|---|
| Limited company | 43 | 230 | 4,857 |
| Sole proprietor | 66 | 409 | 13,563 |
| Cooperative | 31 | 165 | 3,148 |
| Other enterprise | 4 | 42 | 851 |
| Self-employed | 3 | 22 | 333 |
| Central budget organization | 29 | 613 | 10,725 |
| Local government organization | 79 | 284 | 5,936 |
| Social insurance organization | 1 | 1 | 31 |
| Nonprofit organization | 8 | 26 | 447 |
| State enterprise | 1 | 2 | 53 |
| State enterprise to be privatized | 1 | 4 | 51 |
| State enterprise under liquidation | 2 | 10 | 212 |
| Other nonmarket | 1 | 2 | 47 |
| Unknown | 86 | 430 | 12,015 |
| Total | 355 | 2,240 | 52,269 |

Source: Ministry of Labor (1995).

the obvious markets in computer science, languages, and secretarial skills (OECD/CCET 1995). Many are very small, set up to profit from EF contracts. They are required to register with the Ministry of Labor, but effective accreditation or a quality control system has not been put in place to date. Table 1-10 shows the wide range of ownership of training providers for labor market courses in 1995.

As the table shows, small, private organizations run by sole proprietors provided the largest amount of training (by number of participants). State organizations were responsible for less than a third of this type of training. Data on the sectors to which these 355 training providers belong show that more than 65 percent are classified as being in the education sector. In other words, they are training centers rather than factories. Only small amounts of training are done in-plant—mainly in the real estate, manufacturing, trade and transport, and hotel and restaurant sectors.

Total expenditure on labor market training is substantial. In 1993 it amounted to HUF 3,679 million (approximately US$37 million), the largest single item of expenditure on active labor market programs (Frey 1994). The average cost of such courses outside Budapest was HUF 68,000 for a vocational certificate and HUF 47,000 for semiskilled courses.

Pulay (1995) calculated the cost per completer and per placement for retraining courses in 1994 at the regional level. The average retraining cost per completer was HUF 90,000 and per placement was HUF 192,000. (Less than 50 percent of the completers were placed in jobs within six months of completing training.) Completion rates are high in almost all regions, but placement rates vary from 34 to 71 percent. The retraining cost per completer also varies widely, from HUF 31,000 to HUF 128,000, with Budapest having the highest costs. The cost per placement ranges from HUF 73,000 to as high as HUF 262,000.

These figures are interesting, but on their own they are an insufficient indicator of external efficiency. Placement rates show how successful training is in terms of gross outcome. Some of these counties are extremely successful in these terms, others less so. The RTCs appear to have been even more successful: 40 percent of their graduates in 1994 reportedly found jobs after three months and 60 percent after six months (Benedek 1995). However, gross outcome is not the same as net impact. The question is: how much better did these individuals fare in the labor market than they would have done if they had not had this training? To measure the net impact of training in this sense a control or comparison group is needed. Table 1-11 shows the results of a two-stage survey carried out in three counties in November 1992 and 1993. It included a comparison group to measure the difference made by training.

In 1992 a total of 1,574 people were interviewed in three categories: people who first registered as unemployed in June 1991, people who entered retraining in the second half of 1991, and people who participated in public service employment in September 1991. The investigators attempted to interview the same individuals a year later and traced 1,478 of them. The analysis in table 1-11 is based on a sample of 368 graduates of the training and a comparison group of 571 registered unemployed who had not participated in an active labor market program in November 1992, and 445 graduates of the training and a comparison group of 589 in November 1993. Two measures of the impact of the training were used: impact on the probability of obtaining a normal (unsubsidized) job and impact on monthly earnings. As the first row in each part of the table shows, training had a statistically significant, positive impact on employment and a statistically insignificant impact on earnings if the unadjusted mean out-

TABLE 1-11
Retraining and Labor Market Outcomes,
November 1992 and November 1993

| Estimation methodology | Impact on probability of obtaining normal job (percentage) | Impact on earnings gain (HUF per month) |
|---|---|---|
| *November 1992 survey* | | |
| Unadjusted for characteristics | 6.6[a] | 649 |
| *Adjusted for observable characteristics* | | |
| By regression | –4.4 | –3,580[a] |
| By matched pairs | –8.0[b] | –513 |
| *November 1993 survey* | | |
| Unadjusted for characteristics | 19.2[a] | 1,487 |
| *Adjusted for observable characteristics* | | |
| By regression | 6.3[b] | 493 |
| By matched pairs | 1.2 | 2,052 |

a. Significant at the 95 percent confidence level in a two-tail test.
b. Significant at the 90 percent confidence level in a two-tail test.
*Sources:* Godfrey, Lázár, and O'Leary (1993); O'Leary (1994).

comes of the two groups are compared. This is true particularly by the time of the second survey. However, the results are much less impressive if results are adjusted for differences in observable characteristics between the two groups, either by regression analysis or by use of the matched-pairs technique. The first survey shows training to have had a statistically significant, negative impact on earnings, according to the regression analysis, and a negative impact on employment probability, according to the matched-pairs analysis. The second survey shows a positive but small impact on employment probability according to the regression analysis, but all the other results are statistically insignificant.

Even more interesting than the aggregate results are the results of subgroup analysis shown in table 1-12. The statistically significant estimates of the impact on employment probability suggest that the impact increases with age. It is highest for those over 40, about the same for men as for women, higher for those with less schooling and for those in nonmanual specializations, and higher than average in Borsod County, which has the highest unemployment rate of the three.

TABLE 1-12

Impacts of Completing Retraining on Probability of Obtaining
a Normal Job, by Subgroup, November 1993

| Subgroup | Impact estimate | Standard error |
| --- | --- | --- |
| Age 25 or less | 0.072 | 0.051 |
| Age 26 to 40 | 0.136[a] | 0.074 |
| Age over 40 | 0.264[b] | 0.103 |
| Female | 0.112[b] | 0.049 |
| Male | 0.130[b] | 0.048 |
| Education 8 years or less | 0.219[b] | 0.077 |
| Education more than 8 years | 0.071 | 0.043 |
| Nonmanual specialization | 0.079[a] | 0.046 |
| Manual specialization | 0.201[b] | 0.064 |
| Not received unemployment benefits since 6/1991 | 0.049 | 0.066 |
| Received unemployment benefits since 6/1991 | 0.144[b] | 0.043 |
| Worked before 6/1991 | 0.137[b] | 0.045 |
| Never worked before 6/1991 | 0.080 | 0.074 |
| Borsod County | 0.159[b] | 0.051 |
| Hajdú-B County | 0.079 | 0.060 |
| Somogy County | 0.064 | 0.068 |

a. Significant at the 90 percent confidence level in a two-tail test.
b. Significant at the 95 percent confidence level in a two-tail test.
Source: O'Leary (1994).

It appears from this that labor market training may be concentrating on categories of students who can achieve the highest outcomes, but on whom it has the least impact, because, as noted earlier, half of the participants are below the age of 25 and 85 percent have secondary or higher qualifications or a vocational certificate. On the basis of their analysis of flows into and out of unemployment insurance, Micklewright and Nagy (1994) note that those with low levels of education have far lower chances of leaving unemployment insurance for training. They define the situation as follows:

Among men, someone with general or vocational secondary education is over four times more likely to leave UI [unemployment insurance] for a training scheme than is a person who has only completed primary education. Among women, the probability is over five times higher.... This may reflect a variety of factors. The more educated may be more willing to retrain or may react more to the incentives offered (a 10 percent addition to unemployment benefit). They may be more able to find private training courses that the employment office will approve. The employment offices may offer training courses only to the more educated. The part played by selection policy of employment offices (or by national policy in the design of training schemes) seems misplaced given that the more educated have a notably higher probability of finding a job in any case.

Gill and Dar (1995) creatively combine the November 1993 results on impact with estimates of cost to simulate a cost-benefit analysis of training compared with unemployment benefits (table 1-13). If the matched-pairs technique is used, as increases in reemployment probability and earning gains from training are insignificant, it appears that training never pays off regardless of the duration of unemployment benefits. If it is assumed that the gains from training persist over the entire working life of individuals (a rather generous assumption), regression-adjusted estimates yield a benefit-to-cost ratio of 0.97 for an average unemployment benefits duration of six months. That is, it takes more than 30 years for training to pay off. If the average duration for which unemployment benefits are paid is a year, re-training pays off in about 10 years. If, however, the reemployment probability gain from training is transient, training will never pay off, regardless of the duration of unemployment benefits. On the basis of these findings, Gill and Dar (1995, p. 12) conclude that "it seems difficult to justify large scale retraining programs on economic considerations alone."

## Enterprise-Based Training

Little systematic information is available about enterprise-based training, but observers generally agree that it has collapsed, along with many of the large enterprises, and that this is one of the greatest problems the training system faces. An indication of the extent of the collapse is given by the fall in the number of factory workshops available for practical training by apprentice school pupils (table 1-14).

As a result of the virtual halving of the number of factory workshops, schools have been forced to expand their own workshops, thereby considerably reducing their connection with industry. As the large state enterprise workshops have closed, the role of small private enterprises in providing

TABLE 1-13
Simulated Cost-Benefit Analysis of Retraining in Relation
to Unemployment Benefits

| | Average duration of unemployment benefits | |
|---|---|---|
| Evaluation technique | 6 months | 12 months |
| Differences in economic costs (US$) | 1,964 | 900 |
| Differences in financial costs | 1,525 | 900 |
| Differences in forgone earnings | 439 | 0 |
| Matched-pairs analysis | | |
| Benefit-to-cost ratio | 0 | 0 |
| Time taken to recover costs (years) | Never | Never |
| Regression-adjusted analysis | | |
| Benefit-to-cost ratio | 0.97 | 2.11 |
| Time taken to recover costs (years) | 33 | 10 |

*Notes*: Unemployment benefits are assumed to be US$1,250 annually, based on mini-mum unemployment benefits of US$1,030 in 1993 (Burda 1995). Retraining program costs are assumed to be US$900 per participant, and the duration is assumed to be one year (Pulay 1995). Differences are based on monthly earnings and reemployment rates of re-training participants relative to those who only received unemployment benefits. Economic costs include financial costs (fixed at US$900 for retraining and at US$104 per month for unemployment benefit) and forgone earnings (US$0 if the program length is the same as unemployment benefits, negative if unemployment benefits last longer than the retraining program). Forgone earnings for retrainees are computed as follows: the average earnings of unemployment benefit recipients (US$148 per month) are multiplied by the number of months that retraining duration exceeds unemployment benefits duration and the prob-ability of being employed during these months.
*Source*: Gill and Dar (1995).

practical training for school pupils has increased. They now predominate in this role in all sectors except transport and telecommunications. Much of this training is organized by the National Association of Craftsmen, which has also contributed to curriculum development in the schools (Lannert 1994).

The reduced role of enterprises in factory-based training of appren-tices is matched by a reduction in the training of their own employees. The state enterprise workshops that have disappeared or have been sold off or privatized as profit-oriented training centers had been used for this function also. The new joint ventures bring their own in-plant training

TABLE 1-14
Factory-Based Workshops and Training Posts Available
to Apprentice School Pupils, 1990–91 to 1994–95

| Year | Number of factory workshops | Percentage of total workshops | Number of factory training posts | Percentage of total training posts |
|------|------|------|------|------|
| 1990–91 | 3,039 | 76 | 52,338 | 75 |
| 1991–92 | 2,718 | 70 | 46,710 | 67 |
| 1992–93 | 2,304 | 61 | 40,607 | 59 |
| 1993–94 | 1,829 | 52 | 35,237 | 52 |
| 1994–95 | 1,617 | 47 | 32,349 | 48 |

*Source:* Benedek (1995, table 3.1.1).

systems, but little is known about them. The new small enterprises offer practical training to some apprentice school pupils—seen as a source of cheap labor according to Lannert (1994)—but like small enterprises everywhere, they prefer to poach the skilled workers they need rather than to train new workers.

Training for the civil service (currently undergoing a 15 percent cut in staff in two stages) is taken seriously in Hungary. The Public Administration College organizes preservice and off-the-job training and sets two examinations, basic and professional, which all must pass within a set time limit in order to remain in the service. Ministries have a small budget for training of individuals. A number of aid agencies have projects to strengthen the public administration. Britain, Germany, and the European Union's Phare program (1995) have participated in these projects.

Enterprise-based training is regulated by the 1991 Employment Act and the 1993 Vocational Training Act, which defined the responsibilities of the National Training Council, including the allocation of grants from the levy-funded VTF and the award of contracts from the EF. An amendment to the Vocational Training Act, passed in October 1995, has led to some confusion about tripartite arrangements. It sets up a new National Council for Vocational Training, without decisionmaking powers, and merges the VTF, the EF, and various other funds into a single Labor Market Fund under the control of the Ministry of Labor. It also assigns a major role to the emerging chambers of commerce and industry (or employers' associations), particularly in accreditation and examinations—a role assumed temporarily by the Ministry of Labor until the chambers are strong enough to take over. All this leaves the old National Training Council with an uncertain future (Bessenyei 1995).

## Major VET Issues

The major issues for vocational education and training concern organization, costs, and efficiency.

### *Organization and Management*

Organization and management are perhaps the most striking issues in the field of VET in Hungary. As already discussed, the division of responsibility for the system is complex, involving the ministries of Labor and Education; other ministries; local governments; and, through their membership in the Vocational Training Council, employers and employees. Schools in a decentralized system are supposed to have a high degree of autonomy. Inevitably, differences arise in the points of view of the various parties involved. Broadly, the Ministry of Labor favors vocational education, the Ministry of Education and many local governments favor general education, and employers favor a dual training system. Meanwhile, employers, particularly those running private training institutions, tend to dislike the RTCs and want practical training to be located in enterprises. The Ministry of Labor and the trade unions, which tend to represent the teachers, think schools should run their own workshops. More important than these and other disagreements is a lack of clarity about exactly who is responsible, particularly at the local level. As Halasz (1994, p. 58) comments, instruments appropriate for a decentralized system and the sharing of responsibilities have not yet been found. Since 1990, when the 20 counties (including Budapest) lost their jurisdiction over lower level authorities, the middle level of the educational administration has disappeared. This managerial muddle, in which conflicts are not resolved but avoided, is a context for inertia rather than reform.

### *Costs and Financing*

The costs of vocational schools appear to be low, but a high proportion of current expenditure goes to salaries, raising the question of whether the schools spend enough on materials. As for sources of revenue, schools are allowed to earn income and to use it for their own purposes. Lannert (1994) gives examples of schools that use their workshops as enterprises, employing skilled workers and plowing profits back into the schools, and of others that obtain funds from employers under the auspices of the VTF. Sixty to 80 percent of expenditure is still funded by the government, however. The challenge for vocational schools of all types is to expand their nongovernment funding to the point where it covers the entire cost of the vocational part of their curricula.

VOCATIONAL TRAINING INSTITUTES. Cost and financing issues are equally pressing for vocational training institutes. Ideally, the RTCs, which are 30 to 40 percent state subsidized, would be entirely self-supporting. The revenue needed would be even greater if the practical content of their training was increased to the extent that many observers think would be desirable. With skill training for the unemployed probably on the decline, the centers need to attract more sponsorship from enterprises for pre-employment or off-plant employee training, and they should also offer more courses for which individual students are willing to pay full fees. At present the centers recover some 15 to 20 percent of their costs from employer-sponsored and self-funding sources.

LEVY-GRANT SYSTEM. Hungary is fortunate in already having a levy-grant system, which can help to solve some of these financing problems. Although the system has been properly placed within a tripartite structure, the government has tended to exercise control over it because of the weakness of the organizations involved. Mártonfi (1995) asked 340 top managers to assess on a scale of 0 to 100 the influence of various actors on the allocation of the VTF. They judged that government and ministries have the strongest influence (score of 87), followed by local governments (41), schools and training institutions (37), employers' associations (32), and trade unions (21). In the managers' opinion the order of precedence should be more or less reversed, with employers followed by schools exerting the strongest influence and government, central and local, playing a less dominant role. As an example of undue government influence, employers cite the use of the VTF to finance the National Vocational Training Institute. They believe this research and development organization should be financed from the government budget (Lannert 1994). Regardless of how it is allocated, the VTF needs to retain a separate identity if it is to operate as a levy-grant fund increasingly oriented toward enterprise training. The move to combine it with the EF and other funds in a single Labor Market Fund does not seem to be helpful.

*Efficiency*

On the related issue of efficiency, Halasz (1994) suggests that the whole vocational training system is facing a three-fold crisis of legitimacy, institutions, and structures. The crisis of legitimacy arises from the place in the previous regime of vocational training, narrowly specialist, preferred to broad, general education, and tightly linked to unproductive and inefficient state enterprises. The institutional crisis is caused by the decline of industry and the disappearance of workshops and training places. The structural crisis reflects the slow adjustment of schools to changes in the labor market. Many "continue training pupils in fields that are certainly not needed and will probably never more be needed in such a high proportion" (Halasz 1994).

APPRENTICE SCHOOLS. The threefold crisis that affects the system is nowhere more evident than in the apprentice schools. Their institutional crisis is acute, as practical training becomes increasingly difficult to arrange and the growing involvement of small, private enterprises raises quality control problems. Even more acute is their structural crisis in the face of transformed labor markets. With an unemployment rate among apprentice school leavers of 15 percent (only slightly lower than the primary school rate of 19.5 percent), the schools continue to churn out people in unemployable trades. The rate of inflow of apprentice school graduates into the unemployment insurance benefit register is also similar to that of primary school graduates. The impact of apprentice schooling on wages has remained unchanged since 1986—around 10 percent above the rate for completion of primary school. The estimated social rate of return is low, at 2.6 percent, less than half of that for secondary grammar and vocational schools. There are methodological problems with calculating the rate of return to a type of schooling that, as Timár (1994) points out, gets "only poor students, rejected by either of the two other school types." Unless the comparison group is deliberately chosen to reflect the low quality of the intake (for example, confined to graduates of primary school with the lowest grades), the incremental income attributable to this type of schooling is understated, just as it is overstated for schools that have an intake of above average quality. Nevertheless, the external efficiency of the apprentice schools is clearly in doubt.

VOCATIONAL SECONDARY SCHOOLS. The efficiency of the vocational secondary schools is less easy to judge because of the shortage of data. The unemployment rate among their graduates, at 6 percent, is relatively low. The inflow rate into the unemployment insurance register is higher than for grammar school graduates, and the probability of exit to a job is lower for men, but not for women. There are no separate rate of return estimates. The schools are, in any case, in the process of transformation. The new vocational secondary schools based on the World Bank model are popular with parents (Lannert 1994, p. 60), and their ratio of applications to places is near the top of the league table. This suggests that at least the private rate of return to such schooling is high and augurs well for the chances of greater cost recovery.

LABOR MARKET TRAINING. The two-stage survey of those who entered retraining in the second half of 1991 suggested that the impact of labor market training on employment probability and earnings gain in 1992 and 1993 was small or negative. These results combined with cost estimates in a cost-benefit simulation led to the conclusion that large-scale retraining programs are difficult to justify on economic considerations alone.

Training specialists have criticized this conclusion on the following grounds:

• *Training programs under review were still of relatively low quality.* Much has changed since the training under review and the two surveys were carried out. If the training had been of higher quality, its internal efficiency would certainly have been improved. Its external efficiency, however, would depend on whether the low returns to training reflected primarily poor internal efficiency or weakness of demand in the labor market. The improvement in the impact of the same training between the first and second surveys suggests the importance of labor market factors. It reflects the passage of time but also an improvement in the labor market between the two surveys. Although the quality of the best retraining has undoubtedly been increasing, whether this applies to average training is not at all certain given the problems of accreditation and quality control for the burgeoning private training sector.

• *Incentives for placement had not yet been developed.* Incentives tend to increase placement in a given situation. This may or may not have a positive effect on the net impact of training. Such incentives reinforce the tendency of trainers to "cream," that is, admit to courses those who would be able to find a job even without the training.

• *The costs of social assistance after exhaustion of unemployment benefits were not included in the costs of the passive alternative.* Social assistance rather than the provision of insured unemployment benefits is becoming the dominant mode of support for the unemployed. However, this does not necessarily have much effect on the substance (as opposed to the wording) of the assumptions made in the cost-benefit simulation. Those who participate in training courses are in categories of workers (younger and more educated) who do not stay unemployed for long, however financed. The assumptions for the comparison with the passive alternative reflect this.

New evaluations are needed of all types of VET, not just labor market training, that link internal and external efficiency. Such evaluations, with properly chosen comparison or control groups, must focus on net impacts rather than merely on gross outcomes or placements. Types of training that have favorable outcomes (as measured by placement rates) cannot be assumed to have favorable impacts.

One of the most striking issues to arise from the surveys, and from analyses of flows into and out of insured unemployment, is that labor market training may be concentrating on those who need it least in order to get a job: the relatively young and well educated. The Ministry of Labor has recognized this, and the World Bank has welcomed a shift in training emphasis toward the long-term unemployed, who are often men, old and poorly educated, with learning disabilities or marginal disabilities. Criteria for allocating funds will need to reflect this new emphasis.

Special attention has to be paid to the regional training centers, perhaps the most controversial vocational training institutes in Hungary. Economists and trainers disagree about whether it made sense for an extremely indebted economy to borrow US$25 million to help set up these centers. Most economists question the need for such an investment because of the weakness of demand for labor and the existence of other usable facilities that could have been converted more cheaply. By contrast, trainers point to RTCs' symbolic importance, to their effect on teachers' attitudes, and to their role in setting standards of quality and value in competition with private trainers. Realists point to what might be called the political economy of World Bank projects: the centers represented the only chance for the Ministry of Labor to become eligible not only for loan money, but also for counterpart funds that would not otherwise have been made available to it for training purposes by the Ministry of Finance. The RTCs' placement rates are reported to be high, but given the high quality of their intake, this cannot be taken as an incontrovertible indicator of favorable impact. Whatever the verdict on the external efficiency of RTCs, some issues of internal efficiency also need attention. The supervision report at the end of 1994 found evidence of underutilization of expensive equipment. (The norm was a single training session from 8 a.m. to 2 p.m.) Criticisms have also been leveled at the centers' excessively theoretical approach to teaching. Both criticisms may represent national tendencies that go beyond the centers. As the supervision report points out, the role and constitution of the centers within the VET system need to be clarified: are they to be strategic, national institutions in a favored position or autonomous, unsubsidized profit centers competing with other training providers on a "level playing field"?

Because the transition to labor markets has been accompanied by an increase in poverty and inequality, equity has become a more important issue in Hungary. Training can play a role in combating poverty and inequality, but only a small role. Since a person's prior general education determines his or her access to training, an approach to equalization that is confined to training will produce only marginal improvements in the situation of disadvantaged groups. They will still be overrepresented in low education, low-income occupations, and among the unemployed. This is particularly true of Hungary's largest and most disadvantaged minority, the Gypsies. Regression analysis shows that the huge differences in unemployment rates and wages between Gypsies and non-Gypsies are due to three factors: discrimination, location, and education (Kertesi 1994). A national sample survey in 1993 found that 43 percent of Gypsies had less than eight years of primary schooling, and that even for 20- to 24-year-olds, the figure was 25 percent (Kemény, Havas, and Kertesi 1994). Kertesi found that a typical Gypsy child age six in 1981 had 15 times less chance to continue his or her studies in a secondary school and 50 times less chance to study at a university than a non-Gypsy six-year-old.

In these circumstances, the only training programs for which most Gypsies qualify are those that will lock them into relatively low-paid occupations or continued unemployment. Indeed, they are well represented among apprentice school pupils (Kemény, Havas, and Kertesi 1994, p. 11). The Ministry of Labor has been grappling with labor market programs for the Gypsy community, and an excellent nongovernment organization—the Autonomia Foundation—has much experience in this field. However, education rather than training is the key. Kertesi (1994, p. 33) recommends increasing the mandatory school-leaving age for all. This may or may not be necessary, but there is certainly a need for equity-conscious education planners to ensure that all children, whatever their background, complete high-quality primary and lower secondary schooling (Carnoy 1993). Subsidized preschool kindergarten programs for disadvantaged children are the starting point for this (Costarelli 1993). Remedial general education for adults who have not completed basic education may make sense as a precondition for training. The problems of inequality cannot be solved by the training system alone.

## Notable Reforms

Despite the problems identified so far, Hungary has made remarkable progress in reshaping its VET system to meet the challenges of markets. In particular, it has established a framework of laws and institutions within which the system can develop. The National Vocational Training Institute has been set up as the research and development organization for the system, the first institution of its kind in the region. The elements of a levy-grant system are in place, with the potential to eliminate subsidies and to offset disincentives to training that arise from the inability of employers who do train to capture its benefits.

The school system is in the process of restructuring. The age of vocational specialization is due to be postponed, apprentice schools are shrinking and gradually moving closer to the market, vocational secondary schools are increasing the general content of their curricula, the baccalaureate examination is being extended to technical subjects, and all examinations and curricula are undergoing modernization. The system has become increasingly complex. As Lannert (1994) points out, the simple apprentice school "has almost vanished and now in the same institution we find a special vocational school, a vocational training [apprentice] school, a secondary vocational school, and even a grammar school or a primary school."

At the same time marketization and decentralization are beginning to differentiate the more from the less innovative schools. The innovative apprentice/vocational school, as characterized by Lannert (1994), will have the following features: growing or stable enrollment; a fundamentally changed curriculum, including such offerings as craft classes or those associated with the World Bank project; a cooperative attitude toward the RTCs; well-equipped workshops for new forms of practical training and flourishing connections with enterprises; a school enterprise employing skilled workers rather than school pupils; a manager/director rather than a principal; and a staff member responsible for fundraising and keeping in touch with enterprises. An example of an innovative school is one in Csepel. It changed its specialization from textiles to catering and has secured a long-term contract with a luxury hotel in Budapest (Lannert 1994, p. 65). The less innovative school, on the other hand, will have decreasing enrollment, few structural changes other than starting secondary vocational classes, a hostile attitude toward the RTCs, traditional forms of practical training, no school enterprise apart from a shop or rented school buildings, and a pedagogic style of principal.

A striking change in the past few years is the huge increase in the role of private training institutions and in the use of tenders and competition for training contracts. The RTCs compete on equal terms in these tenders, though with the advantage of a substantial government subsidy. An important weakness in the new system is the absence of an accreditation or quality control system. It is gradually being developed, but in its absence, many of the new private training institutions exploit the system (Lannert 1994). Hungary's experience may demonstrate that privatization of training requires a bigger role of government in accreditation (working wherever possible through professional associations) to avoid the risk of wastage.

Criteria are needed for allocating funds from the center to the regions for training and other labor market programs. Hungary (along with Poland) leads the way here with the development of a management system based on performance indicators (O'Leary 1995). For example, an indicator of training program performance is average cost per course completer who is employed at follow-up. It is proposed that this and a few similar indicators should be added to the algorithm for allocation of the decentralized portion of the EF across counties. Demographic data and indicators of regional unemployment are used to adjust national standards for local conditions. Data are already being collected, and the system has been tested in several counties. Progress is impressive, but a few dangers arise from the focus on the gross outcome rather than net impact. Adjusting targets according to local conditions may reduce "creaming," but to know whether training courses are worth supporting at all, data on average cost per unit of impact, rather than on average cost per completer employed, are needed. This, in turn, requires data on a comparison group, which could be drawn from the quarterly labor force survey. The deletion of performance indicators based on earnings from the system is regrettable (O'Leary 1994).

One of the most serious obstacles to the implementation of reforms is the state of the economy and the labor market. The weakness of demand for labor (trained or untrained) means that the government has to take the lead in developing new systems. The inexperience in these areas of the new employers' associations and chambers of commerce and the reformed labor unions reinforces the tendency toward government dominance. The collapse of state enterprises has damaged the institutional basis for apprentice training. Their replacement by a multitude of small firms and the growth of the hidden economy make reviving enterprise-based training and collecting the funds needed for VET difficult.

Attitudes in the education and training sector are changing fast, but teachers still are widely accused of preferring theory to practice. Moreover, trainers understandably prefer to train the easily trainable rather than the difficult cases who will benefit more from training. The academic qualifications of apprentice and vocational secondary school teachers reportedly have fallen. In 1994–95, 21 percent of teachers in the former and 10 percent in the latter were qualified only as primary school teachers. Teachers' lack of industrial experience, however, may be more of a problem. In addition, instructor training for vocational training institutes is not systematically organized, and low salaries make it difficult for public sector institutions to compete with industry for the best talent (Lannert 1994).

Higher education is the most subsidized level of the education system, with a difference of more than 10 percentage points between the social and private rates of return to it. This implies that higher education has probably been expanding at a slower rate than would otherwise have been possible, and that vocational education has been performing the function of rationing the flow of entrants to it from lower levels. Even in 1994 more than 40 percent of primary school completers entered apprentice and other vocational training schools, which did not allow access to higher levels, and the progression rate of vocational secondary graduates to higher education is still much lower than that from grammar schools, which take only 26 percent of primary school completers. However, ongoing reforms are increasing the number of postprimary students who will qualify for higher education.

Finally, the VET system has been reformed despite rather than because of the structures that have been created to manage it. The problem is not the involvement of many parties with divergent interests—a positive rather than a negative factor—but the lack of clarity about the division of responsibilities. Until instruments appropriate for a decentralized system and for the sharing of responsibilities are developed, the reform of VET in Hungary, although impressive, will not reach its full potential.

# References

Árvay, János, and András Vértes. 1994. "The Magnitude of the Private Sector and Hidden Economy in Hungary." *Statisztikai Szemle* 7: 517–529. (In Hungarian.)

Benedek, András, ed. 1995. *Vocational Training in Hungary, 1994.* Budapest: Ministry of Labor.

Bessenyei, István. 1995. *Social Partnership and Vocational Training Policy: Case Study Hungary.* Vienna: Kultur Kontact/ Institute for Comparative Education Research.

Burda, Michael. 1995. "Market Institutions and the Economic Transformation of Central and Eastern Europe." In Simon Commander and Fabrizio Corricelli, eds., *Unemployment, Restructuring, and the Labor Market in Eastern Europe and Russia,* World Bank Institute Development Study. Washington, D.C.: World Bank.

Carnoy, Martin. 1993. "Methodological Guidelines for Measuring the Equity Effects of Training Policies and Programs." Paper presented to the Stanford University Workshop on New Trends in Training Policy, October, ILO, Geneva.

Costarelli, Sandro, ed. 1993. *Children of Minorities: Gypsies.* Florence, Italy: United Nations Children's Fund, International Child Development Centre.

CSO (Central Statistical Office). various years. *Statistical Yearbook.* Budapest.

Fejes, László, ed. 1994. *The Situation of Vocational Training in Hungary in the 1993/ 94 Academic Year.* Budapest: Ministry of Labor.

Frey, Mária. 1994. "The Role of the State in Employment Policy and Labour Market Programmes: The Hungarian Case in International Comparison." Working Paper 16. ILO/Japan Project on Employment Policies for Transition in Hungary, Budapest.

Galasi, Péter, and Gábor Kertesi, eds. 1996. "The Labour Market and Economic Transition: Hungary (1986–1995)." ILO/Japan Project on Employment Policies for Transition in Hungary, Budapest.

Gill, Indermit S., and Amit Dar. 1995. "Costs and Effectiveness of Retraining in Hungary." Report IDP-155. Europe and Central Asian Region, World Bank, Washington, D.C.

Godfrey, Martin. 1994. "Are Hungarian Labour Costs Really So High?" Working Paper 9. ILO/Japan Project on Employment Policies for Transition in Hungary, Budapest.

Godfrey, Martin, György Lázár, and Christopher O'Leary. 1993. "Report on a Survey of Unemployment and Active Labour Market Programmes in Hungary." Working Paper 6. ILO/Japan Project on Employment Policies for Transition in Hungary, Budapest.

Halasz, Gábor. 1994. "Chapter on School Education." National Institute of Public Education. Budapest.

Kemény, István, Gábor Havas, and Gábor Kertesi. 1994. "The Education and Employment Situation of the Gypsy Community: Report of the 1993/94 National Sample Survey." Working Paper 17. ILO/Japan Project on Employment Policies for Transition in Hungary, Budapest.

Kertesi, Gábor. 1994. "The Labour Market Situation of the Gypsy Minority in Hungary." Working Paper 14. ILO/Japan Project on Employment Policies for Transition in Hungary, Budapest.

Kertesi, Gábor, and János Köll. 1995. "Wages and Unemployment in Hungary 1986–1994." Working Paper 30. ILO/Japan Project on Employment Policies for Transition in Hungary. Budapest.

Labor Research Institute. 1995. *Yearly Report of Labour Market: Main Trends in Labour Demand and Supply.* Budapest.

Lannert, Judit. 1994. "Questions and Answers in Hungarian Vocational Education during the Transition Period." Paper presented at the Research Workshop on Managing Vocational Education and Training in Central and Eastern European Countries, December, United Nations Scientific, Educational, and Cultural Organization and International Institute for Environment and Development, Paris.

Mártonfi, György. 1995. "Hungarian Employers on Vocational Training Policy, National Institute of Public Education." Budapest.

Micklewright, John, and Gyula Nagy. 1994. "Flows to and from Insured Unemployment in Hungary." Working Paper 15. ILO/Japan Project on Employment Policies for Transition in Hungary, Budapest.

Ministry of Labor. 1995. *Human Resource and Development Project.* An outline of the human resource project supported by a loan from the World Bank. Budapest.

OECD/CCET (Organization for Economic Cooperation and Development/Centre for Cooperation with the Economies in Transition). 1995. *Reviews of National Policies for Education: Hungary.* Paris.

O'Leary, Christopher. 1994. "An Impact Analysis of Labor Market Programs in Hungary: Based on the November 1993 ILO Survey of Participants." Working Paper 13. ILO/Japan Project on Employment Policies for Transition in Hungary, Budapest.

———. 1995. " Performance Indicators: A Management Tool for Active Labour Programmes in Hungary and Poland." *International Labour Review* 134 (6): 729–51.

Phare. 1995. *Partnerships for Europe 1995: A Guide to Phase II of the Hungarian Ministry of Labor's Program of Innovation in Vocation Education and Training.* Budapest: Ministry of Labor, supported by the Phare Program of the European Union.

Pulay, Gyula. 1995. "Measuring the Efficiency of Employment Policy in Hungary." Paper prepared for Seminar on Evaluating Active Labor Programs, April. World Bank, Washington, D.C.

Sik, Endre. 1995. "From the Multicolored to the Black-and-White Economy (the Hungarian Second Economy and the Transformation Revisited)." Paper presented to the Workshop on Economic Transformation—the Reorganization of Ownership and Finance, November, NSA/NRC, Washington, D.C.

Timár, János. 1994. "Education and Training Now and Its Development till the Year 2005." Budapest University of Economics. Processed.

UNDP (United Nations Development Programme). 1995. *Human Development Report.* New York.

UNICEF (United Nations Children's Fund). 1995. "Poverty, Children, and Policy: Responses for a Brighter Future." Economies in Transition Studies, Regional Monitoring Report 3. International Child Development Centre, Florence, Italy.

World Bank. 1995a. "Hungary: Structural Reforms for Sustainable Growth." Report 13577-HU. Europe and Central Asia Region, Washington, D.C.

———. 1995b. "Poverty and Social Transfers in Hungary." Report 14658 HU. Europe and Central Asia Region, Washington, D.C.

# 2 Poland

PETER GROOTINGS

POLAND EXPERIENCED SEVERAL years of economic crisis during the 1980s, when salaries were low and basic consumer goods and services were in short supply. However, foodstuffs and raw materials were subsidized and therefore accessible. This situation changed dramatically after 1990, when the government gradually removed the subsidies. Savings in Polish zlotys were depreciated, savings in hard currencies lost real value because of exchange rate stabilization, and interest rates rose dramatically. Because most enterprises reacted to the liberalization of markets with sharp price rises, real income levels went down even farther.

By the end of 1993, Poland had become the fastest growing economy in Europe, with a strong private sector and a gradually developing market-based infrastructure. At the same time, however, unemployment rates remained high; the budget deficit was slowly growing; real wages had not recovered; and social conflicts had increased, though no longer in the form of strikes.

## The Labor Market

Within a few years of the start of economic reforms, Poland's labor market changed from one characterized by a persistent shortage of labor into one with some of the highest unemployment rates in Europe, the result of a shortage of jobs rather than a mismatch between education and the labor market's needs. In addition, the system for determining wages and salaries changed radically following the demise of the communist regime.

## Employment Patterns

Between 1990 and 1993 the number of economically active people fell, the number of people employed decreased, the structure of employment fundamentally changed, employment in the informal sector became widespread, and unemployment became massive (table 2-1).

Poland lost more than 2.6 million jobs between 1989 and 1994. Mainly because of the collapse of the state sector in 1994, public sector employment was only 64 percent of what it had been at the end of 1989. In contrast, after an initial loss of almost 200,000 jobs in 1990, employment in the private sector increased by almost 600,000 during this period. However, cooperative organizations, classified as private in the current classification system, almost completely collapsed; an estimated 1.5 million jobs were lost. Although employment in the private sector increased by more than 2 million jobs, this was not sufficient to make up for the loss in public and cooperative employment. Only in 1994 was the increase in private sector employment greater than the loss in public sector employment.

Thus, the structure of employment has changed considerably. Unlike most other Central and Eastern European countries, Poland has always had a private sector—mainly in agriculture, but also in services and handicrafts. However, the majority of people (54.3 percent in 1989) were employed in the public sector, a figure that had dropped to 40 percent by the end of 1994. Since privatization has not been completed and most large

TABLE 2-1

Population Groups, by Employment Status, Annual Averages 1990–93

(thousands)

| Group | 1990 | 1991 | 1992 | 1993 |
|---|---|---|---|---|
| Working-age population | 21,925.7 | 22,008.7 | 22,118.4 | 22,256.9 |
| Labor force | — | 18,692.2 | 18,405.0 | 18,223.0 |
| Employed | — | 17,064.6 | 16,065.4 | 15,500.2 |
| Unemployed | 577.2 | 1,627.6 | 2,339.6 | 2,722.8 |
| Not in the labor force | — | 3,316.5 | 3,713.4 | 4,033.9 |
| Not employed in working-age and nonworking-age populations | — | 4,944.1 | 6,053.0 | 6,756.7 |

— Not available.

*Source*: Author's calculations.

industrial enterprises and banks are still state owned, many of the jobs in the private sector are in new firms, most of which are very small. In 1992–93, the typical private enterprise employed two persons.

The pattern of employment in the various sectors of the economy has also changed. While employment in agriculture remained relatively stable between 1989 and 1994, dropping slightly from 28 to 26 percent, employment in industry fell from 35 to 29 percent, and employment in services rose from 38 to 45 percent. The decrease in agricultural employment has been largely attributable to the collapse of cooperative farms, with the resultant loss of almost 1 million jobs. However, the figures indicate that many of those affected found work in private agriculture. The decrease in industrial employment is the result of almost 1.4 million job losses in manufacturing and of some 400,000 job losses in industrial construction. The increased employment in services between 1989 and 1994 was the result of growth in the retail trade of around 600,000 jobs, in financial services of 80,000 jobs, and in state administration of 90,000 jobs.

The figures for agricultural employment disguise considerable hidden unemployment. Because most private farms are small and poorly mechanized, many people unable to find a job elsewhere work on a farm. Witkowski (1995) estimates that some 450,000 people are in this situation. In addition, an estimated 200,000 people are unemployed but are not registered as such, and they have given up searching for a job.

Regional employment levels vary significantly. Although major cities such as Warsaw, Krakow, Poznan, and Katowice recorded unemployment rates that ranged from 7.5 to 10.0 percent in 1994, rural areas in the North had unemployment rates of 28 to 30 percent, and the region of Walbrzych in the Southwest had an unemployment rate of 27 percent. The authorities have now recognized almost a quarter of all districts as special problem areas, which entitles them to preferential treatment, such as prolonged unemployment benefits and early retirement schemes.

Some of the regions and cities with low unemployment rates (for example, Katowice, Gdansk, and Kielce) have the highest absolute numbers of unemployed. This is a result of the extreme centralization of the population in large cities focused on a single industry.

## Wages and Salaries

Under the previous system, the central authorities set wage differentials and wage increases. They normally based their decisions on political crite-

TABLE 2-2
Monthly Earnings by Occupational Category, 1987, 1991–93

| | Percentage of average annual compensation for all workers | | | |
|---|---|---|---|---|
| | *1987* | *1991* | *1992* | *1993* |
| Professionals and managers | 126 | 126 | 169 | 136 |
| Mid- and lower-level white-collar employees | 84 | 100 | 109 | 88 |
| Service and trade employees | 79 | 80 | 60 | 88 |
| Private entrepreneurs | 204 | 190 | 195 | 188 |
| Skilled workers | 99 | 92 | 69 | 88 |
| Unskilled workers | 65 | 60 | 69 | 60 |
| Farm workers | 88 | 68 | 52 | 80 |

*Source*: Author's calculations.

ria: workers were privileged compared with other occupational groups, and those working in sectors strategically important for the national economy (mining, heavy industry) received better wages than did those working in other sectors. Wage increases depended on the bargaining power of representatives in the central administration and on strike threats by individual occupational groups. As a result, workers in large industrial enterprises occupied a privileged position. There was hardly any relationship between salary and level of education (table 2-2).

Differentiation both in actual remuneration and in wage and salary setting is now much greater. Even though finding accurate statistical data for the 1987–93 period was difficult, some trends became clear: wages in the public sector still depend on political action such as strikes and social unrest, and state enterprise managers and workers (and their unions) still act in partnership when approaching the government with wage demands. Wage differentials and the relative positions of various occupational groups have changed less in the public sector than in the private sector, with the exception of civil servants employed in government institutions, whose position has improved somewhat. In the private sector market forces play a much stronger role, and the influence of unions is less pervasive. The role of education in shaping incomes has increased gradually, especially in the private sector.

## Labor Market Signals for Skill Needs

The high level of unemployment appears to be the result of a shortage of jobs more than of mismatches between education and employment. The job shortage is the result of cutbacks in public employment and the slow growth of demand for labor in the private sector. The large number of very small private enterprises also indicates that many people have become self-employed. The unemployment to vacancy ratio—that is, the number of registered unemployed for each registered vacancy—increased from 13 in 1990 to 87 in 1993.

The employment prospects of secondary school graduates and university and other postsecondary graduates have worsened steadily (table 2-3). In 1989, 41 percent found employment immediately after graduation; in 1994 only 22 percent managed to do so. University and basic vocational school leavers were the most successful, while postsecondary and general

TABLE 2-3

Labor Market Status of School Leavers after Completion
of School, 1989–94

(percent)

| Year education completed and education level | Employed | Unemployed | Inactive | Total |
|---|---|---|---|---|
| *Year of completion* | | | | |
| 1989 | 40.5 | 27.1 | 32.4 | 100 |
| 1990 | 36.0 | 37.1 | 26.9 | 100 |
| 1991 | 28.4 | 46.2 | 25.4 | 100 |
| 1992 | 27.0 | 45.4 | 27.6 | 100 |
| 1993 | 22.5 | 54.8 | 22.7 | 100 |
| 1994 | 21.9 | 58.2 | 19.9 | 100 |
| *Level of education* | | | | |
| University | 34.4 | 41.3 | 24.3 | 100 |
| Postsecondary | 20.2 | 54.8 | 25.8 | 100 |
| Vocational secondary | 28.0 | 50.1 | 21.9 | 100 |
| General secondary | 19.2 | 47.4 | 33.4 | 100 |
| Basic vocational | 32.6 | 47.3 | 20.1 | 100 |
| Primary | 26.0 | 17.0 | 57.0 | 100 |

*Source:* Witkowski (1995).

secondary graduates were the least likely to find employment. In general, the lower the education level, the higher the unemployment rate.

In all age groups more women than men are unemployed, and many women and girls have withdrawn from the labor market. Unemployment is concentrated in the young age groups: almost one-third of the unemployed are younger than 24. Among older workers, those with little education were more likely to lose their jobs.

Signals that come from the labor market in terms of employment patterns, unemployment figures, vacancy levels, and salary levels do not always have direct relevance for the vocational education and training (VET) system, because some of them stem from inherited structures and institutions. Obviously, sectors currently in decline do not offer employment prospects, and the volume of training for these sectors should be adapted accordingly. Similar adaptations are needed with respect to the changing structure of employment. Given the reduced importance of large industrial and bureaucratic organizations, education needs to be less specialized, perhaps even less occupation specific. There is also a need for a stronger training infrastructure that can handle the many long-term unemployed. The fundamental problem of insufficient market demand for labor persists, however. Recruitment levels are such that enterprises can find the skills they need from the pool of unemployed relatively easily.

## The Vocational Education and Training System

A VET system meant to serve a relatively backward centrally planned economy now has to be transformed into one that will meet the requirements of a modern market-led economy.

### Overview of the Polish Education System

The Polish education system is still in transition. Modernization of both its structure and content, planned since the early 1960s, is finally being undertaken.

STRUCTURE Primary school starts at the age of seven and lasts for eight years. Most children attend preschool before entering primary school. Compulsory schooling lasts until the completion of primary school or until the child reaches the age of 17, whichever comes first. Secondary education is not obligatory. After leaving primary school, children can continue their

TABLE 2-4
School Enrollment at Different Education Levels, 1990–95
(number)

| Type of school | 1990–91 | 1991–92 | 1992–93 | 1993–94 | 1994–95 |
|---|---|---|---|---|---|
| Primary | 5,231,300 | 5,259,700 | 5,237,100 | 5,179,300 | 5,118,900 |
| Secondary | 1,896,100 | 1,977,700 | 2,057,800 | 2,136,500 | 2,206,400 |
| General | 445,000 | 499,800 | 555,800 | 602,400 | 648,600 |
| Vocational and technical | 1,451,100 | 1,477,900 | 1,502,00 | 1,534,100 | 1,557,800 |
| Basic vocational | 814,500 | 806,200 | 792,800 | 769,500 | 745,800 |
| Postsecondary | 108,300 | 100,900 | 95,900 | 110,800 | 131,500 |
| Higher | 403,800 | 428,200 | 495,700 | 584,000 | 682,200 |
| Adult education | 224,900 | 210,600 | 212,400 | 223,900 | 245,800 |

*Source:* Witkowski (1995).

education in general secondary schools, in various vocational schools, or in mixed general-vocational schools. General secondary school lasts for four years and can lead to a certificate called the *Matura*. Students that pass the *Matura* can sit for university entrance examinations and enter certain postsecondary vocational schools. Table 2-4 shows enrollment at the various levels.

Basic vocational schools last two or three years, depending on the particular course of study, and lead to a skilled worker certificate. Secondary technical schools last for four or five years. To graduate students must pass the *Matura* and are qualified as technicians. Secondary vocational schools last four years. Students must pass the *Matura* to graduate and are qualified as skilled workers. In the mid-1990s the authorities experimented with a new type of secondary professional school that does not provide an occupational qualification. In 1995 there were 135 such schools.

Students who have trouble completing primary school can enter special schools that prepare them for simple jobs in industry during one- or two-year courses. In addition, factories run so-called job adaptation courses that last from six months to a year for young workers who are paid during the training period.

Graduates of general secondary schools and basic vocational schools can pursue further vocational and technical studies. Those completing a general secondary school can attend a secondary technical school, while those completing a basic vocational school can attend a general secondary school or a secondary technical school.

Poland is the only former socialist country that has maintained a traditional apprenticeship system in the handicraft sector. Such apprenticeships usually last three years, and apprentices can receive either skilled worker or master qualifications. The Chamber of Handicrafts manages this system.

The number of students who receive higher education has always been limited. The apprenticeship system is open to adults (defined as those older than 17) as well as to children. The handicraft apprenticeship system is also open to adults. No distinctions in terms of courses offered and qualifications awarded are made between children and adults who follow the same educational programs.

Institutions of higher education are available at the postsecondary level— namely, higher vocational schools in a few areas that do not provide academic titles and universities and polytechnics (technical universities). Since 1989 a number of postsecondary colleges have been established, mainly to train foreign language teachers. The system is now being expanded to offer higher professional education.

FINANCING. In 1991 expenditure on education and training was about 5.4 percent of gross domestic product (GDP), down from 6.6 percent in 1990. In 1992 the share of GDP increased somewhat to 5.6 percent, but the total amount was less than 75 percent of the 1990 level because GDP had fallen dramatically. During 1991 and 1992 the Ministry of National Education suffered from major budget cuts, resulting in problems paying teachers' salaries. In 1993, 10.3 percent of public expenditures went to education, compared with 11.8 percent in 1989. In 1994 the share increased again to 11.2 percent. Most of the ministry's budget goes to pay teachers' salaries. In 1992, for example, teachers' salaries amounted to 84 percent of all costs for preschools and primary and secondary schools. Maintenance and investment were neglected during the 1960s and 1970s so that by the end of the 1980s, the time when fundamental changes were needed, the state of the educational system had become deplorable.

Students and their families have increasingly been forced to contribute to financing VET by paying for school materials and the upkeep of school buildings. Scholarships for secondary school students have been cut drastically. In 1985–86, 9.5 percent of those in general secondary schools and more than 20 percent of those in vocational and technical schools received scholarships; by 1991 these figures had fallen to 0.5 percent and 1.0 percent, respectively. As a result, households covered 17 percent of all educational costs in 1991–92 and about 25 to 30 percent in 1994–95. For years, salaries in Poland, like in other socialist countries, were low because housing, vacations, education, and transport were heavily subsidized. With the sudden withdrawal of subsidies, many households experienced severe financial problems.

The burden of spending is shifting from the central government to local authorities, which are now responsible for preschools and are gradually taking over the costs of primary schools. Table 2-5 presents a breakdown of expenditures by type of education for primary and secondary schools. Vocational schools received 20.9 percent of the budget in 1980 and 17.4 percent in 1990, when most industrial enterprises closed down their schools. This percentage increased gradually to 26.1 percent in 1993 at the cost of a reduced share for primary schools.

## Vocational Education

All secondary schools (except the basic vocational schools) require entrance examinations. In the past this permitted effective control over the number of students entering these schools. Because the authorities kept the number of students allowed to enter general secondary and secondary technical schools low, basic vocational schools began to be viewed as schools for those who fail to get into other schools. A similar stigma was attached to the secondary vocational and technical schools. Their standards have never been as high as those of the general secondary schools. Nevertheless, the secondary vocational and technical schools have always been popular, because they provided an avenue to higher education. Similarly, many students treated the postsecondary vocational schools as a place to bide their time until they were accepted into a university. This was reinforced by the traditional pedagogical approach, which in both secondary schools and primary schools focused on university preparation.

Links between VET and other types of education. The structure of schooling has changed little in recent decades, although there has been a move to reduce the number of students entering basic vocational schools and to increase the number entering secondary technical schools. There has also been a tendency to introduce more vocational education into general education.

During the 1980s, about 97 percent of those completing primary school continued their full-time education. In 1991–92 the proportion dropped

TABLE 2-5
Public Expenditures on Primary and Secondary Education,
1980 and 1990–93
(percent)

| School type | 1980 | 1990 | 1991 | 1992 | 1993 |
|---|---|---|---|---|---|
| Preschools | 15.5 | 16.9 | 0.4 | 0.3 | 0.2 |
| Primary schools | 52.7 | 55.6 | 64.7 | 61.3 | 59.5 |
| Secondary general schools | 6.7 | 5.8 | 7.1 | 7.7 | 8.1 |
| Special general schools | 2.2 | 2.4 | 2.9 | 3.3 | 3.4 |
| Vocational schools | 20.9 | 17.4 | 22.4 | 24.7 | 26.1 |
| Arts schools | 1.6 | 1.4 | 2.0 | 2.1 | 2.1 |
| Special vocational schools | 0.4 | 0.5 | 0.6 | 0.6 | 0.6 |
| Total | 100.0 | 100.0 | 100.0 | 100.0 | 100.0 |

*Source:* OECD (1995, p. 46).

to 94 percent; of those students, about 26 percent entered general secondary schools, 25 percent attended secondary technical and vocational schools, and 43 percent went to basic vocational schools. All in all, therefore, about 70 percent of primary school leavers enter the vocational education system; half of them are eventually eligible to take examinations for entry into higher education institutions. However, the proportion of students that go on to higher education is low (only 12 percent compared with 30 percent in Organization for Economic Cooperation and Development countries and 15 to 20 percent in other Central and Eastern European countries). Graduates of vocational schools that do not have this opportunity can, theoretically, continue their studies to achieve full secondary level certificates, but only some 23 percent actually do so.

Current policies aim to increase the number of students completing secondary education and, as a result, to reduce the number entering basic vocational schools. Policies also aim at providing higher education that is geared more toward employment than toward traditional academic higher education.

LINKS BETWEEN VET AND THE LABOR MARKET. Almost 50 percent of school leavers entering the labor market in 1989–90 had at most a basic vocational school diploma or incomplete secondary schooling, a figure that had dropped to 40 percent by 1993, while 13 percent could claim only an elementary school certificate.

Vocational education has traditionally been organized along sectoral lines, with the pertinent ministry or agency responsible for determining the vocational curricula and the Ministry of National Education responsible for overall administration, general subjects, and coordination. Schools normally focus on a single sector, and switching from one type of vocation to another is difficult. These characteristics make the system excessively rigid. In addition, skills not required in large enterprises tend to be neglected, and the handicrafts and services sectors have suffered as a result.

The industrial sector and parallel vocational structure have proven to be a major barrier to industrial and regional development during the transition to a market economy. For years educational researchers have pointed to problems in rural areas, where nonagricultural education has been largely absent. With the collapse of state agricultural enterprises, the lack of secondary vocational education in rural areas has become even more of a problem.

At the administrative level, the interaction between schools and enterprises was top-down and bureaucratic. The number of students pursuing particular courses depended on the plans of individual ministries, course content was jointly worked out by representatives of the ministries and teachers, and budgets depended on the bargaining strength of each ministry. The result was a complex, heavily centralized system with uneven and largely unintended outcomes that reflected the ever present gaps between the targets of central administrative planning and realities at the local level in a shortage economy.

All types of vocational schools, even schools with their own workshops, organize part of their training inside enterprises. Most schools have developed relationships with local firms. These firms are keen on having good contacts with schools, because they are a source of labor, which is always needed. However, the training within enterprises is not well integrated into either school work or the work of the enterprises.

ORGANIZATION AND MANAGEMENT. The structure of school-based vocational education and training dates back to 1961 legislation on the development of the educational system. In 1991 Parliament adopted a new law on secondary education, the Education Reform Act, to help cope with the new financial and administrative conditions. The 1991 act maintained the same types of schools that existed previously, and it returned overall responsibility for education to the Ministry of National Education. At the same time, however, it regulated the continued participation of other ministries or central agencies in decisionmaking on curricula and teaching materials, such as textbooks. Details about how this is carried out in practice are settled by separate rulings of the Council of Ministers.

The act also established the rights and obligations of regional education authorities, school directors (who now report directly to the Ministry of National Education), and other staff. It introduced considerable decentralization and gave schools significant discretion in management and in making some decisions about their curricula based on the needs of local labor markets.

The act also allowed for the establishment of any kind of nonstate school. The hope was that this would introduce competition into the school system that would speed up modernization.

COSTS AND FINANCING. All state schools, those under direct ministry control and those governed by local authorities, are financed from the public budget. Other schools that are not state schools but are officially recognized receive subsidies for each student from the state budget that amount to 50 percent of the average cost per student in state schools. The number of private schools is increasing, but private vocational schools are rare.

Formerly, enterprises contributed to the financing of vocational education by running their own schools and training centers. However, this money came indirectly from the state budget, because it was provided by the respective technical ministry, if not directly by the Ministry of National Education. One of the first things enterprises did when they became responsible for their own financial management and budgets at the end of the 1980s was to close their training facilities. The Ministry of National Education was unable to take over all the financial commitments of all the enterprise schools and training workshops. Therefore, it has allowed the remaining enterprise training schools to earn additional income by renting out part of their buildings, by providing private training, or by other means.

ASSESSMENT AND CERTIFICATION. Polish education has been characterized by a high degree of centralized control of inputs, including finances, staff, curricula, textbooks, and numbers of students. The number of graduates was supposed to equal the number of people enterprises planned to hire, but schools were responsible for final examinations. Therefore, the quality of training outcomes was extremely diverse.

Occupations are divided into two broad categories, skilled workers and technicians, depending on the amount of theoretical knowledge required. Unlike the German system, where traditionally a skilled worker can become a technician by pursing further training, in Poland students follow two different tracks after primary education to become either a skilled worker or a technician. This is typical of many Central European countries that had been part of the Austro-Hungarian Empire.

## Labor Market Retraining

In 1990 the Ministry of Labor established the Labor Fund, which is financed from a 2 percent tax on wages. This fund is used, among other things, to refund enterprises for wages paid to vocational education students who do some of their training within the enterprise and to young workers who undergo training within the framework of an employment contract with the enterprise. The fund also finances training for the unemployed. However, the amount the fund spends for training purposes has remained low, and the number of people receiving labor market training has remained few. Table 2-6 shows expenditure on labor market programs from 1990 to 1993.

Several factors are responsible for the low level of retraining activities. The most important one is that few vacancies can be filled on the basis of retraining. Because of the large number of registered unemployed, employment office staff are unable to spend much time on individual cases. In addition, the infrastructure for handling unemployment had to be developed from scratch and has concentrated mainly on benefit payments. Employment offices complain about the difficulties of finding appropriate training organizations that could be contracted to provide retraining courses.

### TABLE 2-6
Labor Market Expenditures as a Percentage of GDP, 1990–93

| Expenditure category | 1990 | 1991 | 1992 | 1993 |
|---|---|---|---|---|
| Labor Fund | 0.63 | 1.65 | 2.00 | 2.01 |
| Passive policies | 0.32 | 1.35 | 1.72 | 1.68 |
| Active policies | 0.29 | 0.26 | 0.25 | 0.31 |

Source: Ministry of Labor and social policy data.

For the moment, secondary schools, private training firms, and large semi-public adult training organizations are involved in labor market training. Most of the unemployed receiving such training are young school-leavers.

## Continuous Training for Adults

For many years Poland has had a widespread system of nonformal training. By the end of 1989, 448 institutions that did not belong to the formal school system provided such training, half of them operated by the Association of Vocational Upgrading Institutions. Some of the institutions operated on a countrywide scale. Courses ranged from short ones—for example, on health and safety (the association has the monopoly on these courses, which are obligatory for all enterprises)—to full vocational education leading to qualifications similar to those provided by the formal school system. By 1993–94 there were more than 2,000 nonformal institutions; 35 percent of them offered foreign language courses.

The large private training organizations and the public school system have suffered from similar problems: outdated curricula and teaching materials for traditionally narrow occupational profiles. Some of these organizations were more or less self-financing through fees and the sale of goods produced by students. Therefore, their problems were also similar to those of school workshops after the liberalization of markets. Some private training organizations have concluded contracts with the Employment Offices for the delivery of retraining courses. Private industries' interest in providing training courses for their employees through commercial organizations has remained minimal.

## Major VET Issues and Reforms

Like the other transition economies of Central and Eastern Europe, Poland faces a dual challenge. Developed to serve a centrally planned economy, VET systems were geared toward heavy industry and technologically backward industrial production. The first challenge is to make them compatible with an economy based on market principles that incorporates a greater variety of industrial production and services. At the same time, the VET system is expected to contribute to the development of a market-based economy—the second challenge.

*Structure and Organization*

Until the mid-1980s, there were three types of secondary schools. About 15 percent of students finishing primary school attended general secondary schools, some 25 percent went to secondary vocational or technical schools, and around 60 percent went on to basic vocational schools. In other words, most students were expected to enter the labor market upon acquiring what often amounted to rudimentary skills. Since the 1960s, training specialists have been pointing out that this should be changed, because technological change requires higher levels of skills, less specialization, and increased educational and occupational mobility for workers. Several attempts to reform the system along these lines met with resistance from enterprise management and manpower planners, who argued that existing jobs were simple in nature and required more practical dexterity than cognitive skills. With the higher levels of uncertainty inherent in a market-based system, Polish authorities appear to have decided that a higher level of general education is the way to handle this challenge.

In 1994, 607,500 pupils completed primary school. Almost 30 percent of them went on to general secondary schools, 5 percent entered secondary vocational schools, 23 percent attended secondary technical schools, and about 40 percent entered basic vocational schools. Thus, less than 70 percent of primary school–leavers entered the vocational education system, down from more than 85 percent before the transition. However, as noted earlier, the proportion of students continuing to higher education is only about 12 percent. The intent of current policies is to increase the number of students who complete their secondary education; to reduce the number of students entering basic vocational schools; and to provide higher education curricula that is different from the traditional academic curricula, in particular, courses more geared to employment.

The changed employment environment and the greater participation of the private sector in the delivery of education require new forms of cooperation between the actors now involved in education. This includes policymakers from the different ministries traditionally responsible for vocational education and training, public administrators at different levels, social partners, and the various providers of education and training. Polish institutions have always had problems when trying to coordinate their activities, and a consensus about how to achieve such coordination on education and training does not appear to exist.

## Management and Funding

Under the old system, vocational schools either were attached to an enterprise, which was responsible for all costs other than teachers' salaries, or were managed by local education authorities, with the budget coming from the Ministry of Education. Companies used to be interested in having control over vocational schools, because this ensured a supply of appropriately trained workers. With the gradual integration of vocational schools into the public education system, companies lost much of this control and became less interested in funding them. At the same time that the Ministry of Education found itself responsible for funding more schools, the government reduced total education budgets as part of its structural adjustment policies and because of falling government revenues. Nearly all firms closed down their facilities for practice learning or canceled their contracts with school workshops. As a result, much vocational education became almost exclusively theoretical.

Because the central government was unable to provide sufficient resources, a 1989 law allowed schools to set up workshops on a commercial basis and to use the profits to buy equipment and to top up staff salaries. By 1990 about 650 schools had workshops, but since their production requirements conflicted with learning objectives, the workshops were closed again in 1992.

Another change has been the shift in spending from the central government to local authorities. In the 1980s the central government's share of education expenditures was more than 90 percent, but by 1994 local authorities' share had risen to more than 30 percent, and this share is expected to increase. There has also been a concentration of expenditure inside the Ministry of National Education once other ministries stopped financing vocational schools.

Since 1992 schools have had a certain degree of autonomy in adjusting parts of their curricula to respond to the needs of the local labor market. Decentralization has, indeed, been predicated on the assumption that responding to labor market needs is best done at the school level. For school management and teachers, however, this has implied taking on new roles in an attempt to bring some order into the labor market uncertainties that surround them. The ministry has been unable to guide schools in their experimental adaptation of courses yet still insists on approving the schools' curricula. Gradually, regional educational authorities are becoming more active in promoting and assisting school-based curriculum change and in providing a mechanism for generalizing and disseminating experience.

The developments to date indicate that policymakers have taken a number of steps to develop an alternative infrastructure for financing, management, and curriculum development of vocational instruction after the collapse of the old system. The new infrastructure is not yet in place, however, mainly because the Ministry of National Education lacks the necessary resources and because of the lack of industry interest. The large international assistance programs financed by the European Community and the World Bank are supporting the development of the new infrastructure, but the three subsystems of vocational education and training (for young people, for adults, and for the unemployed) should be dealt with more consistently within an integrated policy framework (Grootings 1993a, 1993b).

## Curricula and Delivery

The new education policymakers came essentially from the ranks of teachers and educational researchers. Thus it should come as no surprise that they have focused on what had been postponed for so long—namely, revising and modernizing existing curricula and developing new curricula for subjects that had been neglected, such as modern languages, or that had not been in demand, such as financial management, banking, and economic subjects.

The new curricula were to be developed by so-called "author groups" of teachers. These groups were confronted with a challenging task, because the Ministry of National Education had closed down all supporting infrastructure for curriculum research and development. Either private business is not well enough organized yet to participate in such an undertaking, or individual employers have little interest in becoming involved in vocational education, because they have no trouble finding employees with sufficient qualifications. Most curriculum innovation projects have been financed from foreign assistance programs. In 1994 the authorities decided to establish a national curriculum center, and they have now created a special team for curriculum development within the Research Institute for Education.

Early on in the reform process, educators realized that vocational teachers' pedagogical skills as well as their technical knowledge would need a certain amount of upgrading. However, the institutions that once took care of the former had been closed down, and no institutions to provide teachers with further education and training in technical subjects had existed under the old system.

In the meantime the role of teachers has changed considerably. No longer do they merely implement what has been decided by central authorities. They now have to be educational developers themselves and translate labor market signals into educational programs. Some teachers have managed to do this better than others. The authorities have taken steps to reorganize the system for educating vocational education teachers to increase their overall level of qualifications while making them less academically oriented. They have also set up postsecondary colleges for teacher training. These are intended for foreign language teachers but later will accommodate others. The reorganization of teacher training in vocational education has only just begun and remains one of the main challenges facing the Polish VET system.

Because the geographical distribution of VET schools used to be defined primarily by the presence of industrial enterprises, many of whom are now in crisis or have been closed down, the relocation of schools has also been put on the agenda. In addition, individual schools, in consultation with regional authorities, have started to change their course offerings, sometimes with a view to contributing to regional development plans. As a result, some areas of education that had been neglected, such as tourism and commercial studies, are now being developed.

To change from a system that controlled inputs to one that controls output, and to attain standards comparable to those in Western European countries, Polish policymakers will have to agree about relevant occupational profiles. The Ministry of National Education has not yet succeeded in mobilizing the social partners (employers and trade unions) needed for this, so achieving consensus will probably take some time. The slow pace of industrial restructuring is also a hindrance. Except in those sectors that are growing rapidly, industry feels under no immediate pressure to invest resources in such activities.

Policymakers have realized that the problem of developing a set of qualification standards calls for radical improvement of educational provision and the development of a national system of examination and certification. However, perhaps because of the general shortage of funds, they have tended to leave the responsibility for provision to individual schools. Recently, experiments with developing national examinations for general secondary schools have started at the regional level. Yet VET quality control remains largely input oriented through central approval of curricula. In view of increasing mobility, both within the education system and in the labor market, the challenge will be to develop assessment and certification procedures that will lead to generally recognized qualifications.

## New Roles for the Government

Poland's attempts to modernize an anachronistic VET system is complicated by the absence of well-functioning labor market institutions, such as employment offices, and an infrastructure for retraining the unemployed; by the lack of industry involvement; and by the dramatic restructuring of the employment system as a whole, the direction and final outcome of which are still unclear. This problem is particularly acute in the case of retraining programs for the unemployed, which were not required before 1989 and were barely operating even as late as 1992. Retraining policies are crippled by a lack of awareness about future employment prospects, but the number of people enrolled in retraining and training programs has grown more than tenfold since 1990.

## Obstacles to Reform

Few stakeholders are truly interested in the necessary reforms because the supply of qualified labor at this stage of the transition is abundant, and future requirements are unpredictable. Therefore, no clear national strategy for VET reforms exists.

STAKEHOLDERS' LACK OF INTEREST IN VET. Changes in the VET system are largely a by-product of changes in the overall educational system. Vocational education has lost its dominant position in terms of financial and personnel resources, even though it caters to the majority of secondary school students. Policymakers have given priority to developing what was missing in Polish education rather than to improving what was already present.

Individual schools have been forced to bear the burden of adaptation, and the changes taking place are restricted to such basics as curricula, teaching materials, and staff qualifications. With no clear signals from the Polish labor market and social partners reluctant to become involved in mid- or long-term VET policymaking, points of reference are sought elsewhere or are imported through such means as bilateral assistance programs.

Nevertheless, given the country's extremely limited financial resources, Poland's accomplishments should not be underestimated. Its vocational education and training has changed from a closed and centralized system to a system opened up to the outside world. While this has been an ad hoc process based largely on pragmatic, short-term decisions by local actors, it may well prepare the ground for future developments. The time may have come to evaluate what is taking place in schools rather than develop central policy initiatives that do not relate well to local developments. However, educational policymakers may not be able to achieve this without more involvement from industry.

The present economic situation, especially the employment situation, is not conducive to mobilizing social partners for a transformation of the VET system. The labor market has an abundant supply of well-qualified labor for the few new, modern firms that need labor. Most of the immediate skill gaps have been covered, and existing enterprises are not in a position to recruit new labor as they try to protect the workers they have.

If employers and trade unions were more involved in decisions on vocational education, the schools would be more in touch with employers' actual needs. Since planning for skill requirements far ahead of time is virtually impossible, vocational education systems need to have intrinsic flexibility and responsiveness. This can be achieved only when they are able and willing to communicate on a continuous basis with representatives of the employment system.

UNCERTAINTY ABOUT NEEDED SKILLS. The problem of predicting the skills that will be needed is difficult in all transition countries, because of the difficulty of reaching a national consensus on the economy. To a large extent this can be attributed to a political reluctance to change existing industrial employment structures radically, because this would result in considerable social conflict and tension. Moreover, new employment is emerging primarily in small private enterprises.

The experience of Western countries has demonstrated the difficulties inherent in predicting medium- and long-term needs for particular occupations and to structure educational policies accordingly. Moreover, modern technologies and enterprises' organizational structures are now more flexible than before, which makes defining a precise fit between educational qualifications and jobs problematic. In addition, it has always been the case that many jobs could be filled by people with quite different formal qualifications. Finally, there are new "hybrid" occupations that combine skills and competencies that once were the domain of separate occupations (for example, operators of highly automated production lines or auto mechanics, who must now also be familiar with computers).

BOX 2-1
Poland's VET Reforms

The modernization of VET systems has several purposes: to reduce the number of vocational profiles, develop broader occupational profiles, reduce enrollments in basic vocational schools, expand secondary education leading to a *Matura* certificate, and develop postsecondary, nonuniversity vocational education. The reforms involve

- Modernizing curricula. Particular efforts are being made to accommodate modern languages and new technologies. New programs are being developed, especially in services and commercial administration, and obsolete traditional programs (such as in metals and heavy industries) are being phased out. New curricula are being tested in about 600 vocational schools and will gradually be expanded. The Ministry of National Education has set up 15 commissions charged with preparing educational programs.
- Updating teachers' qualifications and educational materials.
- Changing curricula and methods of teaching to provide students with not only technical skills and knowledge, but also the social skills that will enable them to be active in the labor market, and to prepare them for continuous education and training during their working career.
- Helping students make appropriate vocational and occupational choices by developing information systems and an occupational counseling infrastructure.

To cope with the loss of practical training facilities, the Ministry of National Education is developing alternative solutions. Schools that can show that their practice workshops are financially sustainable receive subsidies from the ministry. The ministry has also initiated the establishment of 10 regional training centers that will be well equipped and open to all schools in the region.

Finally, a start has been made in developing a new type of vocational school, the secondary professional school, which will last four years and offer students a general secondary education plus a broad vocational education in 14 fields. Unlike the existing secondary technical schools, the new schools will not qualify students as technicians but will allow them to go on to higher education or to study for an occupational qualification at a postsecondary school.

*Source*: Author's data.

Such developments in the labor market have led Western economies to review their own VET systems and to design new structures for decisionmaking, provision, and control. Polish policymakers appear still to be caught up in modernization rather than in designing a system for the future (box 2-1).

LACK OF A CLEAR CHANGE STRATEGY. During the past few years there has been some discussion about the appropriate method for implementing changes in VET and whether such a method should take a top-down or a bottom-up approach. This debate was related to whether changes should be introduced in the structure of the educational system or in such aspects of the system as curricula, textbooks, teacher qualifications, and so on. In practice, there has long been a mixture of top-down and bottom-up innovation. The problem is how to combine them so that national educational policies support local experimentation, and local developments benefit system development at large.

Sometimes with the help of local enterprises and sometimes with the help of foreign partners, many schools have instigated changes on their own initiative in an attempt to respond to immediate needs and improve the quality of the education they provide. These changes include modernizing curricula, introducing new textbooks, obtaining new teaching equipment, and retraining teachers. What has usually been missing in these activities, however, is a recognition of the systemic change needed to prepare students for functioning in a market economy.

The present policy of decentralization is necessary to cope with the new requirements of the labor market. To this end, teachers require external support and guidance. External support for bottom-up reforms would also provide coherence to what has so far been uncoordinated development of local initiatives. The country does not have the capacity to monitor what is going on at the local level in individual schools. Thus lessons derived from the experiences of innovative schools do not find their way into national training policies.

## References

Grootings, Peter. 1993a. "VET in Transition: An Overview of Changes in Three East European Countries." *European Journal of Education* 28(2): 229–40.

————, ed. 1993b. "VET in Transition: Comparative Analysis and Proposals for the Modernization of Vocational Education and Training in Poland." Berlin: CEDEFOP.

OECD (Organization for Economic Cooperation and Development). 1995. *Review of Polish Education*. Paris.

Witkowski, Janusz. 1995. *Labor Market in Poland in 1994: New Trends, Old Problems*. Warsaw, Poland: Central Statistical Office, Department of Labor Statistics.

# 3 Czech Republic

PETER GROOTINGS

THE CZECH REPUBLIC, a nation of about 10 million people, was established on January 1, 1993, after the Czech and Slovak Federation split up. Before World War II, the former Czechoslovakia was a parliamentary democracy with a gross national product (GNP) per capita comparable to that of Austria and Belgium. Industry was well developed in the western part of the country, and its products were sold on world markets. In 1948 the Communist Party introduced a centrally planned economy, which (after a short interruption during the Prague Spring of 1968) was in place until the Velvet Revolution of 1989. By 1990 GNP was about one-fifth that of Austria and Belgium. By 1994 GNP per capita was about US$3,600, half that in Greece and Portugal, countries with the lowest GNP per capita in the European Union.

By the end of the 1980s, the industrial structure was characterized by a predominance of large nationalized—and increasingly undercapitalized—enterprises in heavy industry and engineering, with markets almost completely concentrated in former Council for Mutual Economic Assistance countries. One of the major challenges Czech industry faced after the collapse of markets in the former socialist countries was to become competitive in world markets.

Basic indicators for 1991–94 show a remarkable turnaround in economic performance, an impressive growth in private employment, and surprisingly low unemployment (table 3-1). As a result, by 1995 Czech policymakers generally viewed their economy as one that was no longer in transition, although external observers argued that the country had merely

TABLE 3-1
Basic Economic Indicators, 1991–94

| Indicator | 1991 | 1992 | 1993 | 1994 |
|---|---|---|---|---|
| GDP (current prices, billions of krona) | 1,037.5 | 716.6 | 791.0 | 910.6 |
| Annual changes of GDP (constant prices, percent) | –14.2 | –7.1 | –0.3 | 3.0 |
| Industrial production (percentage of total production) | –24.4 | 13.7 | –5.3 | 2.5 |
| Ratio of state budget to GDP | –2.1 | 0.2 | 0.1 | 0.1 |
| Inflation (percent) | 56.6 | 11.0 | 20.8 | 10.0 |
| Employed in the private sector (percent) | 18.8 | 31.1 | 46.9 | 55.0 |
| Gross debt per head of population (millions of US$) | 0.6 | 0.6 | 0.8 | 0.8 |
| Registered unemployment (percentage of labor force) | 4.4 | 2.6 | 3.5 | 3.2 |

GDP gross domestic product.
*Source:* Czech Statistical Office data.

postponed some of the problems that had caused social hardship in other countries. These observers predicted that some of the features typical of transition, such as higher rates of unemployment, were therefore likely still to appear. They pointed to the comparatively favorable economic situation in the Czech Republic at the end of the 1980s and to a number of specific factors (such as low labor force participation, low wages, continued labor hoarding in large public enterprises, and the effects of public employment measures). The impact of these factors is likely to weaken in the near future.

A key element of recent economic reforms has been the privatization of state-owned enterprises. As a result, the share of the nonstate sector in GNP reached 56.3 percent in 1994, while its share in industrial production was 56.9 percent. Private sector employment rose from 19 percent in 1991 to 55 percent in 1994. However, the state sector is still relatively large, and future privatization measures may well be accompanied by an increase in unemployment.

## Labor Market Developments

While the Czech population is slowly declining, the large generation born in the 1970s has now reached child-bearing age. In 1994 about 2.0 million

TABLE 3-2
Working-Age Population, Labor Force, and Participation Rate,
Selected Years, 1980–94

| Category | 1980 | 1990 | 1991 | 1992 | 1994 |
|---|---|---|---|---|---|
| Working-age population | | | | | |
| (thousands) | 5,806 | 6,018 | 6,082 | 6,150 | 6,212 |
| Labor force (thousands) | 4747 | 4,627 | 4,871 | 4,644 | 4,699 |
| Participation rate (percent) | 81.8 | 76.9 | 80.1 | 75.5 | 75.6 |
| Men | 87.9 | 81.7 | 86.4 | 81.6 | 81.4 |
| Women | 74.9 | 71.6 | 73.2 | 68.8 | 69.4 |

Source: Czech Statistical Office data.

people were too young to work, about 6.2 million (2.6 million of them women) were of working age, and around 5.0 million (2.3 million of them women) were of retirement age or older. Although the population of working age increased between 1980 and 1994, labor force participation rates, which were relatively high in 1980, decreased both for men and women (table 3-2).

In the early 1990s the Czech Republic saw a decrease in overall employment opportunities, a shift in employment patterns from agriculture and industry toward the services sector, and an increase in employment in the private sector. Table 3-3 provides an overview of employment from 1990 to 1994. The figures show a net decline in employment and a considerable shift from the primary and secondary sectors toward the tertiary sector.

The number of people employed in the private sector increased from 1.3 percent of the work force in 1989 to 31 percent in 1992 and 64

TABLE 3-3
Employment by Sector, 1990–94
(thousands)

| Sector | 1990 | 1991 | 1992 | 1993 | 1994 |
|---|---|---|---|---|---|
| Total employed | 5,435 | 5,387 | 4,889 | 4,766 | 4,759 |
| Primary sector | 826 | 801 | 651 | 491 | 451 |
| Secondary sector | 2,345 | 2,290 | 2,048 | 2,005 | 1,945 |
| Tertiary sector | 2,264 | 2,296 | 2,190 | 2,270 | 2,363 |

Source: Czech Statistical Office data.

TABLE 3-4

Unemployment Rates, by Gender and Education, 1993 and 1994

(percent)

| Education level | 1993 | | 1994 | |
|---|---|---|---|---|
| | Males | Females | Males | Females |
| Primary and not stated | 8.4 | 7.6 | 11.7 | 7.8 |
| Lower secondary | | | | |
| Apprentice | 2.7 | 4.6 | 2.7 | 4.6 |
| Technical | 2.5 | 5.0 | 2.6 | 5.8 |
| Upper secondary | | | | |
| Apprentice (*Maturita*) | 4.7 | 7.3 | 2.4 | 5.0 |
| Technical | 1.9 | 3.1 | 2.1 | 2.6 |
| General | 5.8 | 3.7 | 5.9 | 3.6 |
| University | 1.4 | 1.6 | 1.2 | 1.1 |
| Average | 3.0 | 4.5 | 3.3 | 4.3 |

*Source:* Czech Statistical Office data.

percent in 1995. This is a result both of privatization of former state enterprises and of the growth of small and medium private businesses. Between 1993 and 1994 the number of small and medium enterprises increased from 3,109 to 3,997; half of them were enterprises with fewer than 100 employees.

Although the overall unemployment rate is relatively low, large regional differences resulted from the inherited employment structure. Not only was employment concentrated in large, heavy industrial enterprises, but these enterprises were unevenly distributed across the country, which made some regions and communities dependent on one major enterprise. Unemployment rates also differ significantly by education levels (table 3-4). Czech state enterprises are known to prefer older workers with experience over better educated younger workers, and since they have so far avoided shedding labor, they have not provided many job openings for school leavers. Accordingly, the number of vacancies is still relatively low.

Compared with other countries in transition—indeed, compared with many industrial market economies—the Czech Republic has had remarkably low open unemployment. According to a 1995 report by the Organization for Economic Cooperation and Development (OECD 1995a), the following factors may explain the Czech "unemployment miracle":

• Employment reduction accomplished by pushing people out of the labor force. A much larger component of employment reduction in the Czech Republic was accomplished by pushing people out of the labor force than into unemployment through retirement schemes for working pensioners and early retirement schemes. In addition, a larger number of school graduates at different levels have been retained within the expanding education system, thereby lowering labor force participation by new entrants.

• Workers' acceptance of strong wage moderation. This resulted in a decline in real wages, which were already low compared with those in other Central European countries.

• Favorable initial conditions in terms of employment structure (especially the small share of agricultural employment) and the qualifications of the work force (enabling mobility and flexibility).

• A long industrial tradition.

• Persistent labor hoarding in large enterprises, even after privatization. Because of the nature of the privatization process, in which former enterprise management has played a key role, privatization has taken place largely without enterprise restructuring so far.

• The large absorbent capacity of the newly emerging private sector.

In 1990, 18.7 percent of the economically active population had only a primary education; 43.1 percent had a lower secondary education (most had gone through an apprenticeship system; the rest had acquired technical skills); 27.7 percent had higher secondary qualifications; and only 9.6 percent possessed a university degree. Since then the educational level has improved slightly as a result of the withdrawal of older, less educated people from the work force. The signals emanating from the labor market during this transitional phase have affected the vocational education and training (VET) system.

## The Vocational Education and Training System

The Czech educational authorities since 1990 have increased the flexibility and scope of the education system, including vocational education. After preschool, which is optional, children enroll in so-called basic schools. Basic schools are divided into two levels. The first five years are equivalent to elementary school, and the sixth through ninth years are equivalent to lower secondary school. Basic education was increased gradually from eight to nine years between 1990 and 1996. After leaving basic school, children can apply to attend a secondary general school, a secondary technical school, or a secondary vocational school. All upper secondary schools require children to pass an entrance examination, and those who do not can go to vocational schools that offer one or two years of training for simple manual occupations. Prior to the transition to a market economy, secondary vocational schools were closely attached to, or even part of, industrial enterprises, but this formal relationship has now ceased almost entirely.

Secondary technical schools and secondary general schools offer students the opportunity to take the *Maturita* examination. Students who pass it, can take university entrance examinations. Until recently both types of schools also offered so-called post-*Maturita* courses that enabled students to obtain a professional qualification, to get a second professional qualification if they already had one, or to specialize within a particular field. In 1996 these courses were abolished and replaced by a new system of tertiary-level nonuniversity education.

Of those students who choose to continue their studies at the postsecondary level, about 64 percent have a secondary general school certificate, some 30 percent come from secondary technical schools, and 4 or 5 percent come from secondary vocational schools. The vast majority of those who leave secondary vocational school enter the labor market, although since 1992 more have been staying in school to follow a two-year course that leads to the *Maturita.*

Enrollment data at the secondary level demonstrate the increasing popularity of technical and general education, and they also show the value attached to professional qualifications (table 3-5). With greater flexibility in the system, the share of technical and vocational graduates who can enroll for further studies (that is, pass the *Maturita*) has increased significantly.

## Organization and Management

Until 1989 education was governed through regional and national committees, with the administrative bodies centrally controlled by the Ministry of the Interior and the Communist Party. After the transition, most secondary vocational schools, which had previously belonged to individual enterprises and their respective technical ministries, were placed under the jurisdiction of the Ministry of Economy, while the Ministry of Education took over responsibility for research institutions. The Ministry of Educa-

TABLE 3-5
Enrollment Rates in Secondary Schools, 1989–95
(percent)

| Year | General | Secondary technical | | Secondary vocational | |
|------|---------|---------------------|---------------------|---------------------|---------------------|
| | | *With Maturita* | *Without Maturita* | *With Maturita* | *Without Maturita* |
| 1989–90 | 14.9 | 24.0 | — | 5.6 | 55.0 |
| 1990–91 | 15.3 | 24.4 | — | 5.1 | 49.8 |
| 1991–92 | 16.1 | 23.3 | 4.9 | 5.1 | 48.6 |
| 1992–93 | 15.5 | 24.4 | 3.3 | 5.6 | 46.4 |
| 1993–94 | 16.4 | 27.4 | 2.4 | 6.6 | 46.4 |
| 1994–95 | 18.0 | 34.1 | 1.3 | 6.5 | 40.1 |

— Not available.
*Source:* Ministry of Education (various years).

tion was also responsible for secondary technical schools and some vocational schools. Following the 1996 elections, the government sought greater coordination of VET and placed all vocational schools under the Ministry of Education.

Direct involvement by enterprises in vocational and technical education has largely ceased, although relationships—mostly informal—between individual schools and enterprises persist. Although industry is still represented at the national level in the expert groups that decide on curricula, this participation is largely voluntary and is a continuation of former practice.

Many of the schools' day-to-day responsibilities have been decentralized. School principals can now manage their own budgets—which the state still provides—and they have a large amount of autonomy in matters relating to staff and administration. All secondary schools administered by the state have received the status of legal entities. Nevertheless, there is a general feeling that ministry staff are still heavily involved in operational tasks. To date, decentralization has been largely within the framework of the administrative systems of individual ministries, and it has involved only those people directly involved in education: administrators, teachers, and parents. Horizontal communication and coordinating bodies have not been developed. Nevertheless, those changes that have taken place have made schools and teachers far more responsible for educational matters than in the past.

*Financing*

An important change has taken place in the way schools are financed. In 1992 the authorities introduced a system of formula financing referred to as normative financing. Schools receive a lump sum based on the number of pupils. The amount per pupil varies according to the type of school and the field of study, and an index compensates for certain disadvantages (such as students' disabilities, school location, and so on). Although the criteria for calculating the lump sum remains debatable, this funding mechanism has made schools more responsive to students' and parents' aspirations and to the labor market's needs. The mechanism also allows school management to develop its own policies.

Total expenditures on education increased from 21.1 billion krona in 1989 to 63.1 billion krona in 1994, and as a percentage of gross domestic product, education expenditures increased from 4.0 to 5.7 percent during the same period. Estimates indicate that the state budget covers about 98 percent of total education costs. The major portion of financing (more than 80 percent) comes from the national budget. The municipal share has decreased.

In the VET system about 75 percent of noninvestment expenditures are for salaries and social insurance for teachers and other staff. Finding resources for investments (renovating buildings and buying equipment and teaching materials) has been a continuous problem, especially for the schools now under the jurisdiction of the Ministry of Education.

## Retraining Programs

The labor policies implemented by the Public Employment Service, which falls under the auspices of the Ministry of Labor and Social Affairs, include labor market training. This service was established in 1990 and had to be built from scratch. Training has not had to be implemented on a massive scale given the relatively low unemployment figures. Only a small number of people (less than 0.25 percent of the labor force) have entered retraining programs, and so far only a small amount of money has been spent on them (about 0.1 percent of gross domestic product).

The Public Employment Service does not have its own network of retraining centers, but it enters into agreements with private and public training organizations. Several secondary VET schools have signed such contracts. Increasingly, however, the Public Employment Service is becoming dissatisfied with the quality of retraining provided and the pedagogical approaches adopted both by educational institutions and by private organizations; it feels that it often has to address the resulting problems. These issues are now leading to closer cooperation between education and labor market authorities.

## Postschool Training

While the former system of adult education, as an integrated part of the state educational system, has gradually collapsed, private training initiatives have increased. An estimated 2,000 private training organizations are now operating. The only condition for a private training center to operate is to be registered as a company, but if it wishes to award educational certificates, accreditation by the Ministry of Education is required.

Enterprises have completely withdrawn from financing vocational and technical education because they lost their apprentice and training centers and their soft-budget financing. Recently, however, some enterprises have indicated that they might be ready to invest in training again. These are usually enterprises that have managed to establish themselves on the world market and need skills not readily available in the schools (such as the Skoda car factory), or enterprises confronting severe labor shortages (as in the Ostrava mining region).

## VET Issues and Reforms

Since 1989 the Czech authorities have initiated changes in the structure of VET in an attempt to overcome some of the rigidities of the inherited system. The number and scope of innovations that these measures have encouraged are impressive, but some developments have been less positive.

### Free Choice of Education and the Development of Private Schools

The introduction of freedom of choice at the end of compulsory schooling has dramatically lowered enrollments in vocational schools, which provide courses leading to the apprenticeship certificate, and correspondingly increased enrollments in technical schools, which offer courses leading to the *Maturita*. Encouraged since 1989, private VET institutions have undoubtedly played a major role in changing VET structures in the initial transition years, since most private schools are in the secondary technical school sector.

Private schools have benefited from the same financial arrangements as state schools. In addition, they can elicit financial contributions from students and their parents. These contributions are necessary to cover investment, because state funding only covers teachers' salaries and operational costs. Since public funding depends on the number of students, private schools now seek to attract as many students as possible by offering attractive educational packages.

The inherited VET system catered to 85 percent of school leavers from basic schools, but it channeled them into rigid, narrow educational streams and specialties. The possibilities of transferring from one type of vocational education to another were limited, not only because student quotas were decided centrally, but also because schools were viewed as belonging to the specialized technical ministries and, in the case of the secondary vocational schools, were directly attached to industrial enterprises. In addition, access to schools was possible only after passing the entrance examination. Changing one's educational profile was difficult. Thus occupational mobility among young workers was relatively high.

In response, the authorities have tried to increase the possibilities for horizontal and vertical mobility for students by changing the curricula and by creating new types of educational institutions. A number of secondary vocational schools are being transformed, with European Union PHARE support, into so-called integrated schools, which offer courses at the level of both secondary vocational and secondary technical schools. In addition, a limited number of economic and technical secondary schools have been established that fall somewhere between secondary general and secondary technical schools. (They offer a practical education with a higher level of general theory than that provided by the technical schools, and they expect their graduates to continue their studies at the university level, especially in the technical streams.)

The authorities have diversified further by distinguishing between two-, three-, four-, and five-year courses in both secondary technical schools and secondary vocational schools. The length of the course depends on the requirements for specific occupations. However, because of the extension of basic schooling for one year, the five-year courses were abolished in 1996. Those taking the four-year courses are eligible to take the *Maturita*.

## Development of Higher Professional Schools

Vertical mobility for students has been increased, first by the provision of follow-up courses for graduates of both secondary technical and secondary vocational schools, and second, on an experimental basis, by the creation of higher professional schools. As a result, postsecondary education has been diversified, and students' chances of gaining access to higher education have improved.

Higher professional schools are developing rapidly. In addition to the 25 schools already in existence, about 300 secondary technical schools have applied for status as higher professional schools, of which nearly 150 have a good chance of being accepted. These schools' courses in computer science, foreign languages, and commercial law are in high demand. Admission is selective. Applicants must have a technical *Maturita* and must also pass an entrance examination. Courses last from one to three years, including practical training of at least one day a week.

The status of higher professional schools is problematic, since they are not considered to be higher education institutions. Nevertheless, their position at the apex of secondary technical and vocational education enables them to play a catalytic role in the renovation of VET as a whole.

### The Future Status of Secondary Vocational Schools

Unlike other Central and East European countries, the Czech Republic did not abandon secondary vocational schools to the new market forces. All secondary vocational schools that had belonged to enterprises were placed temporarily under the jurisdiction of the Ministry of the Economy, and the state budget continued to finance their operational costs. Students unable to secure sponsorship from an enterprise are paid for by the state and are known as state apprentices. Since the 1996 elections, all vocational schools have been the responsibility of the Ministry of Education.

Secondary vocational schools, once the central feature of the VET system, now run the risk of becoming the least appreciated type of education. The authorities are interested in continuing to provide vocational education that, in the continental European tradition, offers a combination of theoretical and practical learning that leads students to skilled occupations, and hence involves close cooperation between schools and enterprises. However, the traditional narrowness of courses has come under criticism.

Policy thinking on this matter is not clear. With the development of the integrated schools, the government may well move toward abolishing separate institutions geared to provide skilled worker qualifications. This would be in line with trends in Australia, Japan, the United Kingdom, and the United States. However, there is also the possibility of changing the current system, which differentiates secondary vocational schools from secondary technical schools, into one that distinguishes levels of qualification. Such a system would lead to another type of relationship between the different schools and would be more in line with the VET patterns in a number of continental European countries.

## Modernizing Curricula

The strategy the Ministry of Education has adopted to implement changes in the provision of vocational education in schools has relied primarily on curriculum innovations by teachers. Schools were granted a certain autonomy in changing their curricula: they could adapt 10 percent of a curriculum to local circumstances (and change 30 percent of their syllabuses), and they could make proposals for modernizing curricula with respect to occupations and newly developing sectors. Schools have used changes in their curriculum to attract students. Teachers' and schools' efforts to reorient their curricula are apparent, but the extent to which they have accomplished meaningful innovation is not known. The Ministry of Education has recognized more than 800 different curricula that have resulted from school initiatives, compared with some 500 available before 1989. The sheer number of courses creates problems, however.

Although curriculum change has become part of the competition between schools to attract students, its actual impact on teaching and learning is sometimes limited. This is because some schools have invented new courses that may differ only in title from ones that already exist; having a new curriculum approved is easier than having an existing one changed. Schools have prepared some of these new courses in close collaboration with enterprises that were seeking to re-establish the old enterprise-specific relationships with schools. However, the relevance of these courses is unclear, because no generally accepted list of occupations exists.

One of the positive aspects of school-based curriculum development is that teachers become directly involved in deciding what their students need to know. However, for such a decentralized process to have an impact on the overall VET system, information on schools' experiences must be continuously disseminated to all schools, and policymakers should monitor, evaluate, and make use of such experiences. This is not happening on a regular basis, and thus little use is being made of the experiences of individual schools.

## Governance of VET

A combination of circumstances reveals weaknesses in the governance of VET in the Czech Republic. The relationships between the ministries involved in the various forms of VET are not close enough to allow rationalization of provision, if not of responsibilities. For their part, social partners play only a small role in curriculum development and are not prepared to be involved actively in the delivery, let alone the financing, of vocational education and training. Support structures are too research oriented and lack the authority to implement the changes suggested by their research. Finally, individual VET schools operating independently do not foster a cohesive policy at the national level.

The authorities are now recognizing that the government needs to have a stronger strategic role. If VET is to do more than react passively to short-term changes in the labor market, reform policies cannot rely only on bottom-up initiatives. Monitoring and guidance within a clear policy framework are required, or else VET will be unable to play its part in modernizing and restructuring the economy and employment.

## Lessons Learned from the Czech Experience

The Czech experience has revealed the following lessons for other countries in transition to a market economy:

- *Rely on labor supply adjustment while encouraging private employment growth.* In contrast to other Central and Eastern European countries, the Czech republic has relied more on restricting the labor supply and less on attempting to prop up labor demand through interventions. The two principal instruments for this adjustment were early retirement and delayed entry of youth into the labor market by expanding the secondary education system. The expansion of secondary education, especially technical streams, was financed by limiting public funding of universities rather than by borrowing (table 3-6). However, such measures can only buy time and would not prove effective if the students do not find gainful employment when they graduate. Private employment growth has been encouraged through macroeconomic and labor market reforms. Therefore, these students are entering a relatively buoyant labor market.
- *Generalize vocational education and make it less terminal.* Vocational and technical education has been made more general, and the education system has been restructured to permit students to go on to postsecondary technical education. Although in 1989 only 45 percent of secondary students were eligible to apply for higher study (that is, had a *Maturita*), by 1995 this figure had increased to 60 percent. By introducing postsecondary schools and allowing vocational schools the flexibility to decide on the

TABLE 3-6
Total Expenditures for Different Levels and Types of Schools,
1989 and 1994

| Level and type of school | Billions of krona | | Index (1984 = 100) |
|---|---|---|---|
| | 1989 | 1994 | |
| Kindergartens | 1,948 | 5,528 | 284 |
| Basic schools | 6,055 | 18,299 | 301 |
| Secondary schools | | | |
| General | 644 | 3,042 | 472 |
| Technical | 1,192 | 6,101 | 512 |
| Vocational | 1,651 | 8,832 | 535 |
| Special schools | 640 | 2,423 | 379 |
| Higher education | 3,494 | 8,465 | 242 |
| Total | 22,166 | 62,877 | 284 |

Source: OECD (1995b).

duration and content of instruction, the Czech government was able to increase the attractiveness of vocational education.

• *Keep public training small by maintaining low registered unemployment.* Public training programs, which have a discouraging record elsewhere, have been kept modest in the Czech Republic through a host of measures, especially the reform of unemployment compensation mechanisms. In 1992 eligibility for unemployment benefits was tightened, and their generosity was reduced, resulting in weaker incentives for job seekers to stay unemployed. This reduced the pressure on the government to resort to active labor programs, of which public training is among the most expensive and least effective. This may have allowed the Czech government to maintain its support for formal education.

• *Foster private provision of vocational education by means of favorable laws and industrial growth.* Private provision of vocational education has been encouraged by lenient laws for setting up training centers. Accreditation requirements are more stringent, but they are needed only if certificates are issued or public funds are sought. Although commercial providers are the first to proliferate in the private market, industrial sector growth will encourage a vigorous response from private providers of technical training, particularly if the regulatory environment is not unduly restrictive.

# References

Ministry of Education. various years. *Statistical Yearbook of Education.* Prague.
OECD (Organization for Economic Cooperation and Development). 1995a. *Review of the Labor Market in the Czech Republic.* Paris.
———. 1995b. "Review of Education Background Report." Paris.

# 4 Russian Federation

RICHARD JOHANSON

WHEN THE RUSSIAN FEDERATION was restored as an independent state in 1991, after more than 70 years of rule by the Union of Soviet Socialist Republics, major steps were taken toward a transition to a market economy. These followed earlier experiments with various degrees of privatization and reform under *perestroika*. In the period that followed, prices were liberalized and an ambitious program of privatization was launched. But the period 1991 to 1996 was characterized by a precipitous drop in production and output, high initial inflation, growing interenterprise arrears, and a declining labor force with a surprising stability in the ostensible level of employment.

Between 1991 and 1995 Russia registered a cumulative decline of 47.3 percent in real gross domestic product (Citrin and Lahiri 1995). Part of the decline may be attributed to inflation of production statistics under the previous command economy and incomplete coverage of newly emerging economic activities (Gavrilenko and Koen 1994). Still, the declines have been large.

Other problems arose from the disintegration of the Soviet Union and the collapse of traditional Council for Mutual Economic Assistance (CMEA) export markets. With the loss of those customers, the share of exports to CMEA countries dropped from around 60 percent of the Soviet Union's total trade, to less than 20 percent of Russia's trade with that area alone. At the same time, Russia experienced disruptions in traditional supplies of raw materials and other inputs. Relative prices changed dramatically in response to domestic price liberalization, modifications in subsidies, and changes in the structure of taxes and demand.

The pace of privatization has been rapid. By 1994 more than two-thirds of large and medium enterprises and over 80 percent of small enterprises had been privatized. Over 60 percent of the industrial work force had been employed in privatized enterprises. Privatization, however, cannot be equated with industrial restructuring or competition. Incentive structures for management have not changed much, and privatization has occurred with little discernible impact on enterprise behavior. However, some technological restructuring has begun. About half of all firms by 1994 had introduced some form of capital innovation or some form of work reorganization. These changes have skill implications, mainly by increasing the range of tasks for manual jobs. The size of enterprises has also begun to change. The inherited industrial structure was characterized by large enterprises. These structures have begun to break up into smaller enterprises, and new job growth has been concentrated in smaller firms. Changes in the economy have had significant implications for the labor force.

## The Labor Market

Russia had a population of about 148 million people in 1995. The economically active population was 72 to 73 million people, or 48 percent of the total population. This represented a decline from a labor force of 90 million in 1990. Some 67 million persons were employed in 1995, and an estimated 6 million were unemployed and looking for work. Of this 6 million only 2.4 million were officially registered as unemployed.

The transition period has been characterized by major shifts in employment by sector. In 1990 some 70 percent of the labor force worked in industry, a category that includes transportation, agriculture, industry, and construction, but this proportion fell to 44 percent in 1995. Growth areas include trade, hotel and restaurant businesses, auto service, housing refurbishing, and office repair and refurbishing. Since 1992 some parts of the economy have expanded their work forces, including trade and catering (14 percent), individual economic activity (865 percent), and self employment (163 percent). According to the Ministry of Labor, the service sector grew by 13 percent in 1995 alone. "Informal sector jobs and self-employment are becoming increasingly important. Informal sector employment . . . is a significant source of income in general, and in particular for the 'unemployed'" (World Bank 1995).

However, despite massive declines in output and significant structural shifts in employment, the overall change in employment has been small. The decline in output has not yet translated into high rates of open unemployment, even though geographical imbalances in unemployment rates are becoming more pronounced. Rates ranged in 1995 from 0.5 percent in Moscow to 23.0 percent in the eastern Ingushetia Republic. Overall registered unemployment has increased only gradually; starting from about 1 percent in mid-1992, it reached about 2.7 percent in 1995. Various factors account for the sluggish adjustment of employment to negative output shocks.

First, there have been relatively few mass layoffs. The share of total separations attributable to mass layoffs and enterprise closure was only about 7 to 8 percent at the end of 1994. Layoffs have been relatively infrequent; indeed many state firms have continued to recruit at relatively high rates (World Bank 1995). Second, registered unemployment accounts for less than 40 percent of total unemployment. Third, there is substantial suppressed unemployment in the form of part-time work and unpaid leave. Employers have found various ways to avoid mass layoffs. These include work stoppages, reduced work weeks, and administrative leave.

The proportion of employees with technical and vocational preparation is extremely high. According to the Ministry of Labor, 19.6 percent of all workers have completed higher education; 68.2 percent have completed secondary education—including 32 percent with secondary specialized (technician) training—and only 12.2 percent have less than full secondary education. Among entrepreneurs, the educational qualifications are even higher, with 37 percent having engineering or university backgrounds.

Even though the labor force is highly educated, there has been a mismatch of jobs and skills during the transition. Russian industry initially tended to shed clerical and professional staff; most of the hiring has been of manual workers in production (World Bank 1995). If the demand for production workers is relatively strong, the same cannot be said for those with higher technical skills. About 15 percent of basic vocational school graduates, 60 percent of specialized secondary graduates, and 50 percent of engineers could not get any job in 1994.

The picture is mixed on wage differentials by skill grouping. Commander and Yemtsov (1995) found convergence in changes to nominal wages across the main skill categories. This surely is related to the over 80 percent of cases in which wages remain administratively set rather than bargained. However, the relative stability of wages disaggregated by skill may be breaking down. Occupational wage differentials have widened very rapidly. In mid-1994 the average wage of managerial employees was 3.6 times the average wage of workers in unskilled manual jobs (Standing and Vaughan 1995). Moreover, workers receive nontaxable compensation in the form of bonuses, profit-sharing, some wage individualization, and fringe benefits. These trends have major implications for the vocational education and training (VET) system.

## The Vocational Education and Training System

The Russian education system consists of nine years of basic education for all students, followed by three types of secondary education: academic secondary education of two years' duration; basic vocational education of two to four years' duration; and technical education of four to five years' duration. Higher education consists of four to six years for the first degree, and it may be provided in academies, institutes, or universities. The enrollment ratio is nearly 100 percent for basic education, 90 percent for secondary education, and about 20 percent for higher education. This case study concentrates on basic vocational training, technical education, and continuing education; it explicitly excludes higher education and postgraduate education. Table 4-1 provides information on the destination of basic school completers.

The Russian system of VET has undergone considerable modification in organization, management, finance, and content since 1991, but it is still structured much as it was under the Soviet Union. It can be divided conveniently into three parts: a school-based system for youth; an enterprise-based training system for workers; and a retraining system for adults.

One of the striking features of the system as a whole is its sheer size. School-based education and training includes some 6,900 institutions (al-

TABLE 4-1
Destination of Grade 9 School Leavers, 1990

| Destination | Duration (years) | Number (thousands) | Percentage of total |
|---|---|---|---|
| Academic secondary school | 2 | 970 | 53.6 |
| Technical secondary school | 4–5 | 280 | 15.5 |
| Vocational secondary school | 2–4 | 460 | 25.4 |
| Labor market | — | 100 | 5.5 |
| Total | — | 1,819 | 100.0 |

— Not available.
*Source:* Ministry of Education (1995).

most 4,300 basic vocational schools with 1.8 million enrolled and 2,600 technical schools with almost 2 million students). Enterprise-based training has decreased sharply in recent years, but in 1995 the jobs of nearly 1.8 million blue-collar workers were upgraded, and another 1.3 million workers received training for new occupations. The recently created system of employment training for unemployed adults trained almost half a million adults in 1995. A basic feature of the occupational training system is a heavy reliance on pre-employment and the corresponding lack of a formal, regulated apprenticeship system. An extraordinarily high percentage of all entrants to the labor force (75 to 80 percent) already have some initial occupational qualification.

Until the law changed in 1996, the school-based system had the following main characteristics:

• The enrollment ratio at the secondary level (Grades 10 and 11) was relatively high (about 90 percent of the relevant age group) and was divided into academic secondary schools (about 40 to 45 percent of enrollments), vocational secondary schools (about 40 to 45 percent), and technical secondary schools (about 15 percent).

• Lateral movement between the three types of secondary education was considerable particularly among secondary graduates subsequently enrolling in postsecondary grades of technical and accelerated vocational programs.

• Early occupational specialization was required in vocational secondary.

• Industrial skills were heavily emphasized in the vocational training programs.

• Students were initiated into work in the early years of education; general secondary education included the option of obtaining qualifications in a vocational specialization, and many centralized workshop facilities existed for this purpose.

• Training along with production had a long history in all types of institutions.

In January 1996 the Law of the Russian Federation on Education was amended, and the structure of VET was subsequently divided into the following five levels:

• Basic vocational education. It normally continues two to four years after Grade 9 or one year after Grade 11. Basic vocational education endeavors to train skilled workers for all sectors of the economy.

• Second-level technical education (called "secondary vocational education" or "technical secondary education"). It is normally of three to five years' duration after Grade 9. Second-level technical education gives preparation for middle-level specialists and technician occupations.

• Higher-level technical education. Usually of four to five years' duration, this level provides degree training for engineers and other specialists.

• Postgraduate professional and occupational education.

• Additional professional and occupational education. According to the law, the "key purpose of additional education [is] the continuous upgrading of the skills of workers and employees" (Russian Federation 1996, Article 26, paragraph 1).

The amended law does not specify the minimum number of years for either basic vocational or secondary technical education. This provides a legal basis for flexibility in training duration.

In 1994 the government stopped compulsory secondary education. Students were allowed to leave the education system after Grade 9 or on reaching 16 years. Consequently, a growing number of 14- to 15-year-olds enter the labor market without training and unable to qualify for assistance from the Federal Employment Service (FES), which has a minimum age for access to its services of 16 years.

In what follows I will discuss the system of VET that has existed until recently and focus on basic vocational education, technical education, enterprise-based training for workers, and adult retraining.

## Basic Vocational Education

Russia's extensive system of basic vocational schools (tables 4-2 and 4-3) has three purposes: acquisition of specific vocational skills, continuation of general education, and the unstated purpose of keeping youth engaged in socially useful activities (and off the street). Russia has adopted the European standard of five skill levels, and basic vocational schools impart levels 2 through 4. Structurally, basic vocational education spans both secondary and postsecondary levels. In addition to programs for students completing Grade 9 of basic education, intensive skill programs are offered to graduates of secondary schools (Grade 11). Vocational lyceums, a recent invention, offer an additional year of studies up to the postsecondary certificate level mainly for advanced skill acquisition. About 15 percent of all institutions have been upgraded to lyceums. This confers the advantages of status

TABLE 4-2
Features of the Basic Vocational Education System

| Type | Entry level | Duration | Qualification awarded |
|------|------------|----------|----------------------|
| Vocational school | Grade 9 | 2 years | Certificate, Grade 2 |
|  |  | 3 years | Certificate, Grade 3 + secondary education |
| Vocational school | Grade 11 | 1+ years | Certificate, Grade 3 |
| Vocational lyceum | Grade 9 | 4 years | Diploma, fourth-level (mid-level specialist) |

*Source*: Author.

and modest financial benefits, including an extra 15 percent of each teacher's pay for materials.

According to education administrators and researchers, vocational schools have traditionally been designed for students of lower academic aptitude. Entry traditionally has not been competitive, owing to lack of student demand. Entrants are allocated to various occupational fields on the basis of interviews and examination of school records.

## Teaching Programs

The federal government determines the list of occupations that may and may not be taught. These areas can cover "every basic area of socially-useful activities," and the duration of schooling can vary from one school to another (de Moura Castro 1994). Basic occupational training is roughly one-third theory (academic subjects), one-third vocational subjects, and one-third practical activities and production. Consider the example of an auto repair school with a two-year program of 1,400 hours. Students spend about 62 percent of this time in workshops and production—somewhat less in the first year (40 percent of the time) and more in the second year (60 to 100 percent of the time). In the first semester all the instruction is received in the school, including two days in workshops. In the second semester one day of instruction takes place in the workshop and one day in an enterprise, if the school has managed to arrange sufficient places. In the third semester two to three days of instruction are in the enterprise. Instruction during the fourth semester takes place almost completely at the enterprise.

Vocational and technical schools, unlike general secondary schools, tend to take training cum production activities seriously. Production is not a

TABLE 4-3
Basic Vocational Training, Selected Years, 1991–96

| Category | 1991 | 1993 | 1995 | 1996 | Change, 1991–96 | |
| | | | | | No. | Percent |
|---|---|---|---|---|---|---|
| Number of institutions | 4,321 | 4,273 | 4,166 | 4,214 | –107 | –2.5 |
| Number of students enrolled (thousands) | 1,841 | 1,741 | 1,689 | 1,704 | –137 | –7.5 |
| Number of graduates (thousands) | 1,210 | 1,031 | 1,034 | 955 | –255 | –21.0 |

*Note:* Includes Federal Employment Service, agreements with enterprises, and privately financed individuals.
*Source:* Ministry of Education data.

side activity but a core program. The typical vocational or technical school was built in order to prepare trained personnel for a given enterprise. Located near the enterprise, it depended on the enterprise for equipment, instructors for the practical activities, internships, and jobs for the graduates. In line with this symbiotic relation, the factories subcontracted with the school for the manufacturing or assembly of the parts they needed in their own production lines. This was considered a suitable arrangement for the schools, since it provided practical experience to students and some welcome extra revenue (de Moura Castro, Feonova, and Litman 1994).

In the 1980s an extensive system of contract training grew in which specific enterprises offered workshop experience on or near the enterprise premises. However, this system started to collapse rapidly in 1990 when a new enterprise law freed the enterprises of the responsibility for training students. At present only about 10 percent of the schools have maintained the arrangements with specific enterprises.

*Management*

Basic vocational schools are owned and financed at the federal level, but considerable authority has been delegated to the regions and municipalities for day-to-day operation. In particular, the schools have substantial autonomy in hiring teaching staff, in the teaching process, and in the use of funds. From 1991 to 1995, the number of institutions and enrollments was relatively buoyant, but enrollments by sector shifted considerably. Enrollments in industrial sectors declined markedly, while training in service-related occupations increased substantially.

Teacher and instructor qualifications are high: more than 90 percent of the teachers had higher education qualifications; 85 percent of the instructors had either postsecondary technical qualifications or higher education. Teacher/instructor salaries are reportedly only 30 to 60 percent of the average industrial wage, and this contributes to significant attrition, on the order of 10 percent, primarily among instructors in fields with strong wages in the marketplace.

The cost structure of vocational schools is skewed by the inclusion of student meals, which account for one-third to one-half of total expenditures per student. Utilities make up another 30 to 40 percent of the total. Thus expenses directly related to teaching (for example, teacher salaries at 20 percent of the total) represent a small share of spending per student. The federal government in the 1991–95 period was able to finance only teacher salaries, student meals, and student stipends. It provided nothing for teaching materials, consumable supplies, maintenance, renovation, or utilities. This provoked intensive activity by schools to supplement their income from other sources. The four principal sources are (a) regional and local budgets; (b) production of goods and services for sale in the market; (c) leasing of premises, although the schools can keep only 10 percent of these proceeds; and (d) tuition for additional students, particularly for adult training being financed by the FES. The latter adds about 15 percent on average to school income. Production of goods for sale is increasingly varied in product mix and aimed more at the market in general than, as in the past, at a specific enterprise; on average, schools cover 20 percent of their total expenses from this source.

Student outcomes are tested by the individual school in the absence of overall national standards. National norms (what is called the "state educational standard") are being developed now at the federal level. The external efficiency of the system has been declining. From 1991 to 1995, the demand for skilled workers dropped. The output of graduates from basic vocational training increasingly outstripped effective employment demand, and the rates of employment of graduates fell steadily (table 4-4).

## Technical Education

Technical education and training has the following distinguishing characteristics:

TABLE 4-4
Employment Experience of Basic Vocational School Graduates,
1991, 1993, 1995

| | 1991 | | 1993 | | 1995 | |
|---|---|---|---|---|---|---|
| Destination | Number (thousands) | Per-cent | Number (thousands) | Per cent | Number (thousands) | Per-cent |
| Wage job | 672 | 84.5 | 494 | 66.4 | 393 | 56.8 |
| Further education | 13 | 1.6 | 17 | 2.2 | 33 | 4.7 |
| Conscripted into military | 63 | 7.9 | 66 | 8.9 | 83 | 12.0 |
| Self-employed | 30 | 3.8 | 55 | 7.4 | 65 | 9.4 |
| Unemployed | 18 | 2.2 | 112 | 15.1 | 118 | 17.1 |
| Total graduates | 795 | 100.0 | 744 | 100.0 | 692 | 100.0 |

*Source:* Ministry of Education (1995).

- Four to five years in duration, spanning secondary education (Grades 10 to 11) plus two to three years of postsecondary education
- Recent decline of the secondary level in favor of the postsecondary level (discrete postsecondary institutions are evolving)
- Recent upgrading of a selected one-fourth of the institutions to "colleges" with an extra year of studies
- Frequent changes of administrative responsibility between the Ministry of Education and the State Committee of Higher Education, the latter being responsible at present
- Control of at least 40 percent of the total educational institutions by sector ministries
- Dominance of three sectors in enrollment: industry, health (nurses training), and education
- Shifting enrollments out of industry and health care and into new market-oriented fields such as business and social work.

## Purpose and Structure

Technical education is technician training for middle-level specialists (between skilled workers and engineers) and supervisors requiring a higher level of formal education than the typical skilled worker prepared by basic vocational education (de Moura Castro 1994).

Technical education includes secondary and postsecondary vocational institutions and technical "colleges." Postsecondary technical education spans both the final years of secondary education (Grades 10 and 11) and the first years of postsecondary education (two to three years.) This level is now officially called "secondary vocational education," which is something of a misnomer. The institutions are more a combination of academic secondary schools (the first two years) followed by short-cycle postsecondary institutions of two or three years' duration. The postsecondary cycle dominates in terms of enrollment.

"Colleges" began to be established in 1989 at the request of enterprises. These are independent educational establishments providing advanced training and longer duration training. A third year is added to the program, and graduates can enter the second year of higher education institutions. Many of these institutions offer market-oriented subjects, including commerce, finance, banking, high technology, management, small business, and other services. An institution needs permission to be upgraded from a secondary vocational institution to a college. After submitting a request and presenting its qualifications, the institution is reviewed by the State Committee of Higher Education to determine whether it meets the required standards. Less than one-fourth of the institutions that apply to become colleges succeed.

Russia's 2,600 public technical education institutions enroll 1.9 million students (1.4 million full time) and employ 156,000 teachers and instructors. Included in the overall total are about 680 colleges (SCHE 1996). In addition, more than 40 higher education institutions and 600 basic vocational schools (the lyceums) provide programs of postsecondary technical education. The overall number of establishments has remained fairly constant since independence—that is, there have been no major closings, consolidations, or new openings. There were 2,612 institutions in 1995 compared with 2,605 institutions in 1991.

## Administration

The administration of secondary vocational education has repeatedly shifted back and forth between the Ministry of Education and the State Committee for Higher Education, including four changes in 1993–94 (de Moura Castro 1994). In the mid-1990s the State Committee of Higher Education administered secondary vocational education. However, a significant share of the schools was actually controlled by sectoral ministries like agriculture and industry.

Many of these institutions are considered part of the enterprises. In these cases the State Committee of Higher Education establishes the basic standards, and the sectoral ministry defines the teaching programs. The staff for these institutions often come from the degree-level higher education institutions operated by the sectoral ministry.

Postsecondary technical education confers a diploma that is recognized across the whole Russian Federation. The final certification, which is compulsory, consists of a final examination in general subjects, examination in the occupational qualification, and defense of a graduation paper or project.


## Student Intake

About 15 to 20 percent of the students who complete basic education through Grade 9 (that is, about 280,000 students out of 1,800,000) enroll in Grade 10 in secondary specialized vocational education. However, the bulk of the enrollment is concentrated in the final two or three years of the four-to-five-year program. In addition to the continuation of the 280,000 students entering Grade 10, the postsecondary technical institutions admit to the third year approximately 420,000 students from academic secondary schools—about 40 to 45 percent of the Grade 11 graduates—plus another 50,000 from basic vocational schools (about 5 percent of those who complete the second year). As a result of this entry, the enrollment in the third year of technical education is almost three times greater than enrollment in the first year. The number of students enrolled shows a slight, but steady downward trend from 2.2 million in 1991 to 1.9 million in 1995.

The occupational distribution of enrollments changed markedly between 1990 and 1995 (table 4-5). Enrollments in technical occupations declined dramatically from 349,000 in 1990 to 221,000 in 1995, a decrease of 37 percent. Education dropped from 131,000 to 105,000; health care, from 114,000 to 76,000; and agriculture, from 88,000 to 66,000. The main field registering increases (business and financial occupations) increased by 89 percent from 92,000 to 174,000 (SCHE 1996).

Consistent with their ownership by sectoral ministries, most postsecondary technical institutions are specialized by branch of economy, or sector: occupations in industry and construction (907 institutions), health protection (436 institutions, mainly for training nurses), and education

TABLE 4-5
Postsecondary Technical Education: Occupational Distribution
of Enrollment, Selected Years, 1985–95
(thousands of students)

| Type of studies | 1985 | 1990 | 1993 | 1994 | 1995 |
|---|---|---|---|---|---|
| Technical (industrial) | 422 | 349 | 249 | 222 | 221 |
| Education (teacher training) | 124 | 131 | 109 | 102 | 105 |
| Health care (nursing) | 93 | 114 | 78 | 77 | 76 |
| Agriculture | 80 | 68 | 67 | 45 | 55 |
| Business and finance | 92 | 93 | 161 | 183 | 174 |

Source: SCHE (1996).

(428 institutions, mainly for training teachers in basic general education and basic vocational education).

## Admission

Unlike basic vocational education, postsecondary technical education is open for admission only through competition. This competition takes the form of examinations, interviews, and testing to determine the applicant's suitability and aptitude for the intended studies. There are two alternative entry prerequisites: completion of basic general education (Grade 9) for entry into the first year, and full secondary education or basic vocational education (Grade 11 equivalent) for entry into the third year, called a "contracted intensive program." Competition for available places was strong in 1995: about 1.8 applicants for every available place (SCHE 1996). The proportion of students admitted on the basis of Grade 9 has decreased (only 38 percent of the 1995 enrollment).

## Financing

The federal government establishes enrollment quotas, or targets of the number of students who may be admitted for training at public expense. Like basic vocational education institutions, technical education institutions are relatively free to determine the uses of their budget and off-budget assets. The institutions may admit more students on a fee-paying basis. However, fee-paying students may not exceed 25 percent of the enrollment of students in each area of training specialty. This ceiling prevents fee-paying students from dominating the institutions' teaching program.

## Enterprise-Based Training of Workers

Enterprise-based training has the following characteristics:

- Under the former command system, enterprise-based training was mandated as pre-employment training for students and in-service training for various categories of workers.
- Enterprise-based training has been severely criticized for its ideological content and its often low quality.
- The extensive training provided by enterprises dropped sharply after 1990, when a new law freed enterprises from the requirement to train.
- The worker "qualification enhancement system"—or training to upgrade—still exists, but it has been sharply curtailed because of enterprises' budgetary constraints.
- Enterprise managers have shown a lack of interest in spending on worker training because of more pressing priorities, including finding or maintaining markets, keeping workers employed, and investing in new product development and plant. The threat of workers becoming obsolescent because their skills are no longer in demand is not seen as an immediate priority.
- A marginal tax incentive of up to 1.5 percent of payroll can be deducted from profits for expenditures on training. However, few firms make profits these days from which to deduct training expenses.
- A limited number of enterprises are beginning to recruit workers without qualifications, and they are providing them with systematic pre-employment training for three to eight months. This signals the gradual emergence of an enterprise-specific apprenticeship system.

Large enterprises traditionally have departments of technical training with responsibility for training workers, or they have their own company training centers. Training includes initial training, or apprenticeship, for those who have joined the factory without occupational qualifications; retraining for work in a new field; or retraining for a second occupation that will be practiced in addition to the first.

Initial training may be of two types: apprenticeship training or "formal" training. In the past, apprenticeship training concentrated on the acquisition of skills under the supervision of a skilled worker on the job, but it is now being complemented with formal instruction and a specific individual training program. As with true apprenticeships, the students sign an employment contract and earn money during the entire period of induction training. While in the workshops, the trainees work under the supervision of a qualified master. In the case of formal training, workers may undergo several months of initial training at a training center, at the company's expense, before starting work.

Overall, enterprise-based training has declined. There are two reasons for this. First, the enterprise law of 1990 eliminated the statutory requirement both for training of workers and for training of students from basic vocational education. Second, training of workers is widely considered to be a low priority at a time when production is declining and enterprises are going deeper into debt. A survey in 1993–94 asking enterprise managers to rate the most important factors for production ranked training of workers in 14th place.

The Ministry of Labor has been developing various forms of state support in order to encourage enterprises to develop in-company training. In 1994 a government decree created a network of support among the training departments of enterprises. Under this decree the Association for Personnel Development was created. In 1995 it was active in about 20 of Russia's 89 regions and had a membership of about 2,000 enterprises. The purpose of the association is to analyze the training requirements of enterprises and assist them in their personnel development programs, training of in-company instructors, and exchange of experiences. However, insufficient data have been collected to say with any confidence whether this has led to an increase in enterprise-based training.

## Adult Retraining

Adult retraining aims to prepare unemployed adults for new occupations in demand. The adult retraining system is based on the large and geographically spread Federal Employment Service, created in 1991 by the law on employment of that year. Since then the FES has grown to about 3,000 local offices in 89 regions and 10 municipalities with 36,000 employees.

Some of its distinguishing characteristics are as follow:

• The work of the FES is financed through an employment fund, based on a 1.5 percent payroll tax. The FES pays for the entire cost of training from the employment fund; participants and employers typically do not pay anything.

- The number of adults retrained for new occupations grew from 10,000 in 1991, to about 150,000 in 1993, to nearly 460,000 in 1995.
- The determination of occupations in demand is done through reported vacancies, employer job guarantees, and training for self-employment—which the FES has pioneered in Russia.
- The unemployed are becoming more interested in receiving training. Less than 10 percent were interested in 1991. More than two-thirds of the employed were interested in 1996.
- The FES uses the school-based training infrastructure: over 90 percent of the training financed by the FES is provided by existing training institutions, some of which are selected on a competitive basis.
- The Federal Educational Center of the FES develops the content of adult retraining programs and trains instructors. Training providers must use the FES training programs.
- Overall, there is about a 90 to 95 percent completion rate for the training. About 60 to 67 percent of the trainees find employment after training; 15 to 20 percent of those trainees return eventually to reregister as unemployed.

### Training Purposes

The key question in adult retraining, as in vocational training generally, is "training for what?" The FES uses three basic methods to select the kinds of occupations in which training is given. The first approach is to train for specific vacancies. This method cannot be relied upon solely. Employers prefer to fill most vacancies by other means and tend to register only the most unattractive positions as vacancies (for example, those requiring hard manual labor). The second approach is to rely on the demand of employers. This approach has the advantage of being demand driven. The third approach is to train for self-employment. The reasoning is that if there are not enough jobs to go around, clearly the case in Russia, people should be trained to make their own jobs. Training is given in such areas as clothes making, hair dressing, and small business operation. The FES has pioneered training for self-employment in Russia.

### Training Target Groups

The FES has many more potential clients for training than it can possibly finance and handle. How does the FES select which people to train? The law sets some priorities for selecting clients for training. It specifies the long-term unemployed as top priority. In addition, the FES gives priority to young people (ages 16 to 29), women (60 percent of the registered unemployed), and the disabled.

### Training Methods

In January 1993 the FES established a Federal Educational Center to develop suitable programs for training the unemployed, establish effective training methods, upgrade teachers, and disseminate experience. The center has about 150 staff. Training programs delivered through the financing of the employment service are developed in the center. Training deliverers contracted by the employment service must use the training programs prepared by the FES.

### Results

As in many other countries, in Russia no scientific cost-benefit analysis of these programs has been attempted in order to get the net impact of these programs. Gross data suggest that about 60 to 67 percent of training recipients find a job immediately after undertaking training, which is rather impressive given the employment situation in the country. The number of trained adults who stay on the job is also impressive. In 1995 only 16 percent of people who previously received training were registered as unemployed a second time. However, in the absence of rigorous evaluations, it is not possible to judge the cost-effectiveness of these programs.

## Problems and Issues

The Russian system of occupational training has made considerable progress in orienting itself to changes in the economic system, but there remain several basic problems before the transformation can be effective.

### Structural Problems

Structural problems derive from the overall objectives of the training system, which were developed for another era. In the past it was assumed that everyone had to be trained in a specific occupation before going to work. This meant that the preservice training system had to be large and accommodate virtually all of the secondary age group, and that employers had to do little after employment to upgrade or retrain workers. At the same time, the system required youth to choose an occupation at too early an age. Students entered basic vocational schools at the ages of 14 to 15 and were channeled directly into specific-occupation training. At this age students seldom know the occupation they want to pursue.

The structure of Russian training for vocational qualifications has been rigid in requiring lengthy training for occupations that do not require much training and might be better learned on the job. de Moura Castro (1994) found that 70 percent of the employees in low-skill occupations did not need the vocational skills they learned over several years, and these employees believed they could have learned needed skills on the job in a matter of weeks.

## Organization and Management

The VET system combines the disadvantages of overcentralized coordination and diversified, duplicated management and training bodies. Centralized management has played a dominant role in vocational training. It has developed the content through methodological institutes and allocated budget funds to each of the 6,000 institutions. Schools have achieved greater autonomy, but the view among federal training authorities still prevails that the center should orchestrate and direct the system, which it does through the Ministry of Education and the State Committee of Higher Education. The net effect is overcentralization of the system in terms of budget and definition of teaching programs.

An additional problem is that of duplication. Many other organizations both in the center and outside have responsibilities for vocational training. They include functional ministries with specialist training schools for industries such as oil and gas, ferrous metals, and chemicals. There may be 30 such administrations in addition to the training establishments belonging to large enterprises. According to the Ministry of Education, "because of the proliferation of vocational training institutions under the Soviet system, there may well be three vocational schools catering to the age range 15 to 19 in the same street of the same town serving the same factories and enterprises and teaching the same skills" (Humphries and Dimond 1996).

## Costs and Financing

The government can no longer maintain 100 percent financing for vocational training. The consequences of this are far-reaching. From 1991 to

1996 the Ministry of Education was able to finance only salaries, student meals, stipends, and almost nothing else. Little money was spent on key teaching expenditures. No provision was made for equipment, teaching materials, consumable supplies, maintenance, or repair of facilities. Institutions were left to fend for themselves to finance these items. Utility payments clearly had priority, with the result that virtually nothing was invested in system development (teaching materials or equipment). Equipment was worn out or in disrepair, and textbooks and other teaching materials were in extremely short supply or nonexistent.

Teacher salaries were also comparatively low. As a result, many experienced and high-quality instructors who had the opportunity to employ their skills elsewhere left the profession. New instructors are typically not being hired, in part because salaries are so unattractive but also because school directors (to approximate a living wage) offer double salaries to the remaining instructors to teach double classes.

## Relevance and Effectiveness of Training

With policies and content being developed from the center, either in ministries or methodological institutes, employer participation in these processes is nominal. Very few employers other than large state enterprise managers are being involved in any structured or official way in decisionmaking about vocational training (Humphries and Dimond 1996). In a market economy most demand for skills is local or regional. Groups of employers can best reflect the types of skills needed. At present, however, Russia has no way to get broad involvement by employers. In the 1980s an extensive system of contract training developed in which students spent considerable time in workshops in or near the premises of enterprises (but were never integrated into the enterprise work force). This system virtually collapsed in the early 1990s when enterprises were no longer forced to take interns.

Conversely, vocational institutions have little means or incentive to learn about their graduates' performance in the labor market as a basis for making adjustments in the supply. The already dramatic change in enrollment by occupational grouping does demonstrate a certain responsiveness to changes in the labor markets. However, for sustained progress it is necessary to develop better feedback mechanisms and incentives. Since funding is not tied to performance, there is little information on the external efficiency of the system, and rigorous cost-benefit analysis of training programs is rarely conducted in order to study how training can be better targeted.

## Changes, Innovation, and Reforms

Despite severe problems, the VET system in Russia today differs markedly from the one inherited from the Soviet system with respect to organization, management, finance, training, and content.

- *Organization, management, and financing.* School directors have been given considerable autonomy in a major decentralization of responsibilities; and financial resources have been substantially diversified because 40 percent of school budgets now must come from nontraditional sources.
- *Training.* The system of contract training of students within enterprises was forced on the enterprises, and it collapsed with the adoption of laws giving them independence; a new system somewhat akin to apprenticeship seems to be developing, although many employers perceive little advantage at present in investing in worker training.
- *Clients and content.* Between 1991 and 1996, the official number of occupations taught dropped from 1,200 specializations to 287 integrated skill profiles, which include a range of functions that has broadened along with the range of skills. The composition of enrollments has changed; now in addition to the pre-employment training they may have received at school, adults are being retrained by the new Federal Employment Service. The occupational mix of training has shifted dramatically, away from industrial occupations toward services and new occupations in a market economy (for example, accountancy, small business, bank telling).

Although sometimes the result of deliberate policy, these changes have usually been the spontaneous and natural response to external pressures. Clearly, financial constraints have been a powerful engine of reform in the diversification of financing. Creation of the FES and its role in financing new types of training programs through existing training structures have had a positive effect on training within the formal school system. In addition, exposure to external systems has given new ideas to Russian policymakers, showing them the need to reduce overspecialization and consolidate the number of occupations taught.

### Structural Innovations

The length, location, and type of training have become more flexible. Authorities now can adjust the length of training to the requirements of the occupation. In addition, the law provides for flexibility in the location of training. Specifically, secondary technical education can be given at the first level of higher education institutions, and basic vocational education can be provided at licensed secondary technical institutions. Some efforts also have been made to shorten programs. In Nizhny Novgorod, for example, the training for some simple occupations has been shortened by six months, or 25 percent. Programs have also diversified to allow two years of training for some occupations (without secondary school equivalence), three years for the standard certificate, and four years for the lyceums.

Retraining services are now available through the FES, a major change since the reestablishment of the Russian Federation at the end of 1990. The FES started in 1991 by training 10,000 unemployed workers, and in 1995 it retrained nearly 460,000 adults in intensive courses of four to six months. In response to the declining ratio of jobs to job seekers, the Federal Employment Service devotes as much as 30 percent of its training to preparing the recipients for self-employment. In response to financing constraints resulting from reduction in the payroll tax from 2 percent in 1991 to 1.5 percent in 1995, the Nizhny Novgorod Employment Service began restricting training to training for self-employment or training for enterprises that guaranteed employment to the trainees upon completion of the course. This new form of contract training helps to ensure almost a 100 percent employment rate for trainees.

Regional officials regarded the need to ration training as a problem; however, limiting training to guaranteed employment could be seen as a solution. By providing new content and pedagogical training to existing instructors and training establishments, the FES has had the unintended but positive and widespread effect of improving the quality and relevance of training within school-based training. An example is the adoption of training for self-employment and entrepreneurship, which some basic vocational schools have adopted as a part of their regular programs after it was first introduced in the schools for adult retraining.

## Organization and Management

Since the breakup of the Soviet Union in 1991, the VET system has become increasingly decentralized and open to private management. Under the former Soviet Union, VET decisionmaking was centralized in the Committee for Vocational Education, the equivalent of a ministry, with 350 staff. Now vocational education and training is handled by a section in the Ministry of Education with only 60 staff. Inevitably, some functions have had to be delegated to the regions—part of the government's radical reform of the administration of education. The reforms of 1991 and 1992 assigned considerable authority to individual schools, and this autonomy was reinforced by the 1996 amendment to the education law. School directors became responsible for hiring staff, setting salaries (above a minimum), initiating new teaching programs (for regional approval), managing the teaching process, raising funds, and disposing of self-generated funds (within certain limits). In fact, the pendulum has swung so far that external observers now remark that Russian educational establishments have more freedom and autonomy than do many similar institutions in the West.

In a major change of policy, new education legislation has allowed nonstate institutions to operate. Previously, they were banned. There are remarkably few restrictions on the establishment of private training establishments. Nonstate institutions can legally operate simply by registering. If the schools wish to obtain state recognition, and the possibility for some public financing, they must be accredited. This is a two-step process. The first is to be licensed, which requires an initial appraisal of the resources of the institution. The second step must await the production of graduates, at which point the performance of the institution is assessed on quality standards. Those institutions that pass the accreditation would be able to award certificates with state recognition. In 1995 some 300 nonstate *technikums* and basic vocational schools applied at the federal level for licensing; 260 were licensed and 40 that were previously licensed were accredited (that is, produced graduates whose quality could be assessed).

Privatizing public institutions has proved to be a successful experiment in some cases. One example is the former state training center, Infrakom, in Nizhny Novgorod (box 4-1). However, the federal government in 1995 took action against the "spontaneous" privatization of public institutions. Some public facilities were privatized, then sold off for other purposes by the new owners; the federal government's opposition to this process reportedly led to the closure of 10 percent of educational establishments. In other cases, parts of public facilities were leased out for profit. In vocational schools this meant that some workshops were used by private parties to produce goods for private profits. The Presidential Decree against Privatization of Educational Establishments imposed a three-year moratorium on conversion of public educational institutions into nonpublic ownership. Another decree required that all funds raised by leasing out workshops and other educational facilities for commercial purposes be sent to the federal treasury. The moratorium was superseded by the amendment to the education law prohibiting privatization of education institutions and their social infrastructure indefinitely.

BOX 4-1
Privatization of a State Regional Training Center,
Infrakom, in Nizhny Novgorod

This public training institution is close to 60 years old. Previously a "branch train-ing *combinat*" for the construction industry, it responded to state orders for train-ing people working in municipal infrastructure services. In February 1993—in the midst of a severe financial crisis—budget funds were eliminated for the institution. This was the main factor leading to its conversion. The Department of Construc-tion of the regional administration became the "founder" of the private institution. It allows the institution to use its present premises free of charge but retains owner-ship of the building. The privatized training center cannot dispose of the physical assets of the building for its own benefit.

Under the new structure, the training institution is a nonprofit enterprise. Any excess income after expenses must be channeled back into development of the institution. The institution's director serves on the basis of an employment contract signed by the director of the Department of Construction. As a result of being privatized, the institution lifted restrictions on teachers' salaries. The salaries of teachers then tripled, which greatly increased their motivation. Financial constraints on operation and expansion were also eased. For example, in 1995 the institution got about six times more income than it had received in the last budget from the region.

While maintaining services in its traditional fields (training persons to manage high-pressure equipment and handle dangerous materials and heavy lifting ma-chinery), the institution has expanded training to new fields of study to meet mar-ket demands. Total enrollment grew from about 3,000 trainees in 1993 to about 5,000 trainees (taught in two shifts) in 1996. During this period the share of en-rollments upgraded within their jobs declined from 70 percent to 40 percent; ini-tial training in 1996 covered about 60 percent of the institution's clientele. Students are recruited through advertising in newspapers, radio, and sometimes television.

---

## Costs and Financing

A major difference in vocational establishments in the late 1990s com-pared with earlier in the decade was in sources of income. Previously, the federal budget financed virtually 100 percent of expenses. In the late 1990s it provided only 50 to 60 percent. The balance came from other sources such as the following:

All students or their employers pay tuition, ranging from US$60 to US$300 per course, depending on the term and subject. The school is free to set the tuition fee at whatever level it chooses. About 35 percent of the total income of the center comes from retraining adults on contract with the Regional Employment Service; about 30 percent comes from enterprises sponsoring their workers for in-service upgrading training; and 30 percent comes from individual payments of tuition fees. The balance comes from revenues generated by the institution's own production, including printing facilities for commercial production. This revenue source is expected to grow. The institution has been accepted by the local tax authority (reportedly after a three-year struggle) as being tax exempt in accordance with an existing presidential decree that accords tax-free status to educational institutions. Because income has exceeded expenditures, the institution has been able to invest in new equipment and refurbish its facilities. A new canteen for students opened in the mid-1990s. The director estimated that the center had purchased 60 percent of all existing equipment since it was privatized in 1993.

The main competitors for the training institution come from other former branch training institutions that have also been privatized. However, the other institutions do not have the material basis (that is, equipment) to offer a wide variety of courses. Compared with the 10 to 15 occupations taught in those institutions, the Infrakom center offers training in 30 occupations. Infrakom has an additional advantage: it has its own printing press and desk-top publishing facilities so that it can produce its own teaching materials. This generates some additional income for the school and enhances the quality of instruction and the reputation of the institution in the community.

*Source:* Author's data.

- Regional and local governments. In 1994, 921 out of 2,618 technical schools were being financed from regional and local budgets, which covered mainly teacher training and agricultural and cultural *technikums* (Section Report 1994, p. 16).
- Production of goods and services for the market.
- Tuition from additional courses, such as training of adults for the employment service, or for extra-quota (private) students. In 1994, techni-

cal schools enrolled 46,000 students, or 9 percent of the total, on a commercial basis.

- Lease of premises for use by others for commercial purposes.

It is instructive to learn from failures as well as from successes. Two efforts to introduce major changes in the system related to financing ultimately did not work. The first was the failure to decentralize financing. In 1994–95 the government tried to turn over the complete operation and financing of vocational schools to the regional and municipal governments. However, this was resisted so strongly because of its financial consequences for regional and local governments that six months later the decree had to be rescinded.

Second, attempts to ensure adequate financing for VET (and education in general) through legislation failed. The July 1992 education law stipulated that not less than 10 percent of gross domestic product could be spent on education. In 1995 around 3 percent was spent. Moreover, the law stipulated that the average wage for teachers should not be less than the average for industry. In 1995 teachers' wages averaged 30 to 50 percent below the average wage of industrial workers. This points to the dichotomy between legal documents' good intentions and the realities of allocating scarce resources among competing priorities.

## Relevance and Responsiveness

The content and scope of training offerings have adapted to changes in the market. Enrollments in industrial fields of technical schools have declined nationally by 40 percent. At the same time, interest in market-related fields has grown (table 4-6). Enrollments have increased by about 67 to 90 percent in vocational and technical schools respectively. In training institutions a reorientation has occurred in terms of the breadth of study. The government decided to reduce the number of recognized occupations from 1,200 to 287. Training institutions now offer a broader range of training, from 10 to 15 occupations compared with 3 to 5 in the past. However, as mentioned earlier, there has been no scientific cost-benefit analysis of the effectiveness of these institutions.

## Obstacles to Further Innovation and Reform

The main issue facing policymakers is how to make the system more responsive to changes in the labor market. This requires close and frequent

TABLE 4-6
Changes in Enrollment in Postsecondary Technical Education, 1994–95

| Specialization | Percentage change |
| --- | --- |
| Instrument making | −36 |
| Power machining | −35 |
| Aviation technology | −27 |
| Geology | −23 |
| Shipbuilding | −19 |
| Law | +10 |
| Ecology | +24 |
| Economics | +45 |

Source: Ministry of Education (1995).

links with employers as well as better feedback mechanisms at the local level. Given limited government funding, the policy of providing everyone who enters the labor market with some pre-employment training needs to be reviewed, and other funding sources need to be tapped.

LABOR MARKET CONSTRAINTS. Given the state of the labor market, it is likely that a shrinkage of the education system will lead to growing unemployment among those who would otherwise be in schools. Vocational schools are viewed as a way to keep youth off the street while employment growth picks up. Enterprises face financial crises and mass layoffs. Under these circumstances it is understandable that training of apprentices has low priority. Legislation has been considered to change the tax incentives for training. This draft legislation calls for enterprises to get tax concessions for up to 2 percent of payroll spent on training their own workers; if the firms do not spend the 2 percent on training, the funds would be transferred to approved training institutions. This legislation seems to be misdirected: Russian enterprises already have one of the heaviest tax burdens, variously reported as 80 to 95 percent. The legislation would, in effect, add a mandatory 2 percent payroll tax on top of that burden.

FINANCIAL CONSTRAINTS. The system of technical and vocational education and training has huge accumulated shortfalls of investments from years of neglect of premises and equipment and teacher training and pay. New investments are essential, but the federal, regional, and local governments are limited in their capacity to finance them. The current basis for deter-

mining federal budget allocations to training schools is based on enrollments, size, and past budgets. This makes it difficult to shift resources out
of areas of declining enrollment (for instance, industrial occupations) and
into new areas of high demand (for example, business and finance). New
alternatives must be found to finance the needed improvements. However,
efforts to share the costs of vocational training with the beneficiaries, particularly the trainees themselves, are limited by legislation: initial vocational training is, by law, free to the participants. Furthermore, vocational
schools must transfer to the federal government 90 percent of all income
generated from the leasing and use of school facilities. This applies to commercial leasing of premises and the use of workshops by small businesses
for purposes of production. This gives little incentive to use a potentially
powerful source of additional resources.

INSTITUTIONAL CONSTRAINTS. Russia has not yet begun to address the
fundamental question of how to reform the VET system. Most educational institutions cling to the old ways, and change will require strong
commitment at the central administrative level. Private training provision
has been slow to take root, in part because of the attitude of accrediting
authorities toward private schools, which are viewed as a threat to the public system. The moratorium on privatization of public training institutions
has also prevented legitimate devolution of training responsibilities from
the state to private hands.

## References

Citrin, D. A., and A. K. Lahiri, eds. 1995. "Policy Experiences and Issues in the
    Baltics, Russia, and Other Countries of the Former Soviet Union." Occasional
    Paper 133. International Monetary Fund, Washington, D.C.
Commander, S., and R. Yemtsov. 1995. "Russian Unemployment: Its Magnitude,
    Characteristics, and Regional Dimensions." Policy Research Working Paper
    1426. Economic Development Institute, World Bank, Moscow.
de Moura Castro, C. 1994. "Tradition and Disruption in Russian Vocational Train-
    ing." World Bank, Washington, D.C.
de Moura Castro, C., M. Feonova, and A. Litman. 1994. "Education and Produc-
    tion in Russia: What Are the Lessons?" World Bank, Washington, D.C.
Gavrilenko, E., and V. Koen. 1994. "How Large Was the Output Collapse in Rus-
    sia? Alternative Estimates and Welfare Implications." Working Paper 154. In-
    ternational Monetary Fund, Washington, D.C.
Humphries, M., and J. Dimond. 1996. "Training for Employment: Reforming
    the Russian Approach." Report for the Know-How Fund. Unpublished paper.

Ministry of Education. 1995. Decree No. 44. Moscow, January.

Section Report. 1994. "Current Status and Ways for Transforming Primary and Secondary Vocational Education." Paper presented at the seminar on Education in Russia: Current Status and Ways for Revival, December 18, Moscow.

SCHE (State Committee of Higher Education). 1996. "Secondary Vocational Education."

Standing, Guy, and Daniel Vaughan, eds. 1995. *Minimum Wages in Central and Eastern Europe: From Protection to Destitution.* Central European University Press.

World Bank. 1995. *Country Assistance Strategy.* Washington, D.C.

# 5  Kazakhstan

Alan Abrahart

For most people in Kazakhstan, the transition from a command to a market economy has been traumatic. Life-long security of employment and an interwoven social safety net provided through state-owned enterprises (SOEs) have been replaced by uncertainty. For all people, young and old, the problems are now more or less the same—poverty of immediate opportunity and a paucity of signposts to the future.

In the face of this dramatic change, the government of Kazakhstan has chosen to do little to the system of vocational education and training (VET). This neglect, far from being damaging, can actually be described as benign. Given the circumstances prevailing in the country, far greater dangers could have been realized through precipitate action as has occurred in other countries in transition where major investments in capital and in staff development are proving difficult to sustain and difficult to keep well-directed; insufficient attention is being paid to the policy framework; investments in VET are preceding, rather than following, investments in industry; scarce sources of finance, such as employer levies, are being imposed before it is clear how, or even if, those funds can be put to good use; and policies and investments are enabling existing VET systems to resist rather than to facilitate change.

## An Economy in Transition

Prior to independence in 1992, the economy had been dominated by state ownership, and it still is to a large extent. Agriculture was made up of state owned and collective farms, there was a substantial government defense industry, and the rest of the economy was based on either direct public sector management or SOEs, the latter mainly operated through industry ministries. Each area is now in a critical state and investment remains low. One index of investment declined from 100 to 18 between 1990 and 1995, and it is not expected to recover to the levels of 1990 until 2000. Despite all this, the long-term prospects for economic growth remain good, largely because of the country's extensive natural resources; indeed, this is the only area of significant current foreign investment in Kazakhstan.

The government, correctly, has concentrated on solving general economic problems before considering more detailed issues such as policies on VET. Throughout 1993 and 1994 the government confronted accelerating inflation, reaching 35 percent a month during the second quarter of 1994. The accumulated losses and arrears within enterprises reached a level comparable to total outstanding bank credit to enterprises in early 1994. Losses of nonfinancial enterprises exceeded 20 percent of gross domestic product in 1993 and were similarly large in 1994.

## A Labor Market in Transition

Labor market indicators were all in decline from 1991 to 1994. As table 5-1 shows, after some early increases, both the population and the labor force fell. As I will show, incomes declined most of all. General secondary education and skill levels were also lower, driven partly by shifts in the makeup of the population and the labor force, and partly by declining retention rates in education; and the skills in the labor force were not relevant to the needs of the economy.

Dependence on administrative data collected through SOEs makes it difficult to determine a true employment picture. Employment has certainly declined though not to the extent indicated by the official statistics shown in table 5-1, which fully reflect the decline in state employment but underestimate offsetting increases in the private sector. A study undertaken by the World Bank in 1996 (table 5-2) estimated that over a third of all employment was in the private sector, even though many SOEs were hoarding labor. Although gradual and continual separation from the labor force is taking place, considerable labor shakeout is still to occur.

Apart from the glaring conclusion that labor demand is low, it is difficult to analyze detailed labor supply and demand with any precision. The only data available either come from administrative sources such as the

TABLE 5-1
Labor Market Indicators, 1991–94

| Indicator | 1991 | 1992 | 1993 | 1994 |
|---|---|---|---|---|
| Population (thousands) | 16,721 | 16,892 | 16,913 | 6,679 |
| Rural (percent) | 42.4 | 42.5 | 42.9 | 44.0 |
| Working-age population (thousands) | 9,226 | 9,325 | 9,333 | 9,220 |
| Total employed (thousands) | 7,494 | 7,356 | 6,926 | 6,579 |
| In state sector (percent) | 75.9 | 71.1 | 64.8 | n.a. |
| In rural sector (percent) | 23.4 | 24.4 | 25.4 | 21.6 |

n.a. Not applicable.
*Source*: World Bank (1996).

employment service or are based on the records of nonrepresentative enterprise establishments. Open (that is, registered) unemployment was still low, just over 2 percent of the labor force in 1995, while hidden unemployment was variously estimated by officials as anything from 10 to 20 percent and probably much closer to the latter. Underemployment is widespread, and growth in the informal sector has been rapid.

As table 5-3 shows, the overall employment decline referred to earlier was made up of large falls in a wide range of industry groups offset by generally smaller increases overall in trade and finance. Of these, the largest single increase—53.7 percent—was in trade. It is unlikely that even the relatively large increase in trade represents a major skill imbalance since trade has become the occupation of last resort for many unemployed or underemployed. When SOEs are considered by themselves, the picture is

TABLE 5-2
State and Private Sector Employment, by Gender, 1994
(percent)

| Sector | Males | Females | Total population |
|---|---|---|---|
| State sector | 70.7 | 59.7 | 64.9 |
| Private sector | 29.3 | 40.3 | 35.1 |
| Employees | 17.3 | 25.7 | 21.8 |
| Self-employed, unpaid, etc. | 12.0 | 14.6 | 13.3 |

*Source:* World Bank (1996).

TABLE 5-3
Employment, Selected Industries, 1991 and 1994
(thousands)

| Industry | 1991 | 1994 | Percentage change |
|---|---|---|---|
| Trade | 551 | 847 | 53.7 |
| Finance | 42 | 49 | 16.7 |
| Health care | 465 | 429 | −7.7 |
| Transport and roads | 508 | 551 | −8.5 |
| Agriculture and forestry | 1,754 | 1,419 | −19.1 |
| Education | 1,036 | 827 | −20.2 |
| Manufacturing | 1,533 | 1,201 | −21.7 |
| Construction | 771 | 482 | −37.5 |

*Source:* World Bank (1996).

one of declines in all industries. Growth in labor demand is associated solely with the private sector economy.

Wage levels have deteriorated. In 1992 the country was broadly classified as a middle-income country with a per capita gross national product estimated at US$1,690. Incomes, however, fell along with production, and between March 1992 and March 1994 real average wages more than halved, further increasing the relative importance of the nonwage benefits provided through SOEs. This encouraged employees to remain attached to enterprises even though there was little work available, and wages were often paid weeks or months in arrears.

The legislated minimum wage—which can discourage employers from hiring untrained workers and giving them on-the-job training—has been allowed to fall substantially below the going rate for low wages. During the last quarter of 1995, the minimum wage was US$4 a month compared with average wages of about US$55. Even these figures can be misleading; many people were not actually receiving cash wages or, when they did so, received them up to months in arrears. In essence, there was no effective legislated minimum wage.

Relative wages are also of limited value in assessing skill shortages. During 1993 to 1995, nominal wages increased more in manufacturing and construction (about 16 percent), the industries of greatest employment decline, than in trade or finance (about 13 percent), the only industries with employment growth.

TABLE 5-4
Enrollment, by Type of School, 1991–94
(thousands)

| Population | 1991 | 1992 | Percentage change in year | 1993 | Percentage change in year | 1994 | Percentage change in year | Total percentage change over 4 years |
|---|---|---|---|---|---|---|---|---|
| Under working age | 5,559 | 5,568 | 0.2 | 5,498 | −1.3 | 5,436 | −1.1 | −2.2 |
| In preschool | 1,023 | 868 | −15.2 | 747 | −13.9 | 538 | −28.0 | −47.4 |
| In primary school | 1,192 | 1,209 | 1.4 | 1,227 | 1.5 | 1,220 | −0.6 | 2.3 |
| In secondary school | 1,846 | 1,811 | −1.9 | 1,782 | −1.6 | 1,750 | −1.8 | −5.2 |

*Source:* Asian Development Bank (1995).

Finally, the skill base of the labor force is changing. Some of this can be traced to population shifts: immigration (1,269,000 people in 1990 and 1991) has favored unskilled rural workers, while emigration (1,449,000 people in 1990 and 1991) has taken its toll of the most educated, skilled and, perhaps, employable in the country. But much of the change can be attributed to yet another feature of the transition to a market economy, its impact on the education and training system.

## Education and Training in Transition

Kazakhstan had a well-developed basic education system. In 1990 only 3 percent of the population was considered illiterate, and completions through compulsory schooling were universal. This has changed drastically as schools have found themselves with severely restrained budgets and as the impact of the depressed economy has been felt on family incomes.

The education system began with an extensive system of kindergartens, most of them attached to SOEs, and it is here that the most dramatic declines have taken place (table 5-4). Problems are also emerging in the other levels of schooling. Schooling is compulsory until Grade 11 (to about age 16). However, fewer students are proceeding beyond Grade 9, probably because of the increasing financial difficulties faced by families. In 1995, 13 percent of students who had just completed Grade 9 did not continue their education, and only half of those found work. The effect is more notable for males. The data show that while there were roughly equal numbers of male and female students in Grade 9 (say 13 or 14 years of age), for subsequent grades the proportion of females rose to almost 58 percent, suggesting that fewer than three out of every four males are proceeding to the final two years of compulsory education.

The decline in higher secondary education is being carried through to postsecondary levels where admissions to higher education have fallen by 9 percent since 1990. But in VET the decline has been even greater—25 percent since 1990—and the unused capacity of vocational/technical schools was estimated to be 30 percent in 1995.

## The Vocational Education and Training System

The government has historically considered the VET system to have two purposes: to provide skilled workers required in the command economy and to provide education and training to vulnerable groups in society including those with low academic achievements. The system began breaking down in the early 1990s, and its replacement with something effective has barely begun. In 1995 the government consolidated all institutions under the Ministry of Education's Committee for Vocational and Technical Education, including all those run by line ministries. It then transferred the committee to the Ministry of Labor, before transferring it back again a few months later. The government then abolished the Committee for Vocational and Technical Education. By the end of 1996, it had not replaced the committee with another body.

## Vocational Schooling during the Compulsory Years

Vocational schooling during the compulsory years is provided through the vocational/technical schools (VTSs) and is designed to provide training for students expecting to become skilled workers. Even though the schools form part of the compulsory education system, only 342 of the 471 schools that existed in 1990 were actually administered by the Ministry of Education (through the Committee for Vocational and Technical Education). The remainder were run by industry ministries operating through SOEs. More than one in ten VTSs had closed by 1995 (table 5-5).

The schools offer courses to students who have completed Grade 9 secondary school. The students are required to complete a full-time three-year program; 40 percent of the courses are general education courses. Graduates obtain a diploma of general education (equivalent to Grade 11 school-

TABLE 5-5
Vocational/Technical Schools, 1990–95
(number)

| Year | Schools | Students | Admissions | Graduates |
|------|---------|----------|------------|-----------|
| 1990–91 | 471 | 212,654 | 144,489 | 134,819 |
| 1991–92 | 446 | 203,092 | 152,515 | 142,625 |
| 1992–93 | 439 | 188,740 | 123,739 | 114,773 |
| 1993–94 | 415 | 159,600 | 105,112 | 97,386 |
| 1994–95 | 422 | 160,008 | 79,067 | 76,566 |
| Four-year per- centage decline | 10.4 | 24.8 | 45.3 | 43.2 |

*Source:* Asian Development Bank (1995).

ing) and a specialist vocational diploma. The program includes six months of industrial experience, although the system cannot really be considered an apprenticeship or a dual system. Students are paid for the work experience, but there is no employment relationship covering the whole period of training.

## Postcompulsory Vocational Education

The major providers of postcompulsory secondary vocational education are secondary special schools. Like VTSs, they have suffered a decline in student numbers; unlike VTSs, none of them, all administered by the Ministry of Education, has closed. Secondary special schools in 1994–95 had an average of 850 students each, compared with 400 per school in VTSs (table 5-6).

Secondary special schools provide training for those expecting to become subprofessional or middle-level workers. They are intended mainly for students who have completed compulsory education. Courses are usually three years or slightly less. Students who enter with only a Grade 9 diploma are required to study an extra year. The schools also offer training under contract to the employment service for retraining unemployed people, and they are increasingly offering ad hoc courses-on-demand to meet market needs.

VTSs also may offer postcompulsory school courses. They may offer two-year full-time courses in specialist vocational curricula to students who

TABLE 5-6
Secondary Special Schools, 1990–95
(number)

| Year | Schools | Students | Admissions | Graduates | Teachers |
|---|---|---|---|---|---|
| 1990–91 | 247 | 247,600 | 83,389 | 69,849 | 14,528 |
| 1991–92 | 244 | 238,300 | 80,897 | 69,331 | 14,351 |
| 1992–93 | 248 | 230,800 | 75,269 | 61,827 | 13,921 |
| 1993–94 | 247 | 222,100 | 72,350 | 59,875 | 18,650 |
| 1994–95 | 247 | 214,300 | 69,993 | 62,948 | 13,567 |
| Four-year per- centage decline | 0.0 | 13.4 | 16.0 | 9.9 | — |

— Not available.
Source: Asian Development Bank (1995).

have completed compulsory education to year 11. They may also offer courses-on-demand to all-comers. This may be on a course fee basis, part-time, or by correspondence. A number of standard programs and special retraining programs are offered under contract to the employment service. Almost three-quarters of the students participating in all of these courses-on-demand have only a Grade-9-entry-level education. About 75 percent of the places in courses-on-demand are funded by the employment service.

## Enterprise Training

Despite the collapsing economy and the falling number of students, the system has been remarkably slow in moving away from the concept of training for a command economy. VTSs, closer to the front line of the market economy than secondary special schools, have reacted more quickly to the new circumstances, but even they are proving relatively hidebound. They have, for example, traditionally entered into training agreements with enterprises to supply courses. Financing came out of the VTSs' annual budgets, and it is estimated that 80 percent of training in VTSs was for enterprise agreements. Under the agreements, VTSs trained students to meet the needs of enterprises, while the latter provided an on-the-job training component. Graduates trained under enterprise agreements were guaranteed employment.

Enterprise agreements were the core of the supply-driven model of VET that characterizes command economies. However, the guarantees that backed them have now fallen away. Yet VTSs still operate under preexisting enterprise agreements, including, it is said, with enterprises that no longer exist. Furthermore, VTSs still operate as if students were being "directed" to work in specific industrial groupings, notably in manufacturing and agriculture. Over 60 percent of graduates are employed in these sectors—where employment declines have been greatest and, in the case of agriculture, where relative wage rates have fallen the farthest. Students are still being trained under the system and then being sent to the relevant enterprises covered by the enterprise agreement.

During the command economy, there were over 1,000 specialist vocations (Asian Development Bank 1995). By the end of 1995, they had been rationalized to about 400 vocations although the system had not been fully implemented. The operational list used by VTSs has 42 industry categories and 257 specialist vocations within them (many in more than one industry). Nevertheless, many of the vocations are still regarded by VTSs as irrelevant to the new economy.

The role of employee and employer associations in VET merits interest in this respect. Trade unions still exist in Kazakhstan but mainly as remnants of the previous system when they were part of the establishment. There are embryonic associations of employers, but for the most part individualistic entrepreneurship prevails. The most important joint ventures are in the resources sector, though some major companies have purchased former SOEs. (For example, Philip Morris has purchased a tobacco factory in Almaty, and Nabisco has purchased a biscuit factory in Shymkent.) The immediate concern of joint ventures is with enterprise restructuring, probably involving significant labor displacement. Joint ventures are likely to handle their skilled labor needs either through the use of expatriate labor or internal training. Neither employers nor trade unions can yet be said to be actively engaged in VET, in particular in retraining arising from industry restructuring.

## Current Sources of Funding

Finance for VET has been restricted. In 1995 government funding met an estimated 35 percent of the running costs of vocational/technical schools (Asian Development Bank 1995). Schools are not meeting their bills for many services, particularly utilities. Budgets, traditionally determined on the basis of norms, particularly related to student and teacher numbers, have become restricted. Student numbers have declined, although staff numbers remain higher than the budgets can support, another case of labor hoarding. Staff are unpaid or paid substantially in arrears. Despite the decline of almost 14 percent in student numbers in secondary special schools from 1991 to 1995, the teaching staff declined by less than half this proportion over the same period (from about 14,500 to 13,500). The student to teaching staff ratio was around 16:1 in 1995. VTSs are allowed to supplement their budgets through their own production centers, but this amounts to less than 10 percent of resources. A few rural VTSs with sufficient land holdings are said to be self-supporting.

A significant source of nonbudget financing for VET now comes from the Employment Promotion Fund administered by the Ministry of Labor. The primary purpose of the fund is to finance the operations of the employment service, the payment of unemployment benefits, and to run employment and training programs for the unemployed. Almost its entire revenue comes from a payroll tax of 2 percent levied only on industrial enterprises. In 1995 the fund had limited reserves, having been administered directly by the Department of Finance in the previous couple of years when it was used as a general revenue source. Under advice from the World Bank, the Employment Promotion Fund was returned to the Ministry of Labor in April 1995, although it went back empty.

The employment fund is now seen by the VET system as a means of bolstering its meager funds. But a model of the fund has shown the fund to be relatively unstable. Even small deviations between expected revenues and expected expenditures of the fund will cause substantial changes in the balance over a short period. Although the government can control expenditures, by tightening eligibility requirements for unemployment benefits, it has chosen not to do this for political reasons.

Revenue is no easier to control. Employment is falling, putting revenue on a declining path at the same time as expenditures rise. Avoidance of the payroll tax is high, even among established employers, let alone in the informal economy that, by definition, is not paying. For those SOEs that continue to employ people but are effectively bankrupt, payment of the levy makes little sense since it contributes to enterprise arrears in the country. Policies are now in place to extend the coverage of the levy to all employers (including the government sector) and to introduce an employee contribution, but the government has been reluctant on both counts.

Therefore, the fund cannot be seen as a substitute for budget restrictions. The notion that an alternative training fund can be established is also quite out of the question. The only short-term option for financing the public sector VET system is through increased cost recovery: fees and charges to employers for services. This, of course, raises the question of public versus private provision. Like everything else, VET has, until now, been state business. But with the system still largely unequipped physically or organizationally to handle new demands, a need has grown up for private providers. As yet, the private training sector is poorly developed. The training centers run by SOEs may have offered one major source of private enterprise training, but most of the centers have either discontinued operations or scaled back activities, and it is difficult to imagine them being resurrected. Small entrepreneurs have begun entering the training market, many of them offering short courses, especially in the services sector. The quality of the training may as yet be dubious, but the field can only grow.

## Important VET Issues

Given the plethora of problems facing the economy, the government appears to have concluded that little can be done in the VET sector and that developing vocational education and training policies is a low priority. The government has not been wrong in this. However, the VET system will continue to develop, and mistakes now will be difficult to correct later. The priority should be to invest in change—to get the policies correct, to get the quality of VET properly set. It is arguable that an initiative to stamp a policy agenda for VET is urgently required.

Such a policy would have three essential objectives:

• *To establish a system of VET that is market driven and responsive to employers' needs.* The existing system is still largely dominated by the philosophies and practices of the earlier system. It is not responsive to the needs of the labor market, still preferring to predict industry needs and to train accordingly. The role of employers has diminished to a dangerously low level. Their previous role, exemplified by industry ministries' training agreements with VTSs, is clearly no longer viable, but nothing has taken its place.

• *To increase vocational training throughout the country by encouraging nongovernment training providers.* The system is still built around the domination of the public sector. This has merit for entry-level training, but it is counterproductive for postemployment training such as that required for industry restructuring or for retraining retrenched and unemployed workers.

• *To establish a wider base of funding by recovering from users some of the costs of VET.* Public sector financing of VET has virtually collapsed. Again, this largely resulted from the continued maintenance of an extensive supply-driven public sector training system that simply outgrew its usefulness.

For each of these objectives, two types of VET must be considered: entry-level (that is, pre-employment) training and postemployment training. The urgency of reforms, the nature of reforms, and the management and financing of reforms are totally different in the two types of training.

## Establishing a Demand-Driven System

The single most difficult thing for a VET system to achieve is to convert from being supply driven (essential in a command economy) to being demand driven (essential in a market economy). The change, in its essence, sums up all that is required for a country undergoing a transition in its economy. In general, three developments are required:

• Establishing a mechanism to involve employers and employees in the management of VET. This would cover both entry-level and postemployment training and ensure a connection between the education and training providers and the labor market.

- Decentralizing administrative systems to the regional level to better reflect local economic needs and labor market needs.
- Establishing occupational skill categories and standards suitable for a market economy and then developing the curricula needed for those skills.

ENTRY-LEVEL TRAINING. Young people entering the labor market for the first time need entry-level training. Although other groups cannot be ignored, young people present the greatest political and sociological challenge in Kazakhstan. Given that entry-level training is closely associated with the education system and that the Ministry of Education already manages all existing institutions, there is no doubt that the ministry should remain the primary government agency.

The ministry should be especially concerned with reestablishing a viable entry-level training system, one that is in tune with the changes in industry and meets changing labor demands. The details of how the Ministry of Education should exercise its responsibility can remain open, but the links with the labor market make a form of tripartite management essential. Ideally, employers and employee associations would have an executive role in any future system, but whether this is achievable in the short term is debatable. The role of employers in entry-level training should also be determined. As far as practicable, all vocational training should include elements of on-the-job training.

The government intends that vocational education and training should be administered at the regional level. However, the Ministry of Education proposes to retain substantial central control, particularly in setting standards. While acceptable in principle, this may be unacceptable in practice. The devil is in the detail: the Ministry of Education intends to cover such things as the allocation of teaching time to general subjects and specialist subjects, the designation of specialist vocations, the duration of courses, the classification of VTSs, and the content of general education curricula in VTSs. Much of this detail harks back to the system of norms that once prevailed through all aspects of state business. This degree of centralization may have been appropriate in a command economy, but it is not sustainable in a market economy.

The Ministry of Education's approach suggests that more thought should be given to the development of the school system generally. As many VTSs as possible could be converted to general secondary schools; only those that can be used as postsecondary institutions should be retained. An inventory of other training establishments, covering both government and industry centers, should also be undertaken to determine their effective capacity.

The policies and practices in accredited VET institutions are in need of a thorough overhaul. Accrediting entry-level vocational training involves establishing standards, regulating examinations, and issuing credentials. Occupational skills that are attained below the level of higher education include semiskilled occupations, skilled trades, and some paraprofessional occupations. Obviously, the Ministry of Education must ensure that any occupation within its scope has adequate accreditation procedures. Progress has been made in reclassifying skill groupings, but further developments should proceed on a tripartite basis at the national level. The system needs to be urgently refocused to be responsive to labor market needs, and curricula need to be redeveloped, especially through the importation and adaptation of training materials and procedures used in other countries.

Given financial constraints, the Ministry of Education must determine its priorities carefully. It will be unable to develop all the new curricula it may think appropriate. It should look closely at labor market needs and labor supply and demand. The temptation to seek, for its own sake, an expansion of the system is present in any country, but it is especially dangerous in places like Kazakhstan, where the resources to maintain the system well into the future are severely limited. Donors, for example, may offer expansions or improvements through capital investments, but these will invariably be isolated contributions, and the investments will collapse the moment the government has to fall back on government budgets for maintenance.

POSTEMPLOYMENT TRAINING. The concerns of postemployment training are with industry restructuring and the retraining of retrenched workers, the unemployed, and adults in general. Compared with entry-level training, it has a more short-term focus. Interested in immediate labor market needs and matching labor supply and demand, it is less concerned with accreditation and credentialing and the formalities associated with them. Postemployment training focuses on individual industry sectors, on various geographic regions of the country, or on particular types of vulnerable groups in society.

Postemployment training should be governed separately from entry-level training because of its far wider range of activities and far more ad hoc nature. Primary responsibility for developing policies for postemployment training should rest with the Ministry of Labor, operating through the employment service. Employment service responsibilities could be managed through a tripartite mechanism similar to the one used for entry-level training. Indeed, at the executive level, there is no reason why these mechanisms could not be one and the same. The responsibilities could encompass retraining for the unemployed, retraining for other adults, and support for training within enterprises seeking to restructure their work forces.

The employment service could become a major buyer or financier of postemployment training and refrain from being a supplier of training. As a buyer, it could take full account of labor market circumstances. It could determine the characteristics of labor supply and demand and focus its attention on meeting local labor market needs. Indeed, it could act as if it were in a market, seeking to purchase the courses it required at the best price. For example, it might require potential training providers to bid for specified courses. It would act at all skill levels and in all regions, covering areas of small as well as significant demand. It would act only where the market was apparently failing to deliver what employers wanted.

## Encouraging Nonpublic Training Providers

A great deal of unaccredited training takes place, in both entry-level and postemployment training, typically in the service industries and in high-profile occupations such as those associated with computerization. Nothing can, and nothing should, stop this from happening. In Kazakhstan, where so much is uncertain, unaccredited training should be actively encouraged or, at the very least, not inhibited, even though this may run counter to the traditional inclinations of the Ministry of Education and the Ministry of Labor. Some of this training may be through private training providers, and some may be through on-the-job training with employers. Three main developments are required to encourage nonpublic training providers to enter the training market. The first is by far the most important.

- Legislation should ensure open competition for public and nonpublic training providers.
- Government agencies, such as the employment service, that have an interest in buying courses should involve nonpublic training providers through the use of fee-for-service courses financed by the employment fund.

- Government systems should foster community or cooperative training providers, especially at the postemployment level in areas of high unemployment.

## Reviewing the Need for Legislation

All aspects of life under the former system were regulated. With the transition to a market economy, there is a need to review parliamentary laws as well as ad hoc government, ministerial, or departmental decrees, all of which can have the force of law and can impede change.

Some legislation should be rescinded (for example, legislation that inhibits labor mobility and legislation that restricts some occupations to certain SOEs, giving them a monopoly on providing those skills to the wider community). Licenses to operate in certain occupations may specify a particular credential as a prerequisite, effectively blocking private training from providing skilled operatives in the field. Legislation in Kazakhstan also restricts the Ministry of Education from offering any price for its services other than that derived from outdated norms. Those same norms prohibit anyone else from using the ministry's facilities. This makes it impossible for Ministry of Education trainers to offer courses on a private basis when school is out. The same legislation requires the Ministry of Labor to accept no bids that are lower than the Ministry of Education's, effectively stifling competition.

All current procedures used to accredit courses and training providers should be reviewed. There should be provision for accrediting enterprise training providers. Then enterprises could provide off-the-job training without having to rely on government training institutions. All current standards should be reviewed. Particular attention should be paid to the length of courses and to course prerequisites. As far as practicable, course length should be reduced and prerequisites minimized. Course content also should be reassessed. Testing procedures need to be reviewed as well. Testing should be handled at local institutions, within individual enterprises, or through employer associations, if they exist. Practices that serve primarily to justify large-scale public sector involvement and deny the effective intervention of other providers should be eliminated.

In postemployment training the case for encouraging nonpublic providers is overwhelming. The ad hoc nature of the training, the lesser concern with credentials, and the short-term nature of the responses required all favor nonpublic providers. This is not to say that public sector institutions could not be involved as suppliers. The Ministry of Education is, of course, interested in increasing the role of VTSs in retraining the unemployed. However, given that their main role is to provide entry-level training for young people, meeting ad hoc training needs should be done only on a strictly competitive basis. Anything else would be a diversion from the Ministry of Education's main function.

The government should take advantage of existing training capacities in enterprises and of community groups and associations when marshaling resources to deliver training. The employment service could assist individual enterprises or groups of enterprises that have specific plans to restructure their work forces. Assistance could take the form of financial aid (either direct grants or credits toward their obligations to the employment fund levy). Or the employment service could offer course information, materials, and so on. In providing courses, the employment service could make use of enterprise facilities.

## *Financing Vocational Education and Training*

The VET system, like many government programs in Kazakhstan, is in extreme financial straits. Arguing that it should receive greater support from the annual government budget is not especially useful. That could be achieved only at the expense of other priorities, even such things as making old age pension payments on schedule.

Recommending other financial support systems also is not useful. Employers now, and employees in the near future will, make contributions to pensions and health schemes; and they will make contributions to the employment fund. However, the use the government has made of the employment fund as a general revenue source has been quite deliberate and demonstrates its priorities quite clearly.

Financing the VET system depends on increasing its revenues and decreasing its costs. The latter, in particular, can be supported by the development of a nonpublic sector training market, relieving the public sector budget of a burden it is having trouble carrying and which to a certain extent it does not have to meet. Rationalization of the public sector system will also have an effect on the provision of vocational education and training.

As far as raising revenue is concerned, VET has to increasingly fend for itself. Four avenues are open to the system:

- Establish fee scales to enable government institutes to charge individuals.

- Allow institutes to take private students paying full fees irrespective of the level of training offered.
- Allow the employment service to bid for courses for unemployed or retrenched workers.
- Allow institutes to provide courses on demand.

Yet another avenue has been promoted by others, including the Asian Development Bank (1995) in its study of the education sector. This is to allow institutes to undertake productive activities. They already do this to some extent, since all institutes under the former system were in the production command-chain even if only in some small way. However, increasing productive activities can have a self-defeating element to it, especially in a system that is failing to rationalize and that is hoarding labor much like any SOE. In these circumstances, productive activities could easily become the means by which staff maintain their income. The extent and the quality of training would be incidental.

Entry-level training is the only area of VET that can lay claim to dependency on the government budget. Even so, the Ministry of Education needs to present a new strategy for developing adequate industry and occupational coverage as a basis for determining its budget requirements, and it should demonstrate the labor market relevance of its spending priorities. Because of the likely inadequacy of the budget, finances would still need to be supplemented by fees for services: fees from students who can afford and are willing to pay, and fees for services provided direct to industry. Both have the distinct advantage of forcing the public sector to respond to demand. Courses for the unemployed would be funded from the employment fund but only to the extent of its capacity to do so. Other adults would be able to participate on a user-pays basis. Ministry of Education schools would be allowed to bid, without preference, to run courses.

## Lessons from Kazakhstan

Despite the problems it has faced, the government of Kazakhstan has generally been correct in its decision not to accord VET a high priority. Three major lessons can be drawn from this.

- *Economic realities come first.* Economic development has been slow and uncertain, giving rise to an extremely poor labor market and slowing any investments in VET by employers. Exceptions to this have been few (mining and banking), although even in these sectors the impact on the local labor market has been limited. The government's priorities, quite rightly, have been to reverse this situation by developing a more acceptable macroeconomic framework *within* which growth can take place and *without* which any VET system would operate in a vacuum.

- *Institutional realities have to be faced head-on.* With the government's attention elsewhere, progress in developing VET policies has been slow. Relevant agencies within the government, seemingly caught up in the past and trapped into inactivity by the trauma of their current circumstances, have been unable to define their role or set policies. The priorities of agency employees have been to maintain their own incomes and jobs. They still see the future much as they saw the past—themselves running a supply-driven system dominated by the public sector.

- *Financial realities cannot be ignored.* There are no magic solutions to financing VET in Kazakhstan. There is no replacement for the paymasters who dominated the former Soviet Union. Employers cannot finance everything that was once a state responsibility, simply because they were once indistinguishable from the state. A price has to be placed on the value of VET. To that extent, cost recovery has to be a large part of the answer to financing VET, even in the public sector. No longer is it tenable to assume that growth of the public sector is the objective. Rather, the objective is to achieve an efficient system of VET, where cost-effectiveness demands that the public sector limit its growth.

Benign or not, the neglect of VET should not lead to the long-term desertion of a major policy field by government. Donors are becoming anxious to invest in VET. However, financial assistance should not focus on upgrading the public sector system nor encourage the use of VET institutes in productive activities as a way of financing their activities. The latter would place a major value on merchandise (in a country already littered with moribund factories) rather than on the institutes' primary outputs, educated and trained graduates. Financial assistance, or even technical assistance, of this type is more likely than not to fit the model that has been found wanting elsewhere.

Kazakhstan has reached the point when a more positive approach is required, even if that approach, for the moment, is to continue to do nothing but get the policy framework in place. In the end, benign neglect must be a conscious action: even decisions not to proceed should be taken deliberately.

# References

Asian Development Bank. 1995. "Education and Training Sector Study." Manila, Philippines.

World Bank. 1996. "The Republic of Kazakhstan: The Transition of the State." Washington, D.C.

# High-Growth Economies

PART II ANALYZES the pressures caused by periods of high economic growth on vocational education and training in China, Indonesia, Malaysia, the Republic of Korea, Chile, and Mexico. Many of these countries have experienced a sharp slowdown and even contraction since the mid-1990s. The Republic of Korea, accustomed to unemployment rates in the neighborhood of 2 to 3 percent, saw its GDP shrink by more than 5 percent in 1998, and unemployment rates rose to unprecedentedly high levels. Malaysia is in the middle of a controversial struggle to limit the crippling effects of the Asian crisis on its employment and output, which declined by 7 percent in 1998. Indonesia's woes have been the worst of the six countries discussed in this section. Political uncertainty compounds the problems arising from weaknesses in financial and industrial policies. In China efforts to restructure the economy, through the time and resources afforded by annual growth rates that topped 10 percent, are in jeopardy. The contagion effects of the Asian and Russian crises threaten to overwhelm Mexico, Chile, and other Latin American countries.

These setbacks, which now occupy the attention of policymakers, naturally are affecting adversely the vocational education and training systems in Asia and Latin America. Their funding will decline, and more will be asked of them as unemployment and school dropout rates increase. It is important to remember, however, that the roots of the crises are financial, and many of the afflicted countries' innovations in vocational education and training are still worthy of attention. Moreover, there are signs that, with financial restructuring, growth will resume. Because the horizons explored in this book are broader than the immediate past and near future, its messages remain relevant.

The study on China provides a bridge between the transition economies discussed in Part I and the East Asian and Latin American economies that have grown impressively over the past decade. China is facing the dual challenge of meeting the demand for skilled workers in high-growth coastal areas while downsizing its bloated public enterprises. Korea's experience shows the benefits of an evaluative approach to VET policy. The country has been able to pursue different strategies to encourage investment in enterprise-based training by firms. Malaysia has had success through a well-run levy-grant scheme that has constantly been refined; its experience shows that firms value the products of private training providers and joint public-private institutions much more than the products of public vocational schools. The Indonesia study illustrates another important lesson: by not discouraging private provision of training, poor countries can ensure that a fast-growing economy's demands for skilled workers can be met even when the public VET sector is not operating efficiently.

In Chile the roots of a comprehensive reform of the VET system can be traced to economywide rethinking since the early 1980s. The study highlights the importance of transparent and balanced funding mechanisms and regulations in encouraging vocational education and training at the secondary and postsecondary levels. Finally, the study on Mexico—a country that has experienced both high growth and severe recessions—serves as a bridge to Part III. In that section we examine countries where high labor-force growth, low employment growth, and high unemployment and underemployment rates, especially in the informal sector, are the main challenges facing reform of vocational education and training.

# 6 China

## PETER R. FALLON AND GORDON HUNTING

CHINA HAS SUCCESSFULLY followed a strategy of economic reform since 1978. The strategy focused initially on improving incentives in agriculture and allowing the market to play a greater role in rural areas; later it expanded to include liberalizing measures aimed at reforming the urban industrial sectors. Before 1992 the strategy was highly incremental; reforms were gradually tried out in designated local areas before being extended to the national economy, and they did not signal a clear commitment to a market system. In 1992, however, the authorities announced their intention to accelerate the reform process and open up the economy. Since then reforms signaling a much stronger commitment to the market have been implemented. They liberalize enterprise ownership and governance, allow the central bank to operate an independent monetary policy, develop the financial system, reform foreign exchange allocation, and rationalize the tax system.

Between 1984 and 1993 gross domestic product (GDP) growth was phenomenal, averaging 10.5 percent per year and peaking at 14 percent in 1992. Growth was mainly spurred by the industrial sector, the manufacturing sector, and services, which grew respectively by 13.3, 12.7, and 12.2 percent annually between 1984 and 1993. China's stabilization policies of 1994 and 1995 reduced inflation and nudged GDP growth to more sustainable levels. In 1995 the economy grew at 10.2 percent, while inflation rates that had reached a peak of 25 percent in October 1994 fell to 8.3 percent by December 1995. Since then inflation has fallen even farther.

With close to 1.2 billion people, China is the world's most populous country. It has achieved considerable success in reducing its annual population growth rate from 1.8 percent in the 1970s to around 0.9 percent in 1996. Although China is still a low-income country (per capita GDP about US$600 in 1996), it has made great strides in its social indicators over the past few decades. Between 1970 and 1996, infant mortality rates more than halved, the average life expectancy rose to 69 years, adult illiteracy rates fell to 27 percent, and net enrollment rates at the primary level approached 100 percent. Some of these figures are comparable to those of middle-income countries.

## The Labor Market

Labor market liberalization started relatively late in the reform process. Although progress has been made, labor markets still retain some of their prereform features. Under the centrally planned system, workers were assigned by the state to enterprises that were obliged to give them jobs. Job security was guaranteed for life, and the enterprises paid state-administered wages as well as retirement, medical, and housing benefits. Mobility between employers was largely eliminated in this system, and enterprise management's freedom from market discipline contributed to widespread overstaffing with little or no link at the enterprise level between wages and workers' productivity. The virtual absence of any market mechanism for allocating workers to jobs constrained early industrial reforms. This was an important source of resource misallocation in China as a whole.

There is still much to be done before labor market liberalization is complete. To function properly, labor markets should possess three main features: (a) labor should be able to move freely between jobs; (b) employers should be able to expand and contract their work forces as they choose; and (c) wages should be determined by market forces and not by state regulation or formula. Although considerable progress has been made, China still fails these market tests.

Labor mobility continues to be highly restricted by legislation and a cumbersome system of nonportable fringe benefits. The principal obstacles are legal: a rural resident cannot take a job in an urban area without a work permit, and he or she cannot gain access to state benefits available to urban residents without a residency permit. This policy has insulated the urban population from the much lower living standards of most rural residents, and it has hindered movement from low productivity activities in rural areas to higher productivity activities in cities—a clear example of resource misallocation.

Employment decisions in most urban enterprises are still heavily influenced by the government. Although this is changing, lengthy procedures continue to make it difficult to retrench surplus workers. In rural areas conditions are much better since farms and enterprises have considerable freedom to hire and fire workers.

Wages are largely determined by the state in urban state-owned enterprises (SOEs). Control of the macro wage bill remains an important stabilization instrument, and wage bills are subject to administrative control in the enterprises. There is little evidence that urban wages adjust to the forces of supply and demand. Urban enterprises are obliged to provide a series of services at regulated levels (for example, housing, medical care, education, pensions, and maternity benefits) in addition to wage and bonus payments. In rural areas there are fewer mandatory benefits and greater latitude in wage determination.

## Labor Allocation, Trends, and Imbalances

Out of a total labor supply of 619.5 million in 1994 (table 6-1), 441.5 million worked in rural areas; most of these workers were engaged in agriculture. In urban areas, state-owned enterprises and collectives continue to provide the great majority of jobs, accounting for 91 percent of urban employment in 1994. As statistically measured, unemployment was low by international standards—only 2.9 percent of the urban labor force in 1994—but, as argued below, underemployment is much more severe.

Labor supply and demand growth rates have closely matched each other since 1980, and the unemployment rate has remained reasonably stable at a low level. The composition of labor demand, however, has shifted significantly. In rural areas liberalization of nonagricultural activities led to tremendous growth in off-farm employment in rural enterprises, and the share of such activities at the national level rose from 8.3 percent in 1980 to 24.2 percent by 1994. This was accompanied by a shift in the allocation of labor within agriculture in favor of small-scale farming and away from agricultural collectives. In urban areas a more permissive stance toward growth in the private sector encouraged a shift in the composition of employment away from SOEs and collectives toward privately owned enterprises and self-employment.

These trends hide major imbalances in the Chinese labor market. There is a substantial degree of underemployment in SOEs and collectives in urban areas and a large and growing labor surplus within agriculture. But

TABLE 6-1
Labor Supply and Demand, Selected Years, 1980–94

| Category | Millions of people | | | | Annual growth rates (percent) | | |
|---|---|---|---|---|---|---|---|
| | 1980 | 1985 | 1990 | 1994 | 1980–85 | 1986–90 | 1991–93 |
| Total labor supply | 429.0 | 501.3 | 571.2 | 619.5 | 3.2 | 2.6 | 2.1 |
| Total labor demand | 423.6 | 498.7 | 567.4 | 614.5 | 3.3 | 2.6 | 2.0 |
| Urban labor force | 105.3 | 128.1 | 147.3 | 168.0 | 4.0 | 2.8 | 3.3 |
| State-owned enterprises | 80.2 | 89.9 | 103.5 | 112.0 | 2.3 | 2.8 | 2.0 |
| Collectives | 24.3 | 33.2 | 35.5 | 32.3 | 6.5 | 1.3 | -2.4 |
| Private | n.a. | 0.4 | 1.6 | 10.9 | n.a. | 30.1 | 61.6 |
| Self-employed | 0.8 | 4.5 | 6.7 | 12.3 | 40.9 | 8.3 | 16.4 |
| Rural labor force | 318.4 | 370.7 | 420.1 | 441.5 | 3.1 | 2.5 | 1.5 |
| Agriculture | 283.3 | 303.5 | 333.4 | 297.9 | 1.4 | 1.9 | -2.8 |
| Other | 35.0 | 67.1 | 86.7 | 148.7 | 13.9 | 5.3 | 14.4 |
| Unemployed (urban) | 5.4 | 2.5 | 3.8 | 5.0 | -14.0 | 8.2 | 7.1 |
| Unemployment rate (percent) | 4.9 | 1.9 | 2.5 | 2.9 | n.a. | n.a. | n.a. |

n.a. Not applicable.
Note: Under the statistical methodology used in China, the presumption is that the entire rural labor force is employed. In other words, rural unemployment is assumed to be zero. Data may not sum to totals because of rounding.
Source: Ministry of Labor (1994).

shortages of skilled workers in the cities and in the township and village enterprises also are severe.

Public enterprises in China are grossly overstaffed. The Ministry of Labor estimates that at least 15 percent of the work force of SOEs, or 16.8 million people, could be made redundant with little or no impact on productive capacity. There is also an unknown number of surplus workers in collectives. If the number of surplus workers in SOEs were added to official estimates of urban unemployment, the measured unemployment rate would rise drastically to about 11.5 percent. Despite a doubling of agricultural output between 1980 and 1993, considerable surplus labor in agriculture remains. When applying the labor requirements approach, the Chinese authorities calculate that about 30 percent of agricultural labor is in surplus.

Shortages of skilled workers have emerged following rapid growth in the economy over the past decade. The need to improve international competitiveness and adopt modern technologies in many industries is generating a demand for professionals, technicians, and manually skilled workers that is growing faster than supply.

The government's objective is to move away from a state-administered system of labor allocation toward a market system, while minimizing the inevitable transition costs. Reform and expansion of vocational education and training (VET) are an important part of future labor policy. The government's strategy is to concentrate on five main policy directions. First, encourage rural labor absorption through further development of the township and village enterprises, and continue to limit migration from rural to urban areas. Second, encourage all forms of productive employment growth in the towns. Third, expand and improve urban labor market services. Fourth, progressively allow the market to determine wages and remove barriers to labor mobility within the cities. Fifth, alleviate skill shortages. These policy directions will be implemented by appropriate legislation.

## Vocational Education and Training System

Compared with other developing countries, China has had remarkable success in providing a comprehensive schooling system to its population. Enrollment rates in the first nine years of schooling are higher than in most other low-income countries, with more than 98 percent of the 6-to-11 age cohort enrolled in primary school, and 74 percent of the 12-to-15 age cohort enrolled in junior secondary school (table 6-2). After junior sec-

TABLE 6-2
Schools, Enrollment, and Enrollment Ratios, 1980, 1990, 1994

| | 1980 | | | 1990 | | | 1994 | | |
| --- | --- | --- | --- | --- | --- | --- | --- | --- | --- |
| Level | Number of schools | Total enrollment (thousands) | Enrollment ratio | Number of schools | Total enrollment (thousands) | Enrollment ratio | Number of schools | Total enrollment (thousands) | Enrollment ratio |
| Primary | 917,316 | 146,270 | 93.9 | 766,072 | 122,414 | 97.8 | 682,588 | 128,226 | 98.4 |
| Junior secondary | 87,077 | 45,383 | 61.5 | 71,953 | 39,165 | 66.0 | 68,415 | 43,799 | 74.4 |
| Senior secondary | | | | | | | | | |
| General | 31,300 | 9,698 | 8.9 | 15,678 | 7,173 | 9.9 | 14,242 | 6,649 | 9.5 |
| Specialized[a] | 3,069 | 1,243 | 1.2 | 39,82 | 2,244 | 3.1 | 3,987 | 3,198 | 4.6 |
| Secondary vocational schools | 3,314 | 319 | 0.3 | 9,164 | 2,471 | 3.4 | 10,217 | 3,426 | 4.9 |
| Skilled workers' schools | 3,305 | 700 | 0.6 | 4,148 | 1,332 | 1.8 | 4,430 | 1,871 | 2.7 |
| Higher | 675 | 1,144 | — | 1,075 | 2,063 | — | 1,080 | 2,799 | — |

— Not available.

a. Includes secondary technical schools (STSs) and teacher training schools.

*Source:* State Education Commission (various years); People's Republic of China (1995).

ondary school, students can enroll in senior secondary school. Senior secondary schools can be general or vocational. Since 1980 general senior secondary enrollments have dropped as these schools have been converted into vocational schools.

Most vocational education and training in China is provided through the education system at the senior secondary level. It is also provided by the labor bureaus at the state and municipal levels and by medium to large SOEs. At the senior secondary level there are (in addition to schools providing general education), three types of vocational schools: secondary specialist schools, comprising secondary technical schools (STSs) and teacher training schools; skilled workers' schools (SWSs); and secondary vocational schools (SVSs).

STSs and teacher training schools are run by central technical ministries, state enterprises, or provincial and local education bureaus. They train lower technicians: until the late 1980s all specialist secondary school graduates were guaranteed employment. Under the general control of the Ministry of Labor, SWSs are run by central industrial ministries, local labor bureaus, and enterprises. Students recruited from junior secondary school receive two to three years of skills training. Until the late 1980s the SWS graduates were also guaranteed employment. SVSs were originally established to enroll primary school graduates for skills training in preparation for employment. Discontinued during the cultural revolution, SVSs were reestablished after 1979. They enroll junior secondary graduates in two- or three-year courses and are mainly under the control of local education bureaus. Graduates have never had guaranteed employment.

Since 1980 the volume of vocational and technical education has dramatically increased. Enrollments in specialized secondary schools and SWSs increased by about 10 percent per year, and the growth in SVSs was even more dramatic: about 17 percent per year (table 6-2). From 1980 to 1994, the enrollment in general senior secondary schools dropped by about 2.3 percent per year due to the conversion of these schools into vocational schools. General secondary schools, with their mission of preparing students for college entrance examinations, were the major mode of secondary education until 1985, and they enrolled about 60 percent of upper secondary students. This proportion had fallen to below 50 percent by 1994.

Although the STSs and SVSs are primarily senior secondary-level preemployment vocational education institutions, they have developed and expanded enrollment in part-time and short courses for workers to upgrade skills or be retrained for new employment. By 1994 enrollment in part-time and short courses in secondary technical schools had risen to 130,000 from 75,000 in 1987.

Vocational education is also provided to adults outside the regular school system. More than 60 million persons were enrolled in adult education in 1994. About 50 million were in secondary-level programs, and 95 percent of these students were in technical training schools.

Local labor departments or bureaus also operate employment training centers; the main clients are unemployed youth and retrenched workers. In 1991 there were reported to be 2,200 employment training centers with a training capacity of about 0.9 million. Most large and some medium-size SOEs operate enterprise training centers to meet their training needs. Data on the enterprise training centers are not collected nationwide, but it is clear that many of these centers are in operation.

Vocational education and training is strongly linked to jobs, particularly within the secondary technical schools and skilled workers' schools owned by technical ministries and enterprises. Although the central assignment to jobs of graduates from higher education, specialized secondary schools, and SWSs is being abolished, students sponsored by enterprises and by provincial and local governments are guaranteed employment under the terms of the agreements between the school and the enterprise or local government. Nevertheless, there are reported to be increasing opportunities for employers to select among graduates and for graduates to choose employers.

## Vocational Education

Enrollments in the secondary technical and secondary vocational schools reflect the changing sectoral pattern of employment. Between 1989 and 1994 the share of the services sectors in total employment rose from 18 to 23 percent, while that of industry remained relatively stable at 22 to 23 percent. Meanwhile, the share of agriculture fell from 60 to 54 percent. Enrollment growth in the SVSs and STSs has been largely in the services sectors; training in agriculture has sharply declined (tables 6-3 and 6-4). In the secondary vocational schools the intake in industry and maintenance and repair increased negligibly between 1990 and 1994, while total intake increased by 41 percent. Intake in finance, economics, and administration increased by nearly 220 percent over the same period. By contrast, the intake in agriculture dropped by nearly 30 percent. The pattern for secondary technical schools is similar but less marked. An interesting trend is

TABLE 6-3

Secondary Vocational Schools: Intake and Enrollment,
by Field of Study, 1990 and 1994

(number)

| | 1990 | | 1994 | |
|---|---|---|---|---|
| Field | Intake | Total enrollment | Intake | Total enrollment |
| Industry | 295,492 | 746,200 | 437,784 | 1,043,027 |
| Maintenance and repair | 135,647 | 308,787 | n.a. | n.a. |
| Agriculture and forestry | 251,082 | 523,033 | 154,896 | 394,018 |
| Health | 48,307 | 149,859 | 101,590 | 255,715 |
| Finance, economics, administration | 126,676 | 323,232 | 401,923 | 909,406 |
| Politics and law | 4,553 | 10,498 | 16,088 | 29,096 |
| Teacher training and humanities | 89,170 | 214,740 | n.a. | n.a. |
| Other | 87,443 | 194,926 | 355,280 | 794,166 |
| Total | 1,038,350 | 2,471,275 | 1,467,726 | 3,425,583 |

n.a. Not available.

*Note:* Maintenance and repair and teacher training humanities are not separately recorded in 1994.

*Source:* State Education Commission (various years).

the decreasing percentage of STS entrants who are recruited after graduating from senior general secondary school. This proportion dropped from 30 percent to 20 percent between 1990 and 1994.

The reorientation of vocational education toward the service sectors reflects not only employment patterns but also the lower capital cost of offering nontechnical courses. In recent reviews of provincial development plans, Liaoning province, a major industrial province with about 41 percent of the work force in manufacturing industry, reports over 2,500 programs in its SVSs in finance and economic majors, compared with only 438 courses in engineering.

Private higher and secondary-level education and training have been officially encouraged since 1993. The State Education Commission report for 1994 shows that about 2.3 percent of SVS enrollment was private. The percentage was highest in urban areas at 3.4 percent, dropping to 2.0 percent in counties and towns and 0.4 percent in rural areas.

TABLE 6-4
Secondary Technical Schools: Intake and Enrollment,
by Field of Study, 1990 and 1994
(number)

| Field | 1990 | | 1994 | |
| | Intake | Total enrollment | Intake | Total enrollment |
|---|---|---|---|---|
| Industry | 188,506 | 624,500 | 336,919 | 904,600 |
| Agriculture and forestry | 65,109 | 215,600 | 54,477 | 186,900 |
| Health | 93,261 | 308,400 | 125,815 | 358,200 |
| Finance, economics, administration | 103,299 | 270,800 | 327,750 | 755,400 |
| Politics and law | 20,563 | 43,500 | 34,541 | 68,500 |
| Other | 32,064 | 104,300 | 47,365 | 125,000 |
| Total | 502,802 | 1,567,100 | 929,867 | 2,398,500 |

*Source:* State Education Commission (various years).

Enrollment in the SWSs reflects the predominantly industrial orientation of the enterprises to which these schools belong (table 6-5). Most of the intake (75 percent) is in industry and manufacturing, with only about 2 percent in agriculture.

Expenditure on vocational education is difficult to analyze because there are multiple sources of spending under the control of the schools. Data from 82 leading schools in 5 of the most rapidly developing provinces showed spending in 1993–94 of RMB 2,450 per year per student for the secondary technical schools and RMB 1,590 per year per student for the secondary vocational schools (table 6-6). The average value varied quite widely by region. The share of recurrent expenditure for salaries was on average 58 percent for the secondary vocational schools and about 45 percent for the secondary technical schools. The annual unit costs in the SWSs was about RMB 1,574 per trainee, which is very close to the unit cost for the SVSs. There is little evidence on the relative costs of vocational and general secondary education, but data provided by Guangdong and Shandong provinces suggest that the unit costs of vocational education are higher than those for general education.

The sample of schools also supplied details on the sources of financing for recurrent expenditures. Overall, about 53 percent of revenue for recur-

TABLE 6-5
Skilled Workers' Schools: Intake and Enrollment, by Sector, 1993
(number)

| Sector | Intake | Total enrollment |
| --- | --- | --- |
| Agriculture | 15,205 | 42,313 |
| Machinery/manufacture | 156,984 | 430,628 |
| Mining/smelting | 27,056 | 67,513 |
| Power, oil | 37,825 | 108,659 |
| Chemical, precious metals | 31,983 | 90,723 |
| Light industry (paper, textile, electronics) | 124,103 | 306,474 |
| Construction | 31,593 | 84,789 |
| Transport communications | 58,917 | 140,474 |
| Food and tourism | 71,477 | 160,430 |
| Other | 84,492 | 213,340 |
| Total | 663,073 | 1,715,067 |

*Source:* State Education Commission (various years).

rent expenditures came from the government allocation. But there were wide variations: in 1993–94 the share of government finance ranged from 37 to 64 percent, while that of tuition fees ranged from 2 to 38 percent.

Although there are no nationwide data on employment outcomes for vocational school graduates, evidence suggests that all find jobs. For the STSs and SVSs in the rapidly developing provinces, it was reported that all graduates were employed, though most apparently still found employment in SOEs. For the STS graduates in 1994, 71 percent were employed by SOEs, 15 percent by joint ventures, and 14 percent by township and village enterprises. For the SVS graduates that year the corresponding percentages were 52, 23, and 25.

## Management and Policy

Overall responsibility for the STSs and SVSs, and for coordination of SWSs, rests with the State Education Commission and its Vocational and Technical Education Department. Most of the STSs are managed and financed by central technical departments or the provincial or local technical bureaus. All SVSs are managed and financed by local governments. The State Education Commission sets broad policy and strategy guidelines for STSs and SVSs, and the Ministry of Labor does likewise for the SWSs and training

TABLE 6-6

Annual Cost per Student for Courses at Secondary Technical and
Secondary Vocational Schools, Selected Provinces, 1993–94

(RMB)

| Province | Cost | | Number of schools | |
|---|---|---|---|---|
| | STS | SVS | STS | SVS |
| Guangdong | 2,380 | 2,780 | 5 | 5 |
| Jiangsu | 3,130 | 1,850 | 10 | 10 |
| Liaoning | 1,990 | 1,330 | 3 | 12 |
| Shandong | 1,410 | 1,310 | 4 | 13 |
| Tianjin | 2,720 | 1,660 | 4 | 9 |
| Total | 2,450 | 1,590 | 26 | 49 |

*Source:* Authors' calculations based on questionnaires returned by 82 schools.

centers. Policy and strategy formulation for vocational education is set by
the State Education Commission; the main responsibility for management
of the system rests with the provincial, county/city, and district-level governments. The State Education Commission does not provide direct funding, except for limited pilot projects, but it controls indirect funding from
international bodies. It uses a number of policy instruments including (a)
broad targets, such as the proportion of senior secondary students enrolled
in vocational schools; (b) standards for staffing, including numbers, qualifications, and experience; and (c) guidelines for the curricula for the main
subjects, standard lists of practical exercises to be performed, and lists of
the equipment to be provided in each specialization.

The commission sets targets for the establishment of key schools at the
local, provincial, and national levels. These schools must meet criteria concerning the adequacy and quality of facilities and the number and qualifications of staff. To be recognized as a key school is a high honor, and this
encourages investment and development to meet the criteria.

The State Education Commission exercises control through regulations
and guidelines. A vocational education law was expected that would establish the framework for a comprehensive vocational education system. Among
other objectives, the law would establish occupational classification and
skills standards nationwide and improve linkages between government departments and with enterprises through a skills testing system. The law,

unlike existing State Education Commission regulations, would include penalties for violation.

## Vocational Training

The main suppliers of vocational training through short courses are the employment training centers operated by the labor departments of local governments, frequently through a labor service company. The Ministry of Labor issues regulations governing employment training centers, but they seem to remain relatively uncontrolled in terms of the content and quality of their training. Employment training centers cater to local needs. Their main clients are the unemployed and enterprise workers wanting to learn new skills. Reportedly, 3.0475 million people completed training in the employment training centers in 1993 (table 6-7). Of this number, 2.771 million (91 percent) undertook pre-employment training (and about 77 percent of them were classified as unemployed first-time job seekers).

TABLE 6-7
Employment Training Centers, 1993

| Characteristic | Number of trainees (thousands) |
|---|---|
| Number of employment training centers | 2,525.0 |
| Total number trained | 3,047.5 |
| Pre-employment training | 2,771.0 |
| Of unemployed youth | 2,133.5 |
| *Training authority* | |
| Labor department | 1,327.5 |
| Job training center | 1,129.1 |
| Business management department | 990.7 |
| Society | 205.0 |
| Private | 149.0 |
| Other | 98.9 |
| *Length of training* | |
| Less than six months | 2,190.7 |
| Between six months and one year | 370.1 |
| Longer than one year | 210.3 |

*Source:* Ministry of Labor (1994).

More than 2 million of those undertaking pre-employment training received less than six months of training. A more detailed picture of the enterprise training centers in 1995 has been provided by a few municipalities. Generally, the training was of relatively short duration—less than three months—and mainly for the unemployed. The characteristics of trainees varied between centers. In Shaoxing, for example, all trainees were unemployed, but about 23 percent had been previously employed; in Wuhan about 40 percent of trainees had current jobs. The employment training centers appear to respond to the differing needs of their locations.

Employment training centers are funded by capital grants from the labor bureaus, tuition fees, earnings from subsidiary production activities, and subsidies from the unemployment insurance fund. However, there are almost no data on the costs of employment training center training.

## Enterprise-Based Training

Enterprise-based training is provided in enterprise training centers that are owned and operated by large and medium SOEs. Data on the enterprise training centers have not been collected nationwide, but data from two municipalities (Shaoxing and Wuhan) show that most of the training is short term (table 6-8). Over 70 percent of the training is provided for workers, normally employed by the enterprise owning the enterprise training centers. The regulations governing enterprise training centers are largely determined by the technical ministries to which the parent enterprises are responsible. There is no national standard for courses other than those provided for general education.

## Private Sector Training

Private training centers provided about 4.9 percent of all training in 1993. There are no nationwide data on training centers in private enterprises, nor are there data available on in-service training as distinct from off-the-job training. It appears that many enterprises do not have independent workshops for practical skills training, so practical training aspects of the course are normally carried out in the factory.

## Major VET Issues

Important issues are management and financing of vocational education and training and the relevance and responsiveness of VET to state and student needs.

TABLE 6-8
Characteristics of Enterprise Training Centers
in Selected Municipalities, 1995

| Characteristic | Shaoxing | Percentage | Wuhan | Percentage |
|---|---|---|---|---|
| Number of enterprise training centers in municipality | 10 | n.a. | 176 | n.a. |
| Total number of trainees | 4,420 | n.a. | 280,865 | n.a. |
| Average number of trainees per enterprise training centers | 442 | n.a. | 1,596 | n.a. |
| *Number enrolled in courses by length* | | | | |
| 0 to 50 hours | 2,400 | 54.3 | 150,387 | 53.6 |
| 50 hours to 3 months | 2,020 | 45.7 | 54,360 | 18.9 |
| 3 to 6 months | n.a. | n.a. | 50,830 | 17.8 |
| Longer than 6 months | n.a. | n.a. | 24,488 | 9.7 |
| *Trainees by type* | | | | |
| Young people waiting for employment | 770 | 17.4 | 22,480 | 8.0 |
| Previous workers waiting for employment | 230 | 5.2 | 56,240 | 20.0 |
| Workers employed by enterprises | 1,950 | 44.1 | 105,555 | 37.6 |
| Workers from township and village enterprises | 1,470 | 33.3 | 54,030 | 19.2 |
| Other workers | n.a. | n.a. | 41,760 | 14.9 |

n.a. Not applicable.
*Source:* State Education Commission (1995).

## Management and Financing of VET

The broad policy of the government is to move, incrementally, to a market responsive system. The real question is whether such a system can be achieved if the changes that are made are small and existing structures are maintained. The main problems are as follows:

- Supply-driven systems of VET provision
- Overlap and duplication of course provision
- Schools' lack of responsibility and accountability
- Inadequate financial resources
- Unjustified differences in fees
- Uneconomic enterprises operated by schools.

Although central placement and assignment are being discontinued, and responsibility is being decentralized to provincial and local governments and enterprises, vocational education and training in China is still supply driven. For example, the State Planning Council and State Education Commission have set targets for an increasing proportion of the senior secondary graduates to enter the vocational and technical schools, and local authorities appear to give high priority to meeting those targets.

The multiple systems of management duplicate provision. Both the SVSs and SWSs run three-year pre-employment training programs for junior secondary leavers, while the enterprise training centers include general education as well as secondary technical and vocational school programs. The secondary technical schools and the secondary vocational schools offer an increasing proportion of part-time and short specialist courses for upgrading and retraining workers—supposedly the function of the enterprise training centers.

School managers appear to have a good deal of freedom and power. This may be because they lack legally defined responsibility and accountability rather than because they have been assigned decentralized powers. A more thorough reform of the organization and management of VET would have devolved responsibilities to the training institutions in a clearly defined manner.

In 1995 the State Education Commission proposed the establishment of 2,000 vocational schools (about 16 percent of all vocational and technical schools) by the year 2000. For these schools alone, the investment required from 1995 to 2000 was expected to be about 8 billion RMB per year—eight times the annual capital expenditure on primary and secondary education in 1991. This does not account for the needs of the other 14,000 vocational and technical schools, which are sorely in need of rehabilitation because of inadequate financing. One source of this problem has been the widespread conversion of secondary general schools into secondary vocational schools. Studies indicate that unit recurrent costs for 1994 average RMB 2,500 per year for the STSs and RMB 1,600 for the SVSs and SWSs, which are higher than those of general education.

Analysis of details of source of financing for recurrent expenditure, also supplied by the sample of schools, showed that overall about 53 percent of revenue for recurrent expenditure came from the government allocation. But there were wide variations: the share of government finance ranged from 37 percent to 64 percent, while that of tuition fees ranged from 2 percent to 38 percent. In general, tuition fee and production income was higher for the SVSs, with less than 50 percent of their revenue coming from the government education budget. Students in some government programs pay only about RMB 400, while others pay as much as RMB 2,500. About 6 percent of a sample of schools' operating revenue is obtained from income from enterprises owned by the schools. But some school-owned factory workshops derive profit from special benefits, including low interest loans for investment, freedom from taxation and other controls, and monopoly rights for supply of services.

## Relevance and Responsiveness

STS, SVS, and SWS graduates number about 2 million per year and represent about 17 percent of the total net increase in employment. Until the late 1980s, graduates of STSs and SWSs were guaranteed employment. Although these guarantees have been removed, graduates of these institutions who are sponsored by enterprises and by provincial and local governments are still guaranteed employment. Enrollments in SVSs and STSs reflect the changing sectoral pattern of employment. SWS enrollment reflects the predominantly industrial orientation of the enterprises to which these schools belong.

## Notable VET Reforms

The framework for reform of VET was established in 1985 when the Communist Party of China issued a policy statement "vigorously promoting vocational and technical education" by (a) increasing the proportion of students entering senior vocational education (from 40 percent of entrants to senior secondary education to 50 percent); (b) introducing a system of pre-employment training; (c) including general education within vocational education; and (d) encouraging enterprises, technical departments of government, individuals, and communities to set up vocational and technical education institutions on their own or in cooperation. The policy was further developed in 1993 with an outline for reform of education by the Central Committee of the Communist Party and the State Council (State Council 1993, 1994). Following is a discussion of the main components of the policy.

A major part of the government's education reforms is the introduction of universal nine-year compulsory education. Compulsory education in 2000 was expected to cover 85 percent of the population.

Senior secondary education is to be universalized in large cities and economically developed coastal regions. Enrollment in technical and vocational education at the senior secondary level is to be increased considerably. Each city or county is to set up one or two key comprehensive secondary vocational schools until eventually 2,000 key secondary vocational and technical schools are established around the country. Enrollment in secondary vocational education in 2000 was expected to constitute 60 percent of students in the upper secondary level, with the proportion reaching 70 percent in cities. Postsecondary vocational education and training for graduates of secondary general schools is also to be developed.

The object is for all new job entrants to have access to training, and for job-related training to be available to all employees. A general policy of requiring pre-employment training is to be followed strictly, and jobs requiring skills are to be open only to those with the relevant job qualification certificate. Adult education should be expanded.

The state is to be a major sponsor and source of financing for VET rather than the only sponsor. While basic education will remain the responsibility of government, technical and vocational education and adult education are to be mainly sponsored by trades, enterprises, and public institutions or jointly by all sectors. The central government will be responsible for setting overall policies and guidance, and provincial and local governments will be responsible for administration of the system in line with that guidance.

Nationwide planning of enrollment and assignment of graduates to employment will cease. Schools will continue to recruit some students under plans determined by the schools and administering authorities. In principle, those students will be assigned to employment within sectors, but in practice, students and employing units will exercise mutual choice in actual employment.

The numbers of students sponsored by enterprises and by self-supported fee payments are to be increased progressively. Sponsored students on graduation will be employed according to the training contract between the sponsoring body and the school, or the agreement between the employer and the individual student. With progressive development of the labor market, most graduates should be free to find their own jobs.

Quality is to be improved through a number of steps. Quality standards and evaluation indicators are to be set for schools. Teacher qualifications are to be improved; the hope was that by the year 2000, 60 percent of secondary vocational teachers would have the specified qualifications. Teachers' salaries are to be increased to exceed that of employees in local SOEs, and to rise with rising gross national product. Teachers' salaries and promotion are to be determined by performance, thus overturning egalitarianism and promotion based on seniority in years of service. Efficiency in the utilization of resources is to be improved.

Legislation on vocational education will be introduced to ensure the implementation of the reforms. Local authorities are to follow by formulating local laws and decrees. The system for supervising enforcement of the vocational education law will be established.

Total expenditure on education was expected to rise to 4 percent of gross national product by the year 2000, with budgetary expenditure reaching 15 percent of government expenditure. Government will continue to be the main source of finance, but its assistance will be supplemented by funds from other channels. Low interest loans for setting up school enterprises are proposed. Enterprises and nongovernmental organizations will be encouraged to invest in education, through tax relief on such expenditure. The education tax will also be collected from township and village enterprises and other countryside enterprises exempt from paying value added tax, sales taxes, and consumption taxes. Peasants will also pay an education tax of 1.5 to 2 percent of per capita income. It is to be considered as part of their 5 percent tax burden, to be used mainly to subsidize teachers of schools run by local people and to make up deficiencies in funding of these schools.

## Ongoing and Completed Reforms

The expansion of enrollment in vocational and technical education at the expense of general secondary education is well on the way to being achieved. By 1994 the intake to vocational schools at the senior level was about 58 percent of the total entry to senior secondary education. The budgeted expenditure for education for 1994 was 15.43 percent of the total, thus exceeding the 15 percent target. The growth of nongovernment budget spending for vocational education represents close to 50 percent of total recurrent expenditure in a group of advanced vocational schools in five of the most developed provinces.

The government is experimenting with funding in-service training. Under a pilot project, five municipalities will set up vocational training coordinating committees or similar mechanisms to manage vocational training funds that will become the channel for all municipal finance for provision of in-service training. The vocational training funds will make grants, to both public and private training providers, on a competitive basis using criteria of quality, demonstration of market demand, and cost and outcome benefits. Initially, a bilateral or multilateral loan or credit could be used to upgrade facilities of training institutions, for example, but funds could come from any multilateral or bilateral source or from government grants or allocations. Revenue for the training fund to cover recurrent costs of training would come from multiple sources, including the unemployment insurance fund, education tax, and general budget allocation for training. The vocational training coordination committee will include representatives from government, enterprises, labor, and training organizations.

Management of the VET system has been devolved to provincial, county, and city levels. Indeed, the central government has neither the staffing nor control over financial resources to manage the systems centrally.

### Obstacles to Reform

The major obstacle to the reform of vocational and technical education and training is the capital cost of improving the quality of training facilities and of implementing programs for upgrading staff and revising courses. To establish the target of 2,000 key vocational schools by 2000 required an annual expenditure of some RMB 8 billion—an increase of about 10 percent in the total education budget. Those 2,000 key schools represented only about 10 percent of the formal VET system.

A second important obstacle is the lack of close cooperation between the State Education Commission and the Ministry of Labor, particularly at the central level, and the resulting duplication of functions in the training institutions under their care. The vocational training coordination committees managing training funds from various sources could greatly minimize overlap and inefficiency. To succeed in this regard, however, they must be free from direct control by either the Ministry of Labor or the State Education Commission, and they must operate under the direction of sector training institutions and employers in the private and public sectors.

### References

Ministry of Labor. 1994. *Yearbook of Labor Statistics of China.* Beijing: China Statistical Press.

People's Republic of China. 1995. *Yearbook of Statistics.* Beijing: China Statistical Publishing House.

State Council. 1993. *Outline for Reform and Development of Education in China.* Beijing: Central Committee of Communist Party of China and State Council.

———. 1994. *Suggestions on Implementation of the Outline for Reform.* Beijing: Central Committee of Communist Party of China and State Council.

State Education Commission. various years. *Educational Statistics Yearbook of China.* Beijing: People's Education Press.

# 7  Indonesia

ZAFIRIS TZANNATOS AND HANEEN SAYED

DURING THE PAST 30 years, Indonesia experienced remarkable economic and demographic transformation. Since 1970 the economy has grown at an average annual rate of approximately 7 percent. Aided by a national population policy, the government was able to reduce the total fertility rate from 5.3 children per woman in 1970 to 2.8 in 1993. This combination of rapid economic growth and declining fertility resulted in annual increases in per capita income of 4.5 percent. Other policies that focused on agriculture, regional development, and human resource development helped to reduce poverty from 60 percent in 1970 to 14 percent in 1993 and adult illiteracy from 60 percent to 16 percent during the same period. Today almost all children start school.

A diversified supply of education and training provided by the public and private sectors kept pace with the demands of a fast-growing and transforming economy. As a result, Indonesia joined the ranks of the middle-income countries by the mid-1990s. The financial crisis of 1998 and the resulting economic contraction threatened to reverse many of these gains, but Indonesia may soon recover much of the ground lost. This chapter takes a long-term view and focuses on the pre-1997 labor market and on the vocational education and training reforms carried out over the past two decades.

In the economic sphere the government has engaged in substantial deregulation since the late 1980s to lay the basis for future growth. Indonesia's commitments to free trade under the Uruguay Round of the General Agreement on Tariffs and Trade, and under the Asia Free Trade Agreement, provide for the removal of many trade restrictions by 2004 that will open up its economy further. The challenge is to create a system for producing skilled workers that can readily respond to largely unpredictable changes in the size and composition of future output.

This chapter examines the characteristics of Indonesia's vocational and technical education and training in relation to recent labor market performance and future prospects. It finds that in this connection, Indonesia's strength is a sizable, effective, and cost-efficient private education and training sector. Given this finding, the chapter discusses the role of public policy in vocational education and training and possible reforms in terms of public provision, financing, and regulation.

## Vocational Education and Training

Indonesia's education system produces each year more than 1 million skilled workers, broadly defined to include those with academic and vocational skills at the senior secondary level (ages 16 to 18) and above. This is impressive for a country with a per capita income of US$900 in 1996. Only a generation ago 70 percent of the labor force had no more than a primary education.

Vocational education and training in Indonesia is dominated by private institutions. The number of senior secondary graduates from private schools equals the number graduating from public schools, and the number of graduates from private postsecondary institutions is more than double that from public institutions. Publicly provided training is only a fraction of the training supplied by the private sector. Approximately 1 million trainees are enrolled in private training centers registered with the Ministry of Manpower, compared with 50,000 trainees enrolled in the ministry's public vocational centers. An additional 500,000 trainees attend private training centers registered with the Ministry of Education and Culture. Employer-provided training is also extensive, but it is more difficult to quantify.

A major determinant of the skill level of the labor force in the future will be the number of children who leave the education system before they have completed the basic cycle of nine years of schooling. Approximately 2.0 million students dropped out of the basic education system in 1994 (table 7-1).

When examined against costs, government investments at the higher levels of education are significantly greater than those at basic levels. They predominantly benefit those from higher-income families or employers in

TABLE 7-1

Indonesia's Education System

(thousands of people)

| Level of education | Total output | Portion of total attending private facilities | Drop-outs | Not proceeding to next level of education |
|---|---|---|---|---|
| Primary[a] (ages 7–12) | 3,840 | 256 | 1,200 | 1,200 |
| Junior secondary[b] (ages 13–15) | 1,905 | 522 | 400 | 400 |
| Senior secondary (ages 16–18) | 1,226 | 592 | 300 | 800 |
| General (including commercial and home economics) | 863 | 366 | — | — |
| Vocational | 210 | 129 | — | — |
| Technical (three- and four-year) | 153 | 97 | — | — |
| Diploma | 59 | 39 | 100[b] | — |
| University degree | 155 | 110 | — | — |
| Postgraduate | 2 | — | — | — |
| Selected civil service tertiary institutes | 54 | — | — | — |
| Ministry of Manpower vocational centers | 50 | — | — | — |
| Private training centers | — | 1,500 | — | — |

— Not available.

*Note:* Data are for 1992, 1993, or 1994 (whichever year the most recent data were available).

a. Includes religious schools.

b. Includes diploma and degree dropouts.

*Source:* Ministry of Education and Culture data; Ministry of Manpower data.

the formal sector (where labor costs are only a fraction of value added, typically less than 20 percent). The annual unit cost in primary education averages US$80. The unit cost in senior secondary technical schools is approximately 40 percent higher on average than for senior secondary general schools, where the unit cost is US$170. For public universities the annual unit cost is approximately US$800, but for pre-employment training in a public vocational training center the annual unit cost can amount to more than US$1,000.

The public provision of skills outside the general education system is particularly costly. The discussion that follows takes this as a starting point. We do not deny that training interventions can have many positive developmental effects nor that governments should be engaged in a range of activities that may appear to have low social returns. However, social investments and public interventions should have net social gains and should be fiscally sustainable, and in some cases may be better left to the private sector.

## Vocational Education

Indonesia's human resource policies have been broadly based. The government has focused on expanding primary education, which by 1993–94 had become nearly universal (table 7-2). Junior secondary education has not increased as much and is more likely to lead to senior secondary education than to immediate employment. Senior secondary education and university education, however, have mushroomed as the labor market continues to absorb more educated graduates (although their wage premium over secondary school graduates is smaller than in the past). Because junior secondary vocational education has been phased out, this chapter focuses on senior secondary education.

In 1992–93 almost 4 million students were enrolled in approximately 14,000 senior secondary schools. Senior secondary education takes place in a highly diverse mix of schools. Nearly two-thirds of senior secondary students attend general education schools. The rest are enrolled in 14 dif-

TABLE 7-2
Enrollment Rates, by Level of Education and Output,
Selected Years, 1968–94

| Level of education | Enrollment rate (percent) | | 1992–93 output (thousands) |
|---|---|---|---|
| | 1968–69 | 1993–94 | |
| Primary | 41[a] | 94[a] | 3,700 |
| Junior secondary | 17[a] | 40[a] | 1,900 |
| Senior secondary | 9[a] | 25[a] | 1,250 |
| University | 2[b] | 10[b] | 220 |

a. Net enrollment rate: students in the official age group for a given level of education (see table 7-1) as a percentage of the total population in that age group.

b. Gross enrollment rate: students (irrespective of their age) enrolled in a university as a percentage of the population in the official age group for that level of education.

*Source*: National Development Planning Board.

ferent types of vocational, technical, and specialized schools. Almost 85 percent of the nongeneral schools are commercial or technical schools. The private sector accounts for nearly half of total enrollments.

Vocational education covers mainly commercial fields, such as administration, accounting, marketing, management, and investment and loan management. Technical education includes drawing, surveying and mapping, building construction, water works, electrical installation, electricity supply, machining, communication electronics, automotive mechanics, general mechanics, and ship maintenance. In theory, more than 160 study programs are available, but in practice recognized curricula exist for fewer than 100 programs, of which only 75 are actually offered. On average, schools offer only three to four programs, although a few may offer as many as ten.

The difference between what can be offered at schools and what is actually provided reflects the limited finances of public schools and the unwillingness of private schools to provide courses in fields not required in their local labor markets. Yet the five-year plan for 1993–94 to 1998–99 foresaw a greater increase in enrollments in and output of vocational and technical education (VTE) schools than in general schools, partly as a result of government policy to support VTE. The authorities expected the annual rate of increase in the VTE stream to be nearly 50 percent higher than in the general stream, 7.4 percent compared with 5.1 percent. By the end of the plan period, the authorities expected the ratio of VTE graduates to general education graduates to have increased to two-thirds, compared with one-half at the beginning of the period.

The planned expansion is taking place against a declining wage differential between general and VTE graduates (table 7-3). Urban labor markets no longer differentiate between these two groups, and male VTE graduates now earn less than general graduates. Women VTE graduates continue to enjoy a small, but declining, premium.

The length of job search is similar for graduates of the different senior secondary schools, and apparently little variation occurs in the unemployment rates between graduates from the different types of schools. The incidence of long-term unemployment also does not seem to vary by type of school: around 50 percent of graduates from all schools have yet to find a job after six months.

Despite the fact that the type of school and program "are of limited importance in determining whether graduates are idle or not" (MOEC and USAID 1992), costs in technical senior secondary schools are 55 percent higher than those in general senior secondary schools. The cost differ-

TABLE 7-3

Wage Advantage of Graduates of Vocational and Technical Education
Schools, by Gender, 1977 and 1990

(index, senior secondary general = 100)

| Type of senior secondary school | Men | | Women | |
|---|---|---|---|---|
| | 1977 | 1990 | 1977 | 1990 |
| General | 100 | 100 | 100 | 100 |
| Vocational | 134 | 98 | 127 | 111 |

Source: 1990 labor force survey.

ence between commercial and general senior secondary schools is smaller,
5 percent, but the labor market outcomes of commercial school graduates
is not as good as for those from technical schools. The cost disadvantage of
technical schools becomes even greater if one takes repetition and attrition
into account. The percentage of repeaters among technical school students
is 25 percent higher than for general education schools, and the percentage
of dropouts is nearly three times as large. On average, 13 percent of students from public general education schools graduate at age 20 or above.
The percentage is 20 percent for public commercial schools and 34 percent
for public technical schools (MOEC and USAID 1992, table 26). Combining these findings, we find that general education school students have
a 94 percent probability of finishing the cycle in the allotted three years,
compared with 86 percent for technical school students. This increases
technical schools' costs by another 10 percent.

In terms of exposure to work, on-the-job training of VTE students does
not always match curricula or the needs of students or industry. Rather, it
depends on what is locally available (MOEC and USAID 1992, p. 42).
Ninety-nine percent of students in technical and commercial schools participate in some on-the-job training before graduation. Seventy percent of
commercial school students train in government offices. Twenty-two percent of technical school students train in a government office and 49 percent in industries or business ventures (although whether this is in a private
or a parastatal establishment is not known). The average length of on-the-
job training is only two weeks for commercial school students and three
weeks for technical school students (MOEC and USAID 1992, table 32).

Donor support for the expansion of VTE has not always produced the
desired results. In some instances it has contributed to an oversupply of

vocational schools. It has also created recurrent demands for funds that were simply beyond the reach of the public budget once donor funds ran out. According to the Ministry of Education and Culture and the U.S. Agency for International Development, "The basis for VTE expansion was that economic development would create critical shortages of middle-level technically qualified manpower. However, there is little evidence to suggest that any shortages are being alleviated by the employment of VTE graduates nor is it clear that VTE graduates are, on the whole, being adequately prepared for that type of role in the labor force" (MOEC and USAID 1992, p. 17).

## Public Vocational Training Centers

Many ministries provide training. The Ministry of Manpower, the main supplier of training to the private sector, is officially responsible for coordinating the national training effort. The training programs cover a wide range of areas and vary in design and in methods of delivery. For example, the Ministry of Manpower's vocational training centers aim in theory at school dropouts; secondary school and university graduates; other job seekers (housewives, handicapped people, older people); professionals; employees; and self-employed workers in agriculture, manufacturing, and services. In practice, the programs are targeted at three groups: (a) job seekers such as school dropouts and secondary school graduates, who can receive training in the ministry's vocational centers; (b) workers in private or state-owned enterprises, who can attend fully subsidized training programs; and (c) self-employed workers in small business or agriculture, who receive training either through special courses or mobile training units attached to vocational training centers. We concentrate here on training for job seekers and the vocational centers run by the Ministry of Manpower.

The ministry in 1994 operated 153 vocational centers that were divided into three types: 33 type A centers (BLKs), which are the biggest ones and are located in urban areas; 16 type B centers (BLKs), which are located in smaller urban centers; and 104 type C centers (KLKs), which are the smallest ones and are located primarily in rural areas. The bigger centers provided training in industrial and service skills, while the smaller ones offered training in technologies appropriate for rural areas and in the skills needed for self-employment.

The centers have the capacity to train approximately 120,000 people a year, and government-sponsored enrollments (that is, fully subsidized trainees) reached nearly that figure in 1984 (table 7-4). However, enrollments

TABLE 7-4
Enrollment of Government-Sponsored Trainees, Staff Levels,
and Funding in Ministry of Manpower Vocational Training Centers,
Selected Years, 1984–99

| Category | 1984 | 1988 | 1992 | Five-year plan 1994–99[a] |
|---|---|---|---|---|
| Trainees (number) | 118,000 | 23,000 | 80,000 | 50,000 |
| Staff (number) | 1,600 | 2,240 | 3,200 | — |
| Development budget allocation (billions of rupiah) | 12.6 | 7.6 | 20.0 | — |

— Not available.
a. Planned annual enrollment.
*Source:* Ministry of Manpower data; World Bank estimates.

have fallen over time, reaching as low as 25,000 in the mid-1980s, when project funds dried up and the macroeconomic situation deteriorated, necessitating budget cuts. No new centers have been built in the past decade, although sizable allocations from the development budget have been maintained, and the number of instructors has increased (table 7-4).

Year-to-year budget allocations vary significantly and seem to be unpredictable, as indicated by changes in the number of government-sponsored trainees. Between 1990 and 1991, for example, the number of such trainees in selected BLKs and KLKs increased by 300 percent, only to decline by 11 percent between 1991 and 1992 and then to increase by 18 percent between 1992 and 1993. Reliance on foreign funds and lack of continuity in development budget allocations have deprived the centers of the ability to plan for the long term. The decline in budget allocations (while maintaining the number of centers and increasing the number of instructors) has been accompanied by a reduction in the duration of courses. In addition, the centers have gradually moved to offering less expensive, nonindustrial, short-term training. At the peak of the centers' operations in 1984, more than 60,000 government-sponsored trainees received training in industrial skills; by 1992 this number had declined to only 45,000. Yet during this time employment in manufacturing increased by more than 3 million workers. Currently, most of the courses focus on agriculture, tourism, and commerce, and some centers offer driving lessons. These are low-cost areas already well catered to by the private sector. The initial objective of the centers to provide sophisticated industrial skills remains unfulfilled.

Two other objectives have also been largely pushed aside. First, the centers' original intent was to target weak applicants—those who had not gone beyond a primary school education or who had dropped out of secondary school. In other words, the centers were to provide opportunities to the less fortunate, who for lack of ability or for economic or social reasons could not complete their basic education. Eventually, however, a consistent pattern emerged: those who failed to qualify for entrance were predominantly the school dropouts, and those who gained entry were mainly senior secondary schools graduates. In 1995, 90 percent of trainees were senior secondary school graduates. Students who had less than a senior secondary education often lacked basic literacy and numeracy skills and were unable to handle technical equipment.

Second, based on the centers' original aim of catering to poor students, trainees are exempted by legislation from paying fees. Even though 50,000 trainees are fully sponsored by public funds, cost-recovery measures have gradually been introduced.

STUDENT AND EMPLOYER ISSUES. Student selection is officially the responsibility of the Ministry of Manpower's district offices. Students seeking admittance to a program must be good citizens, physically fit, and at least 18 years old. They also must have registered as job seekers with one of the ministry's district offices, which screen applications, administer the required tests, and select the students. This selection process and the use of criteria that are not related to achievement (for example, being a member of the government party) reduce the quality of the students selected. The BLKs, in particular, feel the effects of this, and some have introduced additional recruitment tests, such as locally administered tests in mathematics.

Individual centers are not involved in placing trainees in jobs. After a typical three-month basic training course, the BLKs and KLKs send a list of successful trainees back to the Ministry of Manpower's district offices, which then place the students. As in the case of student selection, however, placement is increasingly facilitated by BLK teachers through their contacts with local firms.

There have been several studies of BLK and KLK graduates over the years (Clark 1985; MOEC and USAID 1992). Their findings are characterized by significant variation with respect to the employment and wages of graduates compared with some control group. In some studies BLK graduates found employment before nongraduates, but after a year the overall unemployment rate for graduates was not substantially different from that of nongraduates. It is not clear whether the initial differences in employment rates relate to the intensity of placement efforts by the Ministry of Manpower's district offices. In addition, BLK graduates earned more than nongraduates, but both earnings and employment outcomes varied significantly by program, location, and trainees' personal characteristics. More recent evaluations have shown, however, that BLK graduates do not appear to have an earnings advantage over nongraduates, nor do they have a significant advantage in terms of securing permanent or casual employment.

A 1992 Ministry of Manpower study (Patrinos and Clark 1995) presented employers' views about BLK and KLK graduates. It compared the graduates employers had recruited to "similar" workers in the same firms who had not graduated from a BLK or KLK. The supervisors who were interviewed stated that three-quarters of BLK and KLK graduates required basic training on entering the firm, and some required more than three months of training. (The methodology and sample may not be completely reliable.) The supervisors argued that the usefulness of training at BLKs and KLKs is limited because of their lack of modern machinery and tools. They also pointed out that parts of the curriculum at the BLKs are nontechnical, such as physical fitness and mental disciple, which limits the time allocated to instruction in pertinent skills.

FINANCING. The BLKs and KLKs are funded from various sources, including the public budget, donors, and third parties (cost recovery). In 1992–93 the development budget allocation alone was approximately 20 billion rupiah (US$10 million), and the centers enrolled 80,000 trainees. Adding an estimated recurrent budget allocation of Rp 14 billion, the unit cost was approximately Rp 425,000. Since the average course lasts three months, the yearly unit cost is about Rp 1.7 million (US$860), which is equivalent to the average unit cost of studies at a public university. Other estimates of the annual unit cost per full-time BLK and KLK trainee supported by public funds have been more than US$1,200 (World Bank 1991). These high costs derive in part from overstaffing and underutilization of facilities. Public vocational centers have a trainee-per-instructor ratio of 3.3 compared with a ratio of 10 to 15 trainees per instructor in private centers. Estimates indicate that the public funds allocated for the annual training of 50,000 students in BLKs and KLKs could be more than adequate to provide training to 10 percent of all those employed (3.5 million people) in medium and large manufacturing firms.

Foreign assistance continues to be instrumental in developing and assisting the operations of public vocational centers. In addition to supporting building construction and procurement of equipment, foreign grants and loans have funded staff development and upgrading. Donors have financed many of Indonesia's instructor training facilities. Donors have also supported the extensive overseas training of instructors. Foreign funds have helped to develop a system of public vocational training that is now too large to be sustained by local funds and requires continuous injection of foreign monies. Hence, this dependence on foreign funds has become more a liability than an asset. In addition, the stop-go nature of foreign funding means that long-term planning is difficult, and so the operations of public vocational centers are determined by narrow, short-run considerations.

After the financial crunch of the mid-1980s and the depletion of project funds, the government introduced legislation that allows cost recovery for nongovernment-sponsored training. This resulted in individualized training programs for firms (both private and public) or the leasing of facilities for training, teaching, and related activities. The proceeds are largely retained locally and often take the form of supplementary staff salaries. In some BLKs privately funded trainees now outnumber government-sponsored trainees, and the proceeds constitute a significant addition to staff earnings.

The BLKs' ability to contract directly with employers and trainees reflects, above all, desirable market linkages. However, this is not a conventional method of cost recovery, whereby the government recovers costs and uses them to finance activities determined by public (rather than private) interests. Even though they are increasingly demand driven, the BLKs may not be supplying the amount of training privately owned firms would have offered. In a competitive market, an increase in demand normally results in an increase in supply. In the case of third party funding, an increase in demand can be met by an increase in the price trainees have to pay, since staff may be interested in maximizing their own earnings. While this is a testable proposition, no evaluation has been undertaken to date on the effects of incentives on the provision of training services by the public vocational centers.

## Private Training Centers

Indonesia's private training centers are extremely diverse and cater to a wide variety of skill needs. They constitute a vigorous market response to local demand by students for greater job opportunities. The centers range from small, store-front shops that offer a single short-term course, such as hair-dressing or flower arranging, to large, urban institutions with more than 1,000 students. The large centers offer a range of multiyear programs in areas, such as accounting, computer skills, or secretarial work, that lead directly to well-paid employment. They are usually owner operated.

Precise figures on the actual number of centers are not available, but more than 20,000 centers are registered with the Ministry of Education and Culture and the Ministry of Manpower. They enroll about 1.5 million trainees per year. The growth of the private training centers has been dramatic, and much greater than any government planned and financed program could have supported. From 1990 to 1995, private training centers increased by more than 7 percent per year, more than twice the rate of labor force growth.

The growth in the number of private training centers has been largely market driven, reflecting student demand for training in areas that can lead to employment in the expanding services sector. For example, the demand for accounting qualifications rose and fell with the changes in the labor market that followed the deregulation of financial services. The number of students seeking computer-related skills has risen steadily as demand for these skills has increased; the market for office workers has tightened in the last couple of years and reduced the demand for related courses such as typing.

Surveys of the private training centers conducted in 1992 and 1994 by the World Bank, the Ministry of Manpower, and the Ministry of Education and Culture also confirm their market orientation. About one-fifth of the centers reported that they had added or dropped a program in the past two years. The programs most frequently added were in computer fields, and those most frequently dropped were in electronics, welding, and air conditioning.

Overall, private centers employed more part-time instructors (an average of 4.1) than full-time instructors (an average of 3.4). The predominance of part-timers is attributable to a combination of factors, such as the small size of the centers, the need for flexibility from year to year, and the lower costs for contract instructors. Full-time instructors report an average of seven years of related work experience and seven years of teaching experience.

More than half the students were job seekers who had graduated from senior secondary or postsecondary education institutions. One-third were still students, and the rest were employed. The main reason for taking a course was concern for employment. Even among university graduates, the belief that computer skills are a must for finding work was widespread.

Data from the 1992 Indonesian Socioeconomic Survey confirm these patterns. Econometric estimation of the probability of wanting training increases with education after controlling for other characteristics (such as age, location, and income). Those with a junior secondary education are 40 percent more likely to demand training than are primary school graduates, while senior secondary school graduates have a 100 percent greater probability of demanding training than do primary school graduates. Demand for training by graduates holding certificates is still high, nearly double that of primary school graduates, but demand by degree holders is less than for senior secondary school graduates. This is also the pattern observed for employer-provided training: more educated workers receive more training.

Large training centers often run for-profit placement services; other centers offer this service to their graduates as part of their traditional placement and marketing responsibilities. Seventy-one percent of the centers surveyed in 1992 offered some placement services, although only 25 percent of those centers reported that they regularly received job listings from employers. In the 1994 survey nearly half the students found employment through the centers, and most of the rest (38 percent) found jobs through their own efforts. A few found jobs through advertisements, and only 6 percent found employment through the Ministry of Manpower's employment exchanges. Many computer training centers (40 percent of those surveyed) had cooperative arrangements with companies, which in most cases meant the companies provided information about their vacancies. More companies would have approached centers directly if they had not been obliged to report their vacancies to the Ministry of Manpower's employment exchanges and follow that channel of recruitment. Nearly 33 percent of the centers offered job search training, and 10 percent offered interview training. The most common service offered was personal referrals to employers; half the centers that offered placement assistance provided this service. However, many trainees entered the informal job sector after graduation, which meant that such assistance was irrelevant.

## Enterprise-Based Training

Employers cooperate with private training centers and tend to use them as much as they use government training centers. Private training centers have training contracts with employers, and, as already noted, some employers provide centers with lists of their vacancies.

Even when engaged in upgrading their workers' skills, companies are usually reluctant to join formal apprenticeship schemes that involve adherence to ministerial guidelines. Adherence to certain standards and procedures could be beneficial to the economy as a whole, but the companies often argue that the additional equipment needed to satisfy general training initiatives may add to their costs but may not benefit them. A reconciliation between these two views can come from voluntary arrangements and training schemes that are designed in consultation with employers.

Firms that target Indonesia's domestic markets tend to be high-tech firms that manufacture such items as vehicles and pharmaceuticals; they are usually foreign or joint ventures. These firms are more likely to offer training, because they produce expensive products or require complicated and precise production processes that require the development of specific skills, such as dexterity, concentration, and judgment. However, even high-tech products and complex production processes demand only a small number of highly skilled personnel. For example, a few well-trained computer and maintenance and repair staff can keep hundreds of barely literate workers busy when these workers' only task is to put the same component in the same slot over and over again.

Indonesia's export-oriented firms tend to be low-tech firms that specialize in producing labor-intensive products, such as garments and shoes, or simple products, such as plywood and processed shrimp. Many of these firms are domestically owned. The simplicity of the production processes or the low cost of the products suggest that sophisticated skills are unnecessary for these firms.

Firms that invest in technology have greater incentives to provide training or to motivate their workers to learn about new processes than firms that use older, more established technologies. The vast majority of Indonesian firms adhere to simple and traditional production processes for which they can pay low wages. Most workers are semiskilled operators and assemblers who are easily trained on the job in a matter of weeks, rather than months, given the relative abundance of the educated unemployed.

## Conclusions

The current public system of vocational and technical education attracts large amounts of public funds, but its impact on economic development is uncertain. Fiscal unsustainability and dependence on project money result in a lack of continuity. Graduates of secondary-level VTE fare as well in the labor market as do graduates from general schools. Since the costs of general education are much lower than the costs of VTE, the social rates of return to general secondary education should be higher than those for VTE.

This problem is perhaps more understandable in Indonesia than elsewhere. Indonesian VTE systems were developed quickly and were put into practice before they were fully tested. The high rates of economic growth and the initial availability of oil money left little reason to restructure the system. In addition, donors' advice and support were not easy to coordinate. Indonesian policymakers are now aware that the system is not fiscally sustainable or very effective. In the past human resource development attracted considerable attention, and a number of reforms were implemented. These reforms are discussed after we review recent developments in the labor market, which put the prospects for Indonesian labor and human resource development in context.

## The Labor Market

In the past two decades Indonesia easily absorbed a labor force that grew at the rate of 3 percent per year. When female activity rates started increasing, and nearly 10 million women were added to the labor force during the 1980s (compared with fewer than 4 million throughout the 1970s), the pressure on the labor market to create employment was relieved in two main ways. First, the rate of growth of the labor force started to decline because of lower fertility rates (facilitated by family planning) and higher school enrollment rates (brought about by education policies). Enrollments increased because of greater public provision, especially at basic levels and in rural areas, and a laissez-faire attitude toward the expansion of private education at the secondary level and above.

Second, the deregulation package of the late 1980s largely removed provisions that favored import substitution and capital-intensive industries. This created many new jobs. For example, in the first half of the 1980s, growth in manufacturing was driven primarily by the expansion of domestic demand, which accounted for 67 percent of output growth, and of import substitution, which accounted for 16 percent of output growth. Exports accounted for only 13 percent of output growth, while the remaining 4 percent was attributable to technology upgrading. In the second half of the 1980s, exports accounted for 41 percent of output growth and technology for 26 percent. The export effect, particularly pronounced in textiles, was also significant in the wood and chemicals industries. These changes resulted in substantial employment creation in manufacturing.

TABLE 7-5

Occupational and Educational Structure in Manufacturing,
1980 and 1990

(percentage of the labor force)

| Occupation | 1980 | 1990 | Education | 1980 | 1990 |
|---|---|---|---|---|---|
| Professional/technical | 1.0 | 0.4 | Tertiary | 0.5 | 1.6 |
| Managerial/admin- | | | Senior secondary | | |
| istrative | 0.3 | 0.5 | vocational | 2.7 | 5.7 |
| Clerical | 2.1 | 2.9 | Senior secondary general | 2.8 | 8.5 |
| Sales | 1.3 | 0.9 | Junior vocational | 1.4 | 1.1 |
| Service | 2.3 | 0.8 | Junior general | 5.1 | 11.5 |
| Production workers | 91.1 | 93.8 | Primary | 24.3 | 34.8 |
| Others | 2.1 | 0.9 | Below primary | 63.2 | 36.8 |
| Total | 100.0 | 100.0 | | 100.0 | 100.0 |
| Number (millions) | 4.7 | 8.1 | | 4.7 | 8.2 |

*Note:* Figures may have been rounded.
*Source:* 1980 and 1990 censuses.

Employment grew by 2.5 million between 1990 and 1995, while in the preceding five years it had increased by only 1 million.

The result of these two effects was growth driven by exports and favorable to employment creation at more or less constant labor costs. Labor costs did not rise mainly because the education system was expanding faster than the growth of jobs in the formal sector. The significant educational upgrading of the manufacturing labor force (table 7-5) and the reduced distortion in the trade regime explain why Indonesia experienced signs of increasing total factor productivity for the first time in the 1990s.

Despite the relative constancy of wages until the early 1990s, workers increased their overall returns to their labor. Even at stagnant wages, more workers became engaged in wage employment, which constituted an improvement over lower earnings in agriculture or in marginal activities in the informal sector. The annual growth in wage employment was 6 percent in the 1980s; employment in manufacturing and trade increased at more than 10 percent compared with an average of 3 percent employment growth in the economy as a whole.

Workers' labor market outcomes, productivity gains, and economic growth cannot be seen as driven mainly by training interventions. The public training system, put in place in the early 1980s, was by 1990 still vastly underutilized. It has remained largely ineffective for a labor force of more than 70 million.

A more detailed examination of the characteristics and functioning of the labor market can help provide a basis for the design of future training interventions. One way to approach policy design is to pose critical questions about the objectives of education and training interventions or to ask where a market failure is likely to exist. Policymakers are rightly concerned about the following undesirable symptoms: (a) underemployment and unemployment, which can arise from skill deficiencies on the labor supply side; (b) skill shortages and unfilled vacancies on the labor demand side; (c) changes in wages that reflect the interaction of labor demand and labor supply and have a bearing on labor costs and workers' welfare; and (d) credit market failures in the market for training and the fear of poaching of workers by rival firms, which can give rise to underinvestment in skills by workers and employers.

## Can Training Reduce Underemployment?

If we define underemployment as the percentage of the labor force working less than 35 hours a week, more than one in three workers (or 28 million people) fell in this category in 1990 (table 7-6). Underemployment by the year 2000 was projected to be 32 million.

The above definition, however, grossly inflates underemployment. A more appropriate definition of underemployment is those who work short hours and are looking for additional work. As table 7-7 shows, less than 10 percent of workers wanted to work longer hours than they were already working. In addition to workers' unwillingness to work for more hours at current wage rates, conventional statistics overestimate underemployment. People in rural areas often report shorter hours than they actually work. In urban areas many formal sector workers in teaching, the government, and community services are employed for less than 35 hours a week in their main job, but they are engaged in additional employment that escapes statistical enumeration.

Working short hours is particularly prevalent in rural areas. Many rural households, especially in Java, depend on small landholdings as a major source of income. Agriculture has attracted less than 5 percent of total investment since 1980. Most investment has gone to industry, especially to big firms.

TABLE 7-6
Distribution of the Working Population, by Hours Worked,
1980 and 1990
(percent)

| Number of hours worked per week | 1980 total | 1990 | | |
|---|---|---|---|---|
| | | Men | Women | Total |
| Less than 25 | 23 | 16 | 35 | 23 |
| 25–34 | 14 | 14 | 18 | 16 |
| 35–39 | 52 | 58 | 38 | 51 |
| 40 or more | 11 | 11 | 9 | 10 |
| Total | 100 | 100 | 100 | 100 |

Note: Figures may have been rounded.
Source: 1980 and 1990 censuses.

How any training effort can overcome these land and investment constraints is hard to imagine. Even if all underemployment were attributable to skills mismatches and shortages, an expansion of publicly provided training would reduce it only marginally and at great public expense. For example, training 10 percent of the underemployed who are willing to work more would still require a program for nearly 600,000 workers (8 percent of the 10 percent underemployed of 70 million workers). This would affect less than 1 percent of the labor force. If these previously underemployed workers could increase their weekly hours from an average of, say, 20 hours a week to even 40, the total manhours worked in the whole

TABLE 7-7
Percentage of the Employed Seeking More Work,
by Gender and Location, 1990

| Location and gender | Percentage |
|---|---|
| Urban men | 5 |
| Rural men | 11 |
| Urban women | 3 |
| Rural women | 7 |
| Weighted average | 8 |

Source: 1990 census.

economy would increase by only 0.5 percentage points. Existing training programs undertaken in public vocational training centers in rural areas and through mobile training units have high average unit costs (about Rp 300,000). This is twice as much as the annual cost of educating a child, even at the secondary level. Thus training would have only a marginal impact on the reduction of underemployment and at a relatively high cost.

## Do the Unemployed Lack Skills?

Unemployment is an inappropriate labor market indicator in low-income countries with surplus labor that also lack a comprehensive social security system. Few people out of work can afford to seek work. (The combination of "not working" and "seeking work" is needed to qualify a person as "unemployed" by international definition.) The vast majority of Indonesian workers work at whatever jobs they can while trying to improve their employment situation as opportunities arise. Partly for this reason, unemployment is primarily an issue among urban and educated young people from relatively rich families who are looking for their first job.

In 1970 and in 1980 there were approximately 1.0 million unemployed workers. This number had increased to 2.2 million by 1992. This increase mirrors the growth in the labor force in the past three decades from 39 million to more than 70 million. The labor force growth in the 1980s of 3.5 percent per year closely parallels the growth in employment of 3.4 percent per year. So employment constraints have at most contributed only 0.13 percent of the total increase in unemployment (or approximately 150,000 workers). In addition, the unemployment rate has been remarkably constant over time, exhibiting only a cyclical pattern but no discernible trend.

The data profile and an econometric analysis of the unemployed in Indonesia support the views on unemployment cited earlier. That is, unemployment is primarily a phenomenon of the young and educated (table 7-8). The unemployment rates increase among the 15-to-19 age group, when secondary school leavers join the labor force, and then increase further among those ages 20 to 24, when their numbers are reinforced by tertiary education graduates. In the next age group, those ages 25 to 29, the unemployment rate drops by nearly two-thirds and becomes virtually zero at older ages.

Education-specific unemployment rates have changed little over time. If anything, rates have declined for nearly all age groups and for both sexes

TABLE 7-8
Unemployment Rates, by Age Group and Education, 1990
(percent)

| Age group | Unemployment | Education level | Unemployment |
|---|---|---|---|
| 10–14 | 1.5 | No schooling | 0.3 |
| 15–19 | 6.0 | Incomplete primary | 0.6 |
| 20–24 | 9.6 | Completed primary | 1.3 |
| 25–29 | 3.3 | Junior secondary (general) | 4.1 |
| 30–34 | 0.8 | Junior secondary (vocational) | 4.4 |
| 35–39 | 0.4 | Senior secondary (general) | 14.0 |
| 40–44 | 0.3 | Senior secondary (vocational) | 8.3 |
| 45–49 | 0.3 | Diploma | 6.9 |
| 50+ | 0.2 | University degree | 9.7 |
| All ages | 2.5 | All levels | 2.5 |

Source: Labor force survey.

since deregulation. Senior secondary graduates have had significant employment gains, and the apparently better preparedness of vocational graduates for the world of work does not show up in the statistics.

With respect to graduates of tertiary education institutions, it is the increase in the size of tertiary education output, and not an increase in their unemployment rate or the duration of job searches, that has been responsible for the increasing share of tertiary graduates in the unemployment pool. Indonesia now has more than 1,000 postsecondary institutions, and their numbers are growing rapidly. The annual growth rate of degree graduates is 16 percent, followed by 14 percent for diploma graduates (three-year program), and 9 percent for certificate holders (one or two years of study). These expansion rates compare with a labor force growth rate of less than 2 percent.

The average duration of job search among the unemployed has also declined for all education groups. In 1987 it averaged more than ten months, but by 1992 it had declined to nine months. The greatest decline in average duration of unemployment was among those with low levels of education, such as junior secondary school graduates, and the graduates of senior secondary general education programs.

Although graduates of secondary and tertiary institutions represented around 7 percent of those working in manufacturing in 1980, that share had increased to 16 percent by 1990 (table 7-5). Those with less than a primary education lost almost half of their share. Opportunities for improving the quality of workers at lower levels will probably continue to exist for some time. New secondary- and tertiary-level graduates will understandably continue to resist what they regard as downgrading (loss of status and income). Thus the absorption of the unemployed, who are mainly educated, will be gradual unless investment accelerates significantly and more jobs that require more modern skills are created.

To sum up, much of the increase in unemployment has been attributable to the changing demographic characteristics of the labor supply, namely, the increase in the working age population, the increased numbers of people moving from rural to urban areas, the growth of women's share in the labor force, and the increased levels of education among job seekers. From a training perspective, this finding suggests that any mismatch between the output of the education system and labor market needs has changed little, if at all.

## Is the Economy Facing Shortages of Skilled Workers?

Between 1977 and 1990, wage differentials narrowed significantly and for all education levels. In 1990 a male who had completed senior secondary education (which takes at least 12 years) earned on average little more than double the wage of a worker with less than a primary education (table 7-9).

Urban labor markets no longer differentiate between those new entrants who have completed primary schooling and those who have not, and they extend only a small premium to junior secondary school leavers. At the senior secondary level, vocational graduates earn less than do general graduates. Private rates of return for vocational education declined from 1982 to 1989 (McMahon and Boediono 1992) and are about two-thirds of the rates of return to general secondary education. The only category with a relatively resilient premium is university graduates, who continue to enjoy a wage about four times that of an unschooled worker on initial entry into the labor force. However, this is considerably less than the tenfold premium they enjoyed in the 1970s.

Companies do not consider skills shortages to be a major problem. The results of a manufacturing survey (Dhanani 1992) reveal that employers are generally satisfied with secondary school graduates and do not care whether they attended general or vocational schools. Even at the tertiary level, many employers do not expect graduates to possess practical and technical skills.

TABLE 7-9

Wage Differentials, by Education and Gender, Selected Years, 1977–90

(index, less than primary = 100)

| Education completed | Men | | | | Women | | | |
|---|---|---|---|---|---|---|---|---|
| | 1977 | 1982 | 1987 | 1990 | 1977 | 1982 | 1987 | 1990 |
| Less than primary | 100 | 100 | 100 | 100 | 100 | 100 | 100 | 100 |
| Primary | 151 | 142 | 128 | 122 | 149 | 151 | 128 | 126 |
| Junior secondary | 275 | 203 | 170 | 158 | 396 | 290 | 225 | 203 |
| Senior (general) | 245 | 249 | 212 | 214 | 380 | 368 | 304 | 287 |
| Senior (vocational) | 328 | 262 | 214 | 209 | 483 | 375 | 348 | 319 |
| Tertiary | 1,033 | 410 | 372 | 366 | 1,428 | 582 | 551 | 508 |

*Source:* Labor force surveys.

Our previous discussion on the compression of wage differentials over time supports the view that, from the employers' perspective, opportunities for education outside the firm are significant. Competition in the job market has increased because of changing demographics as discussed earlier. Thus workers are motivated to increase their educational attainment or attend training courses in the hopes of landing a job in the still small formal sector, and firms can avoid having to offer their workers specialized training—something especially important to small firms. The training courses workers attend tend to be focused, short, and relatively inexpensive.

Many local surveys reveal that skills upgrading, when required, is primarily internal. Firms rely on in-service training and internal labor markets. Firms are more likely to hire skilled workers from among job seekers than by poaching workers from other companies. Firms did not cite poaching as a major reason for not providing training. Manufacturing enterprises had poached only 1 percent of their skilled workers and 2 percent of their supervisors and technicians during an 18-month period (Dhanani 1992). The firms that did cite poaching as a reason for not providing training were all private Indonesian firms in low-tech sectors, precisely the sectors for which skills are more readily available in the open labor market. The highest incidence of poaching was from firms that were experiencing slow growth in either employment or output. This suggests that the poaching of workers does not depend only on other firms' actions, but also on workers' willingness to leave when their firms are under stress. This can be

TABLE 7-10

Ranking of Production Problems by Manufacturing Firms, 1992

| Rank | Problem |
|------|---------|
| 1 | Quality of raw materials |
| 2 | Quality of final products |
| 3 | Delays in delivery of materials |
| 4 | Availability of electricity and water |
| 5 | Quality of skills of operators and assemblers |
| 6 | Missed production deadlines |
| 7 | Quality of skills of supervisors |
| 8 | Quality of skills of managers; waste of materials |
| 9 | Quality of skills of technicians; quality of machinery; careless use of equipment; absenteeism |

*Source:* Dhanani (1992).

taken as an indication of efficiency: workers find employment where their wages (and, by implication, their productivity) are highest. A tracer study of science and technology graduates (Dhanani 1995a) also concluded that the fear of poaching is not widespread and that employers are likely to be able to pass on some of the costs of training to their employees.

Firms have no effective demand for trained personnel, at least in the types of jobs generally filled by graduates of public vocational centers. A 1989 survey of manufacturing firms found that 31 percent of respondents said lack of skills were problematic (World Bank 1991). This problem ranked only seventh in a list of twelve production problems (and ninth among export-oriented establishments). In the 1991 manufacturing survey (Dhanani 1992), manufacturing firms ranked the quality of skilled workers and operators fifth among the problems they faced (table 7-10).

Those workers already employed do not become unemployed because of a failure to update their skills. In 1980 only half of the unemployed were new entrants into the labor force, but their share had increased to three-quarters by 1990.

*Are Workers Underinvesting in Training?*

Workers may be prohibited from investing in upgrading their skills if unit costs are high. Although demand for training may be buoyant, it may be unmet. Coupled with credit market failures, workers' underinvestment in training can result in serious social losses in the form of workers' lifetime earnings and lower rates of growth stemming from higher labor costs, and possibly from low capital investment in technology. Although credit market failures constitute a serious policy concern and a legitimate reason for certain forms of intervention, there is no evidence to indicate that the amount of private training is insignificant, although we cannot say whether it is still socially optimal.

In 1995, 1.5 million trainees attended private training centers supervised by the Ministry of Manpower and the Ministry of Education and Culture. According to the Indonesian Socioeconomic Survey, expensive training courses, such as those in industrial crafts, have the lowest excess demand. Excess demand is highest for courses in service occupations, which are relatively cheap to provide. Many private training providers offer them at low cost. Among those who would like to be trained but are not currently enrolled in training courses, more than two-thirds stated that they would like to pursue courses in computers, languages, business, or home economics. Training in crafts and industrial skills accounted for less than 15 percent of the excess demand for training.

Underinvestment in training may take the form of low-quality training. This has often been cited as a characteristic of privately provided training in Indonesia compared with the more sophisticated training some public vocational centers offer. In an absolute sense this may be correct: quality could be higher if students were charged higher fees, if study programs lasted longer, and if school accreditation and skill certification were more rigorous. However, the low quality of training that derives from the low costs and short duration of training is not necessarily a reason for concern.

Private training centers will not spend the money to upgrade the quality of training if that means students can no longer afford to attend. Their offerings are driven by the demand for training by students, job seekers, workers, and employers. The centers' most common strategy is to offer inexpensively priced short courses, rather than complete programs. Students, however, may eventually complete a comprehensive program by taking a full set of courses over a number of years. The 1992 survey of private training centers found that median course length was only 72 hours, and the median course fee was Rp 70,000 (US$35). A few longer, more expensive courses raise the average course length to 109 hours with an average fee of Rp 145,000 (US$73). The same survey showed that trainees took such courses when they had spare time, such as during school holidays or between graduating from school and starting university. Thus training complements the education provided by more formal education institutions.

## Are Employers Underinvesting in Skills?

Enterprises often provide extensive training. According to the Ministry of Education and Culture, approximately 2,500 companies operate their own training centers. Ministry of Manpower data suggest that as many as 230,000 trainees are participating in company training. These figures relate more to formal training, and they grossly underestimate in-service training. In a survey of manufacturing enterprises conducted in 1989 (World Bank 1991), 50 percent of the companies surveyed reported providing formal and informal in-service training. The 1991 manufacturing survey (Dhanani 1992) found that 10 to 15 percent of companies had formal training programs with specialized training staff, classrooms, and workshops. These figures are quite high given that at least one-third of the manufacturing work force is classified as unskilled, half are on casual or daily contracts, much training may take place informally, and systems for tracking training activities are not well developed.

Assuming that half of the manufacturing work force is on some form of permanent contract (employers are usually not interested in training casual or temporary workers) and that 10 percent of permanent workers require training in a single year, then medium and large manufacturing firms would have to train approximately 175,000 workers of the 3.5 million they currently employ. Similarly, with respect to the entire formal sector, 400,000 of the work force of 8 million would require training.

By comparing these training needs with the 230,000 people reported as company-based trainees by the Ministry of Manpower alone, one gets an idea of the relatively high levels of in-service training. Training is also high considering the large amount of private pre-employment training taking place in Indonesia.

Estimating how much firms spend on training is difficult. However, sporadic data suggest that firms that employ more than 200 workers spend about 1.7 percent of their payroll on in-service training. For small firms the amount is closer to 1 percent. This is because small firms employ more workers on a casual and piece-rate basis and more unskilled workers. They also hire more women, and since women are more likely to leave the labor force than men, they are offered less training. Training expenditure of 1 percent of the payroll is comparable to the amount spent on training by firms in industrial countries and in the newly industrializing countries.

The ratio of wages to value added in Indonesia's manufacturing sector was relatively constant from 1986 through 1992, when it stood at 21.3 percent. A 1 percent increase in expenditures on training would increase labor costs only by one-fifth of 1 percent. In most cases firms would be willing to incur such an increase in costs if the need arose.

## Will Shortages of Skilled Workers Emerge Soon?

To ascertain whether Indonesia is likely to encounter a shortage of skilled workers in the near future, one can examine the stock of various categories of skilled workers in manufacturing and compare it to the annual output of such workers by the education system. Less than 1 percent of the employees of medium and large manufacturing firms are scientists and engineers. Since such firms employ some 3.5 million workers, around 24,000 of them will be scientists and engineers. A 10 percent growth in manufacturing employment in the next few years will mean employment opportunities for an additional 2,500 scientists and engineers. The annual supply of science and engineering graduates is about 14,000. A shortage of engineers for manufacturing needs is thus unlikely in the foreseeable future. Indeed, many graduates may have to start their careers as technicians, for which demand appears to be quite strong.

Shortages of skilled trades workers (industrial and vehicle mechanics, lathe operators, machine setters, electricians, and so on) are also unlikely. Annual demand is around 40,000. This compares with an annual output from technical senior secondary schools of 153,000.

Finally, semiskilled and unskilled workers, who form more than three-quarters of manufacturing employment, can be recruited easily among senior secondary school graduates regardless of the type of school they have attended.

If Indonesia were encountering skills bottlenecks, wage differentials between skilled and unskilled workers would be increasing and vacancy rates would be high. However, wage differentials are small and have been declining (table 7-11). In the early 1970s, skilled blue-collar workers were paid two to three times as much as unskilled laborers, supervisors were paid three to four times as much, and professionals were paid five to ten times as much. By 1992, however, all these differentials had declined substantially. Overall vacancy rates in the manufacturing sector are small—only 3 percent for skilled operators, 8 percent for tradespeople, and 5 percent for supervisors and technicians. These figures apply to Indonesian firms only. Foreign firms apparently do not have vacancies in these fields.

TABLE 7-11
Wage Differentials, by Skill, 1970 and 1992
(index, unskilled laborers = 100)

| Skill level | 1970 | 1992 |
|---|---|---|
| Unskilled workers | 100 | 100 |
| Skilled workers | 200–300 | 150–200 |
| Supervisors | 300–400 | 200–250 |
| Professionals | 500–900 | 300–400 |

Source: 1970: Manning (1979); 1992: Dhanani (1995b).

## Is the Scarcity of Skilled Workers Deterring Foreign Investment?

Indonesia has been able to attract substantial amounts of foreign investment, especially since deregulation in the late 1980s. Table 7-12 summarizes the views of international investors on the quality, availability, and
costs of production labor and managerial labor in Indonesia and ten other
Asian economies. In most of the economies, foreign investors do not see
the quality of production labor as a major problem, although Indonesia

TABLE 7-12
Labor Ratings in Selected Asian Countries, 1991
(best grade possible = 1, worst grade possible = 10)

| Economy | Production labor | | | Managerial labor | | |
|---|---|---|---|---|---|---|
| | Quality | Availability | Cost | Quality | Availability | Cost |
| China | 5 | 1 | 1 | 10 | 10 | 1 |
| Hong Kong (China) | 1 | 10 | 8 | 1 | 10 | 10 |
| Indonesia | 5 | 1 | 1 | 10 | 10 | 2 |
| Japan | 1 | 10 | 10 | 1 | 1 | 10 |
| Korea, Republic of | 1 | 8 | 7 | 5 | 10 | 9 |
| Malaysia | 3 | 3 | 3 | 5 | 5 | 5 |
| Philippines | 3 | 1 | 2 | 3 | 1 | 1 |
| Singapore | 1 | 10 | 8 | 1 | 10 | 8 |
| Taiwan (China) | 1 | 9 | 8 | 1 | 8 | 9 |
| Thailand | 4 | 2 | 1 | 10 | 10 | 4 |
| Viet Nam | 3 | 1 | 1 | 10 | 5 | 1 |

Source: International Herald Tribune, July 29, 1991; based on research by Political and
Economic Risk Consultancy, Ltd.

and China received the worst ratings in this category. Availability and cost, however, are worrying employers in those economies where labor shortages have emerged, namely, Hong Kong (China), Japan, Singapore, Republic of Korea, and Taiwan (China). Some availability problems are beginning to arise in Malaysia and Thailand but not in Indonesia.

In Indonesia foreign investors are more concerned about the complicated and time-consuming process of licensing. In addition, some Indonesian policies limit the productive capacities of foreign joint ventures and restrict their marketing advantage. China, India, and Viet Nam can take advantage of this in the meantime. To employ an expatriate in Indonesia, firms must submit three applications: to the Ministry of Manpower, to the Municipal Manpower Office, and to the Population Affairs Office. In short, foreign firms are somewhat concerned with workers' skills in Indonesia, but they experience significant difficulties with red tape and access to other local inputs and supplies.

## Conclusions

Indonesia faces two serious problems. Underemployment, although not as high as the conventional definition would suggest, is perhaps the biggest challenge in the labor market, and unemployment is becoming an important issue, especially among urban youth. However, the labor market is providing clear signals as to the direction in which training and more general human resource policies and reform should move. Growth will address the problem of underemployment. Practically the entire increase in unemployment in the past 30 years can be explained by labor supply factors: the changes in the population structure (age and residence); the increase in the labor force participation rate, particularly by women; and an increase in skills availability as proxied by falling wage differentials between those with different skill and education levels. Individual demand for training has been high, as has been the response by private providers. Employers provide add-on training that is sufficient to raise the quality of school leavers so that they meet employers' requirements. These observations pave the way for our discussion of reforms and policy directions for the future.

## Major Issues

The government has already set its policy agenda. It is contemplating changes in VTE, the operations of public vocational centers, and the role of the private sector in financing training. The planning of training is also moving away from manpower forecasts toward practices that place more emphasis on labor market analysis.

## The Dual System

In July 1994 the system of vocational and technical education in Indonesia began to be reoriented as a dual system. The government targeted approximately 250 vocational and technical schools and also expected some 6,000 small and medium companies to participate. Under the scheme students will spend some time working in companies as apprentices. Schools will select the students and seek apprentice slots for them with employers. The apprenticeships will run for three to four years, the typical duration of studies in a senior secondary VTE school. The dual system is based on the view that, on the supply side, it can alleviate future shortages in critical skills, and, on the demand side, that the private sector is unable to appreciate the value of training or its national role in providing training.

Early information on the dual system suggests that it is going to become a complex system with multiple objectives. It aims to increase the ability of the education system to cater to the very diverse needs of the formal sector, the informal sector, emerging technologies, employers' immediate technical production requirements, and students' aspirations. This will not be easy to achieve, though it is not impossible. However, the government has not yet carried out a complete cost-benefit analysis of the dual system. The unit cost as currently estimated may reach approximately Rp 15 million per graduate for the full four years in a vocational senior secondary school, which is more than ten times the cost of completing the general cycle in a senior secondary school.

In addition to unit costs, the success of the dual system will depend on four issues. The first is whether employers are willing to train the apprentices the schools supply. Even if employers could be convinced to take on young apprentices, the quality of training they will provide to students may be questionable. In a labor market where workers are contracted primarily on a daily and casual basis, long-term employment relationships are lacking, and most firms' workers use traditional production processes, training may be offered by near novices to actual novices.

Second, companies may try to mitigate the costs of training apprentices by asking the best vocational senior secondary schools to send a few of their top students. Given that the dual system would target the best technical schools, it could become elitist. This scheme could be an expensive way to develop skills, and it runs the risk of neglecting the needs of the bulk of the student population. In addition, the top students from the best technical schools are almost certain to proceed to higher education. This will leave employers with the weaker students and will reinforce their reluctance to participate in the scheme.

Third, the dual system may be constrained by the views of students (and their parents). Vocational and technical education has low status in Indonesia. Student demand for education and training is driven by available or expected employment opportunities. Because technology is continuously restructuring what people do in the workplace, students do not generally believe it is useful to concentrate on a specific set of skills early on.

The final issue is equity. One premise for intervention in VTE is that the private sector predominates in regions of high market demand—that is, where parents can afford to pay and labor markets are thriving. Indeed, private schools are concentrated in urban and industrialized areas. Urban areas of East Java have four or five times as many private VTE schools as public ones, but some rural areas have one or less than one private school for every public school. However, the presence of public schools does not necessarily solve the issue of equity. The Ministry of Education and Culture and U.S. Agency for International Development study (MOEC and USAID 1992) indicated that more students were enrolled in private than in public general secondary schools outside Java, and that these students were more likely to be from the lower socioeconomic levels of society. These are exactly the two areas (general education and poorer students) where the public sector is expected to be more prevalent: "Students from the highest socioeconomic strata were over-represented in public relative to private STMs [technical schools] in all three provinces. The most expensive type of education was therefore disproportionately taken up by the more affluent" (MOEC and USAID 1992).

## Ministry of Manpower Reforms

The Ministry of Manpower is planning reforms in two areas of training that are important in the present context. The aims of the first set of reforms are as follows: diversify and expand the role of the vocational training centers to accommodate local conditions; change their organizational structure; upgrade training from low- to middle-level skills; and enable the centers to place graduates in jobs, establish industry links, and trace the fate of trainees after graduation. The second set of reforms includes establishing an apprenticeship scheme.

The ministry has not yet fully worked out the practical steps of the first set of reforms, and formal analysis is premature at this time. However, several positive aspects are already emerging. The planned switch of student placement from the Ministry of Manpower's district offices to the vocational training centers is clearly a change in the right direction. The current arrangements do not benefit students, and they isolate training instructors from the labor market. Furthermore, if the placement reforms are properly implemented, there should be no budgetary implications, because existing resources devoted to placement activities will be transferred from one organization to the others.

By far the most important planned reform for the public vocational training centers is the apprenticeship scheme. Although the Ministry of Manpower has always had a program to place students with employers for in-service training, it was never fully implemented, and to a great extent it was supply led rather than demand led. The new scheme, however, is envisioned as company-based training using the BLKs and KLKs to support the companies in their training efforts. The interesting issue is: who will be responsible for the costs of training? The current plan provides for cost sharing between the government and employers. While the division of costs is not known at this stage, companies would probably pay for instructors' honoraria and transport costs, training materials, and facilities, while the government would pay for BLK facilities, office costs, training software, and instructor and administrative staff salaries. The two parties would split the costs of instructor housing, training planning, and skill certification and program monitoring. The apprenticeship scheme represents a move by the BLKs toward on-the-job training, but to what extent it constitutes a departure from the emphasis on pre-employment training is not yet clear. Information about employers' willingness to finance the scheme and workers' willingness to participate in such training is lacking. It is not known whether the apprenticeship scheme will take place with the cooperation of private firms or in government enterprises.

### Financing Training through Levy-Grant Schemes

The government introduced a levy-grant scheme in East Java in 1992 with a view to expanding the scheme to other provinces. The East Java regulations require firms to pay a levy that will be used for their own training purposes. Although companies that already provide training for their employees can opt out of paying the full levy, they still have to pay that portion of the levy that finances the training of job seekers and informal sector workers. Thus the aim of the scheme is not only to create awareness about training and to develop a system driven by the private sector, but also to subsidize training for different groups of workers.

The usefulness of the scheme will depend on whether it becomes a tax on employers and whether additional training will be offered. For example, some employers may engage in token training to reduce their contributions to the fund.

In a levy-grant scheme it is desirable to keep the revenues in a dedicated account. This has not been the case in East Java, where the funds collected have become part of general provincial revenues. They are then allocated at the discretion of government representatives. Instead of committees dominated by government representatives, the private sector should decide which training activities will be funded by the levy-grant revenues, and it should manage the scheme.

Between November 1992, when the levy-grant scheme became effective, and October 1994, nearly 2,000 companies had paid the levy out of an estimated 20,000 that should have paid. More than Rp 850 million had been collected, a relatively small amount considering that it took two years to get this money. Apparently, employers do not consider the scheme's benefits to be worth its costs to them. The number of people trained was also small, fewer than 1,000. Finally, unit costs seem to be high, averaging Rp 900,000. No information on the duration of training is available, but publicly provided training is typically of short duration (lasting from a day to a couple of weeks).

Ideally, training funded by the levy-grant scheme would be in areas where the private sector is absent—that is, where a market failure exists. By 1995 eight training courses had been conducted for job seekers in fields such as the garment industry, beauty, and handicrafts—the low-cost areas easily served by existing providers. More than half of the 35 training programs offered to companies were for supervisory management. The rest included a fair number of other management courses, such as leadership, marketing management, and job analysis.

## Planning

In the past, manpower planning relied to a considerable extent on the manpower requirements approach. The Ministry of Manpower has an economywide manpower demand model that it uses to derive projections of output growth, productivity, and employment. The Ministry of Planning has its own manpower model for monitoring and projecting employment creation using similar industry, occupation, and education matrices. The Ministry of Education and Culture uses a third model.

A major issue for manpower projections in a country like Indonesia is the presence of a sizable informal sector with proven ability to adjust swiftly to changing economic conditions. The economy has shown a remarkable degree of adjustment that makes attempts to derive projections futile and reduces the reliability of forecasts for planning purposes. In addition, the projections are based on an uncomfortable level of aggregation (usually "one-digit" occupations and industries and broad education levels) and outdated information (most often censuses). Gijsberts (1993) and Paauw (1991) have found that sectoral employment elasticities (the response of employment to output changes) vary as much as 500 percent between adjacent periods of time and are often negative. A comparison of projections of shortages and surpluses made at the beginning of one five-year plan with actual outcomes at the end of the plan showed that manpower estimates wrongly predicted half of the changes. Random selection could have resulted in the same outcome.

Reforms should increasingly take into account private training efforts, which so far have not been fully integrated with public provision and financing decisions. This has sometimes resulted in a wasteful oversupply of skills or a crowding out of the private sector. Many of the VTE and apprenticeship plans target areas that are particularly well catered to by the private sector (for example, secretarial, retail, tourism, and dressmaking courses). Instruction in these subjects is already plentiful and is provided in a cost-effective manner, often through employers. Of course, labor market analysis and the incorporation of the private sector would require a better information system, an issue that need not occupy us here.

## Conclusions

The wave of training reforms in Indonesia in the early 1990s was a natural extension of policymakers' interest in improving the performance of the human resource development system. Policymakers moved in the right direction by bringing about greater coordination among government agencies, greater participation by the private sector, and more emphasis on demand-driven, cost-effective schemes.

Public policy will need to identify relatively soon the strengths and weaknesses of the current human resource development system. Our analysis suggests that the country's strength beyond basic education lies in the large private education and training sectors. In this context public policy should be directed less at the direct provision of training and more on the financing and regulatory side. The government can address market failures in the areas of credit markets, skills standards, accreditation of training centers, certification of workers, and occupational licensing. Such interventions should be decided on after close consultation with employers, and they should take into account broad policy objectives, such as equity considerations among job seekers and various groups of workers.

As skills requirements become more complex, the importance of the allocative, rather than the productive, aspect of education and training increases. The former refers to workers' ability to adapt to new techniques and use new information, while the latter deals with narrow, technical aspects directly relevant to production. In this respect training in specific skills is a poor substitute for general education. Skills training addresses narrow situations that can quickly become outdated, and usually it costs more to provide than general education. Therefore, training in occupation-specific skills should be carefully designed: it should take place late in the education system, it should be decentralized, and it should be determined by specific company requirements and specific demands by workers.

Public policy cannot prevent future shortages of critical skills, but even new technologies can be adopted swiftly if the work force has the necessary general education skills. Because productive learning does not end with formal schooling, the education system must provide sufficient mastery in verbal and numerical skills upon which lifetime training can build. The role of public policy is to ensure that children leave school with an adequate education. In 1995 nearly 3 million students left school before they had completed the basic education cycle of nine years. This is the most serious constraint Indonesia will face for decades ahead.

Another issue is whether training should be geared toward highly technical skills. The answer depends on whether a sufficiently clear national technology policy exists. Technology policy can be defined as a comprehensive and consistent set of official guidelines, measures, and instruments that affect the choice, acquisition, creation, and application of technology throughout the economy. Although the Indonesian government treats technology and employment as critical issues, pertinent policies are not yet fully developed, and the relationship between the two areas is not always clear. Policymakers often perceive technology somewhat narrowly. They also emphasize the training of scientists and researchers in such fields as nuclear physics, remote sensing, and aeronautics, and the creation of sophisticated laboratories. However, they do not provide specific suggestions on selecting and applying technologies—technologies that would create jobs and income. The instruments required to distribute income more equitably have not been fully developed. In the 1980s it took about US$135,000 of targeted investment to create an additional job in base metal, machinery, or the chemical industries; the same employment effect in small industry could have come at an investment of only US$630.

Even well-conceived national training policies will not be able to prevent temporary shortages of skilled workers in critical areas, since such shortages are present in neighboring countries. Hong Kong (China) and Singapore, which are noted for their aggressive training policies, have experienced temporary shortages of skilled workers. When computer experts and engineers were in short supply in Hong Kong (China), the government approved the employment of foreign professionals. Indonesia will undoubtedly face similar situations, but the solution does not lie in stockpiling workers with skills that may or may not be needed. Even training policies that prove to be successful in creating critical skills may, through emigration, help meet demands for skilled workers in countries where wages for high-tech skills are higher. To the extent that investment in critical skills is undertaken privately, the government has little role to play either directly in the market for training or indirectly through emigration control. However, if individuals acquire these skills with the support of public funds, they may substitute private investment and satisfy private objectives instead of social goals. Public funds spent in this way may end up subsidizing production in other countries, some of which are Indonesia's competitors in world markets.

## References

Clark, D. H. 1985. "Policy Suggestions from a Tracer Study of BLK Graduates." Jakarta: Ministry of Manpower.

Dhanani, S. 1992. *Findings of the 1991 Manufacturing Employment and Training Survey in West Java, North Sumatra, and East Java.* Jakarta: Regional Manpower and Planning and Training Project.

———. 1995a. "Employment, Remuneration, and Training of Technical Graduates in Indonesia: Findings of a 1994 Tracer Study." Jakarta: Regional Manpower and Planning and Training Project.

———. 1995b. "Skilled/Unskilled Wage Differentials." Jakarta: Regional Manpower and Planning Training Project.

Gijsberts, I. 1993. *Macroeconomic Modeling of Employment.* Jakarta: Ministry of Manpower, United Nations Development Programme, and International Labour Office.

Manning, Chris. 1979. "Wage Differentials and Labor Market Segmentation in Indonesian Manufacturing." Ph.D. thesis, Research School of Pacific and Asian Studies, Australian National University, Canberra.

McMahon, W. W., and G. Boediono. 1992. "Market Signals and Labor Market Analysis: A View of Manpower Supply and Demand." In W. W. McMahon and Boediono, eds., *Education and the Economy: The External Efficiency of Education.* Jakarta: Ministry of Education and Culture and U.S. Agency for International Development.

MOEC (Ministry of Education and Culture) and USAID (U.S. Agency for International Development). 1992. *A Study of the Quality and Efficiency of Secondary Education in Indonesia.* Jakarta.

Paaum, D. 1991. *Employment in the Manufacturing and Trade Sectors.* Jakarta: Ministry of Manpower, United Nations Development Programme, and International Labour Office.

Patrinos, H. A., and D. H. Clark. 1995. "Vocational Training Centers of the Ministry of Manpower." Background notes. World Bank, Education and Social Policy Department, Washington, D.C.

World Bank. 1991. *Indonesia Employment and Training: Foundations for Industrialization in the 1990s.* Document 9350-IND. East Asia Department. Washington, D.C.

# 8 Malaysia

HONG W. TAN AND INDERMIT S. GILL

MALAYSIA'S ECONOMY experienced a sharp turnaround between the 1985–86 recession and the currency crisis in the late 1990s. With gross domestic product growth averaging about 9 percent per year between 1987 and 1995, the economy created almost 2 million jobs (more than 10 percent of Malaysia's population of 19.5 million). A large share of those jobs was in the manufacturing sector. Labor force growth of about 2.9 percent per year, fueled by increased female labor-force participation, was outstripped by a 3.5 percent rate of growth of employment between 1985 and 1994. Per capita income during this period increased by almost 6 percent per year to more than US$3,500 by 1995. In addition, the structure of the economy changed considerably. Between 1980 and 1994 the share of agriculture fell from 22 to 14 percent, while the share of manufacturing rose from 21 to 32 percent. The changes in the sectoral shares of employment were even sharper (table 8-1). The importance of government employment also declined. These developments are testimony to the successful transition of the economy from being mainly a primary goods producer—rubber, palm oil, and tin—to the newest East Asian tiger.

The current crisis is testing Malaysia's determination to continue its policy of export-led development. Although the sharp devaluation of the ringgit has resulted in a preoccupation with the immediate future, especially with regard to capital flows and investment, policymakers will likely return to the problems related to labor markets and skills when the crisis is contained. This chapter abstracts from short-term concerns and focuses on the longer term issues of labor demand, education, and training.

TABLE 8-1
Sectoral Employment Shares, Selected Years, 1970–94
(percent)

| Sector | 1970 | 1975 | 1980 | 1985 | 1990 | 1994 |
|---|---|---|---|---|---|---|
| Agriculture | 51 | 45 | 37 | 30 | 26 | 20 |
| Manufacturing | 11 | 13 | 15 | 15 | 20 | 25 |
| Services | 28 | 31 | 36 | 42 | 43 | 42 |
| Other | 10 | 11 | 12 | 13 | 11 | 13 |

Source: World Bank (1995).

In the 1970s and 1980s Malaysia achieved remarkable progress in education. From 1970 to 1995 primary school enrollment ratios rose from 87 to 100 percent, and secondary school enrollment ratios rose from 34 to 60 percent. Despite their success in both the economic and social areas, policymakers are not complacent. Malaysia has declared that it expects to achieve industrial country status by 2020. As a result of the rapid growth of private sector jobs, the government's policy stance has shifted from a preoccupation with creating employment to one where the upgrading of skills now occupies center stage. Malaysia also recognizes that it may not be able to compete with countries such as China and India in supplying goods that are intensive in the use of low-wage unskilled and semiskilled labor. Thus policymakers increasingly seek strategies to move "up market." Education and training lie at the core of these strategies.

The changing employment pattern and rapid job growth have contributed to a tightening of the labor market. Unemployment rates are the most obvious indicator of this, falling from more than 12 percent in 1985 to less than 3 percent in 1995. Vacancy rates confirm this: in 1987 about 75 percent of reported vacancies in manufacturing were filled within a year; by 1993, 75 percent of vacancies went unfilled. The quit rate remains high, indicating especially high turnover for several categories of skilled workers and professionals, and there are stories of worker poaching in the press. However, labor market tightness is best captured by wage movements. Survey results show that from 1987 to 1992 the average real wage rose 46 percent, while manufacturing sector wages rose 55 percent. Rising wages are not worrisome if productivity growth keeps pace, because this ensures that firms' profitability is not compromised. However, unit labor costs (labor costs deflated by worker productivity) may have risen considerably.

With continuous exchange rate adjustment becoming less of an option, maintaining competitiveness requires a greater effort to upgrade workers' skills.

Between 1987 and 1993 the wages of skilled and semiskilled workers rose by about 10.0 percent per year, those of managers and professionals by about 7.5 percent, and those of unskilled workers by less than 5.0 percent. There are many reasons, not all of which have implications for vocational education and training (VET). First, high rates of investment may have disproportionately increased the demand for technical and managerial personnel relative to unskilled workers. Alternatively, perhaps fewer substitutes are available for technical and managerial workers, and thus an increase in the demand for workers translates into higher wages for a given supply. Unless technology choice has been distorted by policy, these are not "problems" that can or should be corrected by changes in VET supply. However, the supply response of skilled workers to higher wages may be lower than that of unskilled workers, especially in an economy where the shrinking agriculture and plantation sectors have supplied urban areas with labor for the past two decades, and where immigration has been used to ensure a cheap supply of unskilled labor. This would definitely have implications for the VET system.

A World Bank (1995) study disentangles the effects of these three possible influences and draws the following conclusions. First, it is not the level or pattern of investment that has pushed up the wages of skilled workers. In fact, estimates of labor demand indicate that increases in fixed investment raise the demand for unskilled workers more than for skilled workers.

Second, although the demand for skilled workers is less elastic, the magnitudes imply that only a small fraction of the rising wage gap between skilled workers and unskilled workers can be explained by differential demand elasticities.

Third, the most important determinant of the difference in wage growth is the smaller supply elasticity of skilled workers. Estimates indicate that managerial and technical workers have the smallest supply elasticities, followed by skilled workers, then semiskilled workers, and then unskilled workers. Not surprisingly, surveys have indicated that foreign firms in Malaysia view the supply of skilled workers as a serious difficulty (table 8-2).

Improving the supply responses for the required skill categories requires changes in both higher education and VET. With regard to VET, the focus of this chapter, there are various policy concerns: the shortage of techni-

TABLE 8-2
Difficulties Faced by Japanese Firms in East Asia, 1993

| Difficulty | Malaysia | Thailand | Indonesia | Philippines | China |
|---|---|---|---|---|---|
| Labor supply | XXX | XXX | X X | XX | — |
| Employment restrictions | XXX | — | X | — | — |
| Infrastructure | X | XXX | XX | XXX | XXX |
| Inflation | X | X | X | XXX | — |
| Ownership restrictions | X | X | XX | X | — |
| Political risk | — | — | — | XXX | X |

XXX More than 50 percent of responses.
XX Between 35 and 50 percent of responses.
X Between 20 and 34 percent of responses.
—Less than 20 percent of responses.
*Source:* World Bank (1996).

cians, skilled workers, and semiskilled workers and the need for skills upgrading; the inability of public training institutions to meet employers'
demands; and the growing recognition that the private sector will have to
play a greater role in meeting its own skill needs. In the area of industrial
development, policymakers have increasingly recognized the importance
of having a skilled and trained work force to deepen the technology of
firms, improve the competitiveness of small and medium firms, and continue to attract foreign direct investment. In response to these concerns,
the government has expanded resources for public training institutions,
and it has introduced a variety of policy initiatives to encourage private
sector training.

## Supply of Trained Workers

Malaysia's skill development strategy has focused, until recently, on increasing
the supply capacity of public education and training institutions to meet
the skill needs of industry. Vocational and technical education and training
are provided by a plethora of institutions under several ministries, each
charged with specific responsibilities. In total, there are 26 government
industrial and skills training institutes. They include the following:

• Ten industrial training institutes (ITIs) and the Center for Instructors
and Advanced Skill Training under the Manpower Department of the Ministry of Human Resources

• Nine MARA skills institutes (Institutes Kemahiran Mara or IKMs) and Pusat Giat MARA under the Ministry of Public Enterprises

• Seven youth training centers (YTCs) under the Ministry of Youth and Sports.

The government has also set up two advanced training centers, the German-Malaysia Institute and the French-Malaysia Institute, in collaboration with the German and French governments. Finally, the Ministry of Education runs 70 vocational schools, 9 technical schools, and 7 polytechnics that provide vocational education similar to that available in the public training institutions.

Table 8-3 provides an overview of the supply of skilled workers from local public education and training institutions. Between 1991 and 1993 these institutions produced a total of more than 146,000 graduates. Of these, education institutions produced almost 47,000 with degrees (32 percent), some 28,000 with diplomas (19 percent), and close to 14,000 with certificates (9 percent). The remaining 57,600, or about 39 percent,

TABLE 8-3

Production of Skilled Workers, by Education and Training Institutions, 1991–95

| Institution | 1991–93 | | 1994–95 | |
|---|---|---|---|---|
| | Number | Percent | Number | Percent |
| *Education institutions* | | | | |
| Degree graduates | 46,810 | 31.9 | 43,038 | 28.4 |
| Engineering-related | 3,940 | — | 4,770 | — |
| Diploma graduates | 28,340 | 19.3 | 25,720 | 17.0 |
| Engineering-related | 5,540 | — | 6,670 | — |
| Certificate graduates | 13,900 | 9.5 | 12,900 | 8.5 |
| Engineering-related | 8,750 | — | 8,150 | — |
| *Public training institutions* | | | | |
| Skilled/semiskilled graduates | 57,600 | 39.3 | 69,970 | 46.1 |
| Engineering trades | 38,380 | — | 48,460 | — |
| Skills upgrading | 920 | — | 1,560 | — |
| Total | 146,650 | 100.0 | 151,628 | 100.0 |

— Not calculated.

*Source:* Economic Planning Unit (1994).

were produced by public training institutions. Between 1994 and 1995 these institutions produced roughly another 151,000 skilled individuals, with the local public training institutions accounting for a significantly higher proportion (46 percent) of graduates. Considering only the graduates with technical- and engineering-related trade training, the skill group most in demand by industry, public training institutions are clearly the principal source of entry-level industrial skills. However, these public training institutions play a relatively minor role in skills upgrading for the existing work force. Between 1991 and 1993 they provided skills upgrading to only 920 trainees. Several surveys of employers in three regions—Klang Valley, Kedah and Perlis, and Pahang—also revealed a low reliance on public training institutions for retraining and skills upgrading. Despite differences in the level of industrial development across regions, employers reported that only between 2 and 7 percent of skilled workers scheduled for training in 1991 were to be trained in public training institutions. In-plant training was the principal source of training (58 to 93 percent). The two other major sources were training by the parent company (2 to 6 percent) and by equipment vendors (2 to 13 percent), each source being as important or more important than public training institutions.

Table 8-4 shows the output of skilled and semiskilled graduates from these public training institutions. Together, the public training institutions

TABLE 8-4

Production of Skilled Workers, by Public Training Institutions, 1991–95

(number)

| Institution | 1991–93 | 1994–95 |
|---|---|---|
| Industrial training institutes | 6,940 | 5,659 |
| Engineering trades | 2,755 | 2,787 |
| Institutes Kemahiran Mara | 9,905 | 8,225 |
| Engineering trades | 6,879 | 6,293 |
| Youth training centers | 1,254 | — |
| Engineering trades | 971 | — |
| Ministry of Education technical schools | 12,549 | 21,205 |
| Engineering trades | 9,478 | 15,057 |
| Ministry of Education vocational schools | 28,633 | 36,287 |
| Engineering trades | 16,221 | 22,653 |

— Not available.

Source: Economic Planning Unit, unpublished data.

under the Ministry of Human Resources, MARA, and the Ministry of Youth and Sports produce about 7,000 trainees per year with various technical skills, primarily at the basic and intermediate levels. The Ministry of Education's vocational and technical schools produce twice as many trainees per year. All these institutions provide training in overlapping technical and trade areas, including engineering trades (mechanical, electrical, and civil), building, printing, agriculture, and commerce-related trades. Of these, the engineering-related trades are the most prevalent, accounting for between one-half and two-thirds of all training provided in each public training institution.

## Basic Training versus Advanced Skill Training

Higher level skills will increasingly be needed for Malaysian industry to move toward higher value-added production. What role have public training institutions played in supplying these higher level industrial skills? Not all trainees of public institutions take the trade tests administered by the National Vocational Training Council (NVTC), but those who do include trainees from small training programs in other government ministries, the army training center, private training institutes, and places of employment. This latter group of providers is not inconsequential. In terms of output of skilled workers in 1993, as many trainees of private training institutes took the NVTC trade tests as did trainees from the ITIs (4,700 compared with 4,695 trainees).

The test data indicate considerable expansion in the output of trainees at the basic and intermediate skill levels but not at the advanced skill level. The number of trainees taking the NVTC trade test each year at the basic skill level increased fivefold between 1981 and 1993, from about 5,400 trainees in 1981 to 24,500 by 1993. The corresponding increase in the annual numbers of test takers at the intermediate skill level was somewhat less, rising from 1,200 trainees in 1981 to 4,200 by 1993. However, the number taking the trade tests at the advanced skill level rose from only 38 in 1981 to 120 trainees in 1993, when they represented just over half of 1 percent of all NVTC test takers.

The low production of graduates with advanced-level skill training is a matter of some concern. Highly trained technical personnel play multiple roles in industry as supervisors, as trainers of other less skilled workers, and as implementers of new technologies. A shortfall in highly skilled workers will constrain companies' ability to move toward higher value-added, more technology-intensive, production. The government has recognized this, and several centers for advanced skills training have been set up by various ministries and by the government in collaboration with Germany and France. However, even when these centers reach full capacity, their output of trainees with advanced-level skills is unlikely to be adequate.

## Coordination of VET

The NVTC was established in 1989 to promote and coordinate vocational and industrial skills training programs. The NVTC has initiated the establishment of interagency committees to consult on issues relating to training and trade certification, and it has carried out several surveys with a broader focus than the tracer studies that individual ministries have conducted for training institutions under their purview. However, the NVTC does not have the legal standing to coordinate training in all public and private training institutions. Private training institutes are supposed to register with the Ministry of Education. Some do, but many others register only with the Registrar of Companies, so few data are available on their training activities.

This coordination problem is not unique to Malaysia. Many countries' training systems are highly fragmented, with different vocational schools and training institutions being operated by different agencies preparing individuals for broadly similar occupations. Examples include Egypt, where six different ministries provide vocational and technical training, and Thailand, which started the 1970s with two public vocational education systems and ended the decade with four, all offering the same certificates and diplomas. Effective national training authorities coordinate training across different public training institutions, and with participation from the private sector, develop strategic plans for training programs to complement key economic strategies, monitor labor market trends, conduct evaluations of training programs to adjust training to meet new skill needs, and develop and maintain databases on public and private training provision to estimate supply capacity.

In Malaysia inadequate policy coordination raises questions about how efficiently resources are being allocated across training institutions. There have been recommendations that the government enact a national vocational training law to strengthen the NVTC, perhaps based on Singapore's Vocational and Industrial Training Board. The board answers to the Singapore Economic Development Board and is empowered under the

1979 Vocational and Industrial Training Board Act to be the national authority for the development, provision, and regulation of industrial training and the registration and regulation of apprenticeship training and private training institutes.

## Evaluating the Performance of Training Institutions

Evaluations of training institutions can inform decisions about how resources should be allocated to them. At the most basic level, estimates of unit training costs can provide policymakers with an instrument to compare how much it costs different training institutions to produce a trained worker. The performance of public training providers also should be evaluated in terms of external efficiency—that is, how well their trainees do on standardized trade tests, such as those administered by the NVTC—and in terms of labor market outcomes.

This section reports on the findings of such an analysis using data provided by the NVTC. Comparing unit costs was not possible because no centralized collection of unit training cost data is available. The Economic Planning Unit maintains records on the development budgets of different training institutions but not (except on an ad hoc basis) on the operating budgets. These records are needed to calculate and compare unit training costs across training providers. The comparative analysis is restricted to pass rates on the NVTC trade tests and to labor market outcomes.

### Performance on Trade Tests

Table 8-5 shows pass rates on the NVTC trade tests for selected years between 1984 and 1993 for five types of training institutions: ITIs, IKMs, YTCs, secondary vocational schools of the Ministry of Education, and private training institutes. The average pass rate for training institutions as a whole was about 60 percent in 1993. Particularly striking is the increase in the pass rates of all training institutions between 1990 and 1993.

### Labor Market Outcomes: Tracer Study Results

The relative performance of training providers can be evaluated based on four labor market outcomes of their trainees: (a) the probability of finding work after training, (b) the time taken to secure a job, (c) the monthly starting pay, and (d) the relevance of the training to work. An institution

TABLE 8-5
Test Takers and Pass Rates, by Training Institution,
Selected Years, 1984–93

| Institution | 1984 | 1987 | 1990 | 1993 |
|---|---|---|---|---|
| *Test takers (number)* | | | | |
| ITIs | 1,966 | 2,265 | 2,768 | 4,695 |
| IKMs | 3,005 | 3,894 | 5,637 | 1,313 |
| YTCs | 524 | 925 | 1,403 | 1,702 |
| Secondary vocational schools | 483 | 2,746 | 4,020 | 16,011 |
| Private institutes | — | 1,963 | 2,215 | 4,700 |
| Total | 9,931 | 14,166 | 20,244 | 32,860 |
| *Pass rate (percent)* | | | | |
| ITIs | 62.2 | 68.3 | 61.1 | 72.1 |
| IKMs | 70.2 | 59.9 | 51.0 | 78.3 |
| YTCs | 56.3 | 54.8 | 57.9 | 74.6 |
| Secondary vocational schools | 44.7 | 39.0 | 37.5 | 55.6 |
| Private institutes | — | 45 1 | 39 6 | 58 4 |
| Total | 59.8 | 53.2 | 46.7 | 61.4 |

— Not available.
*Source:* Economic Planning Unit (1994).

can be said to perform well if its graduates are likely to find employment, take a short time to secure a job, receive high starting pay, and find their training relevant to their job.

The analysis is based on a 1992 retrospective survey of more than 4,000 individuals who took the NVTC trade tests in 1991—that is, between 6 and 12 months prior to the survey. Since some trainees may not take the trade tests, analysis using this sample of test takers should not be interpreted as reflecting outcomes for all trainees of these training providers. Training providers covered by the survey included ITIs, IKMs, YTCs, army training centers (IKKs), PLK Johor, private training institutions, and training provided by employers and other providers.

Table 8-6 shows the distributions of trade test takers among each of four labor market outcomes by training provider. The statistics shown in this table suggest the following:

TABLE 8-6
Labor Market Outcomes, by Training Institution, 1992

| | | | Percentage of those working in 1992 | | | | | | |
| | | | Time to find a job (months) | | | Starting monthly pay (RM) | | | |
| Institution | Sample (number) | Percentage working in 1992 | Less than 6 | 6–12 | More than 12 | Less than 400 | 401–600 | More than 601 | Job relevance |
|---|---|---|---|---|---|---|---|---|---|
| Vocational schools | 2,621 | 55.4 | 79.3 | 17.1 | 3.6 | 62.0 | 29.7 | 8.3 | 43.5 |
| ITIs | 322 | 84.5 | 86.5 | 9.5 | 3.9 | 23.3 | 49.2 | 27.5 | 69.8 |
| IKMs | 670 | 67.6 | 82.4 | 13.5 | 4.1 | 29.7 | 43.2 | 27.0 | 75.5 |
| YTCs | 81 | 66.7 | 83.3 | 10.4 | 6.2 | 34.7 | 42.9 | 22.4 | 77.8 |
| Private institutes | 159 | 89.3 | 66.9 | 20.3 | 12.7 | 15.8 | 35.3 | 48.9 | 80.3 |
| IKKs | 40 | 60.0 | 65.0 | 30.0 | 5.0 | 10.0 | 65.0 | 25.0 | 37.5 |
| PLK Johor | 90 | 80.0 | 81.7 | 13.3 | 5.0 | 60.0 | 28.3 | 11.0 | 76.4 |
| Other | 108 | 71.3 | 71.7 | 18.3 | 10.0 | 37.5 | 35.9 | 26.6 | 75.3 |
| Total | 4,091 | 62.2 | 79.8 | 15.7 | 4.5 | 47.7 | 35.2 | 17.1 | 56.7 |

Source: 1992 survey by the National Vocational Training Council.

• *Probability of working.* Among public training providers, ITI graduates are the most likely to be employed (84.5 percent), followed by graduates of PLK Johor (80.0 percent); secondary vocational school graduates are the least likely to be employed, with only 55.4 percent finding work in 1992. Of all providers, public and private, the graduates of private training institutes are the most likely to find work (89.3 percent). Trainees trained by employers and other providers (the "Other" category) also do well (71.3 percent find work). Many of those trained by private institutes or by other providers are already employees, so the relatively high percentages in these two categories should not be surprising.

• *Time taken to find work.* Of those who find work, ITI trainees are most likely to find work within six months (86.5 percent). Most trainees from most of the other public institutions, including secondary vocational schools, who find work also do so within six months. Although trainees from private institutes are more likely to find work, they appear to take longer to do so, with 66.9 percent of those finding work doing so within six months, versus the sample mean of 80 percent finding work within six months. There does not appear to be an obvious explanation for this finding.

• *Starting pay.* Of those who found work, trainees of ITIs, IKMs, YTCs, and IKKs are most likely to get starting pay of RM 401 to RM 600 (42.9 to 65.0 percent), while secondary vocational school and PLK Johor trainees are most likely to get starting pay of less than RM 400 (60 to 62 percent). By contrast, trainees from private training institutes are most likely to get starting pay greater than RM 600 (48.9 percent). Some of these variations in starting pay may reflect location effects, an issue addressed later.

• *Relevance of training to work.* Of those who found work, with the exception of those trained by secondary vocational schools and IKKs, 69.8 to 77.8 percent reported that the training provided by most public training institutions was relevant to their work. This figure is consistent with the range of estimates of training relevance reported in studies of vocational school graduates in the United States: 50 to 75 percent. For graduates from secondary vocational schools and IKKs, this figure was much lower: 37.5 to 43.5 percent. Graduates of private training institutes were most likely to report the training as relevant to their current job.

These simple comparisons are useful, but they can be misleading if not interpreted carefully. They do not take into account differences in the clientele of training providers. Providers serve student groups that vary by sex, education and skill levels, occupation, and region. These differences

## TABLE 8-7
### Predicted Labor Market Outcomes Using Regression Analysis

| Institution | Sample (number) | Percentage working in 1992 | Percentage of those working in 1992 | | | | | | |
|---|---|---|---|---|---|---|---|---|---|
| | | | Time to find a job (months) | | | Starting monthly pay (RM) | | | Job relevance |
| | | | Less than 6 | 6–12 | More than 12 | Less than 400 | 401–600 | More than 601 | |
| ITIs | 322 | 79.8 | 85.5 | 11.8 | 2.5 | 36.0 | 43.8 | 20.1 | 66.7 |
| IKMs | 670 | 63.6 | 82.2 | 14.1 | 3.5 | 36.1 | 43.8 | 20.0 | 77.6 |
| YTCs | 81 | 68.7 | 81.7 | 14.5 | 3.6 | 36.7 | 43.6 | 19.5 | 75.2 |
| Secondary vocational schools | 2,621 | 52.1 | 79.5 | 16.0 | 4.3 | 62.9 | 30.7 | 6.3 | 46.2 |
| Private institutes | 159 | 78.6 | 64.7 | 24.8 | 10.3 | 22.2 | 44.4 | 33.3 | 75.8 |
| IKKs | 40 | 42.2 | 69.3 | 22.4 | 8.2 | 33.0 | 44.4 | 22.4 | 33.4 |
| PLK Johor | 90 | 64.3 | 78.4 | 16.8 | 4.7 | 66.4 | 28.2 | 5.2 | 74.3 |
| Other | 108 | 70.6 | 70.4 | 21.7 | 7.7 | 37.1 | 43.5 | 19.3 | 76.2 |
| Total | 4,091 | 58.2 | 79.6 | 15.9 | 4.4 | 51.4 | 35.9 | 12.5 | 57.8 |

*Source:* Authors' calculations.

can have an impact on measured labor market outcomes independent of the effectiveness of training by the institution. A training institution may appear to perform well because its graduates are located in areas of high labor demand and starting pay, compared with others in more remote locations. Private institutes will select locations (for instance, industrialized urban areas) with the greatest demand for their services and with good prospects for job placement and high starting pay for their graduates. Many public education and training institutions, by contrast, may locate in less favorable areas to serve disadvantaged populations. Therefore, these factors should be considered in comparing the performance of different training providers.

Table 8-7 shows the corresponding outcomes by training provider once factors such as gender, skill level, trade area, and residence have been taken into account. The predicted labor market outcomes are based on estimates from several regression models and on the assumption that trainees from all training providers have the sample means of all factors except where they got training. Sample means will primarily reflect the characteristics of secondary vocational school trainees (by far the largest group), so the predicted outcomes for them will be largely unchanged.

The regression analysis indicates the following:

• Group differences in gender of trainees, skill level, trade areas, and state of residence have an impact on measured labor market outcomes. Controlling for these factors both reduces the variation in outcomes across institutions and changes the relative ranking of individual training institutions. Thus simple comparisons are misleading indicators of the performance of various public institutions and of the relative performance of public versus private training providers.

• Female trainees are more likely to receive low starting pay, and their training is more likely to be relevant to work. This result may reflect a concentration of female trainees in low-paying, gender-segregated jobs such as hair dressing. Unlike training in basic skills, higher level skill training improves all measured labor market outcomes. Also trainees with engineering and drafting-related trade training appear to perform best. Trainees in Perak, Johor, Penang, Kuala Lumpur, and Melaka are more successful in finding employment and in getting high-paying entry-level jobs than are trainees in the rest of the country. Unless these location effects are taken into account, training institutions that serve outlying regions of the country for equity reasons will not score well in terms of labor market outcomes.

• Among public training institutions, the relative ranking of ITI, IKK, and YTC trainees in most outcomes remains largely unchanged; however, the differences between them are greatly reduced. As before, secondary vocational school graduates rank lowest among all the different groups of trainees in all labor market outcomes.

• When graduates of public and private training institutions are compared, the record is mixed as before, though the differences between them are greatly reduced. Some outcomes for graduates from private institutes are poorer than for ITI, IKK, and YTC graduates (time taken to find a job). Some outcomes are the same—for example, the proportion working (79 percent for private graduates and 80 percent for ITIs) and relevance of training (76 percent for private institutes and for "other" institutes). Other outcomes are better, as in the proportion with a starting salary of RM 600 or more (33 percent compared with an average of 20 percent in the three public training institutions).

## Labor Market Outcomes: Enterprise Survey Results

The Malaysia Industrial Training and Productivity (MITP) Survey of 2,200 manufacturing firms carried out in 1994 and 1995 elicited information on firm-sponsored training and a wide range of firm attributes, including size, industry, ownership, equipment, technology, quality control systems, markets and exports, work force characteristics, wages and other compensation, and production. These data allow us to document the incidence and characteristics of training in Malaysian industry across firms of different sizes, ownership, and industrial sector.

Table 8-8 shows the incidence of enterprise-sponsored formal training for the manufacturing sector as a whole and by firm size. Two points stand out. First, a high proportion of firms either provide their workers with no training (31.8 percent), or they rely exclusively on informal on-the-job training (47.6 percent). Only 20.7 percent of all employers provide their workers with any formal, structured training. Second, the incidence of training differs markedly by firm size. The proportion of firms that do not provide any training is highest among microenterprises (33.6 percent) and lowest among the largest firms (3.7 percent). Conversely, formal training is most common among the largest firms (70.7 percent) and lowest among the smallest firms (10.1 percent). Most firms that provide formal training also provide informal on-the-job training.

Most firms meet their skill needs either in-house or through largely private sector providers. With the exception of skill development centers and

TABLE 8-8
Incidence of Training in Manufacturing, by Firm Size

| Characteristic | Overall | Micro-enterprise[a] | Small[b] | Medium[c] | Large[d] |
|---|---|---|---|---|---|
| Number of firms with training data | 2,200 | 247 | 959 | 535 | 454 |
| Percentage of firms | | | | | |
| Not providing training | 31.8 | 33.6 | 14.8 | 5.2 | 3.7 |
| Providing only informal training | 47.6 | 56.3 | 58.7 | 43.6 | 25.6 |
| Providing formal training | 20.7 | 10.1 | 26.5 | 51.2 | 70.7 |
| Providing formal and informal training | 17.0 | 6.9 | 24.5 | 48.4 | 66.5 |

*Note:* Overall estimates are weighted. Estimates by firm size are not weighted.
a. 15 or fewer workers.
b. 16–100 workers.
c. 101–250 workers.
d. More than 250 workers.
*Source:* Malaysia Industrial Training and Productivity Survey.

the Center for Instructors and Advanced Skill Training, public training institutions play a relatively minor role in meeting the in-service training needs of private sector firms. Analyses of the determinants of training by firms show that training decisions are shaped primarily by these factors: the firm's size; the education, skill, and gender mix of the employees; the firm's technology level; whether the firm exports; the firm's ownership (foreign or domestic); the type of equipment used; and the firm's emphasis or lack of emphasis on quality control.

Table 8-9 shows the different ways in which firms provide formal in-service training to their employees. It distinguishes between formal in-house company training and external sources of training, both public and private. Of the 20.7 percent of employers that provide formal training, about an equal proportion of them (approximately 13 percent) use in-house resources as use external training providers. The table also shows the external training sources reported by the enterprises. The most commonly cited external sources are private training institutes (34.9 percent), skill development centers (25.8 percent), advanced skills training institutes (21.3 percent), and buyers and material suppliers (11.0 percent). The high proportion of firms that report using skill development centers is striking, especially

TABLE 8-9
Internal and External Sources of Training

| Extent of training and source[a] | Percentage of firms |
|---|---|
| *Firm training status* | |
| Provide any formal training[b] | 20.7 |
| Provide in-house formal training | 12.6 |
| Provide external formal training | 13.0 |
| *Source of training for those providing any training* | |
| Polytechnics | 4.0 |
| Vocational and technical schools | 3.2 |
| Center for Instructors and Advanced Skill Training | 21.3 |
| Skill development centers | 25.8 |
| Institutes Kemahiran Mara | 1.2 |
| Industrial training institutes | 5.3 |
| Youth training centers | 0.5 |
| Other government institutes | 8.2 |
| Joint venture partners | 3.6 |
| Buyers and material suppliers | 11.0 |
| Private training institutes | 34.9 |
| Overseas training | 4.6 |

a. Weighted using 1988 Industrial Survey weights.
b. In-house or external.
*Source:* Malaysia Industrial Training and Productivity Survey.

since most of the centers (other than the Penang skill development center) had been in operation only a few years. The least common external sources of training are government-run training institutions: YTCs (0.5 percent), IKMs (1.2 percent), vocational and technical schools (3.2 percent), and other government institutes (8.2 percent).

The relatively small role of government training institutes reflects their focus on pre-employment training rather than in-service training. This orientation toward pre-employment training is borne out by data on NVTC trade tests taken by graduates from different public training institutes. Most YTC, ITI, and IKM graduates are tested for competencies in basic skills, not in the intermediate or advanced skills that are needed after entering employment.

Table 8-10 disaggregates the different sources of training by firm size. The top panel shows the proportions of firms that provide formal training

TABLE 8-10
Internal and External Sources of Training, by Size of Firm
(percent)

| Characteristic | Micro-enterprise[a] | Small[b] | Medium[c] | Large[d] |
|---|---|---|---|---|
| *Firm training status* | | | | |
| Provide any formal training[e] | 9.1 | 18.2 | 44.7 | 70.6 |
| Provide in-house training | 5.2 | 13.5 | 31.7 | 53.6 |
| Provide external training | 5.2 | 7.6 | 27.0 | 51.4 |
| *External source of training for those providing training* | | | | |
| Polytechnics | 12.5[f] | 2.0[f] | 5.1 | 9.3 |
| Vocational and technical schools | 12.5[f] | 0.0 | 3.1 | 4.2 |
| Advanced skill training institutes | 12.5[f] | 8.2[f] | 6.3 | 19.9 |
| Skill development centers | 25.0[f] | 10.2 | 14.9 | 28.8 |
| Institutes Kemahiran Mara | 0.0 | 4.1[f] | 2.3 | 5.1 |
| Industrial training institutes | 12.5[f] | 0.0 | 11.0 | 18.2 |
| Youth training centers | 0.0 | 2.0[f] | 1.2[f] | 2.1 |
| Other government institutes | 0.0 | 20.4 | 22.7 | 27.1 |
| Joint venture partners | 0.0 | 10.2 | 9.8 | 11.9 |
| Buyers and material suppliers | 25.0[f] | 24.5 | 25.1 | 25.0 |
| Private training institutes | 25.0[f] | 28.6 | 44.3 | 53.0 |
| Overseas training | 0.0 | 8.2 | 12.9 | 212 |

a. 15 or fewer workers. Figures for microenterprises are not reliable because of the small number that rely on external training providers.
  b. 16–100 workers.
  c. 101–250 workers.
  d. More than 250 workers.
  e. In-house or external.
  f. Three observations or fewer.
*Source:* Malaysia Industrial Training and Productivity Survey.

in-house and externally. In general, the use of both training sources rises with firm size, with a higher proportion of small and medium firms training in-house than using external training providers. For those firms that provide external training, the bottom panel shows the proportion of employers citing each external source of training. The table clearly shows variation in the use of different external sources by firms of different sizes. Training provided by private institutes continues to be the single most commonly

TABLE 8-11
Workers Obtaining Formal In-House Training, by Skill Group

| Occupational group | Total number trained | Number of employees | Percentage trained |
|---|---|---|---|
| Supervisors | 17,109 | 67,713 | 25.3 |
| Technicians | 15,105 | 47,396 | 31.9 |
| Skilled production workers | 76,074 | 462,855 | 16.4 |
| Unskilled production workers | 59,327 | 443,051 | 13.4 |

*Note:* Estimates weighted using 1988 Industrial Survey weights.
*Source:* Malaysia Industrial Training and Productivity Survey.

cited external training source. Among the other sources, both small and medium firms are most likely to cite training from buyers and materials suppliers and from other government institutes. Large firms are most likely to cite skill development centers, other government institutes, buyers and suppliers, advanced training institutes and, to a growing extent, industrial training institutes.

Which workers are getting training? Table 8-11 presents estimates of the number of people trained in four broad occupational groups—supervisors, technicians, skilled production workers, and unskilled production workers—as a proportion of the total number of employees in the relevant occupation. On average, a higher proportion of technicians (31.9 percent) and supervisors (25.3 percent) are trained than are production workers; however, skilled production workers are more likely to be trained (16.4 percent) than unskilled production workers (13.4 percent). Production workers are also less likely to get external training (14 percent) than are nonproduction workers (28 percent).

The most important reason why firms provide little or no training is that they use simple technologies requiring few skills. Firms' training and technology strategies are inextricably linked, and any policy discussion of one is necessarily incomplete without the other. Regression analysis indicates the following determinants of formal training by firms:

• *Training probability is strongly related to firm size.* Small, medium, and large firms are, respectively, 14, 35, and 53 percent more likely than microenterprises to provide any formal training. The importance of firm size, controlling for the other correlates of training (including level of technology), may reflect scale economies in training provision, large firms' greater access to resources for training, and unobserved employer attributes associated with improved management and training capabilities. The effects of firm size on training probability differ by skill group: compared with microenterprises, the likelihood of training for skilled workers in large firms rises to 61 percent, although it rises to only 43 percent for unskilled workers, a trend evident in the simple tabulations reported earlier. Large firms are also more likely to use both in-house and external training sources than are their smaller counterparts.

- *The training effects of education stand out.* Employers are more likely to provide formal training for all groups and from all sources the more educated their workers are. A one-year increase in the education of the work force (the sample mean is 8.7 years) is associated with a 2 to 3 percent higher probability of training. The significant positive relationship is strong evidence that the two kinds of human capital—education and training—are highly complementary. Educated workers are better learners and thus benefit more from training than do less educated workers. A higher level of work force education also raises the probability that the firm will train in-house rather than send workers for external training, a result evident from the larger estimated effects of education for in-house training.

- *Firms with skilled workers are more likely to train than are firms with unskilled workers.* Skill mix is measured as the share of managers, engineers, technicians, supervisors, and skilled production workers in the total work force of the firm. Controlling for education and other factors, we find that a 1 percent increase in the skill mix is associated with a 0.5 percent increase in the probability of training. The results also indicate that the skill mix of the work force is a more important determinant of external training than of in-house training. To the extent that training of skilled workers tends to be highly technical and specialized, employers may find it more cost effective to send nonproduction workers to external training providers than to develop in-house programs themselves. There is also evidence that a more highly skilled work force is associated with a greater probability of training for both skilled workers and unskilled workers. Thus unskilled workers enjoy an externality by working in a workplace with a high proportion of skilled workers.

- *Skill and training requirements are shaped by the firm's technology.* Firms that invest in research and development (R&D) are about 10 to 15 percent more likely to provide formal training than are firms that do not invest in

R&D. The results, by skill group, suggest that while firms that carry out R&D are more likely to train production and nonproduction workers than are firms that do not do R&D, the likelihood of their training production workers is higher. To operate mature, well-established technologies, workers typically require little formal instruction beyond informal on-the-job training by co-workers. When new technologies are being introduced, however, production is no longer routine. Under these new and challenging circumstances, formal, structured training becomes critical for all workers, both production and nonproduction, if unanticipated problems are to be detected and fixed, and the productivity advantage of using new technologies is to be realized. The presence of R&D also affects where employers train their workers. The marginal effects of doing R&D on training probability are larger for in-house programs (13.5 percent) than for training by external sources (9.5 percent). These results—firms that invest in R&D are more likely to train their workers in-house—are consistent with the hypothesis that the use of advanced technologies is associated with a greater reliance on in-house training than on external training.

• *Foreign firms are more likely to provide in-house training than are local firms.* This effect persists even after controlling for other factors such as R&D, exports, and firm size. Foreign firms are 8 percent more likely to train in-house. This may reflect well-developed in-house training capabilities, because many foreign firms are large multinationals involved in technology-intensive semiconductor and electronics production and assembly. Finally, foreign firms are no more likely to train skilled workers than are local firms; however, they are significantly more likely to train their unskilled employees.

Training improves firm-level productivity. Firms that train, on average, are about 32 percent more productive than are firms that provide employees with no formal training. Productivity effects of this magnitude are not unusual, and they broadly resemble estimates for Colombia, Indonesia, and Mexico. The productivity benefits of training are particularly large for small and medium enterprises, the group least likely to train. This suggests that small and medium enterprises underinvest in training. Their use of simple technologies means that skill needs are correspondingly low. Small and medium enterprises are also deterred from training by several market failures: limited financing for training; high job turnover, which makes it difficult to recoup training costs; and weak training capabilities. To be effective, training policies targeting small and medium enterprises should not be unidimensional, focusing on just one constraint. An integrated set of policies is required that simultaneously addresses a multitude of constraints, including financing, identification of training needs, information about training pedagogy, technology upgrading, and adoption of high-quality control methods.

The productivity effects of training are larger when new technologies acquired through licensing are complemented by employee training. In contrast, a firm's own R&D has limited effects either on overall productivity or on the productivity of worker training, suggesting that technological capabilities are relatively weak among local firms. The implication is that licensing may be an important source of new technology for most firms and that productivity benefits can be substantive if technology transfer is accompanied by training. This suggests that the government should place greater emphasis on promoting technology licensing and the skills training and technology transfer that accompany such agreements than on encouraging firms to increase their provision of training.

No significant productivity effects were discernible for in-service training provided by public training institutions such as ITIs, IKMs, YTCs, and vocational and technical institutes. Their focus is on pre-employment training, a subject that is not examined in detail here. Nonetheless, the absence of any productivity effects of the in-service training that they provide is striking and may suggest that their training is not well suited to employers' needs. A careful study of the effectiveness and relevance of training provided by public training institutions should be conducted, especially if they are to play an expanded training role—not only in pre-employment training but also in meeting employers' in-service skill needs.

Firms that train also pay higher wages. Overall, training is associated with a 6 percent increase in wage levels, suggesting that one-eighth to one-fifth of the productivity gains from training are shared with workers in the form of higher pay. The patterns of wage increases mirror those of the productivity gains from training—that is, higher in firms that invest in technology, that export, and that are foreign owned. This result holds for training of different worker groups. Skilled worker training is more productive than unskilled worker training, and training of supervisors and skilled production workers is associated with higher pay, but not training for unskilled production workers. The implication is that these productivity differentials will lead to growing wage disparities between skilled and unskilled workers in the absence of training policies to upgrade unskilled workers to skilled status. Technological change, with its associated higher skill requirements, will also put additional upward pressure on the relative pay of skilled workers.

## Reform of Demand-Side Incentives for Training

Policymakers recognize the importance of worker retraining and skills upgrading if industry is to move toward higher value added and more capital- and technology-intensive production. Given the limited role of public training institutions in retraining and skills upgrading of the work force, the government has implemented two training incentive schemes—the Double Deduction Incentive for Training (DDIT) and the Human Resource Development Fund (HRDF)—to encourage companies to play a greater role in meeting their own skill demands.

The employer survey revealed that while most firms do not train because of the low skill requirements of the relatively simple, standardized technologies they use, many firms, especially small and medium employers, did not train because of high labor turnover, lack of knowledge about how to train, and limited resources for training. These latter responses are sometimes used as evidence that Malaysian firms underinvest in training. In this context the results of the DDIT and HRDF training interventions are relevant.

Lack of information about the Double Deduction Incentive for Training was the most important reason why most firms, including many large firms, did not use it. Other reasons pertinent to large firms were bureaucratic application procedures and requirements. With regard to the Human Resource Development Fund, it encountered some teething problems, including what appears to be serious noncompliance in registering for and contributing to the HRDF and failure to take advantage of training reimbursements. Noncompliance seems to be most severe among small firms, firms that are doing little training or rely only on informal on-the-job training, firms with stagnant sales, and firms located on the East Coast and in East Malaysia. These results may be interpreted by means of an economic model in which firms make cost-benefit calculations, weighing the probability of being caught in noncompliance against the benefits of not registering.

Some firms, especially small ones, are also not claiming reimbursements from the HRDF scheme despite their payroll contributions. The data suggest that these firms either provide no training or rely exclusively on informal on-the-job training, which does not qualify as structured training. The data also indicate that these firms have low skill requirements and limited resources for training, and that they can readily hire trained workers from other firms. Although it is too early to judge the efficacy of the HRDF, some evidence suggests that it has indeed promoted training and skill up-grading among the sample of firms that have registered with the Human Resource Development Council.

Several issues arise in evaluating these incentives. How much training goes on in industry, in which firms, and is there any evidence of market failure requiring policy intervention? Have the two schemes had a salutary impact on the amount of employer-sponsored training, and can they be made more effective? We will focus on the take-up of the schemes by firm size and subsector and discuss possible ways to improve their functioning.

## Underinvestment in Training

Policymakers believe that Malaysian companies underinvest in training, especially in relation to the skill requirements of rapidly changing technology and growing international competition. To support this view, they cite (a) technology-related externalities from training; (b) market imperfections in worker retention and imperfect information; and (c) the weak training capacity of domestic firms, especially small enterprises.

The first argument—technological externalities related to training—rests upon the view that a great deal of technology is embodied in workers' skills. New technology usually requires extensive modification and adaptation before it can be used effectively and productivity gains can be realized. This process involves continuous learning and training on the part of all workers, from engineers down to production workers. Just as firms may not spend socially optimal amounts on R&D because they are unable to internalize the benefits of their investments fully, firms may underinvest in training related to technological innovation, some argue. These positive technological externalities may justify government involvement.

The second argument is that firms underinvest in training because of market imperfections in worker retention and information. One argument commonly heard in Malaysia is that poaching of trained workers by other firms prevents employers from recouping their training costs and results in underinvestment in training. Many economists dismiss this view, arguing that firms only poach workers with general (and transferable) skills, but this would not impose costs on firms that train, because they would shift the costs of general training to workers through lower wages. These objections may be diluted, however, if most skills are industry specific or specific to particular technologies. The appropriate policy response is to provide incentives for nontraining firms (poachers) to train, or to share the costs of training provided by firms or other training institutions. A number of countries have used payroll levies, either with public provision of training or with rebates for approved training expenses. Malaysia's HRDF scheme falls into this latter category.

Imperfect information, especially about new technologies and training (the value of training, training needs, and training pedagogy), can also lead to underinvestment in training. Arguably, both technology and training are experiential forms of knowledge, that is, they require learning by doing. To the extent that these forms of know-how are not codified and have value in the market place, firms in the private sector will have incentives to monopolize this information. This could result in less than socially optimal diffusion of best practices, both in technology and in training know-how, and consequently lead to underinvestment in training and technology. The appropriate policy response is to improve the dissemination of best practices in technology and training know-how through industrial extension services (for example, through employer associations and industry groups) and through matching grants for firms or groups of firms to implement best practices. Many of these policy instruments are already in place in Malaysia, although their take-up by the private sector has not been encouraging.

The third argument is that relatively weak management and training capabilities of domestic companies, small firms in particular, have led to underinvestment in training. Certainly, some domestic companies are less likely to train than are otherwise similar multinational firms. This, however, may simply reflect the appropriate amount of training given the firms' level of technology, and not weak management or training capabilities. A stronger case can be made for small firms. Small firms are especially vulnerable to market imperfections in training—namely, lack of access to credit to finance training, poorly developed management and training capabilities, lack of information on appropriate technologies, and high fixed costs in developing in-house training programs for a small number of employees. The appropriate policy response here may be to provide a package of financial services, technical assistance, and education, and to facilitate low-cost group training through industry associations or consortia of small firms or collaboration with larger enterprises.

## The Double Deduction Scheme

There are two ways in which Double Deduction Incentive Training can be used: first, by sending employees for training in approved training institutions; second, by applying to the Malaysian Industrial Development Authority (MIDA) for approval of planned training programs. Firms that send employees for training in approved training institutions (there were 12 in 1994) are automatically qualified to claim the double deduction incentive directly from the Department of Inland Revenue. This facilitates use of the incentive scheme, but because there are no reporting requirements, little direct information is available about the use of, and the number of, employees trained through DDIT-approved training providers. Information about DDIT use through the second route is better developed. Between 1987 and 1993 MIDA approved a total of 591 in-house training programs, involving 3,253 trainees and costing a total of RM 32.5 million. During this period just over 35 percent of applications for in-house training were rejected as incomplete or inadequate.

The DDIT scheme has evolved over time, with an expansion in the number of approved training providers and the addition in 1991 of two additional types of training that would qualify for the DDIT scheme. These changes were made in response to criticisms that the types of training that qualified for the DDIT were excessively restrictive. Originally, training programs had to be directed at (a) the development of craft, supervisory, and technical skills for the manufacture of new products or processes, or (b) the upgrading of craft, supervisory, and technical skills involving existing products and processes. In 1991 two broader categories were added: (c) production-related training for productivity improvements, and (d) training for quality improvements in production. According to MIDA staff, MIDA reportedly has also simplified the application process and reduced reporting requirements.

These changes—in the scope of permissible training, in the number of approved training providers, and in the application process—were associated with a sharp rise over time in the number of DDIT applications and a decline in their rejection rate by MIDA. The number of applications rose from 37 in 1991, to 214 in 1992, and 392 in 1993. However, the numbers have remained low despite the rejection rate of training applications declining over time from a high of more than two-thirds (69 percent) in 1988 to less than 25 percent in the 1990s.

ASSESSMENT OF THE DDIT SCHEME. Several questions arise in assessing the efficacy of DDIT as a training policy. How effective was DDIT in encouraging employer provision of training? Were many firms induced to begin training or to increase training by the public subsidization of training costs, or was the incentive simply a windfall for employers who would have provided training anyway, even without DDIT? Furthermore, now that DDIT is the only training policy for companies with fewer than 50 employees, will it be an effective policy instrument for small firms?

The take-up of Double Deduction Incentive Training through MIDA has been limited, notwithstanding the rise in the number of training programs approved since 1991. Statistics on approved programs overstate the number of firms that use DDIT, because firms submit multiple applications. For example, the 317 training programs MIDA approved between October 1988 and March 1993 were filed by only 159 companies. The total number trained through MIDA-approved DDIT programs by the end of 1993 was only 3,253 workers, with more than half trained in 1993 alone. The take-up of the scheme has been uneven across subsectors, with firms in the electric and electronics subsectors being the main beneficiaries. Between 1988 and March 1993, these subsectors accounted for 57 percent of programs approved by MIDA. On the other end of the scale, the beverage and food industry had no approved programs.

DDIT use has been dominated by multinational companies, again primarily in the electric and electronics subsectors. Of the 68 firms that filed applications in 1992, 48 percent were wholly foreign owned, 45 percent had some foreign ownership, and only 7 percent were wholly Malaysian owned. Finally, the take-up of DDIT by small companies has been low. This pattern of use by firm size is important. As of June 1993, only firms with fewer than 50 employees were eligible for the DDIT scheme, yet during 1988–94 only some 7 percent of DDIT applicants fell into this category. Companies with 50 to 99, 100 to 499, and 500 or more employees accounted for 22, 30, and 41 percent of the take-up, respectively.

These findings raise questions about whether the DDIT scheme can be effective in encouraging new training among domestic firms that are not training intensive. The 1988 survey of labor market flexibility suggests that most multinational and foreign-owned firms would train even without the scheme given the subsectors in which they operate. In the other domestic-oriented subsectors and in the larger group of Malaysian-owned companies, where skill levels are generally lower, the low take-up of the scheme suggests that it has been ineffective in encouraging training.

EVALUATION FROM THE MITP SURVEY. Although the DDIT scheme's coverage of manufacturing firms has been limited, accurate figures on its use have not been available. The figures reported in table 8-12 are thus broadly based and refer to DDIT use in the entire 1987–93 period when it

TABLE 8-12
Participation in the Double Deduction Incentive for Training,
by Firm Size and Industrial Sector, 1993

| Firm size and sector | Number of MITP firms reporting use of DDIT | Percentage of all firms in that firm size or industry |
|---|---|---|
| Overall sample | 183 | 8.3 |
| *Firm size* | | |
| Microenterprise (15 or fewer workers) | 4 | 2.6 |
| Small (16–100 workers) | 14 | 2.2 |
| Medium (101–250 workers) | 74 | 7.8 |
| Large (more than 250 workers) | 91 | 19.8 |
| *Industry* | | |
| Food | 14 | 5.28 |
| Other food, beverages, tobacco | 5 | 39.0[a] |
| Textiles | 7 | 6.5 |
| Apparel | 2 | 1.7[a] |
| Wood and furniture | 16 | 5.2 |
| Paper and printing | 10 | 7.9 |
| Chemicals | 13 | 14.4 |
| Rubber | 12 | 9.2 |
| Plastics | 8 | 6.0 |
| Glass and pottery | 16 | 11.2 |
| Iron and basic metals | 8 | 11.3 |
| Fabricated metals | 18 | 16.7 |
| Machinery | 4 | 4.7[a] |
| Electrical machinery | 34 | 16.0 |
| Transport | 10 | 12.8 |
| Other industries | 6 | 8.3 |

a. Fewer than five observations.
*Source:* Malaysia Industrial Training and Productivity Survey.

was the principal policy instrument for training. (The HRDF scheme was not introduced until 1992.)

Several points emerge from the table and from examination of the MITP data. First, the overall use of the DDIT scheme since its inception has been quite low: only 8 percent of the firms in our sample used the DDIT scheme before 1993. This figure falls to 4 percent when the survey is weighted to reflect the oversampling of large firms in the MITP sample. Second, the take-up of DDIT by firm size and industrial sector has been uneven, and its use by small companies has been extremely low. Across industrial sectors, the primary users of the scheme were firms in the electrical machinery, fabricated metals, chemicals, and transportation equipment subsectors. Its use was low among firms in the food, wood and furniture, and textiles subsectors. Thus use of the DDIT scheme tended to be highest among large firms and industries characterized by a high percentage of firms investing in R&D and having technology licenses, foreign capital participation, and export orientation. Third, firms with foreign capital participation are much more likely to use the DDIT scheme than are purely domestic firms. Only 6 percent of all domestic firms used DDIT before 1993, compared with 14 percent of joint venture firms and 14 percent of fully foreign-owned firms.

The ownership pattern and the uneven take-up of DDIT across subsectors raise questions about the scheme's design and implementation and its effectiveness in encouraging firms to train. Arguably, most multinationals and majority foreign-owned firms would train even without the scheme, given the high-tech subsectors in which they operate and their production for export markets. In the domestic-oriented subsectors and among Malaysian-owned companies, where skill levels and technological capabilities are generally low, the low take-up of DDIT suggests that it has been ineffective in encouraging training among firms that were not training before.

REASONS FOR NOT USING THE DDIT SCHEME. The MITP survey elicited information about why firms did not use the DDIT scheme prior to 1993, and got responses from about 1,500 firms. We classified their responses into 15 categories: not aware of the scheme, do not need training, do not know details of the scheme, bureaucratic nature of the procedures, nonavailability of appropriate training, do not meet requirements, have no training capabilities, small scale of production, high cost of training, confusion with the HRDF scheme, extent of labor turnover, no permission from management, and several minor reasons. Table 8-13 lists the seven principal reasons, with the remaining reasons combined into the "other" category, because less than 1 percent of firms cited each of these.

The most commonly cited reason (45.4 percent of respondents) was unawareness of the DDIT scheme. Some firms (5.5 percent) cited a related reason: did not know the details of DDIT. Thus more than 50 percent of the firms did not use the scheme because they were unaware of it or were

TABLE 8-13
Reasons Cited for Not Using the Double Deduction
Incentive for Training

| Reason | Number of firms | Percentage of firms |
|---|---|---|
| Not aware of the scheme | 682 | 45.4 |
| Do not need training | 260 | 17.3 |
| Do not meet requirements | 163 | 10.8 |
| Do not train | 110 | 7.3 |
| Do not know details | 83 | 5.5 |
| Small scale of operations | 60 | 4.0 |
| No training capabilities | 29 | 1.9 |
| Other | 26 | 1.7 |

*Source:* Malaysia Industrial Training and Productivity Survey.

not sure of its details. This occurred despite considerable effort by the government to publicize its availability. Another cluster of reasons cited were not needing training (17.3 percent), not currently providing training (7.3 percent), or a lack of training capabilities (1.9 percent). Collectively, these reasons suggest that about one-quarter of the firms did not train because they did not need the training. Finally, 10.8 percent of firms did not use the scheme because their training did not meet the requirements and standards established by the scheme, and 4.0 percent did not use it because of the small number of trainees involved.

A decomposition of these responses by firm size shows that lack of information about DDIT was pervasive among firms of all sizes, even among large firms (40 percent). A higher proportion of small-scale firms did not use the scheme—either because they did not need it or did not train (25 to 28 percent)—than large firms (13 percent). This is consistent with the low skill requirements of small and medium enterprises associated with their use of relatively mature technology. A reason for not using the DDIT scheme unique to large firms and not cited by small and medium enterprises is the bureaucratic application procedures.

## The HRDF Scheme

The Human Resource Development Fund was established in 1992 with a matching grant from the government. (The government contributed RM 48.9 million to match projected company levies in the first year, and in each of the following three years it added an additional RM 16.3 million.) The Human Resource Development Act created the Human Resource Development Council, with representatives from the private sector and from responsible government agencies, and a secretariat to administer the scheme. Unlike the DDIT scheme, the HRDF is not a subsidy scheme. Employers who have contributed for a minimum of six months are eligible to claim a portion of allowable training expenditures up to the limit of their total levy (1 percent of payroll) for any given year. The council has set rates of reimbursement that vary by type of training and are generally lower for large firms—companies with 200 or more employees—than for those with fewer than 200 employees. Reimbursement is as follows: (a) technical, craft, and computer training at 60 percent for large firms and 70 percent for small firms; (b) quality-related training at 60 percent for large firms and 70 percent for small firms; (c) supervisory training at 60 percent for large firms and 70 percent for small firms; (d) other retraining at 40 percent for large firms and 50 percent for small firms; and (e) overseas training at 30 percent for both types of firms.

Three training schemes were introduced in July 1993: the Approved Training Program for training in registered training institutions, the Skim Bantuan Latihan scheme for ad hoc in-plant or external training from nonapproved institutions, and the Pelan Latihan Tahunan scheme for firms that wanted training on an annual basis. Under the Approved Training Program employers can send their employees for training without the prior approval of the Human Resource Development Council, and they can submit claims on completion of the course. Employers can select Approved Training Program courses offered by training providers in the PROLUS system. Under the Skim Bantuan Latihan scheme, which is intended to be the main funding mechanism, prior approval of training programs must be obtained from the council. Employers submit structured training plans with specific objectives, areas of training, duration, number of trainees, instructors, and means of assessment. Under the Pelan Latihan Tahunan scheme, which is designed to minimize the burden of multiple filings, employers submit detailed annual training plans covering at least 10 percent of the company's work force and 15 percent of junior employees.

Table 8-14 shows the numbers of firms registered, claims filed, and workers trained under each of the three schemes between June 1993 and March 1994. By the end of the first quarter of 1994, a total of 3,304 companies had registered with the HRDF. Skim Bantuan Latihan had the largest number of training programs (2,010), followed by Pelan Latihan Tahunan

TABLE 8-14

Summary Data on the Operation of the Human Resource Development
Fund, 1993 and 1994

(number)

| HRDF scheme | 1993 | 1994 | Total |
|---|---|---|---|
| Companies registered | 3,273 | 31 | 3,304 |
| *Approved Training Program* | | | |
| Training programs | 446 | 169 | 615 |
| Trainees | 1,308 | 761 | 2,069 |
| *Skim Bantuan Latihan* | | | |
| Training programs | 1,129 | 881 | 2,010 |
| Trainees | 23,780 | 28,269 | 52,049 |
| *Pelan Latihan Tahunan* | | | |
| Training programs | — | 923 | 923 |
| Trainees | — | 56,206 | 56,206 |

— Not available.

*Note:* 1993 refers to the second half of 1993 and 1994 to the first quarter of 1994.
*Source:* Human Resource Development Fund data.

(923) and the Approved Training Program (615). However, in terms of the
numbers of workers trained, the Pelan Latihan Tahunan scheme was the
largest, with 56,206 trainees, followed by the Skim Bantuan Latihan scheme
with 52,049 trainees, while only 2,069 employees have been trained under
the Approved Training Program. This finding is consistent with earlier evidence about employers' preferences for in-plant training over training offered by external private training institutions, because firms can tailor
training to their specific skill and technology requirements.

AN ASSESSMENT OF THE HRDF SCHEME. Several issues arise in evaluating the HRDF scheme. First, is the HRDF having the desired effect of
encouraging companies to begin providing or to increase the provision of
more structured training for their employees? Second, are the differentiated rates of reimbursement by type of training generally eliciting the right
kinds of training? Finally, as currently structured, is the HRDF well organized to administer and to promote training by employers?

The first issue, whether the HRDF is encouraging companies to provide their employees with more structured training, can only be answered with data on the incidence and level of training and its rate of change over time. This was not feasible given the newness of the HRDF in the mid-1990s. Instead the analysis focuses on the rate of take-up of different HRDF schemes. This take-up rate can be used as a benchmark against which outcomes in future years can be compared to evaluate the HDRF's impact on increasing training. The analysis also focuses on take-up rates by firm size and subsector to identify the broad attributes of nontraining firms that might be targeted for closer attention by the fund. The analysis used data for the Skim Bantuan Latihan and Approved Training Program schemes. (Data on the Pelan Latihan Tahunan scheme were not available for this analysis.)

The initial use of the HRDF was low, especially among small firms. For all firms combined, the take-up rate of the Skim Bantuan Latihan scheme was more than 12 percent and that of the Approved Training Program was about 14 percent. About 6 percent of companies used both schemes, while about 80 companies used neither. The rate of take-up in each scheme rises dramatically with firm size, as does the take-up of both schemes. In small firms with fewer than 100 employees, the take-up rate for the Skim Bantuan Latihan and Approved Training Program is 4.3 and 6.3 percent, respectively. In the largest firm size category with more than 1,000 employees, the corresponding take-up rates are much higher—about 52 and 40 percent, respectively. Note, however, that even among large firms the take-up of these schemes is not universal. More than 38 percent of large companies did not file training claims under either scheme. This finding is essentially unchanged if use of the Pelan Latihan Tahunan scheme is considered, because only 24 companies have approved annual training plans.

Small companies are training a lower proportion of their work forces than are large firms. This finding is consistent with evidence from the 1988 survey. Companies with fewer than 100, 100 to 199, 200 to 1,000, and more than 1,000 employees accounted for about 11, 3, 26, and 60 percent of all Skim Bantuan Latihan trainees, respectively. Their share of all employees in companies registered with the HRDF was approximately 15, 16, 52, and 17 percent, respectively. Thus, relative to their share of all employees in registered firms, large firms are providing more employees with Skim Bantuan Latihan training than are smaller employers. A similar pattern is found in the case of the Approved Training Program, but the differences by firm size are less marked. Compared with large firms, small firms are more likely not to use HRDF schemes, and when they do, to use them less intensively.

These data revealed wide variations across subsectors in the take-up of the HRDF. The highest take-up rates of either scheme by employers were in professional and scientific instruments, general machinery, electric machinery, and ceramics and glass. Subsectors with low take-up rates were food, beverages and tobacco, textiles and apparel, and wood products and furniture. With 44 percent of all employees in registered companies, the electric machinery subsector accounted for more than 80 percent of all Skim Bantuan Latihan trainees and 39 percent of all Approved Training Program trainees. In contrast, the wood products and furniture and the textiles, apparel, and footwear subsectors each had less than 2 percent of trainees in either scheme, even though their shares of all employees were 7 and 4 percent, respectively.

The second issue concerns the types of training provided by employers, and whether differential rates of reimbursement are broadly effective in shaping the mix of training. Implicitly, the current rate structure values technical, craft, computer, quality, and supervisory-related training most highly (60 or 70 percent), followed by "other training" (40 or 50 percent), and overseas training (30 percent). With one year of data, we cannot assess the impact of the rate structure on the training mix. All that can be done is to compare the composition of training and the rate structure. Perhaps the more critical question at this point is whether policymakers should be involved in determining the mix of training for firms when their skill needs are so heterogeneous.

Is the distribution of training by type consistent with the reimbursement rate structure? Table 8-15 shows the numbers of Approved Training Program and Skim Bantuan Latihan trainees by types of training. It distinguishes between six types of training: computer, quality, supervisory, technical and craft, overseas, and "other." In both schemes the "other" training category is the predominant type—55.6 percent of Approved Training Program trainees and 37.7 percent of Skim Bantuan Latihan trainees—even though this training category has the lowest rate of reimbursement after overseas training. Note that employers placed the same emphasis on "other" training under the DDIT scheme. This may be because the "other" category is primarily for retraining and skills upgrading of production workers, who typically make up the largest occupational group in industry. The two other largest groups of Approved Training Program trainees are concentrated in supervisory training (12.3 percent) and computer training (10.6

TABLE 8-15

Distribution of Approved Training Program and Skim Bantuan Latihan Trainees, by Type of Training, 1995

| Training type | Approved Training Program total | Skim Bantuan Latihan total | Number of employees | | | |
|---|---|---|---|---|---|---|
| | | | Fewer than 100 | Fewer than 200 | Fewer than 1,000 | More than 1,000 |
| Number of trainees | 2,069 | 54,644 | 5,923 | 1,579 | 14,410 | 32,732 |
| *Percentage in each type of training* | | | | | | |
| Computer | 10.6 | 6.5 | 1.6 | 3.9 | 5.3 | 8.0 |
| Quality | 2.2 | 21.7 | 6.5 | 9.6 | 13.3 | 28.7 |
| Foreign | 0.0 | 1.0 | 0.5 | 1.9 | 1.2 | 0.9 |
| Supervisory | 12.3 | 5.2 | 2.2 | 16.2 | 8.3 | 3.9 |
| Technical and craft | 19.2 | 27.9 | 82.7 | 11.0 | 35.4 | 15.6 |
| Other | 55.6 | 37.7 | 6.5 | 57.4 | 36.4 | 43.0 |

*Source:* Approved Training Program estimates: unpublished Human Resource Development Fund data; Skim Bantuan Latihan estimates: World Bank data.

percent). In the case of Skim Bantuan Latihan trainees, the other large groups are technical and craft training (27.9 percent) and quality-related training (21.7 percent).

What are the patterns of Skim Bantuan Latihan training across firm size? In the smallest firm size category (fewer than 100 employees), by far the most trainees are in technical and craft-related training. This is encouraging, because small firms have traditionally been weakest in technical kinds of training. In contrast, companies with more than 100 employees are most likely to provide training in the "other" category. Furthermore, the proportion of trainees receiving computer- and quality-related training rises with firm size.

The data on Skim Bantuan Latihan take-up by subsector suggest that there are different skill requirements across industries. Compared with the sample mean, quality-related training is emphasized by fabricated metals companies, computer training by food and beverage firms, technical training by scientific instrument companies, and "other" training by the transport equipment subsector. For Skim Bantuan Latihan trainees, the technical and craft category can be further broken down into technical training (25 percent) and craft-related training (3 percent). Craft-related training under the Skim Bantuan Latihan scheme is important in only three subsectors: textiles, apparel, and footwear (21 percent), machinery (5 percent), and electrical machinery (3 percent). In the other subsectors virtually no Skim Bantuan Latihan training is craft related. These large differences in skill requirements by subsector call into question the likelihood of success and the merit of policy intervention to shape the socially desired mix of training.

EVALUATION FROM THE MITP SURVEY. Table 8-16 provides information on the responses of MITP firms about the Human Resource Development Fund. It shows the numbers of firms that were eligible for the HRDF; those that said they were registered with the HRDF; those that reported filing claims under the Skim Bantuan Latihan, Approved Training Program, and Pelan Latihan Tahunan schemes; and those not claiming under any of these schemes. Following the 1995 HRDF guidelines, we define eligible firms as those employing 50 or more workers. Of the 1,450 eligible firms, 402 firms (27.7 percent) reported that they were not registered with the HRDF. Of those that were registered, 44.7 percent claimed reimbursements under the Approved Training Program, 47.0 percent under the Skim Bantuan Latihan scheme, and 9.5 percent under the Pelan Latihan Tahunan scheme. However, 34.5 percent of registered firms reported that they did not claim reimbursements under any of the three schemes.

TABLE 8-16
Operation of the Human Resource Development Fund, 1994

| Category | Number of firms | Percentage of sample |
| --- | --- | --- |
| Firms eligible for the HRDF | 1,450 | 65.9 |
| Firms registered with the HRDF | 1,048 | 72.3 |
| Approved Training Program | 468 | 44.7 |
| Skim Bantuan Latihan | 493 | 47.0 |
| Pelan Latihan Tahunan | 99 | 9.5 |
| Firms not claiming under the HRDF | 362 | 34.5 |

Source: Malaysia Industrial Training and Productivity Survey.

*Noncompliance with the HRDF*

The Human Resource Development Act of 1992 made it mandatory for eligible firms to register with the Human Resource Development Council. Twenty-seven percent of eligible firms did not comply with this regulation. Such noncompliance appears to be significant, even recognizing the possibility of response or coding errors. Noncompliance with the HRDF varies systematically by firm size and industry. Small firms (with 50 to 100 workers) are more likely to be noncompliant (49 percent) than large firms (8 percent). Noncompliance is higher in the food, beverages, and tobacco; wood and furniture; and glass and pottery industries (33 to 50 percent of firms) than in the electrical machinery, chemicals, and textile industries (10 to 20 percent). Noncompliance appears to be concentrated among small firms and firms operating in traditional, domestic-oriented industries.

To identify the factors associated with noncompliance, we estimate a probit model. The results suggest the following. First, medium and large firms are more likely than small firms to comply, possibly because they believe that the probability of their being caught is high given their high profile. Second, firms that do not train or that rely only on informal training are significantly more likely not to comply than those that provide their employees with formal training. This is consistent with the high fixed costs involved in developing and setting up training programs and incorporating the new skills into existing production. Third, systematic regional variations are apparent, with noncompliance being higher in East Malaysia than in the West Coast states. Finally, firms with stagnant or declining sales are more likely not to register with the HRDF.

CLAIMS UNDER THE HRDF. A sizable number (362) of registered firms do not claim reimbursements for training expenditures despite contributing payroll levies to the fund. Their claims for training under any of the schemes are an indicator of the effectiveness of the HRDF in encouraging firms to begin or increase training provision. Tabulations suggest that small firms are less likely to claim than their larger counterparts: 50.2 percent for small firms with 50 to 100 employees, 41.3 percent for medium firms with 101 to 250 employees, and 19.4 percent for large firms with more than 250 workers. This is an important issue, because firms paying the levy but not claiming the rebate in effect pay a tax of 1 percent of payroll without getting any tangible benefits as a result.

Who are these nonclaimant firms, and why are they not training? Table 8-17 presents the distribution of registered firms that do not claim accord-

TABLE 8-17
Registered Firms Not Claiming Reimbursements from the HRDF,
by Training Status, 1995

| Training status | Number of registered firms not claiming | Percentage distribution of firms not claiming |
|---|---|---|
| Firms not training | 22 | 6.1 |
| Firms training informally only | 196 | 54.1 |
| Firms training formally | 144 | 39.8 |

*Source:* Authors' calculations.

ing to their training status: no training for workers, only informal on-the-job training, and the provision of formal training. Note that only 6.1 percent of these nonclaimants do no training. The majority of firms not claiming (54.1 percent) are those that provide only informal on-the-job training. Thus about 60 percent of these firms are not eligible to claim for reimbursements because they either do not provide training or are only training informally. The remaining 40 percent report that they provide formal training, yet do not claim reimbursements for these expenditures.

We estimated probit models to obtain insights into why these registered firms do not implement training programs and claim reimbursements. The results indicate that the firms least likely to claim from HRDF are small firms and firms providing no training or only informal training. This result was evident in the simple tabulations. Having a training plan, however, is associated with a greater likelihood of a claim from the HRDF. This is not surprising, because it indicates a systematic commitment on the part of the employer to training employees. Results from the second model highlight the important factors that employers cite as inhibiting their training: the limited resources available for training, the use of mature technology with low skill requirements, the adequacy of skills provided by schools, and the availability of skilled workers who can be hired from other firms.

HAS THE HRDF INCREASED TRAINING BY FIRMS? We used retrospective responses from employers about how their level of training changed—increased, stayed the same, or decreased—between 1992 and 1995. We can compare the training experiences of two groups of firms: those registered with the HRDF, and those that were eligible but chose not to register. In

TABLE 8-18

Changes in Training Levels from 1992 to 1995, by Firm Registration
(percent)

| Registration status | Increased training | Training is the same | Decreased training |
|---|---|---|---|
| Eligible registered firms | 39.3 | 49.8 | 1.2 |
| Eligible unregistered firms | 47.3 | 27.1 | 5.2 |

*Note:* The percentages do not sum to 100 because of firms responding that they "did not know."
*Source:* Authors' calculations.

principle, the registered group would have increased incentives to train in order to recover its payroll levy contributions, while the unregistered group would not have the same incentives.

Table 8-18 compares the training experiences of these two groups of firms. Of those registered with the HRDF, 49.8 percent said that they had increased training over the three-year period, 39.3 percent firms said that their training had remained the same, and only 1.2 percent said that their training had decreased. In contrast, of the eligible firms not registered with the HRDF, 27.1 percent said that their training had increased, 47.3 percent said that their training had remained unchanged, and 5.2 percent said that their training had decreased over the three years. Thus HRDF appears to have played a role in increasing training provision.

We tested this hypothesis formally using a probit model, which compares the likelihood of increased training over the three years for registered HRDF firms and unregistered firms. The effects of the HRDF are allowed to vary by firm size; we used a set of interaction terms between firm size and an indicator variable for being registered with the HRDF. The model includes a set of industry dummies to control for possible differences in industry composition of registered and unregistered firms. We also include a measure of whether the firm introduced new technologies over the three-year period. The intent was to net out the confounding effects of increased training because of new technology that is independent of the HRDF. Finally, to see if the effects of the HRDF vary by ownership, we estimated separate models for domestic firms and firms with foreign capital.

The HRDF has had a role in increasing training among medium and large firms with foreign capital (table 8-19). Among purely domestic firms,

TABLE 8-19
Probit Estimates of Increased Training under the
Human Resource Development Fund

| Independent variable | Combined sample of firms | Purely domestic firms | Firms with foreign capital |
|---|---|---|---|
| Small firm * HRDF | 0.160 | 0.141 | 0.179 |
|  | (0.122) | (0.151) | (0.215) |
| Medium firm * HRDF | 0.312[a] | (0.101) | 0.171 |
|  | (0.129) | 0.435[a] | (0.179) |
| Large firm * HRDF | 0.788[a] | (0.102) | 0.839[a] |
|  | (0.147) | 0.753[a] | (0.175) |
| Introduced new technology between 1992 and 1995 | 0.428[a] | (0.076) | 0.499[a] |
|  | (0.103) | 0.365[a] | (0.114) |
| Constant | −0.574[a] | (0.083) | −0.616[a] |
|  | (0.099) | −0.516[a] | (0.160) |

*Note:* Industry dummies were included but were not statistically significant. Estimated standard errors are in parentheses.
  a. Significant at the 1 percent level.
*Source:* Authors' calculations.

the HRDF has been effective in increasing training only for firms with more than 250 employees. These results were not affected by differences in industrial composition of the two groups. However, whether or not firms had introduced new technology in the past made a difference: increases in training and introduction of new technology are significantly correlated.

## Conclusions

Between the recession of 1985–86 and 1995, Malaysia's economy experienced a sharp turnaround. The changing employment pattern and rapid job growth contributed to a tightening of the labor market. Unemployment rates fell to less than 3 percent in 1995, and quit rates for skilled and technical workers increased. While average wages have increased considerably, wage patterns show increasing disparities between skilled and unskilled workers. Between 1987 and 1993 the wages of skilled and semiskilled workers rose by 10 percent per year; those of managers, technical workers, and professionals rose by 7.5 percent; those of unskilled workers rose by less than 5 percent. There are many reasons for these wage patterns, not all of which have implications for vocational education and training. High rates of investment may have disproportionately increased the demand for technical and managerial personnel, or there may be fewer substitutes for these workers relative to the unskilled. Studies show, however, that the main reason for widening wage differentials is that the supply of skilled workers has not kept pace with demand. This has implications for the VET system, which tries to ensure an adequate supply of technical, skilled, and semiskilled workers.

### Main Findings

Recent surveys indicate that a high proportion of firms provide their workers with no training or rely exclusively on informal on-the-job training. Marked differences are apparent in the incidence of training by firm size: the proportion of firms that do not provide any training is highest among microenterprises, and, conversely, formal training is most common among large firms. The most important reason why firms provide little or no training is that they use simple technologies that require few skills. The firms that do train either meet their skill needs in-house or rely heavily on private providers. Public training institutions play a relatively minor role in meeting the in-service training needs of private firms. Among employers providing external training, the most commonly cited external sources are private training institutes, followed by skill development centers, advanced skills training institutes, and buyers and materials suppliers. The least common external sources of training are government-run training institutions. The relatively small role played by government training institutes reflects their focus on pre-employment training rather than on in-service training.

### Policy Incentives for Training

Policymakers believe that Malaysian companies underinvest in training, especially in relation to the skill requirements necessitated by rapidly changing technology and growing international competition. Given the limited role of public training institutions in retraining workers and upgrading their skills, the government has implemented two training incentive schemes—Double Deduction Incentive Training and the Human Resource Development Fund—to encourage companies to meet their own skill needs.

Despite changes to the system, use of the DDIT scheme has remained low and take-up has been uneven across subsectors, firm size, and ownership. Initial use of the HRDF scheme was also low, and take-up varied widely across sectors. It is too early to make firm judgments about whether the HRDF has increased training, but a preliminary analysis indicates that the scheme may have increased the incidence of training modestly.

## Lessons from Malaysia's Experience with VET Reforms

In a rapidly growing economy, only careful analysis can identify training policies and institutions that are performing poorly. We offer the following lessons based on Malaysia's experience.

First, formal training is not widespread even in a rapidly industrializing economy. Surveys show that about one-third of firms in Malaysia provide no training for workers, about half rely on informal training alone, and only a fifth provide formal training. Firm size matters: almost one-third of extremely small firms provide neither formal nor informal training, but almost all large firms provide some training, generally both formal and informal. The main reason why firms do not train is that they do not need to train. They cite as reasons mature technology, the high cost of training, and the availability of skilled workers from schools and other firms.

Second, tax incentives have been given to firms that would have provided training anyway. Despite considerable simplification of the scheme, less than 3 percent of small firms used the government's DDIT scheme for training. Most of the participants were large export-oriented firms, primarily multinationals making electric and electronic goods. Surveys indicate that many foreign-owned firms would provide training even without such incentives. This raises serious doubts whether tax incentives can encourage training among small domestically oriented firms.

Third, a well-run levy-rebate scheme has increased training only modestly. Malaysia's levy-rebate scheme is extremely well run, but it still faces considerable noncompliance problems and uneven take-up across industries. Despite being efficient in reimbursing claims and making application procedures easy for employers to comply with, the scheme appears to have had only modest training effects.

Finally, private providers are the most common external source for employer-sponsored training. Employer surveys indicate that in-house and private external training have the highest payoffs and that training in government institutions has the lowest productivity. Not surprisingly, the most popular choices among firms are private institutes and joint venture skill development centers. The least popular external sources used for employer training are youth training centers and vocational and technical schools. Firms use public institutes that offer advanced training somewhat more frequently.

## References

Economic Planning Unit. 1994. "Mid-term Review of the Sixth Malaysia Plan, 1991–95." Government of Malaysia, Kuala Lumpur.

World Bank. 1995. *Malaysia—Meeting Labor Needs: More Workers and Better Skills.* Report 13163-MY. East Asia Region. Washington, D.C.

———. 1996. "Enterprise Training, Technology, and Productivity in Malaysian Manufacturing." East Asia Region. Restricted circulation report submitted to the Economic Planning Unit of the government of Malaysia. Washington, D.C.

# 9  Republic of Korea

INDERMIT S. GILL AND CHON-SUN IHM

THE REPUBLIC OF KOREA, with a population of about 45 million, is smaller in area than Honduras (which has a population of less than 6 million) and is less than one-third the size of the Philippines. Impoverished by years of foreign occupation and internal strife until the 1950s, Korea has since embarked on a path to progress that is nothing short of spectacular. By 1995 Koreans enjoyed a per capita income about ten times that of Hondurans and Filipinos. The mainstays of growth in Korea, which has meager natural resources, were its people and its policies. This chapter explores one aspect of each: investment in the skills of people, and the vocational education and training (VET) policies that made sure that these investments over the long term were consistent with the economy's changing requirements. This chapter also shows that Korean policymakers have made mistakes. In fact, perhaps the single most important lesson from Korea's experience is that successful policymaking is not about being infallible. Rather, it is about being willing to learn from the mistakes that are made.

In 1994 Korea's annual population growth rate was about 0.9 percent, almost half the rate of growth of just 20 years earlier. Between 1975 and 1985, the crude birth rate fell from 25 to 16 per 1,000, with a steady decline since then. With annual real economic growth rates that exceeded 10 percent in some years, Korea's real per capita income grew thirteenfold from less than US$600 to about US$8,000 between 1975 and 1995. In the mid-1980s, when growth was most rapid, Korean manufacturing grew by almost 20 percent every year, and services by more than 10 percent. The share of agriculture in employment fell from more than 45 percent in 1975 to less than 15 percent two decades later.[1] The financial crisis of 1997 contracted Korea's GNP, and Korea is likely to recover only after a few more years. This chapter concentrates on the longer term issues of vocational education and training.[2] The economic crisis is affecting the resources available for further reform. Indeed, rising unemployment has already placed additional burdens on the financial system.

Between 1986 and 1991, gross domestic capital grew by more than 15 percent annually. This investment in capital was paralleled by large investments in human capital. In 1970 almost three out of four Koreans had no more than an elementary school degree; by 1990 this ratio was one in three. The average years of educational attainment rose from fewer than 6 years to almost 10 years during this period. The number of students in vocational and academic high schools rose from fewer than 0.6 million in 1970 to more than 2 million in 1994, and enrollment in higher education rose eightfold from 0.2 million to 1.6 million over the same period. The number of vocational trainees quadrupled between 1970 and 1992: from about 30,000 to 115,000. These investments in physical and human capital paid huge dividends for employers and workers: labor productivity doubled between 1985 and 1993, and monthly wages rose from 200,000 won to 1,000,000 won.

## Vocational Education and Training before the Financial Crisis

Due to these investments in education and training, the large wage differentials between college graduates and workers without a high school diploma that existed in the 1970s fell by half by 1993. But Korea's appetite for education remains unsatisfied. There is a strong demand for more education and of better quality. Fearing either "overeducation" or a mismatch between the economy's "needs" and the output of the education system, Korean policymakers have tried to curb this appetite using questionable interventionist strategies. In 1975, worried about the adverse social effects of competition among parents to enroll their children in a small number of good schools, policymakers instituted a system in which elementary school leavers were allocated to junior secondary schools through a lottery. During the 1970s some of the best private schools came under direct government control in order to curb "credentialist tendencies." Again, in the 1980s, the government outlawed private tutoring to reduce wealthy families' advantage in getting their children placed in the top public universities. These changes have had only limited success in meeting their objectives. Besides, with greater democratization, similarly intrusive measures may no longer be a viable option.

VET has played a pivotal role in this social context, and it contributed greatly to the rapid economic growth in Korea before the economic crisis. In the view of policymakers, VET reduces the pressure on universities to enroll more students, and it meets a "shortage" of skilled and semiskilled workers, especially technicians. But parents see vocational schools as second-best after academic schools, "even though the employability of vocational high school graduates in Seoul and Pusan has been better than for academic high school graduates" (Sorensen 1994), and even though graduate unemployment remains a concern. One reason for this is that social prestige is considerably enhanced by attending university: parental pressure has resulted in successive additions of general subjects in vocational school curricula so that their children have some hope of getting into college. Policymakers lament that Koreans are generally overeducated for the economy's demands but undertrained to fill jobs that are critical for the country's final push toward industrial-country status. Policymakers are carefully evaluating the feasibility of expanding vocational-technical school enrollment or (since there is now a large private industrial base) of shifting more training to the workplace.[3]

After examining the evolution of the labor market, we assess how the VET system has changed in response to developments in the labor market and the economy in general. We identify the general directions that Korean policymakers believed to be appropriate given these developments and the obstacles to moving swiftly in these directions. Finally, we describe how Korea has overcome some of these obstacles to reform and ongoing efforts to deal with the others. Because the focus of this chapter is on long-term issues, we abstract from issues involving the financial crisis.

## Labor Market Conditions

In this section we discuss Korea's labor force, employment, unemployment and labor "shortages," wages, and labor issues relevant to vocational education and training.

### Labor Force

The economically active population in Korea increased from about 10 million in 1970 to about 20 million in 1995, a moderate growth rate of about 2.8 percent annually. During the same period, the total population increased at an annual rate of 1.4 percent, from 32 to 45 million. Overall, therefore, labor force participation rates increased over this period from 58 to 62 percent.

Population growth rates rapidly declined (from annual increases of more than 1.7 in the 1970s to less than 1 percent by the late 1980s). In 1995 the population ages 15 to 24 years began to decline in absolute numbers. Because of increasing advancement to higher education, the labor force participation of persons ages 15 to 19 years fell from 36.9 percent in 1975 to 13.3 percent in 1995. Countering this reduced supply of young workers is a steady increase in female participation, which rose from about 39 percent in 1970 to close to 49 percent in 1995, and increased participation rates of older workers which increased from less than 10 percent to about 15 percent during this period. Korea has moved to a stage where labor quality questions are paramount, since the growth of the quantity of labor has obviously declined to very low levels. The strong emphasis on education and training in the country's economic strategy should be seen in this context.

## Employment

Employment in Korea increased from 9.5 million in 1970 to about 19.5 million in 1994. The share of agriculture declined from 50 to 15 percent over this period, the manufacturing share increased from 13 to 24 percent, and the share of other sectors (mainly construction and services) increased from 35 to 62 percent (KLI 1994). Agriculture, which provided a relatively elastic supply of unskilled workers to the other sectors during the 1960s and 1970s, was no longer a source of cheap unskilled labor by the early 1980s. The rapid expansion of VET in the mid-1980s coincided with the drying up of this source of unskilled labor. This push to substitute labor quality for quantity coincided with Korea's big push into (export-oriented) manufacturing, construction, and service-oriented activities, which require increasingly greater amounts of skilled labor. Compared with when manufacturing dominated the nonfarm sector, the skill-mix required today is more complex.

Shifts in the occupational structure have paralleled these sectoral changes. Between 1970 and 1994, the share of farm workers declined from 50 to 15 percent; the share of professional, managerial, administrative, technical, and clerical workers increased from 10 to 25 percent; the share of sales and service workers increased from 19 to 28 percent; and the share of equipment operators and laborers increased from 20 to 32 percent of employment (KLI 1994). Note that these occupational patterns are clearly indicative of the rising share of skilled workers in the Korean labor force, and they explain why education and training have remained at the forefront of policy discussions.

## Unemployment and Labor "Shortages"

From the mid-1970s until the mid-1990s, the absolute number of the unemployed remained in a narrow range between 400,000 and 750,000 workers, peaking during the recession of 1980–82 at 5.2 percent of the work force. It fell to about 2.5 percent in 1995. But despite the fall in participation of young people, youth unemployment rates remained relatively high: the unemployment rate for males ages 15 to 24 years was about 12 percent in 1993; female unemployment for the same age group was somewhat lower, but was still above 7 percent.[4] Unemployment rates rose sharply during 1997 and 1998 due to the economic contraction that Korea suffered.

Unemployment rates were higher for educated job-seekers in Korea, as in many other countries. In 1994 those with middle school diplomas or less education had an unemployment rate of close to 1 percent. The unemployment rate for high school graduates was about 3.5 percent, and for junior college graduates and those with more education, it was 4 percent. From 1980 to 1993, unemployment declined at a roughly uniform rate for all education groups (KEDI 1994). Although the unemployment rate of high school graduates was the highest of all groups in 1980, since 1985 college graduates have been the most likely to be unemployed. Among high school graduates, unemployment rates are higher for academic school graduates than for those from vocational schools.

With an aggregate unemployment rate of about 2 percent, and with educated job-seekers being a large share of the unemployed, claims of labor "shortages" are common. Unfilled vacancies as a share of employment rose from 2 percent to 7 percent between 1980 and 1991 for skilled workers, but from 5 to 20 percent for unskilled workers; although it stayed at about 1 percent for office workers over the same period, it rose from 2 to 9 percent for production workers (Uh 1993).

## Wages

Labor shortages—in a competitive market—should be eliminated by increases in the wages of workers who are "in demand" and by reduced wages for those whose skills are abundant (for example, the unemployed). Be-

FIGURE 9-1
Wage Trends in Korea, by Education Level, 1975–93

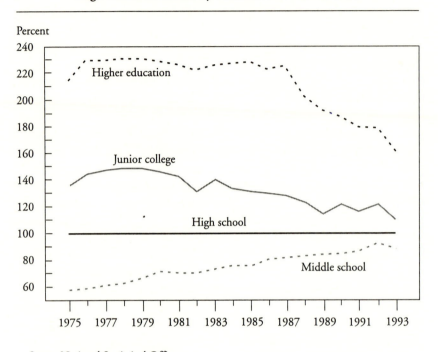

Source: National Statistical Office.

tween 1980 and 1992, wages for workers with a middle school diploma or less education rose 5.5 times, 4.3 times for high school graduates, and 3.2 times for those with a junior college degree or more education. While those with a middle school diploma or less earned a quarter of what college graduates earned in 1975, this ratio had changed to one-half by 1993. The wages of those with a junior college degree, compared with the wages of graduates of high school, steadily declined from 1978 to 1993; and the relative wages of those with at least a college degree fell between 1987 and 1993 (figure 9-1). But note also that the relative wages of less educated workers rose steadily. This implies that, as the supply of educated workers increased, the returns to education fell.

Nominal wages for professionals; technical workers; and administrative, managerial, and clerical workers rose twelvefold between 1975 and 1992. They rose more than sixteenfold for sales and service workers, and more than twentyfold for production workers. Thus, while the average wage for production workers was less than 40 percent of that for professional and technical workers in 1975, it was more than 65 percent by 1993. This finding appears to contradict current claims that technicians were in scarce supply during the past two decades, but more disaggregated data are required to confirm this.

Another noteworthy feature of Korea's labor market is the presence of sizable wage differentials by firm size. This was not always the case. In 1980, for example, average wages in large firms (those with 500 or more employees) were only 8 percent higher than those in small firms (between 10 and 100 employees); by 1993 this differential was more than 35 percent (KLI 1994). The apparent ability of large firms to pay higher wages to workers is widely, but casually, cited as the major reason for their ability to lure (trained) workers from small firms, which are therefore reluctant to invest in in-service worker training.

## Labor Issues Relevant to VET

Three labor issues are particularly relevant to vocational education and training. First, until just before the crisis, unemployment rates remained low (by international standards). The labor-market focus of VET policies was naturally on upgrading workers' skills, not on helping the unemployed get jobs by retraining them.[5] This has changed somewhat since then. In 1995 the unemployment insurance system was introduced, and compensation was combined with vocational training. Public retraining programs for the unemployed—which have a spotty record elsewhere—are likely to become important in Korea.

Second, there is no evidence of increasing unemployment among the educated (despite claims by policymakers that, because unemployment rates of educated workers are higher than for the less educated, Koreans are becoming "overeducated"). The finding that educated job-seekers have higher unemployment rates is not unique to Korea.[6] Viewed this way, the Korean labor market appears to provide little support for the view that more middle school graduates should be diverted from pursuing university education and channeled instead into vocational high schools to be prepared for jobs as skilled workers. This raises serious questions regarding the appropriateness and timing of the recent expansion of vocational school enrollment.

Finally, preliminary evidence on unemployment, labor "shortages," and wages indicates that the demand for higher occupations (professionals, administrators) and middle-level occupations (supervisors, clerical workers, technicians) is largely met, and the market for semiskilled workers (production) and unskilled workers (service workers and laborers) is tight. But this does not imply that enrollments in vocational high schools and pre-employment training institutes—which produce mostly *skilled* workers—should be expanded.

## Vocational Education and Training

In Korea like in most countries, VET is delivered in private and public sector institutions, and by private firms, and it is overseen by the ministries of education and labor. More than 2 million people were trained or educated in Korea's VET institutions between 1987 and 1994. In-plant training accounted for about 57 percent of the trainees, public training institutions for about 27 percent, and authorized training centers for about 16 percent. Table 9-1 sums up the main features.

In 1994 about 758,000 students were enrolled in vocational high schools, which represented about 38.5 percent of total senior secondary enrollment. The graduates of these three-year programs are considered skilled workers. About 500,000 students were enrolled in two- and four-year programs in

TABLE 9-1
Korea's Vocational Education and Training System

| Category | Vocational education | Training |
| --- | --- | --- |
| Implementing institutions | Vocational high schools<br>Junior technical colleges<br>Open colleges | Public vocational institutes<br>In-plant vocational institutes<br>Authorized vocational institutes |
| Ministries concerned | Ministry of Education | Ministry of Labor |
| Period of education | 2 to 3 years | 1 month to 3 years |
| Curriculum | Major field, and knowledge and skill related to major:<br>70 percent theory<br>30 percent practice | Knowledge and skill related directly to major:<br>30 percent theory<br>70 percent practice |

*Source:* Ministry of Labor (1993).

junior technical colleges, which produce technicians and master technicians, respectively. Public vocational training is conducted by the Korea
Manpower Agency (KOMA), a branch of the Ministry of Labor, and by
local bodies. In 1994 there were 41 training centers under KOMA, and 8
under local governments.[7]

Private vocational training is conducted in plants and in "authorized"
vocational training centers. In all sectors other than construction, until
1995, firms with more than 150 employees were obliged to meet a specified minimum training amount, or pay a vocational training levy.[8] In 1994
there were 138 authorized training centers run by nonprofit bodies and
individuals with the approval of the Ministry of Labor. The centers cater to
firms that prefer to not pay the levy, but lack the means to conduct in-plant
training. Enrollment in these institutions increased from about 9,000 in
1987 to 48,000 in 1994.

## Vocational and Technical Education

About 40 percent of Korean students who successfully complete nine years
of formal school at the elementary and middle school levels go on to receive vocational and technical education. Table 9-2 illustrates trends in
vocational education from 1960 to 1994. Nonacademic high schools consist of commercial (45 percent), technical (32 percent), vocational and comprehensive (20 percent), agricultural (2 percent), and fishery and maritime
(1 percent) schools; figures in parentheses denote the share of each in total
vocational enrollment in 1994.[9] The required period of study in all vocational schools is three years, but the amount of time spent in field training
differs: 1 to 12 months for fishery and maritime students, 1 to 6 months
for technical students, and 1 to 3 months for agricultural and commercial
students. Twenty technical schools (with about 3,000 students) began a
new "2+1" system, in which the period of field training is one year, following two years of classroom instruction. (The 2+1 system is discussed later
in the chapter.)

Ever since the 1960s, the government has tried to increase the share of
the vocational track. The government put considerable resources into vocational education. Considerable donor assistance was sought for this, and
policymakers exhorted private business to contribute financially to the expansion of vocational education. But the government was not able to achieve
its target of having two-thirds of high school students in the vocational
track (Takeda 1992). By the mid-1980s, the ratio was closer to one-third.

TABLE 9-2
Trends in Vocational Education, Selected Years, 1960–94

| Category | 1960 | 1965 | 1970 | 1975 | 1980 | 1985 | 1990 | 1994 |
|---|---|---|---|---|---|---|---|---|
| *Technical high schools* | | | | | | | | |
| Number | 196 | 212 | 327 | 294 | — | 408 | 379 | 501[a] |
| Enrollment (thousands) | 63 | 105 | 175 | 283 | 435 | 506 | 440 | 418[a] |
| Percentage female | — | 8.6 | 15.1 | 14.9 | 22.3 | 30.6 | 30.0 | — |
| *Commercial high schools* | | | | | | | | |
| Number | 87 | 100 | 154 | 182 | — | 227 | 208 | 239 |
| Enrollment (thousands) | 37 | 68 | 101 | 190 | 323 | 380 | 371 | 340 |
| Percentage female | 17.4 | 38.3 | 50.2 | 59.9 | 68.2 | 74.2 | 79.0 | — |

— Not available.

*Note:* Includes agricultural, technical, fishery and maritime, and vocational and comprehensive high schools. Therefore, the numbers may not be comparable with earlier numbers.

*Source:* For 1960–90, Chang (1994); for 1995, Ministry of Education.

In 1990, concerned once again that the nation's growing demands for technical skills would not be met, policymakers decided that the size of the vocational track would be expanded so that the ratio of general to vocational enrollment would be reduced from 68:32 to 50:50. This was to be done by expanding enrollment in existing vocational schools, opening new (largely private) vocational high schools, and converting 120 general schools to comprehensive schools. According to the Ministry of Education, this would increase vocational enrollment by about 100,000 at a cost of about US$513 million—that is, at a cost per enrollee of more than US$5,000. Despite these efforts by policymakers (assisted by the World Bank), the ratio of general to vocational enrollment was only 61:39 in 1995. Koreans remained reluctant to enter the vocational track. Vocational high schools have had difficulty in recruiting enough students to satisfy their allotted enrollment quotas (Ihm and others 1993).

ADMISSION TO SECONDARY SCHOOL. In 1995 almost all middle school graduates went on to high school. Ever since the 1970s the government has actively encouraged students to enroll in vocational schools. Since 1974 applicants for vocational high schools have taken entrance exams earlier than those for general high schools. Applicants who had opted for general high schools and those who fail to get admission to vocational schools take another exam; those who pass it are assigned to a school in their district by lottery.

This admissions system—part of the general system of examinations that is believed to have spawned a culture of "testocracy"—allows policymakers to influence the share of students opting for the vocational and general tracks, albeit with a lag. For example, making admission to general high schools harder would, in the following year, result in more students accepting admission in vocational high school instead of taking the (now higher) risk of losing a year.

POSTSECONDARY VOCATIONAL EDUCATION. In 1994 about 45 percent of high school graduates entered institutions of higher learning. The ratio was about 65 percent for general high school graduates and 15 percent for vocational school completers.

Postsecondary vocational and technical education is in two- or three-year programs in junior colleges and in colleges and universities (largely in four-year programs), which aim to produce middle-level "technicians" (in fields such as nursing, technical occupations, agriculture, commerce and business, home economics, and athletics). In 1979 junior colleges were established by merging two-year institutions and two- to three-year professional schools. By 1993 the number of junior colleges had grown to 135 with an enrollment of 507,000, according to Ministry of Education data. The basic requirement for junior colleges is graduation from high school. Entrance is determined on the basis of school scores, a nationwide scholastic achievement test, an entrance exam administered by the college, an interview, and an aptitude test. Between 30 and 50 percent of the freshman quota is reserved for graduates of vocational high schools, certified craftsmen, and experienced industrial workers. Graduates of junior colleges can go on to university.

In 1994 about 1.25 million students were enrolled at 131 colleges and universities, 11 teachers' colleges, and 368 graduate schools. Korea has constantly experimented with admissions procedures for higher education to balance the "educational zeal" of Koreans with the public costs of providing this education and employers' demands for skilled workers. Until 1968 colleges selected students by conducting their own entrance exams. Between 1969 and 1979, a nationwide Preliminary Examination for College Entrance was administered to further deter applicants; only successful examinees could take the entrance exams of individual institutions. In 1980 the Preliminary Examination for College Entrance was replaced by a Scholastic Achievement Examination for College Entrance. Applicants must select universities and colleges *before* they take this exam, and the institutions themselves had some restrictions on how the selection could be done. Since 1994 the institutions have been given more autonomy (especially in selecting students), but restrictions on both students and colleges remain in force.

CURRICULUM. Although the Ministry of Education sets the formal curriculum requirements in general and vocational education, university entrance examinations are an important determinant of what is taught in high schools (Kim 1995). About 45 percent (90 out of 210 units) of the curriculum—for both academic and vocational schools—consists of general subjects such as languages, history, science, and mathematics. Academic students take electives from these general subjects to specialize in either science or humanities (another 100 units). Vocational education or home economics electives also are offered to academic students. Vocational school students take electives from the same general subjects. These electives add up to about 50 units; the remaining electives are the additional vocational element. Perhaps as much as 75 percent of the curriculum for academic and vocational students is common and consists of "general" or nonvocational subjects such as sciences, social sciences, humanities, and moral and physical education.[10]

The general curriculum of vocational schools is perhaps understandable given many Koreans' intense desire that their children receive a university education. Vocational students often do not give up hopes of entering universities. Although education in a vocational high school usually leads children to postsecondary vocational education or the labor market, it does not rule out entrance to a four-year college or university program.

RELATIVE COSTS OF ACADEMIC AND VOCATIONAL EDUCATION. With so much overlap between the curriculum of vocational and academic schools, it would be surprising to observe large differences in unit costs. Nonetheless, it appears that vocational education is about three times more expensive than academic education, although the school fees are the same. Therefore, even if vocational school graduates fare better in the labor market than those with academic high school diplomas, these higher costs imply that the social benefit-cost ratio could still be lower for vocational education. Because the higher labor market returns to vocational education are captured largely by the individual, this may also be considered a reason to charge higher tuition fees for vocational students.

But there are reasons to doubt the claim that vocational education produces a better, quicker match between workers and jobs. Ihm and others (1992, 1993) find, for example, that vocational graduates do not stay long in their first job. This seems to be a result of poor working conditions, lack of promotion opportunities, and a distaste for menial and repetitive tasks, which do not necessarily require three years of technical education.

"DUAL SYSTEM" EXPERIMENTS. As the pace of economic transformation of the economy has picked up, Korean vocational schools have faced increased pressures to ensure that vocational education is relevant (that is, has strong ties to employers). To facilitate this, the dual system was launched in 1994 with German technical assistance. It is called the "2+1" program because two years of vocational education in schools are followed by one year of field training with a firm. Twenty technical schools with about 3,200 students participated in the pilot program in 1995. Although the new system is called "dual" (Chang and Y. Kim 1995), it only loosely resembles the much-vaunted German system of VET in which trainees usually attend school and work as apprentices during all three years. (See chapter 19 in this volume for a description of the German dual system.) Unlike in the German system, the vocational school in the Korean system is responsible for instruction on the factory floor; even though companies participate in the program, they do not have any responsibility for training.

The 2+1 system is not without controversy. The Presidential Commission on Educational Reform has suggested that the 2+1 program be viewed as one way to reform vocational education. If past experience is a guide, it may be difficult to sustain the program given Korea's industrial and labor relations. A similar experiment by the Ministry of Labor between 1980 and 1986 to introduce "cooperative training" between KOMA's vocational training institutes and firms failed to result in increased training of apprentices. Personnel managers did not perceive major differences between the skills of graduates of cooperative training and of other training institutes, and trainees reported no benefits from participation in the experiment. The apprentices were used mainly as low-wage labor (Jeong 1995). Perhaps anticipating this problem, the designers of the 2+1 program have limited the role of employers in the practical training component to allowing use of the plant and machinery. Therefore, the program cannot be classified as an apprenticeship scheme. This may compromise the main objective of the program—namely, to improve the relevance of training in a rapidly changing work environment by strengthening linkages between schools and employers.

SHARE OF PRIVATE SECTOR IN FINANCE AND PROVISION. Korea's public expenditure patterns for education are cited the world over as an example of good practice. Public expenditures are concentrated at primary and junior secondary levels, senior secondary education is financed almost equally from public and private funds, and higher education is financed more by the private sector than by the government. Policymakers have allowed private provision of education to proliferate at all levels of education, but especially at the higher levels. While this has some drawbacks (for example, Korea's policies for regulating higher education may have compromised quality objectives), Korea's public expenditure patterns are praised and recommended to other countries as "best practice."

In fact, the system of financing is somewhat more complicated than a quick look at the share of private provision at each level might suggest. The distinction between public and private provision of education is blurred in Korea, and it is easy to misinterpret statistics on private and public provi-

TABLE 9-3

Share of Private Enrollment, by School Level and Type,
Selected Years, 1965–94

(percent)

| Year | Elementary school | Middle school | High school Academic | High school Vocational | Junior college and university |
|------|------|------|------|------|------|
| 1965 | 1 | 44 | 59 | 39 | 73 |
| 1970 | 1 | 49 | 60 | 48 | 67 |
| 1975 | 1 | 41 | 60 | 52 | 70 |
| 1980 | 1 | 39 | 62 | 57 | 74 |
| 1985 | 1 | 32 | 60 | 62 | 76 |
| 1990 | 1 | 29 | 62 | 62 | 78 |
| 1994 | 2 | 24 | 63 | 58 | 80 |

*Source:* KEDI (1994).

sion as indicators of cost sharing. Table 9-3 shows that the share of private enrollment by school level is exactly what is widely reported and praised: private provision is almost nonexistent at the primary level, and it rises to about 80 percent in higher education.

But this observation does not reflect the rather unique nature of Korea's system of education finance. Parents pay tuition fees in both public and private schools, but these fees are tightly regulated. Private schools—which do not have the option to increase fees to meet increases in operation costs—receive government support, mainly for paying teachers' salaries (which are also regulated). Table 9-4 summarizes this subsidization by the government. In 1994 the share of government spending going to public schools was almost 100 percent at the elementary level, 80 percent in middle school, about 50 percent in high school, and only about 20 percent in higher education. At the high school level, there is little difference between vocational and academic education, other than the fact that public provision is greater for vocational education. This pattern—the government shouldering a larger share of the cost of education at lower levels—has become steadily stronger since 1970.

Despite these efforts to eliminate differences between private and public provision of education, public schools have greater access to Ministry of Education funds. This generally implies that public schools are better equipped or have smaller class sizes. These restrictions on private schools

TABLE 9-4
Government Expenditures on Education, by Level and Type,
Selected Years, 1970–94
(billions of won, current prices)

| Year | Elementary school | | Middle school | | High school | | Higher education | |
|------|-------|---------|-------|---------|-------|---------|-------|---------|
| | Total | Percent private | Total | Percent private | Total | Percent private | Total | Percent private |
| 1970 | 68 | 1.8 | 32 | 50.0 | 19 | 55.3 | 28 | 72.1 |
| 1975 | 148 | 1.8 | 81 | 43.0 | 82 | 53.5 | 83 | 66.3 |
| 1980 | 671 | 1.8 | 389 | 32.9 | 424 | 51.6 | 535 | 68.6 |
| 1985 | 1,565 | 1.5 | 834 | 29.1 | 856 | 56.3 | 1,363 | 73.7 |
| 1990 | 2,757 | 1.4 | 1,591 | 24.5 | 1,797 | 49.6 | 2,378 | 73.3 |
| 1994 | 4,452 | 1.5 | 2,976 | 21.2 | 3,239 | 48.7 | 5,174 | 78.7 |

*Note:* Percent private indicates the share of the government budget going to private schools and colleges.
*Source:* KEDI (1994).

may in part explain why student-teacher ratios are significantly higher in private schools for all levels of education than in public schools.

## Vocational Training Institutes

In 1967 a national training system was formally established with the enactment of the Vocational Training Law. This was followed in 1973 by the National Technical Qualification Law, which set up a system of skill certification. Laws enacted in 1976 introduced and formalized obligatory in-plant vocational training and established a Vocational Training Promotion Fund that was financed through a training levy on firms that did not meet stipulated training requirements. In 1982 the Korea Manpower Agency was founded as the training arm of the Ministry of Labor Affairs. Finally, in 1989 the Korea Institute for Technology and Education was established for higher-level technical training. In 1994 the public vocational training system was reorganized as part of general reforms in the education sector.

By 1995 almost 500 vocational training institutes were providing training at various levels for a broad range of occupations. KOMA is in charge of 38 public vocational training institutes. They aim to provide skills that are commonly needed by industry but cannot be met through in-plant training and skills needed for export-oriented trades. The central government administers 38 vocational training institutes, largely for prisoners. Local governments manage 8 vocational training institutes that mostly administer training programs for unemployed youth and women seeking to increase their incomes. The remainder are in-plant centers (250) and authorized training centers (138) run by nonprofit organizations and private sector firms. Between 1988 and 1993, almost 2 million persons attended training courses in these institutions: about 27 percent in public training institutes, 16 percent in authorized centers, and 57 percent in in-plant facilities, according to the Korea Manpower Agency.

PUBLIC VOCATIONAL TRAINING INSTITUTES. The Korea Manpower Agency administers 38 vocational training institutes, 12 master's colleges, and the Korea Institute for Technology and Education. These institutions together certify about 26,000 craftsmen and master craftsmen annually in almost 100 trades. Between 1988 and 1993, the number of trainees rose from 21,000 to about 26,000. More than 95 percent were trained at the level of craftsman (Ministry of Labor 1993), and more than 90 percent of the trainees were men. All training expenses are fully paid for by the government.

The main clientele of the vocational training institutes are out-of-school youth. These institutes also provide training for employed workers wishing to upgrade their skills. Programs in the vocational training institutes last between one month and three years. For basic training, a six-month program leads to certification as an assistant craftsman, a one-year program leads to certification as a Class II craftsman, and programs lasting two to three years qualify workers as a Class I craftsman. Skill upgrade programs are tailored more specifically to the firms' or workers' needs (Ministry of Labor 1993).

Trainees from vocational training centers reportedly had a high rate of placement in the 1970s and 1980s—about 90 percent between 1974 and 1981 (Takeda 1992). But this may not be a stellar performance: at that time unemployment rates for labor force participants between the ages of 15 and 24 were no higher than 15 percent (KLI 1994). These institutes provide substantial financial support to their trainees and are quite expensive to maintain.

It is now believed that public vocational training institutes would have done better to help employed workers upgrade their skills than to help unemployed youth find suitable employment. The Presidential Commis-

TABLE 9-5
Number of Authorized Training Centers and Trainees, 1987–94

| Year | Centers | Trainees |
|------|---------|----------|
| 1987 | 54  | 9,258  |
| 1988 | 73  | 10,335 |
| 1989 | 58  | 21,671 |
| 1990 | 69  | 17,571 |
| 1991 | 52  | 24,249 |
| 1992 | 62  | 30,276 |
| 1993 | 71  | 35,677 |
| 1994 | 138 | 48,247 |

Source: Ministry of Labor.

sion on Education Reform examined the functioning of these institutes and concluded that there was considerable overlap in the clientele and functions of these institutes and the vocational schools under the Ministry of Education. Contrary to their original mission, the training institutes under the Ministry of Labor have increasingly emphasized the vocational education of students, rather than retraining and upgrading of the skills of currently employed workers.

AUTHORIZED TRAINING CENTERS. In 1994 there were 138 training centers authorized or approved by the Ministry of Labor. The number of authorized centers fluctuates considerably from year to year, indicating either the very short-lived nature of these organizations or sharp changes in the approval rates by the ministry. Enrollment has increased steadily, growing more than fivefold since 1987 (table 9-5). These centers, usually run by nonprofit organizations, provide training for trades that are not catered to by public and in-plant training, such as cooking, hairdressing, wallpapering, and teletypewriting (Ministry of Labor 1993). In a subsector that caters to males, these organizations are exceptional in that their clientele is largely female.

### Enterprise-Based Training

The main law governing employer-provided training is the Vocational Training Law, based broadly on the premise that left to themselves, firms will not train "enough" to meet national growth and equity objectives. Besides laying out the conditions of the training promotion levy, the law forms the basis for government incentives to increase in-plant training. The Vocational Training Law has been amended several times. In addition, the Skill Encouragement Law was enacted in 1989 to exhort employers to provide more training, and to admonish Korean society to accord more prestige to craftspeople and technicians, relative to professionals.

TRAINING INCENTIVES AND LEVIES. A number of incentives are offered to employers to conduct in-plant training. First, employers who offer or intend to offer this training can get low-interest loans (below annual market rates) and long-term loans (a 10-year repayment term, with a five-year grace period) for up to 90 percent of the cost of training facilities. Second, local revenue laws exempt employers whose training conforms with the Vocational Training Law from local acquisition, registration, property, and land taxes. Third, under certain conditions, up to 10 percent of the training costs is deductible from annual corporation or income taxes. Finally, repayments of bank loans taken for in-plant training are considered as payment toward a training levy, which is levied on larger employers.

The system of incentives may have been effective initially. From 1968, when the government introduced a system of subsidies for in-plant training, until 1971, when the subsidy was (temporarily) discontinued, the number of trainees grew steadily. In 1974 the government made in-plant training compulsory for firms with more than 500 employees, and the number of trainees rose sharply from 13,000 to a peak of 96,820 by 1976. In 1976 the government expanded the coverage to include all firms with more than 300 employees, but it provided firms with an option to pay a levy instead of providing the training.[11] The Office of Labor Affairs stipulated stringent conditions for what constituted "recognized training," and the levy was used mainly to subsidize public and joint training institutes through the Training Promotion Fund. The number of registered trainees declined to 15,000 in 1989 (table 9-6), despite an increase in the levy from about 12,000 won in 1977 to almost 100,000 won in 1985. About one-third of covered firms opted to pay the levy instead, sometimes even when they were providing in-house training (Takeda 1992). In 1990 the coverage was expanded to include all firms with more than 150 employees. The government also tried to simplify the requirements, but the levy system failed to promote in-plant training.

In part, this failure can be attributed to the complicated rules for determining the training requirements, the levy, and the criteria for approval.

TABLE 9-6
Rate and Coverage of the Training Levy, 1977–91

| Year | Rate (percent) | Covered firms | Percentage of training centers | Number of training centers | Number of trainees |
|------|------|------|------|------|------|
| 1977 | 5.70 | 1,012 | 66.5 | 558 | 58,709 |
| 1978 | 6.20 | 1,095 | 70.7 | 553 | 73,038 |
| 1979 | 6.70 | 1,223 | 59.1 | 575 | 90,992 |
| 1980 | 3.14 | 1,103 | 60.7 | 472 | 66,213 |
| 1981 | 4.13 | 1,103 | 44.0 | 388 | 48,406 |
| 1982 | 2.44 | 1,106 | 45.8 | 283 | 30,131 |
| 1983 | 1.78 | 1,185 | 32.2 | 172 | 20,960 |
| 1984 | 1.82 | 1,263 | 21.1 | 182 | 22,011 |
| 1985 | 1.73 | 1,341 | 38.7 | 185 | 23,876 |
| 1986 | 1.63 | 1,398 | 25.5 | 179 | 19,042 |
| 1987 | 0.17 | 1,537 | 20.6 | 130 | 14,208 |
| 1988 | 0.20 | 1,573 | 25.6 | 132 | 18,168 |
| 1989 | 0.18 | 1,612 | 24.3 | 110 | 15,019 |
| 1990 | 0.30 | 2,575 | 19.6 | 122 | 25,690 |
| 1991 | 0.48 | 2,675 | 18.9 | 147 | 52,566 |

*Note:* The coverage was of firms with more than 300 employees between 1977 and 1989 and of firms with more than 150 employees after 1989. The levy was calculated as a specified percentage of salaries of workers on permanent contracts until 1986. From 1986 to 1991, the levy was assessed as a fraction of the total wages paid.
*Source:* KEDI (1994).

For example, the formula for calculating the compulsory training ratio is quite nontransparent. The training levy is based on unit costs of training by the Ministry of Labor, but the ministry has considerable power to raise or lower the levy arbitrarily. Regarding the content and duration of enterprise-sponsored training, the laws were even more intrusive. Employers were required to submit annual in-service training plans to the ministry for its approval, the training had to have a substantial theoretical component, and the courses had to be at least six months long to be approved (Kim 1987). With all these restrictions, it is hardly surprising that in spite of huge increases in the levy (for example, from 11,500 won in 1981 to 98,000 won in 1986), many employers chose to pay the levy instead.

Beginning July 1, 1995, the coverage of the training levy was reduced to manufacturing firms with more than 1,000 employees, and the levy may be repealed entirely soon. Claims of poaching by large firms remain widespread, and this is cited as a reason to continue the levy, not as a device to encourage training (which it does not appear to do) but as a mechanism for redistributing resources from large firms to small firms.

Employers that opted to train in conformity with Ministry of Labor stipulations could provide in-plant training, they could arrange cooperative training with other employers, or they could commission a third party to do the training. The number of firms doing independent training has declined over time, while those cooperating with other firms has remained relatively constant (Kim 1987).

Costs. As in other countries, it is difficult to obtain cost figures for in-service training. One study of vocational high schools (three-year programs), public vocational training institutes (one-year programs), and in-service training (varying duration) found that the cost per trainee was lowest for in-plant training and highest for vocational high schools (Lee 1985). But since the education and experience of trainees are likely to be quite different for these three training modes, such comparisons are at best suggestive.

New approach. It is now acknowledged that the government interfered too strongly in the content and duration of in-service training: this forced firms to undertake suboptimal training but did not increase private training expenditures. Korea's lessons in this regard are valuable for countries considering the adoption or expansion of training levies. Korea's new approach to enterprise training marks a retreat from relatively coercive measures (based on a training levy, exemptions, and attempts to tightly regulate training activities) to a noninterventionist system of broad tax incentives and balanced regulations.

## Pressures to Reform VET

Korea is experiencing pressures from two sides to reform its vocational education and training: labor-related pressures and education-related pressures. Policymakers perceive a tightening labor market for technicians that is reflected in a narrowing of wage differentials between the graduates of junior colleges and universities and those of technical secondary schools. This is seen by some as a signal for expanding vocational education. General secondary schooling has virtually been reduced to a vehicle to prepare pupils for the college entrance examination. Preoccupied with making sure that human resource development policies meet "industrial manpower needs," policymakers have paid less attention to individual or social demand for higher education. In this social contest, and given the rapid economic growth from the mid-1960s to the mid-1990s, policymakers view VET as the key to reducing the pressure on universities to enroll great numbers and to meeting a "shortage" of skilled and semiskilled workers, especially technicians.

## The Uncurbed Demand for Higher Education

Although the main goal of VET policies was always to meet industrial demands, once Korea reached near universal secondary enrollment, policymakers began using vocational tracking in high schools to limit entry to higher education. The underlying belief was that if this appetite of Koreans for higher education was left unchecked, there would be a "surplus" of college graduates in the labor market. Manpower requirement projections indicated this, and the higher rates of unemployment for graduates of academic high schools and colleges appeared to confirm it. Given the willingness of Korean parents to pay for their children's higher education, the supply of college places would hardly be a check. In other words, a private sector supply response would be forthcoming.

Vocational schools are seen as second-best by parents after academic schools, "even though the employability of vocational high school graduates in Seoul and Pusan has been better than for academic high school graduates" (Sorensen 1994), and even though graduate unemployment remains relatively high. One reason for this is that *social prestige* is considerably enhanced by attending university (table 9-7). To give their children some hope of getting into college, parents have pressured authorities to keep adding general subjects to vocational school curricula. Presumably this is a rational decision on the part of the parents and pupils in terms of balancing social and job prospects.

Efforts by Korean policymakers to curb this "social" demand for education have not succeeded, despite a decline in the relative wages of more educated workers. In 1975 those with a middle school diploma or less earned a quarter of what college graduates earned; by 1993 this ratio had changed to one-half. This is reinforced by a higher rate of unemployment among academic secondary graduates who cannot pursue higher studies, and among the graduates of both two-year and four-year postsecondary programs. The differences in annual earnings between university graduates

TABLE 9-7
The Purpose of Educating Children According to Korean Parents, 1993
(percentage of responses)

| | Sons | | Daughters | |
|---|---|---|---|---|
| Purpose | Overall education | College | Overall education | College |
| Character and culture | 35 | 43 | 35 | 43 |
| Job | 37 | 28 | 13 | 8 |
| Improvement of nature | 14 | 20 | 21 | 28 |
| Marital advantage | 9 | 8 | 26 | 19 |
| Compensation for education | 6 | 1 | 5 | 1 |
| Other | 0 | 1 | 0 | 1 |

Source: KEDI (1994).

and high school graduates have narrowed.[12] Nevertheless, they remain considerable and continue to rise: between 1980 and 1992, wages rose 3.2 times for those with a junior college degree or more.[13] In part, of course, this demand for higher education is attributable to its considerable non-labor-market benefits (table 9-7).

## Inefficient Public Training Institutes

Academic high school graduates (and high school dropouts) who cannot get admission into a university or junior college are trained for up to three years at vocational training centers run by the Ministry of Labor. The training is free of charge, with additional financial support determined by a means test.

In the 1970s and 1980s, when unemployment rates were relatively high, these training centers were pressed to address the problem of youth unemployment. By the mid-1990s, however, this problem had diminished, largely because of the impressive economic performance and absolute declines in the school-age population. The role, costs, and effectiveness of these centers then began to be questioned.

No rigorous evaluation of the cost-effectiveness of these centers is available. With declining numbers of trainees, these institutes are now competing with vocational schools and junior colleges for students. In 1995 the Presidential Commission on Educational Reform addressed the possibility of consolidating vocational schools and training institutes (under the ministries of education and labor, respectively) into one administrative body in order to increase efficiency and cost-saving. The commission's subcommittee on vocational education recommended that the training institutes concentrate on upgrading the skills of workers who are already employed, rather than providing pre-employment training.

### Unsuccessful Legislative Measures

Since the 1960s, Korea has experimented with various measures to increase in-plant training. Large firms were exhorted to provide in-plant training, and they were forced to pay a levy if they did not or if their training did not meet government regulations. This mandate applied initially to firms with at least 500 employees, but the coverage was later expanded to firms larger than 300, then to firms with more than 150 employees, and finally to firms with more than 1,000 employees. The levy itself has varied, from almost 7 percent of payroll to less than half percent. The measure is now recognized to be ineffective in increasing training by firms.

## Recent Policy Reforms: Constraints and Innovations

The government's efforts to reform VET faced constraints shared by many developing countries: first, a manpower projections approach to decisionmaking that reflected an interventionist stance on matters concerning education and training; second, problems in keeping VET institutions relevant in a rapidly growing economy; and third, a strong social demand for higher education.

### Principal Constraints

Until the 1997 crisis, labor market trends indicated scarcities of lower-level skilled and temporary workers and a "surplus" of white-collar workers. There was also a structural imbalance between the demand for graduates in the scientific and technical fields, on the one hand, and the excess supply in the area of nontechnical and liberal arts, on the other. These imbalances may be related to the fact that the government intervenes in the admission process by setting quotas for different program fields, based on demand and supply forecasted using manpower planning techniques. The reluctance to shift from this approach has proved to be a major constraint.

Efforts to vocationalize secondary schools met serious obstacles. There was the difficulty in funding costly facilities and equipment for existing and new vocational schools to accommodate an increased quota of vocational students. There was also the problem of justifying the practice of forcing children into the vocational track. Parents and children clearly favored the general track, which kept the way open for university education. Many middle school graduates are still reluctant to enter vocational high schools, because of their desire to go on to a university education, and because of the relatively poor quality of instruction in vocational schools.

Not surprisingly, the number of students enrolled in vocational high schools has declined. The strong, perhaps even exaggerated, social demand for higher education is a factor, but so too is the relevance and quality of the instruction received. These institutions had difficulty attracting students despite narrowing wage differentials between university graduates and vocational high school graduates. Problems also have occurred in the employment and utilization of the graduates of vocational programs. Though the rate of employment in recent years has improved, at least at the initial entry point upon graduation, many graduates do not stay long in their first job.

## Vocational Schools and Institutes: Proposals of the Presidential Commission

The Korean government, since 1991, has introduced various measures to strengthen the VET system. The most distinctive effort has been to restructure the secondary school system toward greater vocationalization. The plan called to drastically reduce the enrollment quota of students in the general and humanities track and increase the proportion of vocational track students. Also, special vocational classes attached to general high schools were expanded for humanities students who wanted vocational education. The period from 1990 to 1995 was characterized by an uncomfortable contradiction: vocational/technical education, the sector of education with seemingly the lowest social demand, was expanded in response to government perceptions that it produced workers who were in high demand in the labor market.

In 1994 and 1995 the Presidential Commission for Educational Reform deliberated whether expanding vocational enrollments and encouraging closer industry-school linkages was an effective way to respond to labor market trends. By the end of 1995, it had decided that the on-going vocationalization effort was not adequate and that some of the earlier policy approaches taken were inappropriate. The judgment of the commission was that expanding enrollment in existing vocational programs would not be effective in luring students and parents away from the university race. It was clear that existing vocational school programs did not provide "real" and attractive alternatives to students. And since the vocational track is a dead end, it is unpopular.

Changes proposed by the presidential commission imply a shift from rigid and uniform government control of secondary schools to less coercive policies, and efforts to redesign vocational education to conform to social conditions rather than the other way round. The commission stated that the new system would diversify student choice and make vocational education more attractive to consumers. This emphasis on delivery quality—rather than quantitative targets—and an adequate supply response are the fundamental themes reflected in the commission's specific recommendations.

EMPHASIZING QUALITY TO ELICIT GREATER DEMAND. Recognizing that demand will rise if the quality of education improves, the commission proposed the following:

• *Diversified programs.* One way to improve quality in the provision and management of vocational programs is to diversify programs and institutions to better accommodate the changing needs of the industry and students.

• *Specialized high schools.* One of the commission's proposals is the establishment of specialized vocational high schools. Existing vocational high schools will be encouraged to upgrade to specialized high school status.[14] Specialized high schools will have up-to-date facilities and be easily accessible by public transportation. Proposed measures include improving the external conditions of the school building, playground, and minimum land area. These specialized high schools will allow students, early in their lives, to consider their interests and talents in deciding their future and help them develop marketable competencies in specialized skill areas (for instance, electronic communications, design, popular music). Freed from various regulations imposed on other schools, specialized vocational schools will be given privileges to design programs and select their students. Graduates of specialized vocational schools will be exempt from the requirements of scholastic aptitude test results for college admission, if they apply in the same major field area.

• *Further education for vocational graduates and workers.* To attract students into secondary-level vocational programs, opportunities will be expanded for vocational secondary school completers to continue their education. Exempting admission exam scores for entry into junior technical colleges and other vocational institutions of higher education is an example. Among the innovative programs proposed in this regard is the introduction of a "new college" system to be built on the actual work sites. A business or a consortium of employers may establish a college program, which would allow workers to earn a college-level degree while employed. Lectures for basic courses and theory will be offered through distance learning technology, and on-site duty will count as lab credits.

FACILITATING AN ADEQUATE SUPPLY RESPONSE. The commission has also recommended the following to ensure that the supply response is adequate:

• *Integration of vocational and academic curricula.* Schools that wish to do so can integrate the curricula of vocational and general high schools. This will give students a wider selection of courses irrespective of their fields of study. Schools that integrate and operate both types of curricula will minimize the number of compulsory courses that students must take and increase the number of elective courses. The commission has suggested that integrated schools provide open curricula in which the school curricula are linked to area training institutes or technical schools for lab facilities.

• *Deregulation.* Rigid and uniform regulations and criteria for school charters will be greatly relaxed to allow flexibility in management and utilization of innovative types of vocational programs and new schools. Building, facilities, and land requirements will be eased and simplified. Equipment requirements will be strengthened instead. In addition, distance learning technology will be expanded for area vocational schools.

• *Changes in teacher certification.* To improve the quality of vocational programs, a more open system of teacher certification and appointment is proposed. The recruitment and appointment of vocational teachers will be deregulated and diversified by inviting experienced personnel from industries to teach. Retired but experienced and competent individuals with technical expertise will be given teaching qualification. To upgrade the quality of education for vocational high schools, industry personnel with field expertise will be invited to conduct practice-oriented classes. Also, vocational teachers will be sent to companies for field experience.

• *Expanded financial support for vocational high schools and students.* As the result of a recommendation by the Presidential Commission for Education Reform in 1995, the education budget was expanded to 5 percent of gross national product from about 3.7 percent. Priority was given to vocational programs in allocating the funds that have been increased. The new funding was used to upgrade lab conditions, innovate programs, and attract students with scholarships.

• *More in-plant training programs.* The commission recommended other means to encourage firms to establish in-plant training programs. It hoped to reduce the government's role in training and increase the role by the private sector. The scope of school-industry cooperation will be extended to provide students of vocational high schools with on-the-job training. The 2+1 system will be adjusted so that the duration, time, and type of training will become flexible.

## Enterprise Training

Research at the Korea Labor Institute indicated that the levy had been ineffective in raising the incidence and amount of training. After several changes, the coverage of the training levy was reduced in July 1995 to manufacturing firms with more than 1,000 workers. The levy on large firms was maintained at least in part because it was believed that they "poach" the best (namely, most trained) workers from small and medium-size firms, though there is no rigorous evidence to substantiate this claim. The levy is expected to be eliminated soon. Korea introduced an unemployment insurance system in 1995, and vocational training was integrated into this system. The previous beneficiaries of the training levy were primarily the public training centers of the Korea Manpower Agency. They will have to be funded from the unemployment insurance levy or from general funds, or they must raise finances from students and employers.

The reduction in the levy's coverage and a reevaluation of its role signal a slow retreat from coercive policies to increase training in the workplace. Calls on the Ministry of Labor to focus on occupational upgrading of currently employed workers (rather than on training secondary school students) should also be seen in the light of this retreat.

## Lessons from Korea's Experience

Korea's experience with VET is distinctive for two reasons: its high share of private involvement in provision and financing at all stages of development, and its rare willingness—compared with most other developing countries—to conduct a hard-nosed evaluation of its policies and to discontinue those that are revealed to be ineffective.

These features make Korea's VET system an invaluable "model" for other countries to study. Rather than blindly emulating Korea, they can learn what strategies are effective at various stages of institutional and economic development and under differing labor market conditions. Korea's experience with vocational and technical education and training offers specific lessons with regard to the sequencing of government policies, the difficulty of encouraging private sector participation, and the limits of government involvement.

## Sequencing

By design or by coincidence, Korea invested in vocational education (at the senior secondary level) only after achieving universal primary education. Even when vocational and technical high school enrollments were expanding, their share remained below 40 percent of total senior secondary enrollment. Postsecondary vocational education expanded after near universal secondary enrollment was attained. Even so, the structure of vocational education has to be restructured to reflect changes in economic conditions and the demand of students.

The government encouraged the establishment of vocational training centers outside of formal education. These centers specialized in short courses of up to one year for people with junior secondary schooling. In fact, many of the trainees had higher levels of schooling and work experience.

A similar pattern applies for governmental initiatives to encourage in-service training. Measures to increase in-service training were taken after the working population had achieved high levels of literacy. By the mid-1960s, when the first initiatives were taken, the labor force was largely literate, and almost all new entrants had at least a primary education. The working population without formal education had declined from 40 percent in 1946 to 6 percent in 1960; illiteracy rates had fallen from 78 percent in 1945 to 28 percent in 1960, to 12 percent in 1970. Students and workers in VET programs thus had a sound education base, which means high levels of trainability.

## Private-Public Partnership

The private sector in Korea has always borne a large share of the cost of VET, either through fees charged in publicly provided education, or through direct provision in schools, training centers, and firms. While the government provides financial support for public and (to some extent) private schools and colleges, over 40 percent of junior secondary schools were private until the mid-1970s, and private sector participation was even greater for higher levels of vocational education.

The private share of commercial secondary schools grew from 57 percent in 1969 to 71 percent in 1981 and that of technical secondary schools increased from 40 to 46 percent during this period. To a lesser extent, firms also gave financial support and equipment to schools and to employees enrolling in these schools. While the government established some institutes, its main contribution was to monitor instruction quality.

## Limits of Government Involvement

Because of these investments in education and training, the large wage differentials between college graduates and workers without a high school diploma that existed in the 1970s fell by half by 1993. But Korea's appetite for education remains unsatisfied. There is a strong demand for better quality and more education, and Korea's policymakers—fearing either "overeducation" or a mismatch between the economy's needs and the output of the education system—have tried to curb this demand using questionable interventionist strategies.

For example, in 1975, worried about the adverse social effects of competition among parents to enroll their children in a small number of good schools, policymakers instituted a system in which elementary school completers were allocated to junior secondary schools through a lottery. In the 1980s, when secondary education had expanded to near universal enrollment, the government outlawed private tutoring at the senior secondary school level to reduce the advantage wealthy families had in getting their children placed in the top public universities. But these changes have had only limited success in meeting their objectives. Besides, with greater democratization, similarly intrusive measures may no longer be a viable option.

Korea's experience encouraging enterprise-based training also provides important lessons on what the government can and cannot do. In 1968 the government introduced a system of subsidies for in-plant training. The number of trainees grew steadily until 1971, when the subsidy was discontinued. In 1974 the government made in-plant training compulsory for firms with more than 500 employees, and the number of trainees rose sharply to a peak of 96,820 trainees by 1976. That year the government expanded the coverage to include all firms with more than 300 employees, but it

provided firms with an option to pay a levy instead of providing the training. The Office of Labor Affairs stipulated stringent conditions for what
constituted "training." The number of registered trainees declined to 15,000
in 1989. Despite an eightfold increase in the levy between 1977 and 1985,
about one-third of covered firms opted to pay it. In July 1995 the coverage
was reduced to firms with more than 1,000 workers, after evaluations indicated that the levy had been ineffective in raising the incidence and amount
of training.

## Conclusion

Korea's approach to VET illustrates a general strength in policymaking
that contributed to its stellar economic performance until the mid-1990s:
the willingness to evaluate whether policy actions were effective, and to
alter or abandon efforts if they were less than satisfactory. For example,
government efforts to promote enterprise-based training have been critically evaluated, and the policies changed quite often in the face of evidence
of their ineffectiveness.

   Procedures for selection to higher education have been repeatedly changed
as previous practices have been evaluated and found inadequate for meeting either equity or efficiency objectives. Although some countries would
have been content with the results that Korea's policies have yielded, the
government appointed a Presidential Commission on Education Reform
to re-examine all aspects of education and training so that Korea's changing
demands for skilled workers would be met more efficiently and equitably.

   Korea's most recent VET policies signal a retreat from a relatively coercive approach that involved quantitative targets (for example, in vocational
tracking in secondary education), forced contributions from the private
sector (for example, the training levy), and exhorted private firms and individuals to conform with governmental objectives. The new approach takes
societal and employer preferences as given, emphasizes quality (for instance,
in the case of vocational schools), and relies on realigning government funding mechanisms to improve VET outcomes.

## Notes

   1. The source of all of these statistics is KLI (1994).
   2. Special attention to technical education came in the early 1970s, when vocational schools were established in conjunction with the government's plans to move
into heavy industry and the chemical industry (Sorensen 1994).

3. The Presidential Commission on Educational Reform has deliberated at length on these issues.

4. The data were supplied by the National Statistical Office in 1995.

5. On-the-job training of already employed workers was encouraged by policy measures to increase in-service training in private enterprises. These measures included apprenticeships and financial incentives to train workers, as well as coercive measures. Korea's attempts to increase in-service training are particularly interesting for countries that believe that governments must actively encourage training of workers by private firms.

6. This is because in most countries, the educated generally come from wealthier families and can finance longer periods of unemployment, and because finding a good skill-job match is more difficult in educated occupations.

7. The national government ran 38 training centers for prison inmates.

8. In the construction sector, the cutoff limit was based on the size of business (sales/turnover) in the previous year. The levy was established under the Vocational Training Promotion Fund Law enacted in 1976.

9. There are supplementary (nontraditional) vocational schools (such as civic, trade, correspondence, and other schools), but they are regarded as nonformal institutions that are a part of social education. These schools had an enrollment of more than 200,000 in the early 1990s; two-thirds of the students were female. We do not discuss these supplementary vocational schools in this chapter.

10. In the early 1990s general secondary schools were instructed to expand the teaching of vocational subjects and to strengthen their ties with vocational training centers run by the Ministry of Labor.

11. The covered sectors are mining, manufacturing, construction, utilities, services, transportation, communications, and warehousing. For construction firms, the size is calculated by seeing if the contract amount is equivalent to the stipulated employment size (Kim 1987).

12. The ratio of earnings declined from about 2.1 in 1975 to about 1.6 in 1995.

13. Wages for workers with a middle school diploma or less rose 5.5 times and 4.3 times for high school graduates.

14. The Ministry of Education commissioned a national project to develop specific details on standards and policy guidelines for newly proposed schools.

## References

Chang, Suk-Min. 1994. "Education and Training for the Work Force: Linking Work and Learning in a Changing Society." Korea–OECD Education Policy Seminar, May-June.

Chang, Suk-Min, and Young-Chul Kim. 1995. "Secondary Education in Korea: 1960-90." Report for the Asian Development Bank. Korean Education Development Institute, Seoul.

Ihm, Chon-Sun, and others. 1992. "An Analysis of the Efficiency in High School Vocational Technical Education in Korea." Korean Educational Development Institute, Seoul.

————. 1993. "A Study on the Training and Utilization of Technical Manpower in Korea." Korean Educational Development Institute, Seoul.

Jeong, Jooyeon. 1995. "The Failure of Recent State Vocational Policies in Korea from a Comparative Perspective." *British Journal of Industrial Relations* 33 (2): 237–52.

KEDI (Korean Educational Development Institute). 1994. *Educational Indicators in Korea.* Seoul.

Kim, Sookon. 1987. "In-Service Training as an Instrument for the Development of Human Resources in Korea." Report sponsored by the OECD Development Center and the Korean Chamber of Commerce. Graduate Institute of Peace Studies, Kyung Hee University.

KLI (Korea Labor Institute). 1994. *The Profile of Korean Human Assets: Labor Statistics.* Seoul.

Lee, Kye Woo. 1985. *Human Resources Planning in the Republic of Korea.* World Bank, East Asia Region, Washington, D.C.

Ministry of Labor. 1993. *Vocational Training in Korea.* Seoul.

Sorensen, Clark W. 1994. "Success and Education in South Korea." *Comparative Education Review* 38 (1).

Takeda, Sachi. 1992. "Human Resource Development in Korea: Lessons for Indonesia." World Bank, East Asia Region, Washington, D.C.

Uh, Soo-Bong. 1993. "Employment Structure." In Young-Bum Park, ed., *Labor in Korea.* Seoul: Korea Labor Institute.

# 10 Chile

ALEJANDRA COX EDWARDS

SINCE 1990 CHILE'S gross domestic product per capita has grown by about 5 percent annually. Open unemployment rates fell from more than 20 percent in the early 1980s to less than 6 percent today. Between 1984 and 1994 average real wages grew by 28 percent. By 1995, aided by a system of targeted transfers, headcount poverty had fallen to about half of what it had been in the early 1980s. By 1997 gross national product per capita was US$5,022, and during the first half of 1998 employment growth was 5.4 percent. Chile's performance in improving the most basic labor-market indicators and reducing poverty is impressive and, unfortunately, rare outside of East Asia.

## Background

Chile's reliance on market-friendly, outward-oriented economic policies has been credited with these successes. However, the successes have also invited closer scrutiny of other outcomes of these policies. In particular, observers have questioned whether economic success as measured by average magnitudes—such as per capita income, average labor earnings, and job creation—mask important socioeconomic failures, as indicated by growing inequality in the distribution of income and in the quality of social services such as education and health. Indeed, some observers foresee a frightening possibility in 20 years, with Chile being transformed into a booming economy atop a sea of unskilled and underpaid citizens. The combination of an open economy and a flexible labor market is seen by

294

some to be the cause of growing socioeconomic ills, especially income in-equality. They argue that international trade has led to widening differen-tials in earnings between the poor and the rich, and that labor market reforms have prevented the disadvantaged from stemming this tide.

Increasing or high inequality of earnings can slow growth and may in-duce reversal of earlier reforms, especially the reform of labor legislation. Accordingly, the government is concerned about this development. How-ever, the distribution of income did not worsen between 1987 and 1994. Nevertheless, Chile remains a highly unequal economy despite government efforts to provide targeted assistance to the poorest households (Ferreira and Litchfield 1996). Gill and Montenegro (forthcoming) find that labor earnings have, in fact, become less unequal since the early 1990s. The gov-ernment has been appropriately cautious about changing labor laws, but it views education and training as a major instrument to help poor segments reap some of the reward of economic prosperity. Vocational education and training—traditionally the forms of investment in human capital most rel-evant for poor segments in countries that have attained near universal pri-mary enrollment—occupied an important part of the debate in Chile in the 1990s.

## Patterns and Trends in Labor Earnings and Unemployment

Between 1992 and 1994, average labor earnings for all workers fell by 1.7 percent. Earnings for the lowest three decile groups fell between 2 and 5 percent. The ratio of earnings of the richest to the poorest group stayed steady at about 14. These findings suggest that inequality in earnings re-mained roughly constant between 1987 and 1992, with some redistribu-tion away from the richest 10 percent and poorest 30 percent of households and toward the middle and upper-middle classes between 1992 and 1994. Naturally, labor earnings are observed only for those who work. Unem-ployment may be an important determinant of a household's relative posi-tion in the per capita income distribution. Changes in unemployment rates are important in explaining short-term fluctuations in the income distri-bution through losses in the share of the poorest households.

In Chile, as expected, unemployment is significantly correlated with being in a poor household for both men and women: workers in the poor-est 10 percent of households are almost four times more likely to be unem-ployed than the average worker. This ratio does not change significantly over the years, indicating that unemployment is always critical in determining household income, the variable used to classify households into the decile groups (Gill and Montenegro forthcoming).

Short-term fluctuations in unemployment by income group defy simple characterizations. Between 1987 and 1992, average male unemployment rates fell steadily from almost 9.0 percent to 4.7 percent, and then rose to about 6.0 percent in 1994. Female unemployment rates were higher, but they exhibit similar trends. These changes are fairly uniform across income classes for men between 1987 and 1992: unemployment rates fell by half for almost all groups. Between 1992 and 1994, however, the increases are not uniform: male unemployment rates rose by 25 percent or more for the decile groups 1, 4, 5, and 10, and rose marginally or fell for the other groups. Patterns for women are similar to those for men, with the difference that female unemployment rates for the poorest three groups rose by roughly the same proportion between 1992 and 1994 (Gill and Montenegro forthcoming)

## Returns to Education and Training

The main results of a study of earnings in Chile (Gill and Montenegro forthcoming) are that rates of return to education are systematically higher for higher education levels. These broad patterns also hold for rates of return to education for different decile groups (by household per capita income). Not surprisingly, workers from poor households also have lower levels of education. At the secondary school level, the most immediate and direct impact of improvements in education on poor segments of the population will likely come through improved relevance and quality of technical and vocational education. Poor groups constitute a large share of this stream of education, and this is unlikely to change in the near future. Training programs for unemployed workers are also believed to have been effective in lowering unemployment among certain groups. Therefore, vocational education and training (VET) may be of primary importance in providing labor market skills in a manner that also reduces inequality. This chapter explores the development of vocational education and training in Chile and the lessons for other countries from the many innovations made in the country since the early 1980s.

## Reform of Vocational Education and Training

The objectives of and constraints to reform of VET in Chile are best understood in the context of broader education sector reforms, which began in the late 1970s as part of a comprehensive structural adjustment in response to triple-digit inflation, unsustainable budget deficits, and sluggish economic growth. The new, decentralized approach to funding the social sectors, including education and training, was part of the effort to reduce the public sector deficit, which by the late 1970s had reached 25 percent of gross domestic product, and inflation, which by that time amounted to 600 percent per year. While the expansion of education was deemed necessary for economic and social progress, public expenditures had to be reduced.

The main components of the education reform that affected vocational and training schools included implementing decentralized management at all levels, removing barriers to entry by new providers, and changing the rules for allocating public funds to educational institutions at all levels. At the primary and secondary educational levels the reforms based funding on per student subsidies, expanded the private subsidized sector, and required local governments to administer publicly managed schools. These reforms, which began in the late 1970s, stalled during the recession of 1982 as financial support for reforms declined, but they were resumed and completed in 1986.

In 1990 public spending for education started to rise again, and by 1994 public expenditures were 20 percent above their 1980 level. The expansion of primary, secondary, and postsecondary systems has resulted in universal coverage for primary education, 75 percent coverage for secondary education, and a doubling of postsecondary enrollments. While in 1980 all postsecondary enrollment was concentrated in eight traditional universities, by 1991 these eight universities represented only 46 percent of all enrollment. These educational gains were made despite reduced public funding at all levels of education.

Vocational education in Chile begins at the secondary school level, where about 40 percent of students are in the technical-vocational training track, up from 31 percent in 1980. Postsecondary education consists of instruction at professional institutes, technical training centers, and universities, with professional institutes and technical training centers accounting for up to 40 percent of postsecondary enrollment.

## Vocational Secondary Education Reforms

In the 1980s publicly financed vocational schooling consisted of two types of schools: public schools, which were financed and managed by the Ministry of Education, and religious schools, which were partially subsidized by the Ministry of Education. Technical-vocational schools, henceforth referred to simply as vocational schools, represented 30 percent of total secondary enrollment and were facing fiscal difficulties. The new fiscal reality that came with structural adjustment dictated that vocational schools modernize or disappear. Curricular changes and better coordination between the supply of skilled graduates and the demand for skilled workers had to be instituted for vocational schools to survive.

ENTERPRISE-ORIENTED SCHOOLS. Despite budgetary limitations, the weakness of the private sector in the 1980s, and the lack of experience with private management of vocational schools in countries at a similar level of development, the government decided to keep vocational schools open and to incorporate them into the educational reform. With the encouragement of the Chilean Planning Office, the first vocational schools were legally transferred to private corporations. An important condition of this agreement was the stipulation that guaranteed state funding or a base budget. These regulations favored vocational schools managed by corporations. The hope behind this policy was that, in the future, enterprises could manage all vocational schools. The 1983 curricular framework for vocational schools mandated that those schools respond to job market needs. This directive brought about an important revision in curricula. The first two years of secondary education would have a common curriculum for all students, who would then specialize in the third year according to occupational demands.

MONEY FOLLOWS STUDENTS. The funding formula that the reform introduced left the question of the relative size of vocational schooling open to market forces. Money, in this case public subsidies, follows students. Nevertheless, the state maintains control over two key variables that influence school choice, namely, the basic curriculum and financial support.

The law establishes the basic subsidies for all schools, with the exception of vocational schools transferred to corporations. The value of the subsidy increases with the grade of the student and allows for additional funds to cover the expenses of handicapped children. In some cases transport is covered. Schools that comply with ministerial requirements related to maximum number of students per class, basic curriculum regulations, and physical facilities are permitted to apply for funding.

The government has responded to pressures to increase subsidies in line with higher costs, even though the original intent was not to finance the entire per student cost. The structure of the subsidy was modified in 1987 and in 1993. The 1987 law introduced a unit of account that automatically adjusted the subsidy with the adjustment of public sector salaries; modified the payment structure to approximate more closely the costs per school grade, with significant increases given to the secondary vocational track; and introduced special coefficients for allocating additional payments to "low density schools." Since 1993, aided by changes in the law, schools have relied more on voluntary contributions from parents to augment funds.

Agricultural schools receive a subsidy that is about twice the size of the one given to general secondary schools, plus a living expenses allowance in the case of boarding schools. The per student subsidy given to industrial schools in 1993 was about 60 percent higher, and that given to commercial schools was about 25 percent higher, than that directed toward general secondary schools (table 10-1). In 1992 in municipal and subsidized schools, the per unit cost of secondary general education was about US$1,700, while that of vocational education was about US$2,500; in corporation-run vocational schools the corresponding figure was US$3,200 (table 10-2).

TABLE 10-1
Per Student Subsidy, 1980, 1987, 1993
(U.S. dollars)

| Type of education | 1980 | 1987 | 1993 |
|---|---|---|---|
| Preschool | 8.5 | 9.6 | 11.6 |
| *Primary* | | | |
| Grades 1–6 | 8.5–9.6 | 10.5 | 12.8 |
| Grades 7–8 | 10.3 | 11.7 | 14.2 |
| Adult education | 2.9 | 3.3 | 6.1 |
| Special education | 21.5 | 21.0–31.5 | 38.4 |
| *Secondary* | | | |
| General | 11.6 | 13.1 | 15.9 |
| Adult education | 3.5 | 3.9 | 7.2 |
| Technical-vocational | 6.8–11.6 | — | — |
| Agriculture and seamanship | — | 21.1–31.6 | 25.2 |
| Industrial | — | 16.9–23.2 | 18.9 |
| Commercial | — | 10.5–13.7 | 16.6 |

— Not available.
*Source:* Government of Chile data.

TABLE 10-2
Total Cost of a Secondary Graduate, 1992
(U.S. dollars)

| School type | Municipal | Subsidized | Private | Corporation |
|---|---|---|---|---|
| General secondary | 1,697 | 1,643 | 4,329 | n.a. |
| Vocational | 2,573 | 2,465 | n.a. | 3,223 |

n.a. Not applicable.
*Note:* August 1992 U.S. dollars converted at the rate of US$1 = Ch$375.
*Source:* Salas Opazo and Gaymer Cortes (1993).

JUSTIFICATION FOR HIGHER SUBSIDIES TO VOCATIONAL SCHOOLS. The 1980 reform established a funding structure that differentiated schools by level and made allowances for distance. Municipal and subsidized schools enrolling first-year students in vocational programs get less funding than if they enrolled them in the general track. The government was willing to continue funding vocational schools more generously only if they were transferred to corporations, but in 1987 the funding structure changed and improved incentives for maintaining the vocational track in municipal and other subsidized schools.

The financial support that the government gives to vocational schools over and above that offered to general secondary schools has efficiency effects. The evidence on private returns to vocational education indicate that school-to-work transitions for vocational graduates are faster than transitions for general secondary graduates, and that vocational graduates earn more than their general secondary counterparts. Butelmann and Romaguera (1994) show that rates of return to vocational and general secondary schooling are not significantly different when the sample is restricted to males. They argue persuasively that a positive selection bias affects the comparison for females, because those that choose vocational schooling are more likely to make a transfer to the labor market. Therefore, measured differences in rates of return between vocational and general secondary education for females are an overestimate of differences in returns for a random sample.

The financial support that the government gives to vocational schools also has equity effects. There are reasons to believe that students who choose the vocational track are typically less well off than their counterparts in the general secondary track. Parents' education is correlated with parents' income, and there is a correlation between parents' education and the types of schools their children attend: parents of general secondary students have three to four more years of schooling than do parents of children in vocational schools. This means that the extra support for vocational schools does benefit a relatively poor segment of the population (table 10-3).

DIVERSIFICATION OF FUNDING SOURCES. In addition to the per student funding from the state, all subsidized schools can receive payments of tuition fees from parents. Schools are free to decide their fees, but they cannot make entry conditional on tuition payments, and therefore parents are not obliged to pay. Until 1993, unaffiliated, private subsidized schools depended almost exclusively on subsidy payments for their revenues. The possibility of accepting voluntary contributions from parents gained new impetus in a law passed in 1993 that referred to this option as shared funding. Monthly incomes from voluntarily paid tuition fees must be reported, and the Ministry of Education has the legal right to reduce the state subsidy in proportion to the amount received as fees. This right is currently being exercised, and about 40 percent of the tuition fees collected is discounted from the state subsidy. The new law also established a threshold for tuition fees equal to two to three times the basic subsidy, above which schools would be disqualified from receipt of the subsidy.

TABLE 10-3
Schooling of Parents and Type of Schools their Children Attend,
by Gender, 1992
(years of schooling)

| Gender of children and school type | Schooling of parents | | | |
|---|---|---|---|---|
| | General secondary | Commercial | Industrial | Agricultural |
| *Males* | | | | |
| Private subsidized | 14.2 | 7.9 | 7.6 | 7.2 |
| Municipal | 11.3 | 8.4 | 6.6 | 4.5 |
| Corporation | 9.9 | 9.3 | 7.9 | 7.3 |
| *Females* | | | | |
| Private subsidized | 14.2 | 7.3 | 7.2 | 4.2 |
| Municipal | 11.3 | 7.8 | 7.2 | — |
| Corporation | 9.2 | 8.2 | 8.3 | — |

— Not available.
*Source:* Cox Edwards and Dar (1994).

Private subsidized schools affiliated with business or religious organizations receive both public subsidies and donations from their sponsors. In 1979 a reform of the tax law allowed taxpayers to treat donations to schools and nonprofit organizations as expenses for tax purposes. Vocational schools have an additional avenue for generating their own resources through selling products or services. Unlike municipal and corporate schools, which were granted the land and infrastructure, newly private subsidized schools were compelled to make large investments in fixed capital.

Municipal schools have seen distinct advantages on many fronts as a result of reforms. In addition to the advantage of being granted both the land and the school buildings, municipal schools have access to municipal funds, which in wealthy municipalities can be substantial. Municipal governments receive funding from three main sources: the Ministry of Education; the Ministry of the Interior, which is traditionally responsible for their budgets; and the Ministry of Planning, which is responsible for poverty alleviation programs, taxes, and user fees. The Ministry of Education provides per student subsidies and extraordinary funding to cover all teacher salary increases. The Ministry of the Interior provides funding for the construction of new schools, for the expansion of buildings, for repairs, and for upkeep. The Ministry of Planning, through the Social Investment Fund, provides funding for secondary education. These additional budgetary sources have changed the funding formula in favor of municipal schools.

TEACHERS' PAY AND PREROGATIVES. Responsibility for teachers' pay was decentralized along with the transfer of schools. Prior to reforms, public school teachers were paid according to the public sector pay scale and were promoted according to seniority rules. After the reform, teachers had two options: they could continue being paid according to the public sector pay scale, or they could accept the private sector rules for voluntary negotiation of pay. Both alternatives were to be regulated by the new Labor Code introduced in 1979, which eliminated the special statutes for teachers.

Facing the risk of dismissals and wage losses, municipal teachers started to exert a great deal of pressure to recover the statutory rights that teachers employed under the auspices of the Ministry of Education still enjoyed. This brought the Ministry of Education back into management of municipal schools in terms of (a) restricting the opening of new schools in a given jurisdiction whenever schools already in existence had places available; (b) preventing municipalities from firing teachers; and (c) mandating wage adjustments, even after municipal school teachers had received full severance pay for the transfer. However, further funding crises in the mid-1980s, this time arising from the municipalities, forced the Ministry of Education to substantially revise downward its guarantees of salary supplementation, which eventually led to the removal of job guarantees (Castaneda 1992). The restrictions on school openings were removed in 1986, but municipal schools cannot be closed without prior approval of the Ministry of Education.

In 1991, a decade after the reforms were initiated, and under mounting pressure from teachers' unions, Congress approved a new statute that regulates teachers' contracts with municipalities in detail, including allocation of time, activities, and hourly salaries. The statute unified the individual contract clauses of all teachers, except those hired by private schools or by corporations, which are regulated by the Labor Code. Moreover, article 52 gives municipal teachers job stability. Employment stability created a formidable constraint on budget allocations during the late 1980s, especially during the period when enrollments declined. The difference between teachers and administrators is that the latter come under the rules of the general Labor Code. However, both groups have the right to organize in unions and bargain collectively.

To hire new teachers, private subsidized schools and corporations use their own procedures, as long as their candidates conform with the minimum eligibility established in the statute. In the case of municipal schools administered by municipalities, teacher selection is handled at the municipal level and not at the school level. The municipalities also determine the number of openings in a given school, with the approval of the Provincial Department of the Ministry of Education. Up to 20 percent of the personnel can be hired on fixed term contracts, and in this case job openings do not have to be publicly advertised. Each school has the freedom to determine the salaries of its personnel or to enter into a collective bargaining agreement. However, the salaries must conform to the minimum standards established in the statute. The statute also established norms regarding teacher training, and it leaves to the Ministry of Education the responsibility of deciding which courses grant certificates to trainees. While training in the private sector is a decision that involves managers and teachers, it can be a unilateral decision of teachers in the case of municipal schools.

THE SYSTEM'S INITIAL RESPONSE. The number of students classified as being in the vocational track declined suddenly in 1983, as all first- and second-year students were reclassified into a common track. Many schools that had originally offered vocational programs were not considered ready for approval under the new guidelines. As a result, the relative size of the

TABLE 10-4

Enrollment in Vocational Track, Selected Years, 1980–93

(thousands of students)

| | 1980 | 1983 | 1985 | 1988 | 1990 | 1992 | 1993 |
|---|---|---|---|---|---|---|---|
| Enrollment | 541.6 | 613.5 | 667.8 | 735.7 | 719.8 | 675.1 | 652.8 |
| General secondary | 371.6 | 488.6 | 539.2 | 601.8 | 464.4 | 410.9 | 391.5 |
| Technical-vocational | 170.0 | 125.2 | 128.7 | 134.0 | 255.4 | 264.2 | 261.4 |
| Percentage of enrollment in vocational track | 31.4 | 20.4 | 19.3 | 18.2 | 35.4 | 39.1 | 40.0 |
| Percentage of enrollment in general secondary track | 53.0 | 65.0 | 76.0 | 82.0 | 80.0 | 76.0 | 75.0 |

*Source:* Ministry of Education data.

vocational track fell from 31.4 percent in 1980 to 18.2 percent in 1988. Decree 130 of 1988 greatly simplified the process of approving curricular reforms in vocational schools. The decree allowed specialized programs to begin in the first, second, or third year of secondary school, and it shortened the minimum requirement to four years. The result was a reclassification of many secondary students back into the vocational track (table 10-4).

QUALITY AND PRIVATE SECTOR RESPONSE. Between 1980 and 1986, many vocational schools that had been administered by the Ministry of Education were adopted by private corporations or were transferred to municipalities or municipal corporations. In 1990 private corporations managed 70 vocational schools, or 18 percent of all vocational schools, 32 of them in the Santiago metropolitan area. The participation of the private sector continued to increase. In 1993 a new foundation, the Fundacion Educacional Arauco, set up by Celulosa Arauco y Constitucion, a large cellulose company, initiated steps to take over 22 schools in a southern region where wood-related production had grown considerably. In some cases entities such as CODESSER have incorporated schools that were originally transferred to municipalities (box 10-1). Table 10-5 summarizes the changes in enrollment by funding type between 1980 and 1993.

## Postsecondary Training

Postsecondary technical education training is highly diversified and for many years went officially unrecorded. Traditionally, worker training was

TABLE 10-5
Enrollment in Vocational Secondary Schools,
by Funding Type, 1980 and 1993
(percentage of enrollment)

| Type of funding | 1980 | 1993 |
|---|---|---|
| Ministry of Education | 71.8 | — |
| Municipalities | — | 44.3 |
| Private subsidized | 28.0 | 37.6 |
| Corporation subsidized | — | 17.7 |
| Private unsubsidized | 0.2 | 0.4 |

— Not available.
*Source:* Cox Edwards and Dar (1994).

considered a remedial step for individuals who entered the labor force without formal education.

Key elements of the postsecondary education reform were (a) the establishment of three types of postsecondary degrees: university, professional, and technical; (b) the passage of labor legislation that eliminated the 1 percent payroll tax earmarked for workers' training and the introduction of tax credits to encourage voluntary participation in training by private employers; (c) the changes in labor policy that reoriented the focus of the Ministry of Labor in targeting certain groups in the labor market; and (d) the opening of markets that increased competitive pressures on firms, thereby encouraging firm-specific research and development and worker training.

PRE-EMPLOYMENT TRAINING. Before the reforms, pre-employment education, both general and technical, was concentrated in eight universities. They were the only institutions that were allowed to offer postsecondary degrees. State support of these universities accounted for 35 percent of the education sector budget in 1980. Two of the eight institutions were oriented toward technical degrees, and roughly a quarter of all students enrolled were taking short professional or technical degree programs.

Since these eight universities were the only entities allowed to offer technical degrees at the pre-employment level, the entry of private providers was limited. Two public institutions created in the 1960s, INACAP and DUOC, were the key arms of public sector training policy until 1981, and they offered a variety of training courses for workers. Funding for these

BOX 10-1
Vocational Education for Chilean Farming: The CODESSER Model

CODESSER (la Corporación de Desarrollo Social del Sector Rural) is a nonprofit organization created by the National Society of Farmers in 1976. Initially, it administered four schools. Their reputation was so low that attracting enough students was difficult. By contrast, in 1995 some of the schools received more than 300 applications for 45 first-year openings. Additional schools were incorporated later, including two industrial schools in 1987, and by 1993 CODESSER was managing 17 schools.

The management style of CODESSER schools is unique, and merits special attention because it has produced graduates that easily make the transition to jobs in their field. In 1995 more than 75 percent of the graduates in agriculture schools were working in mid-level management jobs in agriculture. This figure is a far cry from the 15 percent match between vocational training and the job descriptions of the schools' graduates in the 1970s. In industry, where CODESSER's impact is more recent, the percentage in 1995 was close to 62. When examining the reasons for the program's success, one should not overlook the healthy growth of labor demand in the Chilean economy from the mid-1980s to the mid-1990s.

The CODESSER model includes the following six distinguishing features:

• *Private sector participation in management.* A regional directorate made up of seven farmers or industrial entrepreneurs oversees each school. The participation of the private sector ensures greater job-skill matches, a direct connection to the labor market for graduates, and an effective medium through which to bring about organizational and productive innovations in the schools.

• *Teachers hired as private sector employees.* As part of the transfer process, all contracts for teachers and other personnel are voided. CODESSER has established a clear personnel policy, including selection and promotion criteria, and new contracts conform with the general Labor Code as do contracts for other private sector employees. Teachers' salaries are about 50 percent higher than in municipal schools, and there has been a consistent effort to upgrade teachers' training. Currently, at

---

institutes was derived in part from a 1 percent payroll tax. However, in 1978, 571 unregulated private establishments offered technical training. Entry into these private institutions did not require candidates to have completed secondary school.

The reforms in the 1980s successfully restructured the eight traditional universities. The following legal changes occurred in 1981:

least in the San Felipe schools, some 60 to 70 percent of the personnel once taught under the old system.

• *Educational programs.* The aims of educational programs are to deliver a solid general knowledge in humanities and sciences, prepare students to work in a variety of occupations, teach the students to be problem solvers, and encourage them to continue learning. The schools also emphasize general growth and the development of responsibility, leadership, and personnel management. To give the curriculum local relevance, CODESSER updated the programs after a thorough field study and approval by the Ministry of Education.

• *Curriculum revisions.* CODESSER conducts periodic surveys of job requirements in the areas around each school. Currently, the surveys, which vary slightly by locality, are a list of tasks that potential employers are asked to identify. CODESSER uses the results of the surveys to adjust vocation-specific components in the curriculum and to prepare teachers in those areas.

• *Student selection.* In Chile grades range from one to seven, where seven represents excellence. To be considered for admission, students must have achieved a minimum of grade five in each course in levels seven and eight. Prospective students must also present a recommendation letter, spend two days at the school to take written examinations in four basic areas, go through a personal interview and psychological tests, and undertake a farming activity. The school selects the best applicants.

• *Funding and budget allocations.* The real value of public subsidies fell in the early 1980s and declined again by about 15 percent between 1987 and 1991. CODESSER schools have developed independent means of funding. While in 1982 the public subsidy represented the bulk of the schools' budget, by 1992 public sector support represented about 50 percent of the schools' combined budget.

*Source*: Compiled by author.

• The establishment of basic requirements for opening educational institutions, including universities. This law eventually came into effect in 1989, and during 1980-89 official approval of new institutions was conducted on a case-by-case basis.

• The diversification of pre-employment education into three levels: universities, professional institutes, and technical training centers. The law classified universities as institutions that confer academic degrees in 12 professional areas, professional institutes as entities that confer professional degrees in other areas not exclusively reserved for universities, and technical training centers as institutions that confer postsecondary technician degrees after relatively short programs. However, universities can also offer professional and technical degrees and professional institutes can also confer postsecondary technician degrees. Entry to any of these institutions requires completion of secondary education.

• The offering of incentives for creating new postsecondary institutions with minimum requirements and access to a new public funding formula. In 1980 the eight traditional universities received all their funding directly from the state. The plan was that this direct funding would decline over time, and the government would open up two additional areas of funding: indirect support (initially attached to the best 20,000 students of each entering cohort, or about 20 percent of total enrollment) and a new credit program (see Brunner 1992 for details). As in the case of secondary education, the plan was that competitive forces would enhance opportunities, especially for the poor.

In practice, however, budgetary allocations for postsecondary education did not evolve as planned. There were budget cuts associated with the 1982 recession and changes to the legislation regarding the indirect funding formula. Until 1990 access to public funding was reserved for the universities, and the expectation was that professional institutes and training centers could recover their costs through tuition fees. Since 1990 professional institutes and technical training centers have been allowed to apply for indirect funding as they compete for the 20,000 best graduates of each cohort.

Table 10-6 shows the evolution of actual funding for postsecondary education in relation to planned allocations. The allocations for credit programs were on target until 1982, but from 1984 to 1990, the plan was significantly greater than the allocation. Once it realized that demand was greater than the amounts allocated, the Budget Office started to allocate funds by establishment. Since the creation of the University Credit Fund in 1987, each postsecondary education institution that receives direct public funding has administered its own credit allocation.

The initial reform and the norms that defined its application were perceived as too permissive by some groups inside and outside the government. Several attempts to regulate curricular programs followed, and until 1988 the approval of new institutions was determined on a case by case basis.

TABLE 10-6

Funding for Postsecondary Education as a Percentage
of Planned Allocations, Selected Years, 1980–90

| Transfer mechanism | 1980 | 1982 | 1984 | 1986 | 1988 | 1990 |
|---|---|---|---|---|---|---|
| Direct funding | 100.0 | 86.2 | 58.7 | 47.9 | 41.6 | 33.4 |
| Indirect funding | 0.0 | 11.0 | 9.4 | 7.8 | 7.8 | 10.8 |
| Credit program | 0.0 | 14.7 | 22.7 | 17.7 | 15.6 | 9.4 |
| Development Fund and other funds | 0.0 | 0.3 | 0.4 | 1.0 | 7.1 | 5.6 |
| Total funding | 100.0 | 112.2 | 91.3 | 74.4 | 72.1 | 59.1 |
| Total planned | 100.0 | 115.0 | 130.0 | 150.0 | 150.0 | 150.0 |

Source: Ministry of Education as cited in Cox (1992).

Some 20 professional institutes were created during 1981-83; virtually all of them originated as a result of the reorganization of the eight traditional universities. During this initial period, the government introduced constraints on the creation of new institutions. When it lifted these controls in 1987, a new wave of private expansion followed, along with the disappearance of some of the public institutions. As table 10-7 shows, by 1990, 80 of the 82 professional institutes were private.

Enrollment in technical training institutes grew within institutions that existed before the reform but were not officially recognized. Estimates indicate that enrollment in those institutions was about 66,000 in 1980.

The reforms quickly met their objectives of expanding enrollments and increasing cost recovery. Enrollments in postsecondary institutions with direct public funding fell in 1981, recovered in subsequent years, and started to decline again in the late 1980s because of competitive pressures. In 1993 postsecondary enrollment in institutions with direct public funding was about the same as in 1980. The new universities, which operate without public funding, and the professional institutes have seen steady increases in enrollment since 1983. Technical training centers exhibit the fastest growth, and in 1990 represented about one-third of total postsecondary enrollment. Figure 10-1 shows the expansion of postsecondary education in its diversified form, and figure 10-2 shows expansions of enrollment by funding source.

All postsecondary education institutions, both with and without public funding, charge tuition fees (table 10-8). Tuition fees are typically highest

TABLE 10-7

Postsecondary Institutions after Reforms, Selected Years, 1980–90

(number of institutions)

| Type of institution | 1980 | 1983 | 1984 | 1985 | 1986 | 1987 | 1988 | 1989 | 1990 |
|---|---|---|---|---|---|---|---|---|---|
| *Universities* | | | | | | | | | |
| With public funding | 8 | 17 | 17 | 18 | 20 | 20 | 20 | 20 | 20 |
| Without public funding | — | 3 | 3 | 3 | 3 | 3 | 6 | 14 | 40 |
| *Professional institutes* | | | | | | | | | |
| With public funding | — | 7 | 7 | 6 | 4 | 4 | 4 | 2 | 2 |
| Without public funding | — | 17 | 18 | 19 | 19 | 19 | 26 | 39 | 80 |
| *Technical training centers*[a] | — | 86 | 102 | 102 | 122 | 116 | 123 | 133 | 168 |

— Not available.

a. Do not receive direct public funding.

*Source:* Ministry of Education as cited in Cox (1992).

## FIGURE 10-1
Postsecondary Enrollment in Chile, by Type of Institution, 1980, 1983, 1990

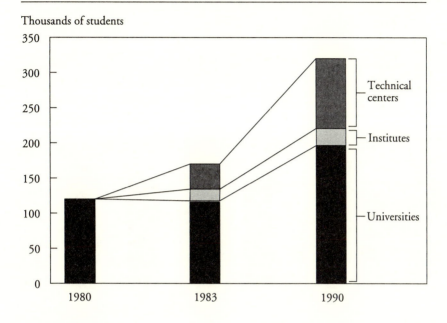

*Source:* Cox (1992).

in private universities, followed by universities with public funding and professional institutes. Technical training centers charge the lowest annual fees. Average values mask considerable variation across programs. Within specific institutions, fees vary directly with demand and supply conditions. Technical fields command low tuition fees relative to management fields.

IN-SERVICE TRAINING REFORM. The most important incentives for investing in training workers are intrinsic to market forces. As real wages increase, employment must be more productive. Productivity increases are achieved through improvements in the organization of production and through a shift from labor-intensive activities to more capital-intensive activities. Achievement of production increases in this way requires knowledge, training, and skilled labor. The concept of skills in this context includes schooling, which improves an individual's capacity to learn on the job, and training. Firms and their workers gain from investments

FIGURE 10-2

Postsecondary Enrollment in Chile, by Funding Source, 1980, 1983, 1991

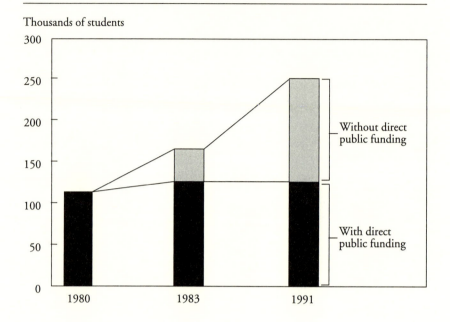

Thousands of students

*Source:* Cox (1992).

in training, and they can normally arrive at agreement to share the costs of such investment.

Before the economic reforms of the 1970s, many distortionary factors reduced incentives for private sector investment in training, and the public sector was extremely active in encouraging such training. Since the reforms the incidence of training within the private sector has increased significantly. Nevertheless, the government chose to subsidize worker training using tax credits. Enterprises that take the initiative to train their workers can obtain tax credits under three, often complementary, formulas.

• Tax credits may fully compensate an enterprise for the cost of training, up to the equivalent of 1 percent of its payroll. The National Service for Training and Employment, a division of the Ministry of Labor with offices in the central metropolitan area and in the regions, certifies if and how much credit an enterprise obtains. The procedure, while not automatic, is relatively straightforward.

TABLE 10-8
Average Annual Fees in Postsecondary Education, 1990 and 1991
(U.S. dollars)

| Type of institution | 1990 | 1991 |
|---|---|---|
| *Universities* | | |
| With public funding | 974 | 992 |
| Without public funding | 1,257 | 1,306 |
| *Professional institutes* | | |
| With public funding | 535 | 575 |
| Without public funding | 735 | 784 |
| Technical training centers | 425 | 471 |

*Note:* U.S. dollars at an exchange rate of US$1 = Ch$305 in 1990 and US$1 = Ch$349 in 1991.
*Source:* Ministry of Education as cited in Cox (1992).

• Member enterprises' contributions to their technical assistance institution are also eligible for the tax credit. Technical assistance institutions are intermediate-level organizations that represent sectors of economic activity or regions and support their members through training activities and diffusion of technology. They can charge for their services, but they are established as nonprofit organizations.

• Wages paid to workers under the apprenticeships program are also eligible for tax credits. This program consists of temporary work contracts aimed at training young workers. It is limited to workers up to 21 years of age, and up to 60 percent of the salary paid (with a limit of 60 percent of the minimum income) can be added to the tax credit.

In short, direct expenditure on training or indirect support to the market for training through contributions to technical assistance institutions is partially tax deductible. For example, in the case of agriculture, the technical assistance institution is CODESSER, whose presence in secondary vocational education, technology diffusion, and worker training has been growing.

## Reforms and Challenges

Chile diversified institutional options for vocational education and training, introduced decentralized management of schools, and implemented student-based funding.

*Notable Reforms*

Schools were eligible for public subsidies as long as they met six requirements, including curricular conformity with official requirements; basic approval of school direction; basic standards for school facilities; enrollments per course within a ratio of 1: 45; qualified teachers; and the prohibition of payments as entry barriers other than one annual basic fee, which was set at less than half of the monthly subsidy for primary education.

Schools were transferred to municipal governments or to private corporations. The transfer agreements presented different challenges in the case of municipal versus private administrators. Under a special legal formula, municipalities were guaranteed autonomous management of school infrastructure. School infrastructure was transferred to private corporations in exchange for an agreement to administer the schools and design their curricula, but the corporations had to accept financial and pedagogical supervision by the Ministry of Education and report on annual enrollments and expenses.

The funding formula left the question of the relative size of technical vocational schooling open to market forces. Money, in this case public subsidies, would follow the students. Nevertheless, the state maintained control over two key variables that influence school choice: basic curriculum requirements and financial support. Per student payments are made available on an equal basis to private and municipal schools, in the expectation that the two sectors will compete for students and upgrade schools' quality. Incentives to improve attendance and retention are built into the funding. In the first five days of each month, schools deliver the previous month's attendance roll to the corresponding provincial directorate, which in turn sends the information to the central office of the Ministry of Education. The per student subsidies are delivered to each school during the last five days of that same month. Actual attendance is checked by inspectors who randomly visit schools, and differences between real and declared attendance result in financial penalties.

*Daunting Challenges*

To implement these reforms, the Ministry of Education had to increase its expenditures substantially. Real government expenditures for education rose by 6 percent between 1979 and 1980, 20 percent between 1980 and 1981, and 2 percent between 1981 and 1982, when the transfers were suspended.

Expenditures increased to bring subsidies to private schools to the level of municipal ones, to pay severance to teachers that were losing their public sector contracts, and to finance special incentives for the municipalities to accept the transfers of schools (Castaneda 1992). By 1983, 83 percent of all public establishments had been transferred to local authorities (Matte and Sancho 1991). At the same time, the increase in funding to privately managed schools compared with what they had been receiving resulted in an explosion in the number of private establishments, from 1,674 in 1980 to 2,643 in 1985.

The 1982 economic crisis severely affected the public sector's capacity to sustain this reform process. With 17 percent of students still enrolled in schools totally dependent on the Ministry of Education, school transfers were suspended because of the lack of funding for severance payments. The crisis was severe enough to force a freeze in the per student subsidy, which resulted in a real decline of 20 percent between 1982 and 1985, and by 1990 it had fallen 30 percent in real terms. The government restricted the opening of new schools in areas where municipal schools had vacant places. The municipalities faced deficits in their administration costs, a large part of which the Ministry of Education eventually covered, but differences among municipalities in their capacity to absorb deficits began to affect the school system. Estimates indicate that in 1981, 7 percent of education expenditure was funded by municipal funds.

A second major challenge concerned the hiring and firing of teachers. In 1986 teachers had become opposed to the change because of their experience during the 1982 recession, which demonstrated the vulnerability of their employment status with municipal administrations. They lobbied for the re-establishment of job security guarantees and for automatic indexation of salaries. This culminated in the approval of the new statute in 1991. The statute legally re-established job security for teachers and took away much of the freedom to negotiate employment conditions at the local level.

A final major challenge involved disadvantaged families. Rising demand for places in some schools has led to enrollment expansion, and ultimately to stricter criteria governing student selection. Enrollment expansion within schools has natural limits, and rising demand is bound to generate rents among students who succeed in gaining entrance into popular schools. Thus parents' willingness to pay for better services in some schools is not surprising. Similarly, other schools whose services are deteriorating relative to alternatives face declining enrollments. Declining enrollments, in turn, create financial difficulties and probably a further a decline in services, precipitating an even faster decline in enrollment.

The current system does not deny good education opportunities to the poor, because access to schools is not limited by location. As long as alternative schools are accessible by public transportation, good schools are within the reach of poor students. Students who live in sparsely populated areas have fewer choices or have to spend more on transportation. To make up for this disadvantage, the state is more generous with schools located in sparsely populated areas, adjusting subsidies by a rural factor and allowing those schools to compete with smaller enrollments. The system is tough on poor achievers, who cannot get entrance into well-managed schools, and with schools that lose enrollment. Schools that cannot attract a minimum number of students have no choice but to close. However, school survival ultimately depends on funding, and funding depends on the number of students, thus there is a danger of matching low achievers with poorly managed schools.

## Lessons Learned

Chile's reforms provide the following valuable lessons for countries attempting to improve their VET systems:

• *Reforms are not always smooth and painless.* Changes trigger resistance. However, Chile's experience shows that the judicious use of public funds is an effective instrument for overcoming resistance to reform, as illustrated by the stalling of reforms during the severe budget crunch of 1982. Another obstacle was strong resistance from teachers' unions, which continue to this day, but this obstacle can probably only be fully overcome in the long term.

• *Public funding is often more important than public provision.* Privately provided vocational and technical education is growing faster than general secondary education. This is convincing evidence that a private sector response can be forthcoming even in low- and-middle-income countries if public funding mechanisms encourage private provision, instead of promoting public provision, which crowds out private providers. Chile's experience also shows that both equity and efficiency objectives can be well served through simple financing mechanisms.

• *The regulatory environment is sometimes more important than public funding.* The sharp expansion of postsecondary technical education after

1989, after rules had been made transparent and the in-service certification process for tax credits had been streamlined, points to the importance of a friendly regulatory environment for training provision. Note that publicly funded organizations were a small part of the additional supply of VET at the postsecondary level.

• *Matching instruments to target groups is important.* While the mechanisms through which VET is supplied (for instance, public, private, or subsidized private) are important, VET programs must target the groups that will benefit the most. Thus Chile put in place regulations to favor underprivileged students and implemented special measures for children traveling some distance to school; introduced competition to improve the relevance of VET to the economy; and unbundled policy, planning, financing, and management to increase institutional options and lower public costs.

• *The government's role in facilitating VET is vital.* Often preoccupied with providing, regulating, or financing VET, the government should not neglect its role as a provider of information about the availability and effectiveness of vocational programs. In Chile a heated and publicized debate about Chile's economy helped the general public learn about VET.

• *A vigorous private sector response can be expected.* In Chile regulations concerning governance and financing were designed to increase the share of private VET providers. Within 10 years enrollments in private subsidized schools had grown dramatically and several corporation-sponsored schools had been opened. Postsecondary training saw a dramatic shift toward private sector provision.

• *Political will, not institutional capacity, is the key to comprehensive reform.* The experience in Chile points to strong political will as the main factor behind comprehensive reform. Successful reform comes from determined and sustained effort. Although the 1982 economic crisis may have slowed the pace of reforms, Chile's political will saw the country through the crisis and allowed it to pursue its reform policies.

## References

Brunner, Joaquin. 1992. "La Educacion Superior en Chile: Tres decadas de desarrollo." In J. Brunner, H. Courad, and C. Cox, eds., *Estado, Mercado y Conocimiento: Politicas y Resultados en la Educacion Superior Chilena 1960-1990.* Santiago: Foro de la Educacion Superior.

Butelmann, Andrea, and Pilar Romaguera. 1994. "Educacion Media General vs. Tecnica: Retorno Economico y Desercion." Cieplan, Santiago.

Castaneda, Tarsicio. 1992. *Combating Poverty: Innovative Social Reforms in Chile during the 1980s.* San Francisco: International Center for Economic Growth.

Cox, Cristian. 1992. "Genesis y Evolucion de los Institutos Profesionales." In J. Brunner, H. Courad, and C. Cox, eds., *Estado, Mercado y Conocimiento: Politicas y Resultados en la Educacion Superior Chilena 1960–1990.* Santiago: Foro de la Educacion Superior.

Cox Edwards, Alejandra, and Amit Dar. 1994. "Technical-Vocational Education in Competition: Evidence from the Chilean Reform of the Early 1980s." World Bank, Washington, D.C.

Ferreira, Francisco, and Julie Litchfield. 1996. "Calm after the Storm: Income Distribution in Chile, 1987–94." Policy Research Working Paper 1960. Washington, D.C.: World Bank.

Gill, Indermit, and Claudio Montenegro, eds. Forthcoming. *Stabilization, Fiscal Adjustment and Beyond: Quantifying Labor Policy Challenges in Argentina, Brazil, and Chile.* Latin America and Caribbean Region. Washington, D.C.: World Bank.

Martelli, Mariana, Guillermo del Campo, and Rodrigo Martino. 1994. "Marco normativo que regula las differentes formas de gestion de la educacion media tecnico profesional en Chile." Santiago: Sociedad Nacional de Agricultura.

Matte, Patricia, and Antonio Sancho. 1991. "Sector Educacion Basica y Media." In Cristian Larroulet, ed., *Soluciones Privadas a Problemas Publicos.* Santiago: Editorial Trineo.

Salas Opazo, Victor, and Mario Gaymer Cortes. 1993. "La Evaluacion Economica de la Educacion Media en Chile." Final report of the MECE Media IV.3 project.

# 11 Mexico

MARI MINOWA

MEXICO IS A MIDDLE-INCOME country with a population of 90 million people. In 1996 gross national product per capita was around US$4,000. During the Mexican "miracle" from 1950 to 1981, Mexico's gross domestic product (GDP) grew at an average rate of 6.5 percent per year. This growth was based on an inward-looking, import-substitution model and was sustained by foreign exchange earnings, initially through agricultural exports and later through petroleum exports. In the early 1970s, with expectations of growing oil income, the government abandoned policies of fiscal equilibrium and private-sector-led economic growth and adopted policies of public-sector-led growth, with expansion of direct public investment in the productive sector and expansionary fiscal policies. By the early 1980s, at the peak of the parastatal era, public enterprises accounted for 24 percent of GDP. Private sector development became increasingly constrained as a result, and in 1982 rising world interest rates and falling oil prices led to a collapse of these unsustainable policies.

After the 1982 financial and economic crisis, structural reforms began gradually with some limited privatization of state enterprises and the beginning of trade liberalization in mid-1986. Mexico moved rapidly from being a closed economy to an open economy, with the aim of improving the productivity of the tradables sector and encouraging efficiency in both export and import substitution activities by opening the economy to international competition. After the stagnation of 1982–88, GDP growth resumed during 1989–92 to an average of 3.6 percent per year, or 1.6 percent in per capita terms. However, Mexico was unable to repeat the growth rates

319

achieved in earlier decades, and at the end of 1994 it became immersed in a financial crisis from which it has yet to recover fully.

## The Labor Market

Mexico's labor force grew at an average rate of 3.1 percent per year from 1980 to 1993 to reach 33 million workers. This means that about 1 million new entrants were added to the labor force every year. Despite the rapid expansion of the public sector during the 1970s, the private sector in 1980 continued to account for 83 percent of total employment, a much larger share than that prevalent in the countries of the Organization for Economic Cooperation and Development (OECD).

The Mexican private sector exhibits a growing duality: a large traditional sector coexisting alongside an expanding modern sector. The former, which consists primarily of microenterprises and small and medium-size enterprises (defined to include firms with up to 250 workers), employs a large fraction of the labor force but accounts for a much smaller portion of output and exports. These enterprises account for 71 percent of total employment, 53 percent of employment in manufacturing, 95 percent of employment in the retail sector, and 73 percent of employment in services. Productivity growth in this traditional sector has been slow, and output growth has been sluggish. In contrast, the modern sector has experienced faster productivity growth and stronger output and export performance.

Labor productivity growth in the manufacturing sector has been slow. While some studies have shown that the manufacturing sector has become more efficient as a result of trade liberalization, with gross labor productivity increasing at an annual rate of 3.5 percent rate during the 1986–91 period, this rate was still low compared with that in other developing countries, and about the same as in the United States. Between 1982 and 1989, output per hour of labor in the manufacturing sector grew at a rate of 1.5 percent per year. In contrast, output per hour of labor grew by 4.2 percent per year in the United States and 2.5 percent per year in Canada. Other countries of the OECD also experienced productivity increases in the manufacturing sector during the same period that were higher than Mexico's.

One explanation for this slow growth in labor productivity is the lower education level of Mexican workers and the resulting deficiency in on-the-job human capital accumulation compared with their counterparts elsewhere. Supporting evidence for this hypothesis is provided by the fact that experience-wage profiles for Mexican workers are flatter than those estimated for workers in other countries. The increase in wages associated with an additional year of work experience for men is 3.8 percent in Mexico, compared with 8.1 percent in the United States, 8.4 percent in Japan, and 9.1 percent in France. This rate is low even when compared with the rate in countries at a similar level of development and with comparable education indicators, such as Brazil (6.2 percent) and Colombia (5.8 percent). Given the well-documented correlation between wage growth, on-the-job training, and productivity observed in many countries, these differences are consistent with the hypothesis of less postschool investment in human capital and resulting lower productivity growth.

The observed low level of investment in human capital can also be explained by the incentive structure of labor regulations. Labor laws regarding job security and promotion policy have important implications for employers' incentives to provide in-service training. A strict interpretation of the Mexican Labor Law would suggest a restrictive and overregulated labor market, where labor mobility is highly restricted because of job security considerations and promotion is based on seniority and a rigid job assignment scheme, and not on individual performance or flexible job rotation. However, in practice, firms appear to enjoy more flexibility than a strict interpretation of the law would suggest. In particular, firms appear to have substantial flexibility in hiring categories of labor that can be dismissed without significant costs; they seem to be relying increasingly on performance-based promotion and compensation schemes and moving away from the more traditional seniority-based mechanisms; and they seem to have flexibility in defining job assignments and pay scales.

In sum, deficiencies in the education and vocational education and training system in Mexico present a significant bottleneck to human capital accumulation. In the next section I turn to a description of that system.

## National Education System

To strengthen basic human capital, the government in 1993 extended compulsory education from six years to nine years. Thus, as established in the General Education Law, the national education system includes nine years of basic education (six years of primary education and three years of lower secondary education), followed by upper secondary and higher education in the form of either formal, in-class instruction or nontraditional extension programs. During the 1993–94 academic year, the public sector, its decentralized agencies, and private accredited institutions provided education services to about 25 million students: 14.5 million were in primary education with public schools accounting for about 94 percent of the enrollment, 3.1 million students (72 percent of total lower secondary) were in general academic middle schools, and 1.2 million students (28 percent of total lower secondary) were in technical middle schools.

At the upper secondary level, two tracks are offered: an academic track, which includes technical specialization (*bachillerato tecnológico*), a prerequisite for higher education; and a technical vocational track (*profesional técnico*), which does not lead to higher education. Thus those students who plan to pursue a technical career have to choose either a vocational-technical curriculum and be prepared to enter the work force on graduation, or a technical college preparatory curriculum that qualifies graduates to enter undergraduate programs in technical fields. During 1993–94 some 1.3 million students (58 percent of total upper secondary enrollment) were in general academic high schools (including teacher training schools), and 530,300 (24 percent of total upper secondary enrollment) were in technical academic high schools, both leading to a high school diploma *(bachillerato)*. The remainder (406,500 students) were in technical professional schools and were not eligible for higher education.

The national education system also offers job skills training programs in a formal classroom format, with courses ranging from a few hours to three to four months. These courses have no academic prerequisites and provide job skills training for entry-level technical positions. Most students in job skills training programs have a primary education background. The system also encompasses adult education, including nontraditional job skills training in self-instructional formats, special education, education for indigenous and rural populations, and open education at all levels.

## National System of Technical Education

The public sector offers both formal and informal technical education and training through the Education Secretariat and the Labor Secretariat. The Education Secretariat's Office of Undersecretary for Technological Education and Research is responsible for managing the National System of Technical Education.

### Public Technical Education and Training

Formal technical education and training are given at four levels: (a) job skills training with no formal academic requirements, (b) upper-secondary-level (high school) training with completion of middle school required, (c) undergraduate-university-level training, and (d) graduate-level training. In the 1992–93 academic year 973,000 students were registered in the National System of Technical Education—about 45 percent of upper secondary school enrollment or 3.8 percent of the total student enrollment in the entire education system. Table 11-1 presents key statistics of the National System of Technical Education, and table 11-2 further disaggregates enrollment.

Formal job skills training without academic requirements prepares skilled workers and craftspeople, and it is provided through 196 industrial training centers (CECATIs). They enrolled 91,700 students in 1992–93. The CECATIs offer short courses ranging from 100 to 450 hours of technical skills training, both in their training centers and at the place of employment. Of total enrollment in Mexico's formal job skills training, the CECATIs' share was about 24 percent. Nearly 65 percent of those enrolled were trained in private institutions and the rest in state and autonomous institutions. While CECATI programs concentrate on the industrial sector, particularly on manufacturing, private sector job skills training is primarily oriented toward the commercial and services sectors.

The upper secondary level public technical programs are divided into (a) terminal technical and vocational programs; and (b) *bachillerato tecnológico* programs whose graduates can go on to university-level education. The terminal vocational and technical programs enrolled 210,500 students in 1992–93, preparing them to be technicians. During 1992–93, enrollment in the National System of Technical Education programs represented about 53 percent of total enrollment in the mid-level, terminal, vocational and technical education track nationwide, with about 30 percent enrolled in private training institutions and the rest in state and other independent training institutions. Of the 210,500 students enrolled in the National System of Technical Education terminal programs, 81 percent were enrolled in 253 schools run by the National College of Professional Technical Education (CONALEP), 18 percent were enrolled in either the Center for Industrial and Service Technical Studies or the Center for the Industrial and Service *Bachillerato Tecnológico* managed by the General Directorate for Industrial Technical Education, and a small number of trainees were enrolled in the National Polytechnic Institute. These terminal programs offer three-year courses in a total of 164 career specializations in engineering and technology, agriculture, livestock, health sciences, and administration.

While the Center for Industrial and Service Technical Studies and the Center for the Industrial and Service *Bachillerato Tecnológico* train some

TABLE 11-1

Formal Training Offered by the National System of Technical Education, 1992–93

(number)

| Type of technical education and training | Total enrollment[a] | New enrollment | Schools and centers | Courses | Educational services | Instructors | Other personnel | Graduates | Facilities | | | |
|---|---|---|---|---|---|---|---|---|---|---|---|---|
| | | | | | | | | | Classrooms | Laboratories | Workshops | Other |
| Job skills training | 93,149 | 92,994 | 217 | 57 | 209 | 4,460 | 3,761 | 40,683 | 523 | 28 | 1,175 | 4,145 |
| Upper-secondary-level training | 675,082 | 341,796 | 944 | 331 | 1,354 | 45,170 | 34,312 | 124,680 | 11,342 | 3,090 | 4,970 | 21,260 |
| Terminal | 210,487 | 109,517 | 264 | 183 | 413 | 14,934 | 11,461 | 39,061 | 2,916 | 1,025 | 1,415 | 13,968 |
| Bachillerato tecnológico | 464,595 | 232,279 | 680 | 148 | 941 | 30,236 | 22,851 | 285,619 | 8,426 | 2,065 | 3,555 | 7,292 |
| University-level training | 200,610 | 55,370 | 129 | 141 | 179 | 19,567 | 13,388 | 24,871 | 4,302 | 1,156 | 594 | 4,907 |
| Graduate-level training | 4,136 | 1,128 | 16 | 168 | 73 | 1,867 | 815 | 701 | 59 | 260 | 23 | 229 |
| Professional | 505 | 126 | 0 | 21 | 12 | 0 | 0 | 179 | 0 | 0 | 0 | 0 |
| Masters | 3,309 | 963 | 16 | 109 | 50 | 1,867 | 815 | 491 | 59 | 260 | 23 | 229 |
| Doctorate | 322 | 39 | 0 | 38 | 11 | 0 | 0 | 31 | 0 | 0 | 0 | 0 |
| Total | 972,977 | 491,288 | 1,306 | 697 | 1,815 | 71,064 | 52,276 | 190,935 | 16,226 | 4,534 | 6,762 | 30,541 |

a. At the beginning of the school year.
Source: Education Secretariat (1994).

students in their terminal programs, most of their students are enrolled in the *bachillerato* track or high school diploma program, and on graduation obtain a technical high school diploma. In 1992–93, 464,600 students were enrolled in technical high schools; 75 percent of those students were enrolled in the General Directorate for Industrial Technical Education system (Center for Industrial and Service Technical Studies and Center for the Industrial and Service *Bachillerato Tecnológico*) and about 9 percent in the National Polytechnic Institute. Although this diploma allows those graduates to enroll in universities, the actual progression rate is not high: of the total of 381,531 graduates with a *bachillerato* diploma in the 1993–94 academic year, only 56,556 (14.8 percent) went on to higher education.

In addition to the formal training programs, the public sector provides informal training programs in the form of short courses to upgrade the skills of employed and unemployed adults. The informal training programs are provided in training institutions and at the workplace. In total, about 230,000 trainees received informal training during 1992–93. Preservice informal training is offered in training institutions of the National System of Technical Education through short courses of 15 to 350 hours, and in-service informal training is part of employer-provided training required by the Federal Labor Law. For the latter, employers often contract the National System of Technical Education institutions to provide short courses for their employees. Finally, the Labor Secretariat finances the Labor Retraining Program for Unemployed Workers (PROBECAT). The program's beneficiaries are trained at one of the many training institutions nationwide or at enterprises, which are obligated to employ at least 70 percent of program participants on completion of the training. The program finances the stipend equivalent of the regional minimum wage plus a transportation allowance during the duration of training courses, which last from two to three months. Since 1984 the National System of Technical Education has participated in this program, training more than 50,000 unemployed workers per year in its training institutions.

## Private Technical Education and Training

Skills development of workers after entering the workplace has been left to employers. However, in reality, training for employed workers is limited. While large firms provide their own training programs, small and medium-size firms, if they offer training for workers, rely mostly on contracting out

## TABLE 11-2
### Enrollment by Training Institution Units of the National System of Technical Education, 1992–93
(number and percentage in parentheses)

| Responsible unit | Job skill training | Upper secondary | | University-level training | Graduate-level training | | | Total |
|---|---|---|---|---|---|---|---|---|
| | | Terminal | Bachillerato tecnológico | | Professional | Masters | Doctorate | |
| DGCC | 91,700 (98.44) | 0 | 0 | 0 | 0 | 0 | 0 | 91,700 (9.42) |
| CONALEP | 0 | 171,142 (81.31) | 0 | 0 | 0 | 0 | 0 | 171,142 (17.59) |
| DGETI | 0 | 37,735 (17.93) | 348,340 (74.98) | 0 | 0 | 0 | 0 | 386,075 (39.68) |
| CETI | 0 | 0 | 2,208 (0.48) | 670 (0.33) | 0 | 0 | 0 | 2,878 (0.3) |
| UECyTM | 0 | 0 | 11,025 (2.37) | 1,628 (0.81) | 0 | 0 | 0 | 12,653 (1.30) |
| DGETA | 0 | 0 | 58,404 (12.57) | 5,853 (2.92) | 0 | 107 (3.23) | 0 | 64,364 (6.62) |
| DGIT | 0 | 16 (0.01) | 0 | 133,623 (66.61) | 311 (61.58) | 1,058 (31.97) | 13 (4.04) | 135,005 (13.88) |

| | | | | | | | | |
|---|---|---|---|---|---|---|---|---|
| ODE | 1,449 (1.56) | 1,594 (0.76) | 4,095 (0.88) | 1,941 (0.97) | 0 | 0 | 0 | 7,501 (0.77) |
| IPN | 0 | 0 | 40,523 (8.72) | 56,895 (28.36) | 194 (38.42) | 1,536 (46.42) | 73 (22.67) | 100,815 (10.36) |
| CIEA – IPN | 0 | 0 | 0 | 0 | 0 | 608 (18.37) | 236 (73.29) | 844 (0.09) |
| Total | 93,149 (100.00) | 210,487 (100.00) | 464,595 (100.00) | 200,610 (100.00) | 505 (100.00) | 3,309 (100.00) | 322 (100.00) | 972,977 (100.00) |

DGCC — *Dirección General de Centros de Capacitación*
CONALEP — *Colegio Nacional de Educación Profesional Técnica*
DGETI — General Directorate for Industrial Technical Education
CETI — *Centro de enseñanza Técnica Industrial*
UECyTM — *Unidad de Educación en Ciencia y Tecnología del Mar*
DGETA — *Dirección general de Educación Tecnológica Agropecuaria*
DGIT — *Dirección General de Institutos Tecnológicos*
ODE — Decentralized state government institutions with federal participation
IPN — National Polytechnic Institute
CIEA-IPN — *Centro de Investigación y de Estudios avanzados del Instituto Politécnico Nacional*

*Note:* Enrollment at the beginning of the school year.

*Source:* Education Secretariat (1994).

to specific training courses in public training institutions. In all cases training provided by employers has served only as a complement to the basic technical education and training provided by public training institutions.

In recent years, with the support of the World Bank, the Labor Secretariat has been implementing the Total Quality and Modernization Program (CIMO), a program of technical and financial assistance to microenterprises and small and medium-size enterprises to improve their productivity and competitiveness through worker training and related advisory services. Between 1984 and the mid-1990s CIMO helped about 4,000 enterprises per year to develop their human resource strategies and to design and implement training and retraining courses for their workers.

In addition to the training provided by employers in the private sector, there are about 500 privately managed training institutions currently listed in the Education Secretariat's registry. The private training institutions offer programs mostly in the nonmanufacturing areas that do not require a large capital investment. The relative shares of subject areas are as follows: secretarial and clerical (32 percent); computers (25 percent); accounting (19 percent); construction, trades, and manufacturing (12 percent); services, including health and personal services (9 percent); and other areas (3 percent). Little information is available on the quality of the training these institutions provide.

## Enterprise Training

Given the lack of systematic information on training provided by enterprises, the administrative registry of the Labor Secretariat serves as a useful source of information on the general characteristics of enterprise-based training. This registry maintains information on mixed training commissions, training plans and programs, certification of workers' skills, and training providers, which are all part of the system that the Federal Labor Law has established to promote enterprise-based training.

In the early 1980s, faced with the absence of a legal framework to promote enterprise-based training, the authorities amended both the Constitution and the Federal Labor Law to declare that training was a right guaranteed to all workers. The law stipulates that every enterprise set up a bipartite mixed training commission to oversee whether training plans and programs are properly prepared and to authenticate the labor competency certification. In 1989 enterprises registered a total of about 108,000 mixed training commissions with the Labor Secretariat. That same year about 509,000 firms were registered with the Social Security System, implying that only about 20 percent of firms were complying with the requirement to establish a mixed training commission. However, in terms of the number of workers, firms that had set up mixed training commissions represented about 61.6 percent of all workers who were insured by the Social Security System. Only about half of the workers in firms with fewer than 100 workers have mixed training commissions; this figure increases to 71 percent for those in firms with more than 100 workers.

In the early 1990s only about 28 percent of firms with mixed training commissions had registered their training plans and programs. The percentage of firms with mixed training commissions and registered training plans and programs increased from 26 percent for firms with fewer than 5 workers to 39 percent for firms with more than 250 workers. Employers attribute the insufficient level of training in small firms to scarcity of resources; lack of knowledge about externally available training opportunities; organizational deficiencies; or the operational characteristics of the firms, where workers perform multiple functions and are thus difficult to train in specific skills.

By law, firms are required to provide proof of workers' skills and to register training providers for their training programs. In the early 1990s just over 1,800 training institutions with 28,000 instructors were registered with the Labor Secretariat as external training providers. Of these training institutions 62 percent were in the public sector, both federal and state. The remaining 38 percent correspond mostly to private institutions and a few social sector institutions (for example, union training centers).

More than 90 percent of training institutions in the public sector at the basic and upper-middle level had registered as external training providers for enterprise training by the mid-1990s. While this could indicate a high level of effort by the education sector to establish links with productive sectors, more detailed analysis is necessary to evaluate the level of success in forging such links. Private training institutions participate much less in enterprise-provided training: only 27 percent were registered with the Labor Secretariat as external training providers. This could be because most private training institutions offer courses in business or administration of extremely diverse quality.

The Federal Labor Law established three levels of organizations auxiliary to the Labor Secretariat that have authority over training activities. As an intermediary between the Labor Secretariat and the firms, these organizations are responsible for providing advisory services, including analyzing problems related to training and promoting training within firms. Sectoral national training committees are auxiliary bodies that help determine training requirements. They have the authority to propose training that they deem pertinent within their particular sector. In 1995, 14 different sectors had national training committees. The Federal Labor Law also established the national-level Consultative Council, which consists of representatives of national labor organizations, employers' associations, the Labor Secretariat, the Education Secretariat, the Secretaría de Comercio y Fomento Industrial, the Energy Secretariat, and the Social Security System. Its function as a consultative body covers virtually all aspects of training, from the formulation of policy and national programs to the establishment of criteria for forming enterprise-level mixed training commissions. Consultative councils have also been established at the state level. Their functions are similar to those of the sectoral national training committees and the national Consultative Council. By 1995, 31 state-level consultative councils had been formed.

## Vocational and Technical Education and Training Issues

Despite the progress made during the past 25 years, Mexico's training system still does not meet the requirements of the labor market. The most critical weaknesses of the vocational and technical training system are (a) poor preparation of workers for vocational and technical education and training; (b) supply-driven programs, which lack flexibility and relevance to changing labor market needs; (c) the uneven quality of training programs, with no objective measures available to gauge the quality of outputs; and (d) lack of an adequate institutional framework for private sector involvement in training design and provision.

### Poor Preparation of Workers for Vocational and Technical Education and Training

The existing labor force has an average of six years of schooling; new entrants to the labor market typically have finished eight years of education. While the average worker has low levels of trainability because of low schooling levels, new entrants may also suffer from low levels of trainability because of the poor quality of their education in primary and secondary schools.

Issues related to primary education include the following:

- Low educational achievement. A 1992 study found that primary school students mastered only 53 percent of the national core curriculum in Spanish and 30 percent of the national core curriculum in mathematics.
- Inappropriate curriculum. In 1992 the curriculum was revised for the first time in 20 years.
- Inadequate teaching quality.
- Teacher absenteeism and misallocation, especially in rural and remote areas because of poor salaries and harsh physical conditions.
- Inadequate supervision.
- Shortage of library books and other materials and deficiencies in textbook distribution.
- Dilapidated infrastructure.
- Insufficient community participation to ensure teachers' attendance and students' motivation.
- Inadequate managerial capacity.

To overcome these obstacles, the government has been increasing investments in basic education to improve its quality, especially in the poor southern and central states with low educational indicators, and to extend free compulsory basic education from six to nine years.

### Supply-Driven Programs

A predominant characteristic of the training system has been its supply orientation. Even though some training programs (including courses in CONALEP, CECATIs, and the Center for Industrial and Service Technical Studies) have been strengthening their ties to employers and involving them in the design of curricula, many training programs still follow the academic model of the vocational and technical schools. Even when employers ask for specific courses, curricula tend to be driven by academic subjects and related to obsolete occupational classifications that bear little resemblance to the needs of the workplace today. Many of the degree-granting courses tend to be rigid programs that are inaccessible to most of those already employed. This rigidity makes training not only long and costly, but also irrelevant, unattractive, and unresponsive to changes in the labor market.

## Uneven Quality of Training Programs

Given weak traditions of training in Mexico, standardization of the output of training institutions has been minimal. The quality of training varies substantially across institutions and courses. Even within the public sub-systems of CONALEP, the Center for Industrial and Service Technical Studies, the Center for the Industrial and Service *Bachillerato Tecnológico,* and CECATI schools, the quality of training provided by each school system can vary substantially. Across the systems, the quality differences are even greater (box 11-1).

---

### BOX 11-1
### Impact Evaluation of Three Training Programs in Mexico

It has not been a common practice in the public sector in Mexico to conduct rigorous impact evaluation studies of programs that have been implemented. However, such evaluation studies were carried out for the CONALEP, PROBECAT, and CIMO programs.

CONALEP (Colegio Nacional de Educación Profesional Técnica; the National College of Professional Technical Education). This program's graduate tracer study compared the placement rates and earnings of CONALEP graduates to those of control groups. Unfortunately, the findings are not conclusive because of the failure to control for other factors that could account for different labor market outcomes by the two groups. With this caveat, the results suggest that CONALEP graduates actively participated in the labor market at a higher rate than the similar age cohort of the general population, and at a much higher rate than graduates of traditional vocational high schools. On average, CONALEP graduates found jobs faster, and about two-thirds of CONALEP graduates worked in jobs related to the specialization they had studied. Using cross-cohort comparisons, the study results also suggest that CONALEP graduates' earnings increased rapidly within the first two to three years of employment.

PROBECAT (the Labor Retraining Program for Unemployed Workers). Two impact evaluation studies have been conducted for this program: one for the 1990 cohort of trainees and a control group of unemployed workers drawn from the 1990–91 national urban employment survey, and the second study for the 1993 cohort of trainees and the control group from the 1993–94 national urban em-

---

## Lack of Private Sector Involvement in Training Design and Provision

Preservice training, considered an integral part of the education system, is governed accordingly and dominated by the public education sector. Most of the technical training programs are highly subsidized by the government. Few policy measures and strategic incentives have been employed to induce more active participation by employers in worker training. As a consequence of past policies, which did not provide incentives for employers to invest in human resource development, the financing of skills forma-

ployment survey. The survey design and the data analysis were better in these studies than in the CONALEP evaluation. The findings of both studies were consistent, and showed that PROBECAT was fairly effective in shortening the duration of unemployment for certain target groups, namely, trainees with prior work experience (both men and women). The program also appeared to have improved the likelihood of employment for participants over a longer period of time. In addition, the evaluation suggested that program participation raised the post-training earnings of men but not of women.

CIMO (Total Quality and Modernization Program). Evaluation of the CIMO program involved a comparative analysis of various quantitative indicators of training, production, production processes, organizational structure, markets, employment, and remuneration using a sample of 248 firms assisted by the CIMO program during 1991–93 and a sample of 316 firms in a control group selected from the industrial survey to match the CIMO sample. The study showed that participation in the program helped firms increase their productivity faster than those in the control group. The initial productivity level was lower for CIMO firms than control group firms, but this gap diminished after program participation. However, the corresponding gap in the wage level between the two groups did not diminish even after program participation. Thus the benefits of the CIMO program appeared largely to be reaped by employers.

*Source*: Compiled by author.

tion has been perceived as a responsibility of individuals or of the government, and not as a responsibility of employers.

In recent years some efforts have been made to enlist the involvement of the productive sector in training program design, such as the industrial advisory committees of the CONALEP system. However, such efforts need to be expanded significantly. Furthermore, the government has established the National System of Labor Competency Standards, which emphasizes involving the private sector in defining competency standards for each skill area. The governing body of the new system is a tripartite council with representatives of the government and of employers' and workers' associations; the private sector has majority representation.

## Notable Reforms

The government has launched several efforts to improve primary education to make future workers more trainable and to help workers and job seekers to acquire skills relevant to jobs. The success of the reforms depends on the financial sustainability of the new vocational education and training system since the government proposes to reduce gradually its financial contributions.

### Improving Primary Education

Increasing access to and improving the quality of primary education is a priority issue, and visible progress has been made. Since 1950 Mexico has made great strides in increasing both access to and the quality of basic education: school enrollments have increased sevenfold while the total population tripled, and adult illiteracy has decreased from 40 to 12 percent. The government implemented a comprehensive reform of the education sector from 1990 to 1995, with an emphasis on improving literacy and numeracy.

### Improving Technical Education and Training

Faced with new pressures brought about by international competition, and drawing from the lessons learned from existing training programs, the government has undertaken a comprehensive overhaul of the country's technical education and vocational training programs. In 1994 it launched the Technical Education and Training Modernization Project to help achieve this objective. The specific aims of the project were to (a) establish the

National System of Labor Competency Standards, (b) redesign training programs into modular courses based on the new standards, (c) promote private participation in training design and implementation by providing incentives to enterprises and individuals, and (d) establish an information system and undertake studies to improve training programs.

## Establishing National Skill Standards and Stronger Links with Employers

Financial sustainability will be attained only if the new system brings the expected value added to employers and workers. The government is studying how to achieve this self-sufficiency, using a mechanism similar to the franchising of certification agencies to generate resources. The National System of Labor Competency Standards will serve as the measure against which both workers and training programs will be judged. The system will also provide a reliable basis for updating curricula, training equipment, and instructor training. Links between training institutions and potential employers will be strengthened through employers' participation in course design and through arrangements whereby businesses provide practical training opportunities for trainees.

## Reference

Education Secretariat. 1994. *Estatistica Básica Sistema Naciónal de Educaion Tecnologica, 1992–93, Inicio de Cursos.*

# III Low-Growth Economies

The countries discussed in Part III—South Africa, Tanzania, Zambia, the Arab Republic of Egypt, Jordan, and the West Bank and Gaza Strip—have high labor-force growth, low employment growth, and high unemployment and underemployment rates, especially in the informal sector. Training reform in South Africa is best seen in the context of the dramatic changes in the political arena. With the breakdown of the apartheid system in the early 1990s, policy reform and institutional change began. The roots of South Africa's poor development of human resources lie in the legacy of black citizens' lack of access to a basic education and in the poor quality of that education. Training provision takes place within this context. Two-thirds of the South African labor force is employed in the formal sector; industrial training boards collect and disburse training levies and organize training in companies. There is no structured system of training in place to meet the needs of informal sector workers. The reform of vocational education and training in South Africa is based on consensus building. Rather than creating new institutions to develop and implement reforms, the authorities have relied on existing institutions.

Tanzania is one of the five poorest countries in the world, and it is not surprising that the financing of social sector investments has been inadequate. Vocational education and training (VET) in Tanzania has been plagued by the inefficient use of resources, inequitable educational opportunities, poor labor market linkages, and a lack of coordination between donors and the government. Reforms were initiated in response to these problems, but the preliminary diagnosis of their results is discouraging.

Inefficiency in the allocation of resources continues, leading to high unit costs in public secondary schools and training institutions. The quality of training remains poor. Students who enter secondary schools and training institutions are mainly from upper income households. Although the government is still a major employer, the private formal sector has grown relatively rapidly over the past decade. Public training institutions have done poorly in catering to this new client, or to the large informal sector.

Zambia's vocational education and training system faces similar constraints relating to its purpose, clientele, management, and product quality. Current training efforts reach less than 3 percent of those entering the labor market every year, and programs are focused on providing youth with skills for formal sector jobs that are almost nonexistent. The government's capacity to collect and analyze information for policy development or implementation is weak. Donors are important, but their role is not always clear. Not surprisingly, the quality of training is poor. Following the election of a new government in 1991, concern about the deplorable state of skills development in the country led to several policy reviews and reform initiatives. Of these, vocational education and training reforms have perhaps been the most innovative in terms of procedures and proposals. These reforms, however, face formidable obstacles: a sluggish economy, lack of consensus, and unwillingness to accept a reduced role of government in the finance and provision of VET. Among the most promising measures are efforts to strengthen nonformal training by making it easier and financially attractive for private providers and microentrepreneurs to train informal sector workers.

In Egypt the main problems seem to be an oversupply of technical and vocational skills to a sluggish economy and a fundamental mismatch between the needs of a largely informal economy and the VET system, which is designed to meet relatively formal needs. In the former centrally planned system, vocational and technical graduates were guaranteed employment. Now that employment cannot be guaranteed, the rationale for attending vocational and technical training has shifted from educational to social reasons. Even in unrealistically optimistic scenarios, the likely supply-to-demand ratios for university and secondary school graduates are greater than 400 percent. The system is inequitable as well: Egypt spends almost half of its education budget on fewer than one million university students, while primary and secondary schools enroll about 13 million students. The study concludes that there are few ways to reform the VET system without transferring resources from higher education.

Despite lacking natural resources and being constrained by a small industrial base, Jordan has developed good education and training programs. Its workers have achieved high education and skill levels, and they have proved to be the most successful export of the economy. Jordan is exceptional in terms of economic performance within the region, and it compares favorably with other countries with low-middle incomes. As in Egypt, however, VET faces problems of low relevance, quality, and efficiency. Vocational school students tend to specialize quickly and narrowly upon entry into training centers, and community colleges are out of touch with community demands. But the high levels of cost recovery in postbasic education make the system equitable, and laissez-faire labor policies have hidden weaknesses in the VET system. The high education of Jordanians and employment opportunities in neighboring countries have acted as a buffer for surplus or mismatched labor and put little pressure on the VET system to reform. The emphasis has been on public training; relatively little is known about the provision of VET in the private sector. The Jordan study optimistically concludes that the existing structure of the education and training system is adequate. What is now required is consolidation and selective expansion.

The West Bank and Gaza study is special in that it describes efforts undertaken by an authority not yet a government, and by territories not yet a country. Since 1948 education in the West Bank has been modeled after the Jordanian system; Gaza adopted the Egyptian model. The Palestinian Authority assumed control of education in 1994 and has taken steps to unify the system. Only a small proportion of secondary enrollment is in vocational schools; graduates can continue education at the tertiary level in community colleges or universities. Training for school-leavers is provided in vocational training centers. A major expansion of the Palestinian training system would, naturally, raise the issue of financing and sustainability. Unit costs are three times those in neighboring Jordan and Egypt. Like in Egypt, in the West Bank and Gaza there is little or no cost recovery. Instruction in government vocational centers and schools is of poor quality, and these institutions rate their contact with industry as mediocre at best. Having decided that such constraints are no excuse for inaction, Palestinian authorities have embarked upon a reform process that promises to be gradual, substantive, and even innovative. Vocational education and training enrollments are to be expanded using a modular format that is integrated with the general education system, and greater cost recovery is to be used to overcome problems of efficiency and finance.

# 12 South Africa

ADRIAN ZIDERMAN AND ARVIL VAN ADAMS

WITH THE BREAKDOWN of the apartheid system of separate racial development in the early 1990s, the beginnings of a process of appraisal, policy reform, and institutional change became evident in many areas of South African life. This process is both remedial—to correct the ill effects stemming from the legacy of apartheid—and innovative, witnessed in a wave of sweeping moves to fashion a "new South Africa." The reform of the vocational education and training system (VET) is a central element in the broad process of social and institutional change in the country. Indeed, the development of the education and training system and of efficiently functioning labor markets are two areas that were particularly stunted during the apartheid period. There is broad consensus on the pressing need for change in the area of human resource development in general and VET in particular, as a necessary condition for achieving national objectives in the economic, industrial, and social fields.

The root of poor human resource development in South Africa lies in the historical legacy of black citizens' lack of access to basic education and in the poor quality of education received by those that gained access. Results from the 1991 census indicate that 30 percent (41 percent for blacks) of the adult population ages 20 to 64 were functionally illiterate, that is, with an educational level of Standard 3 or below. Similar ratios have been estimated for labor force participants. If illiteracy is defined as failure to complete Standard 8, then 12.5 million people may be regarded as illiterate (NTB 1994a); some 60 percent of them are estimated to be economically active. Yet the provision of adult basic education by industry, nongovern-

341

mental organizations, and the Ministry of Education combined reaches less than a quarter of a million individuals. The dramatic changes in the political arena have led to growing optimism on the part of the black population and to an inflation of expectations in the economic sphere, especially in relation to job opportunities and living standards.

## The Economy and Labor Force

Training provision takes place within the context of a sluggish economy.[1] While the gross national product (GNP) per capita of some US$3,000 is considerably in excess of that in neighboring countries, annual output growth has declined. Gross domestic product (GDP) per capita fell at the rate of 2 percent per year from 1980 to 1993; gross output per employee stood at only 75 percent of 1980 levels in 1993; gross investment declined by 4.7 percent per year during the 1980–93 period; and the investment-to-GDP ratio, which stood at 30 percent in 1980, was only 15 percent in 1993. In addition, the economy suffered from limited technological advancement, high unemployment, and continued widespread poverty.

South African labor is mostly urban: only 38.5 percent of the labor force was in rural areas in 1995. Despite attempts to restrict Africans to their homeland areas during the apartheid era, 49 percent of African workers were urban. Agriculture accounted for only about 10.7 percent of the labor force.

The formal sector is by far the largest employer. Estimates of the labor force and employment in 1995 suggest that about 49.9 percent of the labor force held formal jobs. This proportion varied across racial groups: Africans (42.6 percent), Asians (64.1 percent), coloreds (66.8 percent), and whites (71.6 percent). Yet it remains true that the formal sector generates the most employment for every group. Estimates based on the Poverty Survey are similar. The survey also shows that the formal sector is the biggest employer for both men and women. Regular wage jobs provide the bulk of employment for all workers regardless of gender or racial group (table 12-1).

In 1995 formal employment was quite highly unionized by developing-country standards. It accounted for 26.6 percent of formal workers. Unions are especially strong in mining and much of manufacturing, but as in most countries are weak in agriculture and most services sectors. Whites are the least unionized racial group among regular employees (table 12-1), and

TABLE 12-1

Employment Status of Adults Ages 16 to 70, by Gender and Population Group, 1995
(percent)

| Status | Male | | | | Female | | | | Total |
|---|---|---|---|---|---|---|---|---|---|
| | African | White | Colored | Asian | African | White | Colored | Asian | |
| *Regular wage employment* | | | | | | | | | |
| Public sector | 8.4 | 16.8 | 12.9 | 16.7 | 4.7 | 16.3 | 8.1 | 8.1 | 8.3 |
| Private sector | 26.6 | 49.9 | 41.2 | 41.7 | 13.3 | 29.5 | 28.2 | 21.7 | 23.8 |
| *Informal employment* | | | | | | | | | |
| Casual wage employment | 4.3 | 2.8 | 6.0 | 3.8 | 2.8 | 4.7 | 5.9 | 1.2 | 3.7 |
| Self-employed | 4.1 | 8.3 | 2.7 | 9.8 | 4.7 | 5.1 | 2.2 | 3.7 | 4.6 |
| Total employed | 43.6 | 77.9 | 62.7 | 71.6 | 25.5 | 55.7 | 44.5 | 34.6 | 40.5 |
| *Unemployment* | | | | | | | | | |
| Looking for work | 7.2 | 2.1 | 8.5 | 5.2 | 5.3 | 1.9 | 9.9 | 3.4 | 5.7 |
| Discouraged | 14.9 | 0.8 | 4.4 | 0.8 | 14.7 | 1.1 | 4.5 | 3.4 | 11.5 |
| Total unemployed | 22.1 | 2.9 | 12.9 | 6.0 | 20.0 | 3.0 | 14.4 | 6.8 | 17.2 |

*(Table continues on the following page.)*

TABLE 12-1 (continued)

| Status | Male | | | | Female | | | | |
|---|---|---|---|---|---|---|---|---|---|
| | African | White | Colored | Asian | African | White | Colored | Asian | Total |
| Total out of labor force | 34.3 | 19.2 | 24.4 | 22.4 | 54.5 | 41.3 | 41.1 | 58.6 | 42.3 |
| Total | 100.0 | 100.0 | 100.0 | 100.0 | 100.0 | 100.0 | 100.0 | 100.0 | 100.0 |
| Union members as percentage of regular employment | 34.9 | 18.7 | 40.9 | 39.4 | 20.6 | 10.7 | 39.7 | 34.6 | 26.6 |
| *Percentage of labor force* | | | | | | | | | |
| Regular employment | 53.2 | 82.5 | 71.6 | 75.3 | 39.6 | 76.7 | 50.6 | 72.0 | 55.6 |
| Informal employment | 13.2 | 13.9 | 10.8 | 17.0 | 16.4 | 18.2 | 25.0 | 11.6 | 14.6 |
| Unemployment | 33.6 | 3.6 | 17.6 | 7.7 | 44.0 | 5.1 | 24.4 | 16.4 | 29.8 |
| Total | 100.0 | 100.0 | 100.0 | 100.0 | 100.0 | 100.0 | 100.0 | 100.0 | 100.0 |

*Source:* Fallon (1997).

consistent with experience in other countries, women are much less unionized than men.

There is a great contrast between the incidence of unemployment among Africans and whites (table 12-1). White unemployment is modest by international standards, but African unemployment is high. In 1995, 33.6 percent of males and 44 percent of females in the labor force were unemployed. Unemployment is particularly severe among young people (table 12-2). More than two-thirds of African males ages 16 to 19 are unemployed under the broad definition, and extremely high unemployment rates prevail among teenagers in other racial groups. In virtually every country unemployment among young people is more severe than for other age groups, because as first-time job seekers they often experience a period of unemployment before securing a job; however, the South African problem is one of the worst in the world.

Census data point to another troublesome fact: unemployment has been rising over time. Changes in unemployment rates for South Africa, as measured in the censuses of 1980, 1985, and 1991, are roughly consistent with the movements in the percentage of the labor force outside formal employment shown in figure 12-1. (These numbers do not include discouraged workers.) The figure shows that black unemployment rates nearly doubled in the 1980–95 period, while white unemployment rose less sharply.

To some degree labor allocation by race can be reinterpreted according to skill levels. Even though levels of education and skill attainment between the racial groups have narrowed significantly over the years (Fallon 1992), large gaps still remain. Whites tend to have much more education and skills than other groups, among which Africans lag well behind Asians and coloreds. One can make the following observations about labor allocation: (a) skilled workers are more likely to work in the formal sector than are semiskilled or unskilled workers, (b) unskilled workers are more likely to end up in the informal sector than are skilled workers, and (c) unskilled workers experience much higher unemployment rates than do other workers. But the likelihood of being unemployed or employed in the formal sector depends not only on skill levels. It also depends on other characteristics, including race.

As unemployment rates have risen, so have real wages, especially for Africans; however, rising wages have dampened the demand for labor. Figure 12-2 shows real product wage behavior from 1970 to 1996. The most striking feature is that wages for whites were virtually stationary, while wages for Africans grew in a somewhat erratic manner. Wage differentials thus

TABLE 12-2

Unemployment Rates, by Gender, Population Group, and Age Group, 1995

(percent)

| Status | Male | | | | Female | | | | Total |
|--------|------|------|--------|------|--------|------|--------|------|-------|
| | African | White | Colored | Asian | African | White | Colored | Asian | |
| All ages | 33.6 | 3.6 | 17.6 | 7.7 | 44.0 | 5.1 | 24.4 | 16.4 | 29.8 |
| 16–19 | 66.9 | 40.0 | 54.3 | 0.0 | 74.3 | 9.3 | 48.0 | 43.0 | |
| 20–24 | 57.0 | 3.8 | 29.6 | 18.8 | 68.9 | 10.1 | 44.2 | 25.7 | |

Source: Fallon (1997).

## FIGURE 12-1
### South African Labor Force Outside Formal Employment, 1970–95

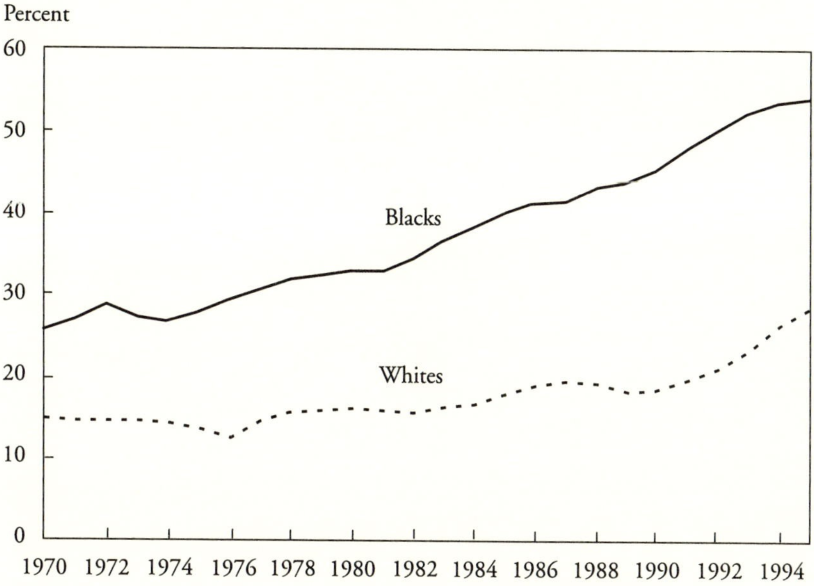

Percent

Source: Fallon (1997).

narrowed considerably between whites and other groups of workers. Growth in real wages for Africans largely ceased after the economic recession deepened in 1989, but Asians and coloreds continued to make some gains, although at a slower pace than before. These slowdowns are broadly in line with the behavior of real GDP per capita. Although figure 12-2 is based only on manufacturing, the picture is broadly similar in other major sectors.

Rising real product wages have had a substantial dampening effect on the demand for black workers. Labor demand equations indicate an average long-run wage elasticity across the sectors of –0.71. (A similar value is quoted in the 1996 Presidential Labor Commission's report.) In other words, a 10 percent increase in the real product wage would eventually lead to a 7.1 percent decrease in black employment. Furthermore, markets clear for skilled workers but not for the unskilled. Econometric analysis indicates that unskilled wages have been much less responsive to unemployment levels than those of the skilled. Although average unemployment prob-

FIGURE 12-2

Real Manufacturing Wage Index in South Africa, 1970–96

(1970 = 100)

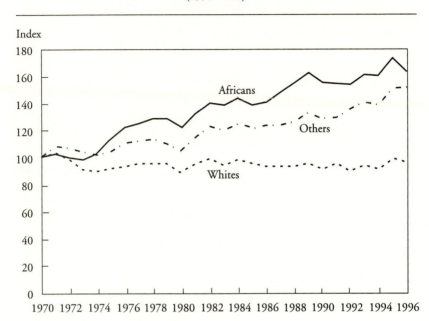

*Source:* Fallon (1997).

abilities are much higher for nonwhites than for whites, these probabilities fall off sharply at high education levels, indicating that markets clear for skilled nonwhites.

However, as noted earlier, educational attainment levels for nonwhites are significantly below those for whites. Segregated education limited funding for black education: in 1975 average educational expenditure on white students exceeded that on black students by a factor of more than 15. Although resources were then shifted toward black education, they were directed toward expanding enrollments rather than improving quality. It is within this context that the VET system operates.

## The VET System

The South African education and training system displays the classic division of responsibilities between the labor and education departments. Technical education institutions at the postsecondary level (68 technical colleges and 15 *technikons*) are run by the Department of Education and financed from central budgetary appropriations. Secondary schools offer mainly academic programs, but a few schools provide technical courses, including practical workshops in such traditional vocational education areas as woodworking, metalworking, electrical and electronics, motor mechanics, and, more recently, bricklaying and plastering. South Africa does not appear to have traditional secondary vocational schools. The greatest area of concern is the poor levels of mathematics and science teaching across the system (Department of Labor 1996).

The main institutional players in the vocational training system are the Department of Labor, the National Training Board (NTB), industrial training boards (ITBs), employers, and public and private training providers. The Manpower Training Act, as amended in 1990, places primary responsibility for formal sector vocational training firmly on the shoulders of employers. The Department of Labor assumes a mainly supportive role. The amended act paved the way for the introduction of a largely new training system based on the establishment of industry-based training boards, the mechanism through which business assumes responsibility for training within its sector, including the structuring and control of apprenticeship training. In practice, this new system has displayed a number of weaknesses, particularly in relation to coverage, control, national accountability, and financing. Proponents of reform are seeking to understand the nature of these shortcomings. They want to introduce appropriate reforms in the context of best-practice international experience.

While the major thrust of this section is on training provision and financing for formal sector employment, it also looks at training for the informal sector and special needs groups, such as the unemployed and the poor. Training for these diverse groups is recognized as the responsibility of the state. Although it does not provide training courses directly, the Department of Labor funds programs for these groups through special budgetary allocations. However, current funding is inadequate to meet needs, training efforts are insufficiently focused on particular needs, courses are too short and of a low standard, and coverage is poor.

Information on the extent of these training submarkets and emerging training gaps is meager. Coopers and Lybrand estimated that between 3.7 and 5.4 million workers in 1994 were unemployed and at the subsistence level or attached to the urban informal sector. (Even higher estimates of more than 7 million have been suggested.) Government training programs in 1994 reached less that 5 percent of this sector (Coopers and Lybrand 1995).

## Department of Labor

The Directorate for Manpower Training at the Department of Labor holds the view that employers are primarily responsible for training and retraining workers, and the department's role in training workers for the formal sector is a supportive one. The department's total training budget in the early 1990s represented only some 3 percent of training expenditures (NTB 1994a, p. 67). This supportive role comprises a number of functions, including creating an appropriate legal and administrative framework. In particular, the directorate administers the national apprenticeship scheme and runs the national trades tests through its Central Organization for Trade Testing; establishes and accredits industrial training boards; and runs the national program for training the unemployed (Department of Labor 1995).

Unlike the situation in many other African countries, the Department of Labor's role in both the provision and financing of training is marginal. It does not operate its own vocational training centers, nor does it finance training to any major extent. However, the department does participate in financing training through the partial subsidization of a number of training programs, as well by bearing part of the administrative costs of the apprentice training scheme and the costs of running the trades test centers. The only major program that is financed wholly by the department is training for the unemployed: 100 percent cost coverage includes a daily allowance for trainees and payment of the pre-set instruction costs of courses provided by the nine regional training centers (RTCs) and their satellites and by registered private contractors.

## National Training Board

There is no central control or steering of the national training effort. The NTB does not function as a national training authority in the sense defined by the World Bank (1991), and it has no executive powers. Established under the 1981 act, the NTB advises the minister of labor on policy matters arising from the act and, more generally, coordinates, facilitates, and promotes training. The NTB was a tripartite body, with the bulk of its membership drawn equally from business, labor, and government, until 1995, when it was restructured to be more representative of the main stakeholders in education and training. Representation of training providers, community organizations, and special interest groups was increased to half of the board's membership. The NTB's main work is conducted by committees, such as those concerned with artisans, in-service training, and the disabled. Specialist regional training committees also exist.

The NTB ran the task team the minister of labor appointed in 1993 to develop a national training strategy for South Africa and to coordinate the activities of its eight specialized groups. This work culminated in the publication of the National Training Strategy Initiative a year later (NTB 1994a, 1994b). This influential report was instrumental in establishing a national integrated framework for education and training qualifications. The report also provided the point of departure for initiatives relating to reform of the national system of training management, control, and financing.

## National Economic Development and Labor Council

The National Economic Development and Labor Council (NEDLAC) was launched in February 1995 as a tripartite forum for reaching consensus on economic issues. The three main stakeholders—unions, business, and government—have equal membership. Representation of community and development interests is more limited. NEDLAC presides over four chambers. Its Trade and Industry Chamber has assumed the leadership role in reform (based on broad consensus) of the financing and management of the training system.

NEDLAC set up the Counterpart Group, composed of nominees representing the three main constituencies, to oversee research projects on training financing commissioned by the NTB. The objective was to develop and agree on a financing model suitable for implementation in South Africa using a process of engagement and consensus building. The idea was that group members would be responsible for reporting back to their constituencies on progress made and concerns that arose.[2]

## Industrial Training Boards

South Africa's industrial training boards are a unique feature of its training system and operate under regulations outlined in the 1981 act. In terms of comparative international practice, the 27 ITBs are unusual: they are sector based and voluntary. Industries may voluntarily decide to establish an ITB. The functions of ITBs vary. While all are concerned with accreditation and setting standards, most do not engage in training provision (BMI Industrial Consulting 1995); most impose a training levy on members;

and most are bipartite, following amendments to the act in 1990 that permitted black union representation on ITBs. (Board membership had previously been restricted to state officials, business representatives, and white union members.)

Only about a third of South African industries are represented by an ITB. ITBs are noticeably lacking in the government sector and in service sectors such as retail, banking, insurance, and health. Because each ITB does not represent the entire industry (coverage varies between 50 and 100 percent), only about one-fifth of formal sector employees are represented by an ITB. However, ITBs strongly focus on artisan training. In 1995 some 90 percent of all registered apprentices were represented by ITBs (Rockey 1993). However, the number of trainees and apprentices enrolled in artisan training declined from 37,000 in 1982 to some 22,200 in 1994 (Department of Labor 1996).

### Training Providers

The flagship training institutions in South Africa are the nine regional training centers. They operate as autonomous organizations, each with an independent governing body, although they maintain close ties with the Department of Labor. Together with some 60 satellite campuses and 165 mobile units, RTCs mainly provide training for the unemployed. They train more than 60 percent of the unemployed receiving training under the Department of Labor–financed Scheme for the Training of Unemployed Persons, launched in 1985. The RTCs also have sole responsibility for providing training under the Employee Training Program, which caters to the training needs of small enterprises (those with fewer than 200 workers). Under this scheme, the Department of Labor covers 60 percent of approved course fees (70 percent for agricultural workers).

Almost all of the RTCs' income comes from Department of Labor contracts, particularly under the Scheme for the Training of the Unemployed (Coopers and Lybrand 1995). Constant Department of Labor budgets and rising course costs have led to a decline in the numbers of trainees at RTCs and satellites (Department of Labor 1995). Capacity utilization at RTCs is low, estimated at less than 50 percent (Rockey 1993), and a number of satellites have closed in recent years because of a lack of funding. While training courses for the unemployed and heavily subsidized short training courses for workers from small enterprises dominate their activities, RTCs may offer courses to any organization (or individuals) prepared to finance the training. However, they have not proved successful in broadening the scope of their nonsubsidized activities in this way. Historically, links between RTCs and industry have been weak, with few courses offered being recognized or accredited by the relevant industry sector (NTB 1994a). In 1995, 26,500 people were trained at RTCs.

There were some 1,400 private training centers in 1995 established by employers registered with the Department of Labor. These centers provide certain skills training for the unemployed under contact with the Department of Labor. In 1995 more than 130,000 people were trained under this scheme but with questionable effectiveness. Follow-up support was limited and placement rates were low. The 66 technical colleges (under the aegis of the Department of Education but with parastatal status) had a student enrollment of 62,000 in 1994 (Central Statistical Service 1995). Somewhat less than 30 percent of students were registered as apprentices. Generally, however, the colleges have limited links with ITBs.

## Strengths and Weaknesses of the Training System

The following paragraphs explore some of the strengths and weaknesses of the training system for the formal and informal sectors.

### Training in the Formal Sector

About 56 percent of the South African labor force was in formal sector employment, including government employment, in 1994. Thirty percent of these workers were in small enterprises with fewer than 200 workers (Coopers and Lybrand 1995, p. 62). Yet it is widely accepted that training provision for formal sector employment falls considerably short of needs. Updating earlier BMI estimates, the NTB (1994a, p. 67) estimated training expenditures by the private sector at R 5 billion in 1993, less than 1 percent of total employment costs. This contrasts poorly with a training expenditure of 5 percent of employment by major trading partners.

ITBs are responsible for collecting and disbursing training levies and organizing training for companies in their sectors. However, the ITBs have not constituted a comprehensive, well-financed, and integrated national training system. In retrospect, the system's two central features—its sector-based structure rather than national board and its voluntary nature—are built-in weaknesses mitigating against an effective system able to meet the needs of a changing economy.

The advantage of industry-based boards is that they can concentrate more directly on meeting the particular needs of the industry in question. This may be difficult to achieve in nationally based schemes. Diverse practices among ITBs are apparent not only in their different functions and activities (BMI Industrial Consulting 1995, p. 153), but also in different levy schemes in terms of type of levy, categories of workers covered, and disbursement policies. (Note that a small minority have not introduced a levy scheme.) There are positive features of levy schemes linked to given industries: they provide a self-financing mechanism and place control of funds in the hands of those directly concerned, while minimizing direct intervention by the state.

The voluntary nature of the South African scheme is also unique. Under the 1981 act, the government is not empowered to establish ITBs where it deems a need is present. The initiative for accreditation of an ITB by the Department of Labor comes from the industry itself, whether a group of employers, employers' associations, or trade unions. The minister may impose a binding levy on employers in the industry but only with general board agreement. The voluntary system perhaps reflects a local ethos, but it also may have been introduced to assuage opposition from business interests.

The following are weaknesses of the ITB system (Adams 1995) that stem from its two central features:

• *Inadequate ITB coverage of the work force.* In 1994 only 27 industries had voluntarily chosen to form ITBs under the Manpower Training Act. In addition, there was less than full worker coverage in industries with ITBs. As a result, only about 20 percent of workers in the formal sector were covered by an ITB. Most enterprises and their workers fell outside the ITB system.

• *Inefficient levy collection by ITBs.* Not all ITBs have a levy system in place. Although most of them do, compliance with regard to levy payments is not always satisfactory (Coopers and Lybrand 1995, pp. 17–18; Adams 1995). Given minimal funding from government appropriations (the only notable contribution being Department of Labor–subsidized training courses for workers of small enterprises at regional training centers) and the limitations and gaps of the existing sectoral funding framework, formal sector training as a whole remains underfunded. [3]

• *Limited capacity for flexibility across sectors.* A major shortcoming of a system of training boards, each linked to a particular industry, is that it may produce a narrow approach to training, with duplication of effort and a failure to develop a functional approach to common core skills transferable across industries. It is also poorly adapted to meeting regional needs.

• *Failure to target key economic sectors.* In sectors where ITBs have not been established, the absence of a coordinating institution may lead to gaps in provision for key economic groups, such as the informal sector (which in 1994 absorbed some 15 percent of the work force), survival-oriented microenterprises, people retrenched during industrial restructuring, and dynamic small enterprises. While some ITBs have been proactive in developing pioneering training programs for some of these key economic groups, ITBs dominated by large and medium firms may fail to meet their needs.

• *Lack of national coordination or strategic planning.* The lack of a central coordinating institution means an absence of any national strategy, targets, or agreed priorities for funding and promoting training. The system does not facilitate the shifting of resources between industries to meet the needs of emerging sectors. These shortcomings are of particular concern in an economy such as that of South Africa, which is undergoing considerable structural change, with major shifts in the composition of output and employment.

• *Weak research capacity, monitoring, and evaluation.* ITBs possess neither the resources nor the expertise to identify strategic trends and introduce cost-effective, efficient management of the training system. No central body has been charged with these tasks.

• *Failure to contribute to meeting social equity needs.* The ITB system has failed to address the nonformal segments of the labor market in any meaningful way. The emphasis on sector-based training and the lack of national coordination of the training system have resulted in considerable underprovision of skills development to meet social needs, particularly in relation to school leavers, the unemployed, and rural populations.

## Training for the Informal Sector and Special Groups

No structured system of training is in place to meet the needs of informal sector workers. Under its program for training the unemployed, the Department of Labor finances courses for the informal sector. The courses are aimed at equipping unemployed people with appropriate skills for informal sector employment or to operate as independent entrepreneurs. However, the outcomes are poor. Only one-quarter found work in the sector; a third of these workers started their own businesses. Programs meeting the needs of special and disadvantaged groups (including the long-term unemployed, the disabled, and retrenched workers) are limited in coverage and poorly responsive to market needs. The biggest program is the Scheme for the Training of Unemployed Persons, administered and financed by the Department of Labor. In 1995 funding was disbursed to some 450 public and private training contractors. Funding was on a cost basis, according to a pre-set formula, rather than on the basis of outcomes, such as achieving a qualification, finding a job, or starting a business. Placement rates were low, around 20 percent.

## The VET Reform Process

The VET reform process is internally driven and is based on consensus building. Rather than creating new institutions to develop and implement the reform process, preference has been given to using existing institutions to run the reform initiative. Much emphasis has been placed on the main VET stakeholders assuming ownership of the reform process and on the building of consensus. The core of the team designing the reform strategy was drawn from the NTB, with additional membership constituted so as to provide broad representation from the four central stakeholders: employers, unions, government, and education and training providers. The result was the National Training Strategy Initiative. The NEDLAC Counterpart Group was also presented with options for reform of the system. However, none of the proposals from the National Training Strategy Initiative or NEDLAC for new governance structures or financing of the system has received broad support because of major stakeholders' conflicting interests. Furthermore, the proposed reforms were unconvincing. The National Training Strategy Initiative attached great importance to the establishment of a national qualifications framework; however, governance and financing issues were accorded a secondary role.

Given this impasse, the Department of Labor moved ahead with its own comprehensive proposals for training reform. These were included as part of the government's new skills development strategy, outlined in a green paper issued in March 1997 (Department of Labor 1997). Independent of but complementary to the national qualifications framework, set up under the South African Qualifications Act of 1995, the skills development strategy seeks to address issues of investment and prioritization for economic growth and development. The national qualifications framework addresses two key aspects of the learning system: quality and access. Both the national qualifications framework and the core proposals of the skills development strategy will be discussed in the sections that follow.

## National Qualifications Framework

The national qualifications framework provides a comprehensive mechanism for awarding qualifications based on credits for achieving learning outcomes. The South African Qualifications Authority develops and implements this framework.

Attainment of credits goes toward the achievement of eight levels of nationally recognized qualifications including both training and education. Thus the framework provides formal qualifications, against clearly defined standards, for a wide range of training programs. Moreover, it provides portability of learning outcomes by cutting across the training-education divide through the development of equivalencies of learning achieved within the education and training systems. Integration of the education and training systems will facilitate maximum flexibility for horizontal and vertical mobility between different levels. For example, on-the-job training and prior informal learning are recognized on an equal basis with skills and knowledge acquired through the formal education and training process, leading in each case to appropriate certification.

The system facilitates entry into higher levels of training based on hitherto unrecognized skills achievement and provides greater portability of existing skills. Thus it attempts to narrow the disparate skill distribution among black and white Africans. Ultimately, the system would lead to a more flexible training approach, adaptable to new developments in the labor market, the workplace, and education and training (BMI Industrial Consulting 1995).

The national qualifications framework has been widely welcomed, but a note of caution is in order. Although the advantages of the new system are manifest, it is likely to be extremely costly. Moreover, by making skills more portable, the framework will increase the probability that workers will leave for other employment after training. This may lower firms' expected returns from training investments and reduce their willingness to participate in training (Katz and Ziderman 1990).

## Learnerships

The learnership system broadens the apprenticeship system now in decline. Apprenticeships had been the traditional framework for combining structured learning with work experience. Learnership coverage extends beyond the traditional blue-collar confines of the apprenticeship system to include a wide range of services. Access includes those in formal employment, in self-employment, in the informal sector, and in pre-employment, as well as members of special target groups, including unemployed young people and women in rural areas.

Through learnerships, structured learning and work experience are organized for accreditation within the national qualifications framework. Learnership contracts are formulated between the learner, the provider of structured learning, and the organization providing work experience. Learnership contracts must be registered with a sectoral education and training organization to qualify for public support. The learnership system is highly original in its breadth of client coverage, sectoral spread, and potential range of skills to be covered. Its development will be monitored with much interest.

## Funding the Public Training Delivery System

Budgetary allocations would continue to fund training programs for special groups, including the unemployed and young people, as well as pre-employment public sector training. Proposals for the disbursement of public funding for training programs aimed at target groups envisage the removal of protection from all providers. A new system of competitive tendering for long-term training contracts would be introduced. These measures would end the privileged position of regional training centers in relation to private sector institutions. The system would encourage competition between education and training providers, both public and private, and it would enhance providers' responsiveness to the performance criteria governing the allocation of public funds.

## Sectoral Intermediaries

The Department of Labor proposed the introduction of sectoral agencies, or intermediaries, to promote high-quality and relevant education and training provision under the skills development strategy (Department of Labor 1997). The new sectoral education and training organizations will be developed from existing ITBs, whose functions will be appropriately broadened. Current training levy powers at the sectoral level will be replaced by a national training levy, which will fund sectoral education and training organization activities.

## National Coordination

Broad agreement has been reached on the need for national coordination and strategic direction of the training system. The advisory status of the NTB has not provided scope for these activities, however.

The NEDLAC Counterpart Group favored a tripartite coordinating body. Given the traditions of volunteerism in the training sector, this body would not exercise the strong degree of central control found in national training authorities in many other countries, but it would assume overall responsibility for developing national policy, national research capacity, and monitoring and evaluation studies. It also would coordinate the activities of ITBs and provide them with advice and support.

The government's proposals for governance of the training system are a far cry from this scenario. The NTB is to be restructured into a new tripartite National Skills Authority. Although it will be given "much stronger advisory powers than the old NTB," it will remain purely as an advisory body to the minister of labor (Department of Labor 1997). It appears that the minister and the Department of Labor will assume greater control over the governance of the national training system as a whole. Rather than run the new Research and Strategic Planning Unit, the National Skills Authority would only have "access" to it. The Research and Strategic Planning Unit would be based in the Department of Labor.

In sum, these proposals provide unions and employer representatives with an advisory role only, thereby denying these stakeholders any real role in the governance of the national training system. The opportunity to create a central, tripartite training authority to coordinate the system and to assume overall responsibility for control over training development and policy has been passed by.

## Funding of Skills Development

The government intends to replace sectoral training levies with a national levy-grant scheme, based on a national payroll levy, to fund industry-based training. The case for a national levy-grant system is set out in Department of Labor (1997, p. 67). For a more comprehensive discussion, see Middleton, Ziderman, and Adams (1993, chap. 4) and Whalley and Ziderman (1990).

The system will be flexible in relation to the needs of different industries and sectors. The sectoral education and training organizations will be responsible for managing the sectoral dimension of the levy scheme using sectoral skills development funds (80 percent of total levy revenue). The remaining 20 percent of revenues will go toward a national skills fund (perhaps supplemented by allocations from relevant government departments and donor funds). The national portion of the levy scheme will target learnerships and employee training in priority sectors and skill categories.

## Conclusions

Much can be learned from South Africa's ongoing experiment in training reform. The national qualifications framework represents an important effort to equalize the training and education experiences of black and white Africans and to create a level playing field between formal and informal training modalities. The proposed skills development strategy is comprehensive in its coverage of in-service and pre-service training. Learnerships are an innovation to broaden apprenticeship and dual training systems and to link training more firmly with work experience. Public technical training institutions will now have to compete with the private sector for public funding.

The approach of building on present institutional structures is sound. Retaining and expanding the role of the industrial training boards will keep training decisions close to beneficiaries and provide a mechanism for coordinating the national qualifications framework and in-service training expenditures at the sectoral level. Of all the ingredients of the skills development strategy, the design of a new financing mechanism has proven to be the most contentious. Opposition by the business community to a national training levy and failure to agree on a national coordinating mechanism have prompted the government to move forward with its own proposals.

In sum, we applaud South Africans' comprehensive, participatory, consensus-building approach to reform and welcome their innovations in training. Yet a note of caution is in order. By screening employers and labor representatives out of the system of governance, the government has adopted a risk-prone strategy that could lead to serious problems in the long term.

## Notes

1. Note that this section draws heavily on Fallon (1992, 1997).
2. These comments are based on the minutes of the group's first meeting held on March 17, 1995.

3. Under the Employee Training Program in the early and mid-1990s, some 20,000 workers from enterprises with fewer than 200 workers attended courses for four to five weeks. In 1992–93 the Department of Labor budgeted 0.93 million Rand, or 60 percent of the cost; most of the remainder came from employers, partially via the levy system. The average course cost was R 290.

## References

Adams, Arvil V. 1995. "National Training Strategy Initiative: Proposed Research into the Financing of Training and the Implementation of Recommendations." Pretoria: National Training Board.

BMI Industrial Consulting. 1995. "Education, Training, and Development in Business: A Training Perspective 1995." Rivona, South Africa.

Central Statistical Service. 1995. *RSA: Statistics in Brief.* Pretoria: Government Printer.

Coopers and Lybrand. 1995. "Funding Mechanism Research Project Studies 3 and 4: Funding of Training in South Africa." Johannesburg.

Department of Labor. 1995. *Annual Report 1994.* Pretoria.

———. 1996. "South Africa: Country Report." In David Atchoarena, ed., *The Financing and Management of Vocational Education and Training in Eastern and Southern Africa.* Report of a United Nations Education, Scientific, and Cultural Organization subregional workshop in Mauritius, March, 18-21. Mauritius: International Institute for Educational Planning and Industrial and Vocational Training Board.

———. 1997. *Green Paper: Skills Development Strategy for Economic and Employment Growth in South Africa.* Pretoria. March.

Fallon, Peter. 1992. "An Analysis of Employment and Wages Behavior in South Africa." World Bank Discussion Paper 3, Southern Africa Department, Washington, D.C.

———. 1997. "Labor Markets in South Africa." World Bank, Washington, D.C.

Katz, Eliakim, and Adrian Ziderman. 1990. "Investment in General Training: The Role of Information and Labor Mobility." *Economic Journal* 100: 1147–58.

Middleton, John, Adrian Ziderman, and Arvil V. Adams. 1993. *Skills for Productivity: Vocational Education and Training in Developing Countries.* New York: Oxford University Press.

NTB (National Training Board). 1994a. "A Discussion Document on a National Training Strategy Initiative: A Preliminary Report by the National Training Board." Pretoria.

———. 1994b. "Executive Summary. A Discussion Document on a National Training Strategy Initiative: A Preliminary Report of the National Training Board." Pretoria.

Rockey, N. 1993. "Audit of Existing Training Practices." BMI Industrial Consulting, Rivona, South Africa.

Whalley, John, and Adrian Ziderman. 1990. "Financing Training in Developing Countries: The Role of Payroll Taxes." *Economics of Education Review* 9(4): 377–89.

World Bank. 1991. *Vocational and Technical Education and Training.* Policy paper. Washington, D.C.

# 13 Tanzania

Amit Dar

Tanzania is one of the poorest countries in the world. Since gaining independence in 1961, its economy has undergone a series of internal and external shocks. Tanzania inherited an economic system based on private enterprise with some government regulation. The economy remained largely laissez-faire for some five years after independence, but in 1967 the Arusha Declaration turned Tanzania into a socialist state that was supposed to be self-reliant with regard to national development. The government considered this move necessary to achieve economic equality, and it considered it essential that the state should be responsible for providing education, including vocational education and training (VET), and health services. This led to a surge in government involvement in the economy and a concomitant rise in government employment. All major firms were nationalized, many parastatals were created, and agricultural cooperatives under state control were encouraged. Unfortunately, these policies did not turn out to be beneficial. On the contrary, exacerbated by oil shocks in the 1970s, a fall in export prices, and drought, the growth rates of the gross domestic product fell drastically. The public sector became overstaffed, while the private sector shrank. Simultaneously, real wages fell between 1967 and 1986 because of poor macroeconomic conditions.

Given these adverse economic conditions, the government in the mid-1980s launched the Economic Recovery Program with the objective of liberalizing the economy. The authorities liberalized agricultural input and output prices and industrial policies, removed quantitative controls on exports and imports, established controls on interest rates, reformed the parastatal sector, and deregulated private investment. These reforms have succeeded to some extent: while progress in implementing structural reforms has been modest, Tanzania has accomplished its basic liberalization objectives and has phased out the regime of pervasive and restrictive government intervention. Gross domestic product growth rates increased from 0.8 percent per year in the early 1980s to more than 4.5 percent by the late 1990s. Employment in the private formal sector has been growing rapidly, and public sector reform has led to a decline in the growth of government employment. The client of the VET system, for all practical purposes, is now the private sector.

The reforms and economic recovery have also improved household welfare. The incidence of rural poverty declined from about 65 percent in 1983 to 51 percent in the early 1990s. However, this decline in poverty has yet to be reflected in most human resource indicators. Social indicators deteriorated during the 1970s through the mid-1980s when the economy stagnated. Some progress has been made, but the signs are still not encouraging. Access to secondary education remains low, less than 5 percent. Primary enrollment rates fell from more than 90 percent in the early 1970s to 70 percent in 1990, and school outcomes are worsening. Life expectancy, infant mortality rates, and morbidity rates have either stagnated or declined. Tanzania lags substantially behind other low-income countries in basic social indicators, including education enrollments at all levels. Beyond the primary level, opportunities for formal education and training are tightly rationed, inequitable, and expensive. In addition, the quality of the education is substandard, and it is not aligned with the needs of the labor market.

## The Labor Market

Until very recently, government employment dominated the formal labor market. The remainder of employment was mostly agricultural, with a sizable informal urban sector that absorbed the large annual additions to the labor force.

### The Labor Force, Employment, and Unemployment

Tanzania's population has been growing rapidly. For more than a decade, until the early 1990s, the growth rate was around 3 percent per year. In 1994 the population numbered some 27 million. The high population

TABLE 13-1
Profile of the Labor Force, by Education Level and Gender, 1991

| Category | Total | Male | Female |
|---|---|---|---|
| Total labor force (millions) | 8.9 | 4.5 | 4.4 |
| Participation rate (percent) | 76.8 | 80.9 | 73.1 |
| Formal education participation rate (percent) | | | |
| None | 29.2 | 19.3 | 39.4 |
| Primary | 66.8 | 75.4 | 58.0 |
| Secondary | 3.8 | 5.0 | 2.5 |
| Postsecondary | 0.2 | 0.3 | 0.1 |
| Training (any level) | 8.3 | 12.8 | 3.8 |

Source: World Bank (1995).

growth rate has led to a skewed distribution of population by age: about half the population consists of children younger than 15 years of age. The growth in labor supply matches the growth in population. Between 1984 and 1994 the working-age population grew by some 3.5 percent per year. One outcome is that the work force is becoming younger, with a third below the age of 25 and half below the age of 30. This has resulted in a surge of inexperienced and unskilled job seekers. These trends are expected to continue, since population growth rates have not dropped significantly in the past few years and are not expected to do so in the near future.

The level of education of the labor force is extremely low. In 1991, 29 percent had received no education at all, 5 percent of the male labor force and 2.5 percent of the female labor force had more than a primary education, and just over 8 percent of the labor force had received any formal training (table 13-1).

Tanzania is an agricultural economy. In 1994 the agricultural sector absorbed more than 80 percent of the work force, mostly in subsistence agriculture. The informal sector was small but growing rapidly. More than 10 percent of the work force was employed in this sector, while the formal sector employed less than 10 percent of the work force. Until the mid-1990s the public sector dominated the formal sector.

The vast majority of agricultural workers have low levels of education (primary or below). The demand is low for skilled workers in a sector that remains primarily subsistence farming. This suggests that the demand for

TABLE 13-2

Employment Levels in the Formal Sector, by Employer,
Selected Years, 1978–91

| Employer | Number of people employed (thousands) | | | Annual change (percent) | | |
|---|---|---|---|---|---|---|
| | 1978 | 1984 | 1991 | 1978–83 | 1984–91 | 1978–91 |
| Private sector | 150.1 | 145.7 | 275.2 | –0.5 | 9.5 | 4.8 |
| Government | 186.2 | 302.1 | 331.6 | 8.4 | 1.3 | 4.5 |
| Parastatals | 199.6 | 185.6 | 185.6 | –1.2 | 0.0 | –0.6 |
| Total | 535.9 | 633.4 | 792.4 | 2.8 | 3.2 | 3.0 |

*Source:* Abe (1995).

VET is likely to be limited in agriculture. The informal sector is the most
rapidly growing source of employment in Tanzania—probably a result of
the high rate of labor force growth coupled with the decline in the supply
of public sector jobs. Furthermore, entry into the informal sector is relatively easy, not only because of the low skill requirements (only about 10
percent of informal sector workers acquired their skills through a formal
training program or apprenticeship), but also because the capital requirements to start up an informal enterprise are modest (Abe 1995). Thus expansion of the urban informal sector does not appear to depend on a supply
of skilled workers.

The formal sector, where the demand for skilled workers is likely to be
the greatest, is relatively small and accounts for less than 8 percent of total
employment. Tanzania's formal sector consists mainly of the civil service
(42 percent of the formal sector work force), parastatals (23 percent), and
medium and large private enterprises (35 percent).

Until the mid-1980s Tanzania relied excessively on the public sector for
generating employment. Since then economic and political liberalization
and civil service reform have encouraged private sector growth and reduced
the government's role as the country's major employer. Between 1984 and
1991 the private formal sector grew from 23 percent of total formal employment to 35 percent (table 13-2). Constraints in the supply of skilled
workers do not appear to have slowed the growth of the private formal
sector.

Because of the highly informal labor market, measuring unemployment
does not make much sense in Tanzania. However, with the public sector

shrinking, recent government figures indicate that unemployment is becoming a growing problem in Tanzania. Official unemployment rates are still below 5 percent.

### Earnings and Returns to Education

Because labor force data are not regularly collected, data on earnings are outdated. According to the 1990–91 labor force survey, only a small proportion of Tanzanian workers, 9.3 percent, received income from paid employment. Wage data point toward wage compression in the public sector but high returns to education and training in the private sector. Table 13-3 presents private and social rates of return to education. For men annual private rates of return increase sharply with level of education; for women the rates of return are higher than for men at all levels of education but are fairly constant across education levels.

The social rates of return to education are small for secondary education and negligible for training and higher education (table 13-3). This is primarily because public expenditures per pupil (unit costs) in postprimary education are high, a result of inefficient government spending in this sector. Given that most of the beneficiaries of vocational education and training come from the better-off segments of society, the high private and low social rates of return provide a rationale for reducing government investment in VET and increasing private investment in the sector.

TABLE 13-3
Private and Social Annual Rates of Return to Education and Training,
by Level, 1991
(percent)

| Group | Education level | | | Vocational training |
|---|---|---|---|---|
| | Primary | Secondary vocational | University | |
| *Private rates* | | | | |
| All | 3.6 | 6.9 | 9.0 | 19.4 |
| Male | 1.9 | 6.6 | 9.9 | 17.8 |
| Female | 10.8 | 9.0 | 11.4 | 20.2 |
| *Social rates* | 3.6 | 1.5 | 0.0 | 0.0 |

*Source:* Author's calculations based on the 1990–91 Tanzania Labor Force Survey.

Although employment in the economy is growing, labor shortages are not apparent. One study even predicted that the supply of graduates from technical training institutions in the industrial, mining, transportation, and agricultural fields would far exceed the demand (ESAURP 1992). Recently, private and semiautonomous training institutions are providing instruction in skills for the services and trade sectors, which constitute the majority of private formal sector employment. With this as a background, I now turn to a description of the VET system in Tanzania.

## An Overview of Vocational Education and Training

The Tanzanian education system follows a seven-four-two-three pattern. After seven years of primary school, pupils who qualify for further education by passing an examination administered by the Ministry of Education can choose to pursue four years of lower secondary education at a public school or training at a postprimary training institution that provides basic vocational training. Lower secondary education is followed by two years of higher secondary education. Individuals can also enter training institutions after completing either lower secondary or higher secondary education.

In 1993–94 some 350,000 students completed primary education, but fewer than 70,000 places in secondary education (lower secondary schools and postprimary training institutions) were available in public and private institutions. About 16,000 openings were available in upper secondary schools and other vocational institutions for the 35,000 students who finished lower secondary school (World Bank 1996). These figures illustrate the tight rationing of educational opportunities following primary education. Table 13-4 presents the situation in public sector institutions in 1993–94. Equivalent data for private institutions were not readily available.

Despite the tight rationing, Tanzania has many public training institutions. The 1967 Arusha Declaration, which emphasized socialism and self-reliance and stated that Tanzania should be self-sufficient in manpower needs by 1980, led to the proliferation of these institutions. The authorities believed that training individuals at the postprimary and postsecondary levels would lead to self-sufficiency. They started crash training programs. With the nationalization of large companies and the creation of many parastatals, a large public sector sprang up. To be self-sufficient in high-level manpower, the sector needed trained employees. The rallying theme was that only Tanzanians could be truly dedicated to the work at hand. Public training institutions multiplied in proportion to the number of

TABLE 13-4

Enrollment in Public Education and Training Institutions, 1993–94

| Program | Number of students entering yearly | Total enrollment (number of students) | Enroll- ment rates (percent) | Females as share of entrants (percent) |
|---|---|---|---|---|
| *After higher secondary* | | | 1 | |
| University | 2,000 | 5,700 | | 11.3 |
| Other | 3,200 | 6,200 | | 27.0 |
| *After lower secondary* | | | 2 | |
| Upper secondary | 4,300 | 8,300 | | 32.2 |
| Other | 5,500 | 14,900 | | 34.0 |
| *After primary* | | | 3 | |
| Lower secondary | 20,000 | 73,000 | | 43.5 |
| Other | 10,200 | 29,500 | — | — |
| *Primary* | — | 1,800,000 | 70 | 50.0 |

— Not available.

*Source:* Bureau of Statistics (1993); Ministry of Education and Culture (1994).

parastatals, ministries, and departments created. Private training became almost nonexistent (Omari 1994).

## The Complex System of Training Institutions

Tanzania now has a multitude of ministries that deal with the provision of technical and vocational education and training at various levels. The most important ministries in this connection are (a) the Ministry of Education and Culture through its diversified secondary schools and postprimary training centers; (b) the Ministry of Science, Technology, and Higher Education, which operates 14 nonuniversity training centers and teacher training colleges; (c) the Ministry of Labor and Youth Development through its vocational training centers; (d) a number of other ministries, government agencies, mission trade schools, and parastatals that have their own specialized training institutions; and (e) private training institutions.

MINISTRY OF EDUCATION AND CULTURE. The Ministry of Education and Culture operates all public secondary schools as well as various postprimary training institutions that admit students who could not gain entrance into secondary schools.

The perceived failure of secondary education in preparing students for wage employment or self-employment led to the diversification of the secondary school curriculum in 1978, including making it more vocational. All public lower secondary schools were converted into so-called diversified schools that focused on agricultural, commercial, industrial, and home economics courses. Private schools were also required to offer courses in at least one specialization. However, upper secondary schools were not required to specialize. In 1994 Tanzania had about 164 public lower secondary schools and 258 private lower secondary schools.

Because of the rationing of secondary school places, the government opened postprimary training centers in 1976 to provide primary school leavers with the skills that would make them employable. Some 300 centers offer two-year (on average) training programs in such fields as carpentry, masonry, sheet metal work, home crafts, and electrical work.

MINISTRY OF SCIENCE, TECHNOLOGY, AND HIGHER EDUCATION. In addition to operating all three of Tanzania's universities, this ministry is responsible for overseeing the technical training centers and teacher training colleges. The ministry operates 14 nonuniversity training centers. These intermediate-level colleges are dedicated to training students in specific professions, such as management, accountancy, teacher training, journalism, and social welfare. Entry into the colleges is predicated on completion of lower secondary school, plus extended academic exposure to senior secondary education. Courses last two or three years and students graduating from these institutions are awarded diplomas or certificates.

MINISTRY OF LABOR AND YOUTH DEVELOPMENT. The Ministry of Labor and Youth Development is responsible for operating the 19 national vocational training centers. The passage of the 1974 National Vocational Training Act led to the creation of the National Vocational Training Division within the Ministry of Labor and Youth Development in 1975. The fundamental building block of the training system developed by the division is basic training at a national vocational training center, which teaches the rudimentary skills needed for employment in one- or two-year courses. The programs are open to primary school leavers who are at least 15 years old, but for some courses a lower secondary completion certificate is also required. Students spend 60 percent of their time on practical work and the remainder on theory and general education. To receive a certificate of basic training, they must pass a test at the end of the course. The National Vocational Training Division can place those who pass the test in two-to-three-year apprenticeships in industry. Apprentices are expected to attend evening classes run by a national vocational training center. On fulfillment of all the requirements, apprentices receive a certificate of apprentice completion.

The system is focused almost exclusively on training young people to become craftspeople. In the mid-1990s training was provided in 34 trades. The general opinion is that the centers are unsuccessful. After two decades, only basic training is in place, and what passes for apprenticeship is usually placement (or self-placement) in a semiskilled job without any organized training within the firm. Thus apart from the mandatory evening classes, for the vast majority of trainees organized training ceases at the end of basic training. Studies conducted in the late 1980s (Lauglo 1990) estimated that for every 100 trainees entering basic training, 93 completed their courses, 66 were recorded as placed in an industry, 13 signed an apprenticeship contract, and only 4 were awarded an apprenticeship certificate.

Recognizing that the old system was failing to produce graduates suitable for the labor market, the government passed a new Vocational Education and Training Act in 1994 (Government of Tanzania 1994). The main provisions of this act were (a) the establishment of the Vocational Education and Training Authority (VETA), an autonomous body that took over the functions of the National Vocational Training Division; (b) the introduction of a vocational education and training levy, a 2 percent payroll tax on all employers used to finance VETA activities; (c) the establishment of a vocational education and training fund to receive levy payments and pay for activities approved by the VETA; and (d) the establishment of regional VET boards responsible for coordinating and supervising VET in the regions. The new system, supposedly demand driven, is expected to meet the skill needs of both the formal and informal sectors.

OTHER VOCATIONAL TRAINING INSTITUTIONS. The Ministry of Culture and Women's Development is responsible for running 52 folk development colleges. Established in 1975 with support from the Swedish International Development Authority (SIDA), they provide programs related to the needs of rural communities. For example, they offer short courses (one day to six months) and long courses (six to eighteen months) on a wide variety of topics, including carpentry, masonry, electrical work, dressmaking, and domestic crafts.

A number of training institutions fall under the jurisdiction of a ministry or parastatal agency. They operate mainly at the postsecondary level and cater to the needs of the specific ministry or agency. For example, in 1994 the Ministry of Agriculture ran 18 training institutions that offered certificate and diploma courses in animal husbandry and veterinary sciences; the Ministry of Health operated 43 training institutions that offered courses for medical assistants, nurses, midwives, and others lasting two to four years; and the Ministry of Natural Resources and Tourism operated about 10 training institutions with courses on such varied topics as bee keeping, wildlife management, and hotel management. Most other ministries also operate training institutions on a smaller scale. Parastatals—such as the Tanzania Portland Cement Company, the Tanzania Electric Supply Company (Tanesco), the Tanzania Post Corporation, and the Sugar Development Corporation—run their own specialized training institutes. These provide on-the-job training to their own employees. In 1995 about 10,000 students were enrolled in parastatal training institutions. Tanzania also had 58 registered mission trade schools (run by the church) that mainly provided skills for the informal sector.

PRIVATE TRAINING INSTITUTIONS. The number of private training institutions, which was virtually zero in the early 1990s, has increased. Most private sector involvement in education has been at the secondary level, where private schools outnumber public schools and private enrollment outnumbers public enrollment. Private training institutions mainly teach secretarial, commercial, and computer skills. While the number of such institutions is unknown and relatively scant data are available, estimates suggest that private training institutions enrolled about 16,000 students in 1995 (World Bank 1996). The lack of information about this increasingly important subsector is worrisome, because it may reflect neglect of this subsector on the part of policymakers.

## Costs and Financing of VET

In Tanzania the government has historically been the major financier of VET, with assistance from donor agencies. In fiscal 1995–96 the government of Tanzania planned to spend 23 billion Tanzanian shillings (about

## TABLE 13-5
## Recurrent Government Expenditures on Education and Training, Fiscal 1993–94 and 1995–96
### (T Sh millions)

| Program | 1993–94 | | | 1995–96 | | |
|---|---|---|---|---|---|---|
| | *Actual expend-iture* | *Percent of total spend-ing* | *Percent of VET spend-ing* | *Budgeted expend-iture* | *Percent of total spend-ing* | *Percent of VET spend-ing* |
| Primary education | 23,997 | 53 | n.a. | 45,766 | 66 | n.a. |
| Secondary education | 6,741 | 15 | 42 | 7,310 | 11 | 43 |
| Universities | 5,772 | 13 | n.a. | 6,512 | 9 | n.a. |
| Vocational training in government and parastatals | 8,251 | 18 | 51 | 8,271 | 12 | 50 |
| Technical training under MOSTHE | 1,106 | 2 | 7 | 1,124 | 2 | 7 |

n.a. Not applicable.
MOSTHE Ministry of Science, Technology, and Higher Education
*Source:* World Bank (1996).

US$46 million, or 2 percent of budget expenditures) on recurrent costs for its postprimary education and training institutions. Of this figure, T Sh 16.7 billion was expected to be spent on training at the secondary and tertiary levels and on diversified secondary education (table 13-5).

Of the total recurrent spending on vocational and technical education and training, in fiscal 1995–96, close to T Sh 7 billion, or about 43 percent of recurrent expenditure, was devoted to diversified government secondary schools operated by the Ministry of Education, while T Sh 1.1 billion, or 7 percent, was spent on running the technical training institutes under the Ministry of Science, Technology, and Higher Education.

The rest of the recurrent expenditure—around T Sh 8.3 billion—was divided among the many vocational and technical training institutions operated by several parastatals and by the ministries of Health, Education and Culture, Home Affairs, Agriculture, Labor, Community Development, and others. Among the various vocational programs, teacher training absorbs the single largest share of recurrent spending, closely followed by training programs in the Ministry of Health.

## Selected Issues

As we have seen, Tanzania has a complex system of public VET institutions. As the economy has liberalized and the government has had to face tight budget constraints, the system's efficacy has increasingly been called into question. The main issues facing the VET sector concern costs, labor market and training linkages, and the role of donors.

### Unsustainable Training Costs

The inefficient allocation of resources has led to extremely high unit costs in public secondary schools and training institutions, while the quality of training remains low because of insufficient expenditure on developmental and learning materials. The cost of educating one student varies widely across programs and institutions. In public institutions the recurrent cost per student for any type of training is at least ten times the comparable cost for primary school (table 13-6). Although the greater cost of higher level education is not surprising given the more costly inputs required and the more highly trained staff needed, some of the unit costs are extremely—and unsustainably—high. For example, the unit cost of a year of education at one of the technical training colleges run by the Ministry of Science, Technology, and Higher Education (some US$1,500) is 75 times the unit cost of a year of primary school (US$21) and about 10 times the unit cost of a year of secondary school (US$154).

Vocational education is an expensive venture in any setting, but it is particularly costly in Tanzania. Many of the government financed and operated training institutions that were created to provide alternatives to lower or upper secondary education are far more costly than secondary schooling. For example, vocational training in the folk development colleges, which are intended to equip students who could not go on to receive a secondary education with skills for the informal sector, are nearly three times as expensive per student year than are secondary schools.

The government faces high costs in the postprimary subsector because it is the main, and in many programs the sole, financier. Cost sharing would, by definition, reduce the financial burden on the state. However, many types of training in Tanzania cost more than necessary. The reasons for this include low capacity utilization and poor use of available facilities; low student-to-faculty ratios; large amounts spent on student room and board and welfare; and large wage bills despite low salaries. The government ab-

TABLE 13-6
Recurrent Expenditures per Student on Selected Public Programs,
1994–95
(thousands of T Sh)

| Program | Recurrent expenditures per student | Multiple of expenditures on primary education | Multiple of expenditures on secondary education |
|---|---|---|---|
| Primary education | 12.5 | 1 | n.a. |
| Secondary education | 92.7 | 7.4 | n.a. |
| Teacher training | 131.7 | 10.5 | 1.4 |
| Folk development colleges and other training institutions under the Ministry of Community Development | 267.6 | 21.4 | 2.9 |
| Health worker training | 415.9 | 33.3 | 4.5 |
| Technical training under MOSTHE | 937.4 | 75.0 | 10.1 |

n.a. Not applicable.
MOSTHE Ministry of Science, Technology, and Higher Education
Source: World Bank (1996).

sorbs most of these costs since the proportion of costs borne by students is still small.

LOW CAPACITY UTILIZATION. According to one study (ESAURP 1992), many public training institutions are operating at low capacity, with only about 50 percent of available places filled. At the Muhimbili College of Health Sciences, capacity utilization was 51 percent (Mukyanuzi 1994). Data from agricultural training institutions in particular show a large decline in enrollments (Omari 1994). Another approach to capacity utilization is to consider the intensity of use of facilities, including human resources. While few hard data on the intensity of use are available, some indicators are illustrative. For example, many public training institutions follow government working hours and close by 4 P.M. instead of offering evening classes. A study by the Food and Agriculture Organization of the United Nations (FAO 1994) showed that in many of the Ministry of Agriculture's training institutions, farm utilization was well below capacity and tractors and farm machinery were either unused or in a state of disrepair.

LOW STUDENT-STAFF RATIOS. Compared with international standards, student-staff ratios in Tanzania are low across the board in government secondary and tertiary institutions. Government secondary schools have about 14 students per teacher compared with an average of 24 in the rest of Sub-Saharan Africa. Twenty-eight students per teacher is the ratio recommended by the Tanzanian government. Many of the vocational and technical training institutions have even lower ratios, perhaps ten or fewer students per instructor. For example, at the National Social Welfare Training Institute, two faculty members are available for every student; at the Institute for Rural Planning and many agricultural training centers, the student-staff ratio is 1:1; and in the technical colleges operated by the Ministry of Science, Technology, and Higher Education, the average ratio is 8.8:1.0. By employing fewer teachers and administrators, the institutions could allocate resources to critical nonpersonnel inputs that improve achievement, such as textbooks and equipment.

SPENDING ON ROOM AND BOARD AND STUDENT WELFARE. Excessive spending on student welfare is endemic throughout Sub-Saharan Africa, and Tanzania is no exception. While public training institutions in Tanzania spend about 33 percent of their budgets on student welfare, Asian countries devote about 7 percent of their budgets to such expenditures. All institutions use a significant share of the funds invested in education and training for nonteaching-related inputs (table 13-7). Across the board, expenditures on student welfare take up at least one-quarter of the budget for education and training at each level. Even though the government has begun to institute cost-sharing measures, welfare expenditures still make up a significant proportion of recurrent expenditures.

SPENDING ON WAGES AND SALARIES. In most VET institutions more than 50 percent of recurrent expenditures goes to pay salaries (table 13-7). Although teachers and nonacademic staff are not overpaid relative to other civil servants in Tanzania, overstaffing has contributed to the large wage bill. Thus the high proportion of expenditure on salaries is directly related to the low student-staff ratios. Another reason for the high wage bill is the sizable allowances and other benefits available to teachers (as well as to other civil servants) in the form of reimbursement for housing rent, medical and travel allowances, and so on. The civil service reform under way is in the midst of monetizing these benefits.

Given these excessive expenditures, few resources are left to cover developmental expenses—namely, teaching and learning materials, operations

TABLE 13-7
Budgeted Recurrent Spending on Selected Programs, by Input, 1995–96
(percent)

| | Percentage of total spending | | |
| --- | --- | --- | --- |
| VET institution | Salaries | Student welfare | Other |
| Technical | 35 | 43 | 22 |
| Commercial | 60 | 27 | 13 |
| Agriculture and home economics | 52 | 32 | 16 |
| Teacher training | 53 | 33 | 14 |
| Health worker training | 21 | 47 | 32 |

Source: Government data; Kaijage and Abayo (1995).

and maintenance, examination costs, and other miscellaneous inputs. This results in a substandard quality of education and training. By contrast, private training institutions allocate funds more efficiently. The student-staff ratios are higher, and even though the salaries are more competitive than in the public sector, a smaller proportion of expenditure is spent on the wage bill. Furthermore, private training institutions' low expenditures on student welfare ensure that a greater proportion of funds is spent on developmental expenses, such as teaching and learning materials. This leads to the provision of higher quality education (box 13-1).

## Poor Linkages between the Labor Market and Training

Policies pertinent to training have undergone major changes. On the macroeconomic level, past policies supported a centrally planned economy; restricted trade; provided universal subsidies across many sectors; and nationalized or prohibited most private sector enterprises, including those delivering health and education services. Since the late 1980s, however, the government has introduced public sector reforms to stimulate the private sector to produce and deliver goods and services, including social services. These changes have revealed weaknesses in Tanzania's VET system, which was designed to cater to a largely public sector clientele.

Although labor force data are extremely limited and somewhat outdated, one can get some idea of the labor market conditions facing graduates of the education and training system. In the past the vast majority of students who completed primary school and did not go on to additional formal

BOX 13-1
Recurrent Expenditures on Public and Private Training Institutions

To analyze the main determinants of recurrent expenditures, Kaijage and Abayo (1995) examined spending in eight public tertiary training institutions and one private training institution (Microtex). Their analysis revealed that staff salaries and student welfare expenses constituted about 80 percent of the expenditures in the public training institutions. Student-staff ratios were low in all the public tertiary training institutions.

The largest proportion of the recurrent education budget went to pay teachers' salaries and allowances. In 1993–94 this figure amounted to more than 42 percent in the eight public tertiary institutions but less than 30 percent in Microtex. A significant reason for these differences is that the public tertiary institutions were overstaffed, while Microtex was not.

The second large expenditure item for the public institutions in the sample was student welfare. About a third of recurrent expenditures was spent on student welfare, mostly on room and board. The private institution did not provide food for its students; hence, Microtex's expenditure on student welfare was less than 15 percent of total recurrent expenditure. Microtex spent less than T Sh 30,000 per student on welfare, but more than T Sh 150,000 per student was spent by the public training institutions. Given this large amount, they had relatively little money to spend on teaching materials and other inputs (5 percent). In comparison, Microtex spent 34 percent of its recurrent budget on such items.

*Source:* Kaijage and Abayo (1995).

education or training worked in agriculture or were engaged in labor-intensive informal sector activities. The same holds true today. In the past those students who obtained a postprimary education were guaranteed secure employment in the public sector, either in the civil service or in parastatals. The government, however, has eliminated such employment guarantees. Private sector opportunities are slowly emerging, and the labor market has changed markedly as a result. These changes—along with the reforms to liberalize the economy, reduce government involvement, and encourage the growth of the private sector—imply that the education system must change to become more responsive to the labor market's future needs.

As noted earlier, the formal sector in 1995 constituted less than 8 percent of total employment. Although the government is still a major employer, the private formal sector has grown rapidly. Public sector employment is likely to remain stagnant, but employment in the private sector is expected to grow quite fast. However, demand for graduates of government tertiary institutions is not high in the private sector. In 1993 about 20 percent of educated youth were unemployed, compared with 10 percent in the mid-1970s, when the government hired most of them (Omari 1994). Studies to examine demand for these trainees in the private sector have not been conducted, but informal interviews with employers suggest that government tertiary institutions are not providing their students with skills needed in the labor market. Two private enterprises, D. T. Dobbie, an automotive sales company, and the New Arusha Hotel preferred to hire students from private training institutions to fill their secretarial and accounting positions. In some cases the companies had found that if they hired employees who had been trained in public institutions, they had to send them to private training institutions for short courses to attain the requisite skill levels (Sumra 1995).

Another means of examining the demand for trainees in the labor market is to look at job placement rates for trainees from public institutions. A World Bank–sponsored study (Olomi and Assad 1995) that examined differences between public and private training institutions sheds some light on this issue. The study examined costs, financing, and training relevance in five institutions: one private, one semiautonomous, two public, and one parastatal.

The study concludes that private training institutions allocate their expenditures more efficiently while providing relevant and demand-sensitive training. Public institutions did badly on both counts. In the two institutions not under government control, teachers and support staff are fully qualified and student-staff ratios are adequate. By contrast, the three public sector institutions are overstaffed, and fewer academic and support staff are fully qualified.

The main sources of funding for these institutions are fees, government assistance, grants, and self-generated incomes. The nongovernmental institutions obtain most of their resources from fees and self-generated income, while the public training institutions depend almost entirely on the government for their revenues. This dependence is proving to be unsustainable.

As noted earlier, expenditures on salaries, administration, and student welfare leave little to be spent on teaching and learning materials, especially

TABLE 13-8
Performance of Public and Private Training Institutions

| Indicator | Institute of Information Technology | Institute of Financial Management | National Social Welfare Training Institute | Ministry of Agriculture training institutions | Tanesco Training Institute |
|---|---|---|---|---|---|
| Program demand | High | High | Low | Low | Low |
| Job placement | High | High | Low | Low | — |
| Return on assets (percent) | 58 | –2 | –6 | — | — |

— Not available.
*Source:* Olomi and Assad (1995).

in the public institutions. Private training institutions try to keep abreast of the latest technological advances to maintain their niche in the market-place, but public institutions appear to be unresponsive to market demand.

It comes as no surprise that the private institutions have the best quali-tative performance indicators. Their programs are in great demand because their job placement rates are high. By the same token, demand for pro-grams in the other three institutions is low because students and their fami-lies perceive that employment opportunities are poor for those graduates. The complete government support these institutions receive insulates them from the market. Therefore, their management sees no need to change courses to meet labor market demands (table 13-8).

Most graduates from the private institutions had been hired by the time they completed their training. The picture was less rosy for public training institution graduates. With the abolition of government employment guar-antees in the early 1990s, graduates of the sampled government institu-tions were finding it increasingly difficult to gain employment in the private sector.

An FAO (1994) study of 15 Ministry of Agriculture training institu-tions found similar results. Graduates' employability was low once govern-ment employment guarantees were removed, and most sought employment in the informal sector.

Faced with a low demand for their skills in the private sector, many graduates from public training institutions are joining the informal sector or the ranks of the unemployed. The skill requirements in the informal sector are generally low, and the training acquired in public institutions is not useful for these jobs; however, training programs do not seem to be responding to these realities.

## Dependence on Donors

The main donors to Tanzania's education sector are Denmark, Norway, and Sweden. Other contributors include France, Germany, Ireland, the Netherlands, and the United Kingdom. Multilateral agencies such as the World Bank and the United Nations Children's Fund have also been involved in this sector.

The government has become largely dependent on donors for its nonrecurrent capital expenditures. Donors mainly lend for activities in the postprimary subsector. Funding for VET composed about 64 percent of total donor assistance in 1993 (table 13-9).

Data on the actual amounts committed to each activity are not available. Donors primarily fund such items as staff development, infrastructure creation and rehabilitation, educational materials, curriculum development, and technical assistance. They may provide some support to maintenance, research, transport, central administration, and national education trust funds, but this is less common. Despite the large donor contributions, their effectiveness is limited by the following constraints.

UNSUSTAINABILITY. Most projects funded by donors do not include phasing out mechanisms that give local institutions a period for learning and

### TABLE 13-9
Donor Funding to Postprimary Education and Training, 1991–93
(T Sh billions)

| Sector | 1991 | 1992 | 1993 |
|---|---|---|---|
| Secondary education | 3.0 | 5.2 | 9.1 |
| Vocational and technical training | 5.5 | 6.7 | 6.0 |
| Total VET funding | 8.5 | 11.9 | 15.1 |
| VET funding as a percentage of total donor funding for education | 53.0 | 58.0 | 64.0 |

Source: Materu and Omari (1995).

taking over the project when donor aid stops. In some cases little dialogue takes place with local administrators while the aid is being supplied, and so the work ceases as soon as aid is no longer provided. In addition, the long-term impact of aiding institutions is sometimes given little thought. A classic example is the support the Swedish International Development Authority gave to the folk development colleges. These institutions produce poorly skilled graduates at high costs both to the government and to SIDA. Reluctant to write off these institutions as failures, both sources continue to fund them at the expense of other, more important, programs (for example, primary education).

LACK OF COORDINATION. Lack of coordination among donors and between donors and the government is a related problem. Donors, sometimes unintentionally, are working at crosspurposes with the government. For example, they may invest in institutions that should not be the top priority in terms of meeting the country's needs. In the long run, when donor funding for such institutions declines, the government must bear the usually unsustainable costs of running them. Similarly, donors do not coordinate with each other. Not only does this work against capacity building, it also leads to less flexibility in operations. Often it results in duplication of efforts and wasted resources, a criticism that donors frequently level at government ministries.

LACK OF TRANSPARENCY. Institution administrators do not know how much money is being committed to projects in their institutions. Donor agency representatives use their own discretion to decide what or how much to provide, often after little consultation with local counterparts. Lack of transparency also obscures the institutional lines of accountability, since materials and equipment received in this manner are not recorded in institutional budgets. In this situation even parent ministries are not aware of institutions' real budgetary needs.

TOO MUCH TECHNICAL ASSISTANCE. Many countries are once again tying aid to technical expertise. While the original objective of technical assistance was to close the technology gap between industrial and developing countries by accelerating the transfer of knowledge, skills, and expertise, this outcome is rarely achieved because technical experts are not always of the highest quality. The large proportion of aid that is usually devoted to technical assistance and the excessive dependence on expatriate staff for management and implementation diminish the funds that can be devoted to educational activities. For example, of the US$2.4 million that was spent to upgrade a vocational training center at Morogoro as part of the VETA initiative, close to 45 percent was used for technical assistance from international consultants, and only 25 percent for staff development, equipment, and materials (World Bank 1996).

## Reforms and Obstacles to Reform

At the sectoral level the government's policies represent a shift in the state's conceptualization of its role. The Education and Training Policy and the Higher Education Policy put forward in the mid-1990s emphasized the government's continued responsibility to finance and provide more and better basic education opportunities. At the same time the policies reduced untargeted subsidies by increasing cost sharing, liberalizing private education and training at all levels, and decentralizing authority. The higher education policy highlights the importance of rationalizing the government's contribution to higher education. It advocates competition for grants to institutions, cost sharing to reduce the government's expenditure, and a student loan scheme to ensure that students from the poorest segments of society have more access to education and training. The authorities have also established the VETA to ensure that the training provided meets the labor market's needs. While some of these reforms are steps in the right direction, the efficacy of others is questionable.

### Fiscal Sustainability and Cost Sharing

Because of the financial constraints facing the public sector and the high expenditures incurred in recent years, the government recognized that it could not fully finance education at the higher levels or use its resources efficiently. The result has been the gradual introduction of cost-sharing schemes: some government-owned institutions have begun to charge fees for instruction, and room and board. This will reduce the government's expenditure in connection with pre-employment training.

Cost sharing is most significant at the secondary education level. In 1994 parents bore about 37 percent of total expenditures on public institutions and only around 10 percent on training institutions. In comparison, households absorbed 62 percent of educational expenditures at the secondary level in Kenya (World Bank 1995). In Vietnam households bore 22 percent of the costs of public tertiary education; both Botswana and Ghana have eliminated subsidies for student meals (World Bank 1996). Clearly there is ample scope for greater cost sharing at all levels of education in Tanzania (Galaitsi 1995).

Although no official policy on cost sharing for training institutions exists, many institutions have instituted cost-recovery schemes to alleviate severe budget constraints. In these institutions students tend to bear the costs of transportation, stationery, uniforms, bedding, and personal hygiene items. In some institutions students are required to pay examination and registration fees and to buy some of their food.

Official documents on the subject of cost sharing lack clarity. They do not specify the fees that should be charged institutions. (With no official policy, training institutions charge what they want.) Furthermore, the government circulars do not state what measures to take when students do not pay their fees. In the mid-1990s at least 20 percent of students were not paying any of the costs of their education (Mushi, Baisi, and Mbamba 1995). In some cases this was because the households were unable to pay, but some students from better-off households were simply not paying. An adverse impact of the policy has been delayed starting times for schools. Students' failure to pay for transportation leads to late arrivals, and schools end up starting three or four weeks late. Failure to make up this lost time further diminishes the quality of education the students receive.

The government continues to allocate resources inefficiently. Cost sharing will reduce the government's burden, but until it closes poorly performing schools, retrenches staff based on clear criteria, lowers expenditures on student welfare, and recycles some of the money saved back into the institutions in the form of quality-enhancing inputs, the quality of education in public VET institutions is unlikely to improve.

## Cost Sharing and the Poor

As in other countries, the better-off in Tanzania have greater access to postprimary education and training opportunities than do the poor. To ensure that access to education by the poor does not become even more limited, the government has initiated loan schemes for students in training institutions.

To make user charges workable, the government should exempt poor students from payment. However, the cost of obtaining information to differentiate between poor and better-off students is often prohibitive.

Moreover, in a society where income is difficult to measure, it is hard to identify households that can afford to pay. The means-testing scheme relies on grassroots-level institutions to identify parents with the ability to pay (Mushi, Baisi, and Mbamba 1995). If students cannot pay the fees, they apply to the village government for exemption. If the village government determines that a particular student is unable to pay, then it is required to foot the bill, and this is where the system is prone to abuse. If the village government is also unable to pay, it passes the burden on to the district council. Even when their resources are limited, village governments tend to approve the applications submitted to them. Thus the burden is passed on to the district councils. In this way the government ends up paying, often for students who can afford to pay for themselves.

In response to growing student unrest over the cost-sharing policy, the government of Tanzania started a student loan scheme in 1994–95. The scheme covers students enrolled in tertiary institutions, and it is designed to help meet the room and board expenses of students who cannot afford to pay. Students are supposed to fill out an application form that sets out their sources of income, and local district commissioners must endorse these forms, which have the status of legal contracts. The repayment terms are generous: the loans are interest free (in a country where the inflation rate is between 30 and 40 percent a year), and the loans can be repaid up to 16 years after graduation. A student who borrowed T Sh 200,000 in 1994–95 would end up having paid only the equivalent of T Sh 33,000 16 years later given the current rate of inflation. Thus, even in the best-case scenario (no defaults and low administrative costs), the government will be repaid only a small fraction of the worth of the loans.

Currently, almost all students receive loans. This suggests that the information collection procedure is not working. Furthermore, the loan collection mechanism is unclear: the means by which the government plans to trace students and recover loans after they leave the institutions have not been spelled out. The problems the government faces in administering this loan scheme are similar to those facing other developing countries where loan schemes have proved a dismal failure (Ziderman and Albrecht 1995).

## Alternative Financing Mechanisms and the Cost of Labor

Evaluations of vocational education and training in Tanzania reveal the following shortcomings: (a) training centers are insensitive to the labor market, and employers are not involved in curriculum development; (b) training facilities are inadequate because of the lack of funds and the inefficient use of existing funds; (c) the quality of training is unsatisfactory; and (d) the apprenticeship system has not worked successfully.

Realizing that its training institutes are operating inefficiently, the government of Tanzania has set up the VETA, which it expects to provide tailor-made training courses not only to meet the training needs of the formal sector, but also to help the unemployed attain skills that they can use in the informal sector. This training will be financed through a payroll levy on firms that equals 2 percent of gross emoluments payable by the employer to all employees (Government of Tanzania 1994). The authorities believe that because enterprises are bearing the costs of training that will benefit them, such a tax is fair.

This innovation was implemented in 1995, but its efficacy has not yet been assessed. Research from industrial countries suggests that, in reality, either labor bears the cost of these taxes or, since payroll levies are a tax on labor, they tend to raise the price of labor relative to capital, thereby encouraging a shift to more capital-intensive techniques and inhibiting employment growth. In addition, enterprises are likely to resist this because their experience with graduates from government vocational training institutions has not been positive. Given that public enterprises are not subject to this levy, the private sector is, in effect, subsidizing their training—something that private employers will be reluctant to do.

## Donors, Efficiency, and Labor Market Linkages

The shortcomings of the VET system triggered the establishment of the Vocational Education and Training Authority. The Danish International Development Agency and the Swedish International Development Authority are working with the government to implement the VETA's strategic action plan.

Under the VETA, vocational training centers will provide short, tailor-made courses for the formal and informal sectors, skill upgrading and updating for craftspeople and laborers, entrepreneurial courses and other support for people who want to be self-employed, and advisory services for the local business community. To achieve this the national vocational training centers will be transformed into vocational training and service centers. Each region will have one vocational training and service center; all other centers registered with and managed by the VETA will be referred to as vocational training centers. Regional boards will govern vocational training and service centers and coordinate training activities in the regions.

The government envisages that the system will be more responsive to the needs of the labor market than the old system. By involving employers' associations (such as chambers of commerce and trade unions) in curriculum design and trade testing (testing whether students are proficient in the trade), the government hopes to respond more successfully to changes in demand. New courses offered at the vocational training and service centers will be designed specifically to meet the needs of local labor markets. Whether employers will show an interest in curriculum development is not yet clear.

# References

Abe, Yasuyo. 1995. "The Labor Market in Tanzania: The Status of Unemployment and the Prospects for Employment Growth." Working paper. World Bank, Washington, D.C.

Bureau of Statistics. 1993. *Education and Training Statistics.* Dar Es Salaam: Government of Tanzania, Planning Commission.

ESAURP (Eastern and Southern African Universities Research Program). 1992. *Tertiary Training Capacity in Tanzania.* Dar Es Salaam: Tanzania Publishing House.

FAO (Food and Agriculture Organization of the United Nations). 1994. *Assessment and Evaluation of Middle Level Agriculture and Livestock Education and Training System in Tanzania.* Report TCP/URT/2357(A). Dar Es Salaam.

Galaitsi, E. C. 1995. "International Experiences in Organization, Governance, and Financing of Post-Primary Education." Working paper. World Bank, Africa Region, Washington, D.C.

Government of Tanzania. 1994. *Vocational Education and Training Act.* Dar Es Salaam.

Kaijage, E. S., and A. G. Abayo. 1995. "Economic Efficiency of the Secondary and Tertiary Education and Training Sector in Tanzania." Working paper. World Bank, Africa Region, Washington, D.C.

Lauglo, Jon. 1990. *Vocational Training in Tanzania and the Role of Swedish Support.* Dar Es Salaam: Swedish International Development Authority and Ministry of Labor and Youth Development.

Materu, P. N., and I. M. Omari. 1995. "Donor Participation in Postprimary Education and Training in Tanzania." Working paper. World Bank, Africa Region, Washington, D.C.

Ministry of Education and Culture. 1994. *Basic Education Statistics in Tanzania, 1988–1992.* Dar Es Salaam: Government of Tanzania.

Mukyanuzi, F. 1994. "Undergraduate Training and Muhimbili University of Health Sciences." Internal document. World Bank, Africa Region, Washington, D.C.

Mushi, R., M. Baisi, and U. Mbamba. 1995. "Cost-Sharing Schemes and Financing Strategies in the Postprimary Education Sector." Working paper. World Bank, Africa Region, Washington, D.C.

Olomi, D. R., and M. J. Assad 1995. "Institutional Case Studies." Working paper. World Bank, Africa Region, Washington, D.C.

Omari, I. M. 1994. "Government-Financed Training in Tanzania." Internal document. World Bank, Washington, D.C.

Sumra, Suleman. 1995. "Students', Parents', and Employers' Attitudes towards Education and Career." Working paper. World Bank, Africa Region, Washington, D.C.

World Bank. 1994. *The Role of Government: Public Expenditures Review for Tanzania*. Report 12601. Washington, D.C.

———. 1995. *Tanzania Social Sector Review.* Washington, D.C.

———. 1996. *Postprimary Education in Tanzania: Investments, Returns, and Future Opportunities.* Washington, D.C.

Ziderman, Adrian, and Doug Albrecht. 1995. *Financing Universities in Developing Countries.* The Stanford Series on Education and Public Policy. Washington, D.C.: The Falmer Press.

# 14 Zambia

## Fred Fluitman and Wim Alberts

ZAMBIA, A LANDLOCKED COUNTRY in the southern part of Sub-Saharan Africa, has a land surface area of 753,000 square kilometers. Its population in 1995 was 9.4 million, and its population growth rate in the mid-1990s was 2.9 percent per year (World Bank 1994, 1996a,b,c). Despite vast mineral resources, copper in particular, and an abundance of fertile soil, Zambia is a low-income country. In 1995 gross national product per capita (US$370) remained well below the average in Sub-Saharan Africa (US$490).

Zambia's economy suffers from a very high debt service burden, heavy reliance on a single export product (copper), and excessive public sector direction of, and direct participation in, the production of goods and services. Soon after independence in 1964, Zambia moved toward a public sector–led economy dominated by inefficient parastatal monopolies and further characterized by a pro-urban, anti-agricultural bias. The situation derived, in part, from a distrust, rooted in colonial experience, of the private sector. Rising copper prices helped Zambia to grow at an average rate of 2.5 percent over the first decade, but since 1975 the declining production and falling world prices of copper, the general deterioration in Zambia's terms of trade, and the country's failure to develop a dynamic and diversified economy have caused economic decline. With copper prices down, many social indicators stalled and even reversed. Per capita income fell by more than 50 percent from 1974 to 1994. Life expectancy and access to safe water are estimated over the years to have fallen below Sub-Saharan averages; female primary school enrollments and per capita health spending are among the lowest in the Southern Africa region, and infant mortality is almost twice as high as the average for low-income countries. By the mid-1990s more than 60 percent of all Zambians were living in households with expenditures below the level considered sufficient to provide for basic needs.

In 1990 Zambia decided to undertake a major structural adjustment program to counter its rising problems. By this time many parastatals had experienced large losses, private investment had collapsed, social sector budgets had declined, physical infrastructure had deteriorated, and basic goods and services were in short supply. The structural adjustment program combined trade policy reforms, deregulation, and exchange rate adjustment with stabilization policies designed to restore fiscal and balance of payments equilibrium and price stability. While improvements were reported for several key economic indicators, gross domestic product remained more or less constant during 1991–95, mainly as a result of one major and two minor droughts, necessitating maize imports, and a further drop in copper production. Nevertheless, medium-term prospects for renewed growth are believed to be reasonably good.

## The Labor Market

In the decade following independence, Zambia witnessed considerable changes in its labor force. People moved away from subsistence agriculture into nonagricultural activities and, conversely, from rural to urban employment. Initially, there was a significant increase in the number of formal sector wage jobs, but these jobs never represented more than 20 to 25 percent of the labor force. However defined or measured, formal sector employment stalled in the mid-1970s and has continued to decline in the wake of the country's economic misfortunes. With Zambia's labor force growing at 3 percent per year in the early 1990s, the share of formal sector employment in the labor force dropped to between 10 and 15 percent during this period.[1]

A comprehensive survey in 1993 estimated that 41 percent of all Zambians participated in the labor force; participation was higher in rural than in urban areas, both in absolute and relative terms. Two-thirds of the national labor force resided in rural areas. Moreover, the rural labor force represented 46 percent of all rural dwellers, with men and women participating in almost equal proportions. In urban areas, where one-third of the national labor force resided, overall participation was lower at 33 percent, with 41 and 25 percent for men and women, respectively.

TABLE 14-1
Employment Status in Urban and Rural Areas, 1993
(percent)

| Employment status | Urban areas | Rural areas | Total |
|---|---|---|---|
| Self-employed | 31 | 52 | 46 |
| Unpaid family worker | 6 | 44 | 34 |
| Public sector employee | 40 | 3 | 13 |
| Private sector employee | 21 | 1 | 6 |
| Not stated | 2 | — | 1 |
| Total | 100 | 100 | 100 |

— Not available.
*Source:* Central Statistics Office (1993).

Some 3.3 million people, most of them under the age of 25, were part of the country's labor force. Around 0.5 million (15 percent) were reported to be employed, most of them for wages, in the formal sector of the economy. Some 2.1 million workers (68 percent), whose number includes subsistence farmers, were counted to be employed in the informal sector, most of them self-employed or unpaid family workers. The remainder, some 0.6 million people (17 percent), were reported to be unemployed.

Eighty percent of workers were either self-employed or unpaid family workers. Wage employment was an almost exclusively urban phenomenon, and two-thirds of all wage employees worked for the public sector—that is, for the government or a parastatal company (table 14-1). Almost three out of four Zambians employed found work in the agricultural sector, where most of them were subsistence farmers. Even in urban areas some 14 percent of those who worked were involved in agricultural activities. Manufacturing employed only 4 percent of the national work force, or 12 percent of urban workers; the figures for mining were are 3 and 9 percent, respectively. Employment in the services sector, 18 percent of the national total, was also concentrated in towns and cities.

Unemployment was much lower (11 percent) in rural areas than in urban areas (30 percent). Whereas in rural areas men and women were believed to be equally affected, in urban areas women were worse off than men, with unemployment rates of 40 and 24 percent, respectively. Three out of four among the unemployed, both in urban and rural areas, were youth under the age of 25. A large share of youth, after having been to school, pass through a phase of unemployment. Except for the few who have had access to higher education, unemployment rates hardly vary by level of education. Periods of unemployment appear to last longer in urban areas than in rural areas. A typical scenario would see most young school leavers "hang on" in town and look for a job, at least for a while; gradually some of them would return to their villages and be quickly absorbed in the never-ending activities of the subsistence farm.

Survey results indicate that the Zambian labor force has become increasingly educated, reflecting considerable investment in schooling, at least until the early 1980s. The proportion in the labor force without any schooling was reported to have declined from 24 percent in 1986 to 16 percent in 1993; the proportion of those who had completed all or part of primary school remained about the same during this period (56 to 58 percent). The percentage of those who had completed all or part of secondary education increased from 18 to 24 percent. While there is little doubt that the average level of schooling among labor force participants in all categories went up, differences among such categories have remained intact. Average education levels are higher for men than for women. Education levels are higher for wage workers than for the self-employed and, therefore, higher in urban areas than in rural areas and higher for those who are in the formal sector than for those in the informal sector. The unemployed, as a group, are not necessarily less educated than the employed, since unemployment is concentrated among young people who have typically had more education than their parents; there are, in fact, a sizable number of educated youth, including university graduates, looking for suitable jobs. That being said, observers of the Zambian education system agree that the quality of education provided, never satisfactory, deteriorated considerably during the 1990s.

## The Vocational Education and Training System

Vocational education and training in Zambia is provided by a diverse group of government ministries. The private sector is also slowly becoming a player in this sector.

### General Education

Primary school in Zambia begins at age seven and lasts seven years. Thereafter, selected pupils may go on to secondary school, comprising a two-year junior secondary cycle (intended eventually to form part of basic education) and a three-year senior secondary cycle. Further education and training is available after Grade 12, at the university level or in institutions forming part of the country's technical education and vocational training system.

It is evident from enrollment data that Zambia has made remarkable efforts since independence to provide all its children with primary education. Enrollments steadily increased from around 380,000 in 1964 to 1.5 million in 1995. Over the same period, secondary school enrollments increased from around 14,000 to 228,000 (table 14-2). Enrollment rates, particularly for primary education, compare favorably with those of other Sub-Saharan African countries. In 1994 net enrollment rates for primary school (excluding overage pupils) were 86 percent for boys and 80 percent for girls; net enrollment rates for secondary school were 19 and 14 percent, respectively.[2] This relatively positive picture conceals the fact that, in recent years, primary level enrollment rates have been gradually declining and drop-out rates have been increasing. After "catching up" until the mid-1980s, with enrollment growth exceeding population growth, primary school enrollments increased, on average, by 1.6 percent per year between 1985 and 1990, and by only 1.1 percent per year between 1990 and 1995, compared with a population growth rate of close to 3 percent per year over the past two decades.

Upon completing primary school, only one in three pupils (62,000 out of 183,000) entered secondary school in 1994; progression to senior secondary, after Grade 9, was a mere 18 percent in 1994. Of students who left secondary school upon completing Grade 12 ("Ordinary" levels), at best 20 percent is believed to have pursued some form of further education or formal training. It should be noted that formal, pre-employment training opportunities are available only for those who complete Grade 12 (because there are far fewer training places than applicants). In other words, formal

TABLE 14-2

Primary and Secondary School Enrollments, Selected Years, 1964–95

(thousands of pupils)

| School level | 1964 | 1970 | 1975 | 1980 | 1985 | 1990 | 1995 |
|---|---|---|---|---|---|---|---|
| Primary | 378 | 695 | 872 | 1,042 | 1,343 | 1,451 | 1,534 |
| Secondary | 14 | 52 | 73 | 95 | 132 | 182 | 228 |

*Source:* Ministry of Education data.

vocational education and training in Zambia is all at the tertiary level, regardless of whether, in the context of that country, a completed secondary education is essential (for example, for tailors or masons).

The University of Zambia in Lusaka and the Copperbelt University, which was established in the early 1990s, had a combined enrollment in 1995 of 6,000 students, considerably more than the 4,000 students enrolled in the 1980s. The focus of this chapter, however, is on VET other than that provided by universities.

## Vocational Education and Training

VET in Zambia is officially administered by the Department of Technical Education and Vocational Training (DTEVT), established by an act of Parliament in 1972. The act provides for the department to put in place and operate a centralized, publicly supported training system. Its goal is to produce specialists at the crafts, technician, and technologist level for employment in the formal sector of the economy. In addition, the act makes DTEVT responsible for registering and monitoring private training providers and for training standards and certification throughout the country. A 1996 national audit of training providers found 231 functioning institutions with 19,181 students, 48 percent of them women; 39 percent of the institutions were run under the auspices of different government ministries, 21 percent by private-for-profit providers, 32 percent by church groups, nongovernmental organizations, donor agencies, trusts or cooperatives, and 8 percent by industry.

The Department of Technical Education and Vocational Training, an autonomous body under the Ministry of Science, Technology and Vocational Training, is directly responsible for managing 17 public training institutions—namely, the country's trades training institutes, the Evelyn Hone College of Applied Arts and Commerce, the Northern Technical College, the Luanshya Technical and Vocational Teachers College, the Zambia Air Services Training Institute, and the Zambia Institute of Business Studies and Industrial Practice, opened in 1993. Primarily to meet their own manpower requirements, other government ministries operate colleges offering formal, pre-employment training, notably for teachers, health workers, and agricultural specialists. For example, the Natural Resources Development College near Lusaka and the Zambia College of Agriculture in Monze, with 430 and 240 students respectively, fall under the Ministry of Agriculture.

The institutions under DTEVT management offer two-to-three-year, full-time programs, resulting in diplomas or certificates. These programs cover a broad spectrum of subjects, including applied arts, teacher training, engineering, automotive repair, electrical training, construction, tailoring, paramedical studies, journalism, and clerical and business courses.

Each trades training institute typically offers a limited choice of subjects. Therefore, students may come from far away places, and most of them are boarders. Crafts-level students are expected, after two years in their respective institutions, to spend a year in an industry job. It appears, however, that a majority do not succeed in finding employers prepared to take them on, thus greatly reducing the practical element in their program. In an effort to diversify its programs and make them more responsive to the labor market, DTEVT introduced on a limited basis skill training programs for those who do not qualify for regular pre-employment programs. In addition, it offered a few competency-based modular training courses and entrepreneurial training modules in all its programs. The department did this "so that graduates of these programs do not necessarily have to look for paid employment because nowadays formal employment is difficult to find" (DTEVT 1995, pp. 10–11).

Total enrollments in DTEVT institutions varied between more than 3,000 in 1971 and nearly 5,000 in 1994 (table 14-3), and annual outputs usually did not exceed 1,600 graduates. In 1991, 3,619 students were enrolled, 54 percent of them at the crafts level. Twenty-eight percent of enrollees and 25 percent of graduates were women. Just over 30 percent of graduates obtained a crafts certificate, 24 percent graduated in secretarial and business studies, and another 14 percent as vocational teachers.

Training institutions under the DTEVT, some of them far away from Lusaka, have very limited autonomy and depend on headquarters for decisions on course offerings, curriculum and training modes, and staffing and student places. Moreover, they depend for almost all of their income on government subsidies, which the department administers. Frequently, money allocated (for example, for salaries) arrives late, and when it arrives it may have lost much of its value because of high levels of inflation. Threatened with court action or food supply boycotts by creditors, several training institutions have reportedly been unable to settle their bills. Funds for necessary repairs and maintenance ran out a long time ago in most institutions.

In 1996 the Zambian government allocated 3.4 billion kwacha (US$2.7 million) to the department, or approximately 3.5 percent of total govern-

TABLE 14-3

Full-Time Enrollments in Pre-Employment Programs Offered
by the DTEVT, Selected Years, 1971–94

| Institution | 1971 | 1981 | 1991 | 1994 |
|---|---|---|---|---|
| Trades training institutes | 1,226 | 2,182 | 1,714 | 2,456 |
| Evelyn Hone College of Applied | | | | |
| Arts and Commerce | 812 | 1,160 | 1,068 | 1,395 |
| Northern Technical College | 795 | 559 | 559 | 596 |
| Technical and Vocational | | | | |
| Teachers College | 88 | 390 | 278 | 264 |
| Zambia Air Services Training | | | | |
| Institute | 375 | 238 | — | 87 |
| Zambia Institute of Business | | | | |
| Studies and Industrial Practice | — | — | — | 90 |
| Total | 3,296 | 4,529 | 3,619 | 4,888 |

— Not available.
*Source:* DTEVT (1995).

ment expenditure on education and training.[3] In real terms the 1996 budget was 27 percent lower than in 1990. In 1995 the DTEVT estimated the actual cost of training a student at the crafts level at US$1,593 per year and at US$2,007 per year at the technician level. In the same year crafts-level students were expected to pay an annual fee of US$115 (US$83 for boarding and US$32 for tuition); students assigned to an industry had to pay an additional US$85 per year. The basic fee for crafts students therefore covers approximately 7 percent of actual cost. During the 1990s, the public training system also received significant support from donors. In 1994, 40 percent of all donor assistance for human resource development in Zambia was channeled to VET. The value of this assistance rose from US$9 million in 1990 to US$19 million in 1994. Donor funding is largely channeled to capital investment and technical assistance.

There exists a variety of private-for-profit colleges, as well as training institutions run by public or private enterprises. Little information, however, is available on these institutions. Private-for-profit colleges, registered and, at least on paper, monitored by the DTEVT, concentrate on pre-employment, secretarial and business, and computer courses; their fees vary considerably, but in 1995 some were said to be charging up to K 300,000

(US$240) per term. Training organized by enterprises is mostly technical training for their own employees; firms such as the copper mines, the railways, or the national electricity company have developed well-functioning, in-house training centers. The National Institute for Public Administration, which provides in-service training for civil servants, can also be mentioned in this context. The majority of private training institutions adhere to the DTEVT curricula in order for graduates to be certified by the Examination Council of Zambia. The council also oversees a trade testing scheme, administered by the DTEVT, to recognize competence acquired outside the formal training system—that is, in nonformal training centers or on the job (for example, as an apprentice).

## Major Issues in Vocational Education and Training

Zambia's VET system is set in an exceedingly harsh socioeconomic environment. It faces multiple constraints that may be categorized in terms of purpose, clientele, management, and product quality.

The first issue deals with the relevance of training. Training efforts reach less than 3 percent of the population entering the labor market. However modest in size, the system has been targeting the wrong clientele for years. Programs are essentially focused on providing a limited number of youth with skills for wage-jobs in the formal sector, jobs that have all but vanished. Individuals entering the Zambian labor market have little choice but to make a living as self-employed microentrepreneurs or as family helpers in the informal sector or in subsistence farming, a situation for which they are usually ill prepared. Part of the problem is the lack of a comprehensive national training policy. Current training efforts are dispersed and mostly uncoordinated. The capacity of government officials to collect and analyze information necessary either for policy development or for administrative purposes remains weak. The involvement of nongovernmental stakeholders, such as private training providers and those who represent the world of work, in directing the system is strictly limited, and the precise management role of external donors is not always clear.

Not surprisingly, the quality of training is quite poor. Staff are untrained, and there are plenty of vacancies. Funds earmarked for training are not released or released only after long delays and with financial regulations requiring numerous signatures to get a check ready. Curricula are outdated. Equipment is broken down for lack of maintenance, buildings are dilapidated, the library facilities are inadequate, and such essentials as writing paper, chairs, or light bulbs are often missing. Staff utilization is poor, with an apparent student-staff ratio of about 6 to 1. Moreover, the ratio of non-teaching staff to teaching staff is inordinately high (2 to 1 in 1997).

## Reform Proposals

Following the election of a new government in 1991, concern about the deplorable state of skills development in the country led to many policy reviews and reform initiatives. Of these, VET reforms have perhaps been the most innovative in terms of both procedure and proposals.

### A New Policy Framework

The government's plans for the training sector are radical: a new training authority has been established, the government has begun privatizing its own training institutions under the supervision of autonomous management boards, and there is a commitment to establishing a level playing field for private providers. The reform process began in 1996 when the government issued a policy document entitled "Technical Education, Vocational and Entrepreneurship Training (TEVET) Policy." This document identified the problems facing the economy and the training institutions and formulated a broad national policy on technical education and vocational training. In 1997 the government produced a strategy paper—"Strategy Paper for Technical Education and Entrepreneurship Training (TEVET) in Zambia"—that spelled out strategies for implementing the new policy and an action plan.

The government in 1998 signaled its commitment to a thorough reform of the sector by passing the Technical Education, Vocational and Entrepreneurship Training Bill. A statutory instrument in late 1998 implemented the legislation. The Board of the Technical Education, Vocational and Entrepreneurship Training Authority (TEVETA) has now been constituted, and terms of reference for the director general and senior management of the authority have been developed. Individual public training institutions are in the process of constituting their management boards.

### The National Training Board

The main feature of the new structure of technical education and vocational and entrepreneurship training in Zambia is the National Training

Board, which endeavors to coordinate an efficient response to training demands and provides technical assistance to public and private training providers. The DTEVT was transformed into a support structure and integral part of the National Training Board, with three directorates to deal with training standards, training support services, and finance. A large measure of autonomy was granted to colleges and trades training institutions hitherto under the DTEVT. This enables them to tailor skill requirements more closely to demand and to increase opportunities for entrepreneurship in the informal sector.

## Cost Sharing with Students and Employers

A greater portion of the cost burden of training will be shifted to beneficiaries, including those in the informal sector. More realistic fees will be charged, and a loans and grants facility will assist disadvantaged groups. A payroll levy scheme involving industry will be established to increase and diversify sources of funding for public and private providers alike. Public training institutions will be encouraged to augment their income by engaging in commercial activities.

## New Pathways for Formal Sector Training

Because there have been no opportunities for people to move from one level of training to the next and programs have been highly biased in favor of Grade 12 certificate holders, the new system allows for progression on the basis of credits obtained from completed, lower training levels and relevant experience. Based on competence acquired in institutions, on the job, or as a result of distance learning, persons now can move from the trades test level, via the crafts level and technician level, to the technologist level. A reform of trades testing and of the examination system was proposed to achieve this aim.

## Training for Entrepreneurship and Work in the Informal Sector

The capacity of the country's education and training system to enhance skills needed to succeed in self-employment will be strengthened. A series of measures will be taken to introduce entrepreneurship development in the formal curricula. Immediate attention will be given to the establishment of community-based, multipurpose resource centers by reconverting existing facilities and providing them with trained staff and relevant train-ing materials. Nonformal training will be strengthened by making it easier and financially attractive for private training providers and microentre-preneurs to train informal sector workers, by enhancing the quality of their training by upgrading trainers, by assisting in training needs assessment, and by promoting informal sector apprenticeship.

## Notes

1. The data on the labor market are derived from a 1986 labor force survey; Central Statistics Office (1991 1993); and World Bank (1995).

2. Gross enrollment rates (the total school population as a percentage of the 7-to-13 age cohort) were 103 percent for boys and 93 percent for girls at the primary level; at the secondary level they were 25 percent for boys and 16 percent for girls.

3. Reconversions from kwacha to dollars indicate mere orders of magnitude. High levels of inflation gave rise to considerable exchange rate variations within short periods. Different sources may yield widely different dollar figures.

## References

Central Statistics Office. 1991. *Priority Survey.* Lusaka.
———.1993. *Priority Survey.* Lusaka.
DTEVT (Department of Technical Education and Vocational Training). 1995. *Technical Education and Vocational Training in the Republic of Zambia—Current Status.* Lusaka.
World Bank. 1994. "Zambia Poverty Assessment." Washington, D.C.
———. 1995. *Review of the Literature on Labor Markets in Zambia.* Washington, D.C.
———. 1996a. *Trends in Developing Economies.* Washington, D.C.
———. 1996b. *World Development Report 1996.* New York: Oxford University Press.
———. 1996c. "Zambia Second Economic and Social Adjustment Credit." Washington, D.C.

# 15 Arab Republic of Egypt

INDERMIT S. GILL AND STEPHEN P. HEYNEMAN

STATE-LED ECONOMIC growth in the Arab Republic of Egypt, averaging 4.5 percent per year in the 1960s and 1970s, had slowed to 0.5 percent per year by the mid-1980s. Regional conflict and declining remittances because of the return of migrants provide some explanation, but structural problems and other more problematic issues were also involved. High growth had occurred during an era of high petroleum prices and protection for agricultural and manufactured products and services. After 1985, however, public debt became burdensome, oil prices fell, and workers' remittances declined as labor in the Gulf was replaced. Egypt needed to adjust to these problems, but unlike during earlier eras, a return to previous policies was infeasible. The Mediterranean world changed in the 1990s, and the circumstances that predated the change were unlikely to return.

Part of the change was exogenous. Economies in Eastern and Central Europe and the former Soviet Union were suddenly open to new trading relationships with Western Europe. Western Europe was beginning to position itself for a more coordinated trading relationship both internally and outside the region. No longer would bilateral tradition determine trading relationships. Agricultural products could be found offshore with outsourcing located in such places as Budapest or Alexandria. Choice would be determined by a set of well-understood characteristics, including efficient labor markets, low barriers to trade, and repatriation of profits.

Part of the change was internal. In reaction to exogenous pressures, internal policies in Egypt had to shift. Private enterprise was increasingly accepted as a requirement for growth, along with an economy open to free trade. It was also accepted that a healthy economy would require a significant increase in productivity, the attraction of private capital, and the ability to compete successfully with alternative trading partners in the European Union.

What is the role of vocational and technical education in this overall shift? Does competitiveness in Egypt require an increase in the current form of vocational and technical education, or does it require something new? If the latter, in what way should the education be different? Should vocational and technical education employ the same structures as found in Egypt today, or should different structures be used? If the structures need to change, how would this affect the rest of the education system, including general secondary education and criteria and mechanisms for entry into higher education? How would labor markets, employment guarantees, and restrictions on mobility and flexibility be affected?

This chapter suggests that the health of the Egyptian economy depends on the extent to which it can continue to shift away from the past assumptions of central planning. This will require making changes in vocational and technical education. However difficult institutionally and however problematic in terms of recent tradition, these changes may not be any harder for Egypt than for other countries whose economies are shifting away from central planning.

We conclude with recommendations concerning compulsory education; the definition of vocational and technical education; the audience for such education; and mechanisms for financing, managing, and delivering it. While these suggestions are not simple or risk free, we believe they are necessary. Moreover, we believe that the Egyptian educational authorities could benefit from the general discussion of the economic background that makes these changes in vocational and technical education so necessary.

## The Supply of Skilled Workers

The formal education system is an important supplier of skilled workers in Egypt as in most other countries. In the late 1980s more than two-thirds of unemployed males and almost all unemployed females were first-time job seekers, so the only skills they possessed were those they acquired in school. The education system is four-tiered: elementary school (five years), preparatory school (three years), secondary school (three years), and tertiary education (two, four, or more years).

## The Formal Education System

Table 15-1 shows the growth in enrollments from 1990 to 1995. With an enrollment of more than 12.4 million in primary and secondary schools and roughly 750,000 in postsecondary institutes and universities, the formal education system is the largest supplier of workers with pre-employment skills.

The enrollments in secondary and higher education are of special interest, because a large share of these graduates is expected to look for work in the private sector. Table 15-1 shows that about 500,000 graduates of universities, technical institutes, and secondary schools enter the labor force each year. About 90 percent of general (nontechnical) secondary enrollment is in government schools, although there are almost 300 private general secondary schools. The Ministry of Education administers or regulates both three- and five-year technical and vocational education programs and two-year technical institutes. In 1994–95 enrollments in these programs totaled about 1.75 million (table 15-2), more than twice the enrollment in general secondary education. Seven hundred thousand of these students are enrolled in 385 industrial schools, 754,000 in 524 commercial schools, and 187,000 in 90 agricultural schools. In 1994 there were more than 250 private commercial schools, but only 4 industrial secondary schools and no private agricultural schools. The Ministry of Education aims to have 70 percent of secondary school students enrolled in industrial, agricultural, and commercial schools; however, the rationale is not to meet the economy's

### TABLE 15-1
Enrollment, by Level and Type of Education, 1990–91 to 1994–95
(thousands of students)

| Type of education | 1990–91 | 1994–95 | Change (percent) |
|---|---|---|---|
| Primary | 6,402.5 | 7,313.0 | 142 |
| Secondary | 1,648.9 | 2,788.2 | 66 |
| General | 576.4 | 894.4 | 47 |
| Technical-vocational | 1,026.2 | 1,893.8 | 85 |
| Higher | 215.8 | 224.5 | 5 |
| Universities | 74.3 | 148.4 | 200 |

Source: Ministry of Education (1995).

TABLE 15-2

Enrollments in and Graduates of Vocational-Technical Schools, 1993–95

(thousands of students)

| Type of school | 1993–94 students | 1994–95 students | 1993–94 graduates |
|---|---|---|---|
| *Industrial* | | | |
| 3-year schools | 710.0 | 776.0 | 167.5 |
| 5-year schools | 33.6 | 35.4 | 15.3 |
| Vocational | 14.0 | 27.9 | 3.6 |
| *Agricultural* | | | |
| 3-year schools | 183.2 | 197.2 | 40.1 |
| 5-year schools | 1.4 | 1.3 | 3.2 |
| Vocational | 3.1 | 6.7 | 0.8 |
| *Commercial* | | | |
| 3-year schools | 734.0 | 674.6 | 153.0 |
| 5-year schools | 20.3 | 22.7 | 1.4 |
| Total | 1,699.7 | 1,741.8 | 384.8 |

*Source:* Ministry of Education (1995).

demand for technical and vocational skills, but to ease the burden on higher education.

Higher-level technical and managerial skills are taught in universities and technical and commercial postsecondary institutes. Enrollment in higher education is increasing rapidly: in 1990–91 the total enrollment in higher education was 0.7 million students, up from about 0.5 million in 1988. Egypt has 13 universities, and 12 of them have faculties of engineering. About 10 percent of enrollment in higher education is in faculties of engineering and about 20 percent in technical institutes. Technical institutes offer two-year programs after general secondary schooling; universities offer five-year engineering programs after general secondary education and management and accounting courses (postsecondary, degree, and diploma programs). Enrollment in technical institutes has risen by more than 10 percent per year in some years, but this is attributable to government attempts to ease the pressure on universities rather than to meet private sector skill needs. Overexpansion has led to widespread deterioration in quality: teachers are underpaid, and equipment is outdated or lacking entirely. Most faculty members teach in more than one institution and give private lessons that are estimated to provide up to 10 times their salaries. Thus while private higher education is limited to the American University and institutes that provide short courses, cost sharing by students is considerable. The irony is that this parallel system of higher education is neither free nor adequately funded (World Bank 1989).

## Training in Ministries and Enterprises

Training activities in ministries other than the Ministry of Education and in enterprises proliferate. Vocational training in some ministries, such as Industry and Housing, compete with the vocational education provided by the Ministry of Education. The Ministry of Industry's Productivity and Vocational Training Department (PVTD) administers programs for vocational training, productivity improvement, and management development in its 40 centers. In 1994 these centers had an annual enrollment of roughly 40,000 students in three-year programs and shorter "made-to-order" programs. The three-year programs use a dual system: all instruction, which is 80 percent practical and 20 percent theoretical, is in the centers during the first two years, but in the third year more than 80 percent of training is on-the-job instruction in participating enterprises. Roughly 25 to 30 percent of participating employers are private firms. By all accounts, employers prefer PVTD graduates to graduates from the Ministry of Education's industrial schools. In 1994, of the roughly 50 percent of PVTD graduates who were not drafted into the military, more than half (or about 25 percent of all graduates) found private sector jobs for which they were trained. The traditional clientele of these schools has been public enterprises, but PVTDs now face the challenge of reorienting their training to meet private sector needs.

Other training centers managed by ministries include the Training Organization of the Ministry of Housing and Reconstruction (TOMOHAR). More than 50 centers enroll about 70,000 students. These centers, which cater to the demand of the public construction and housing sector, are largely ineffective in supplying skills to an overwhelmingly informal private sector (Assaad 1993).

The Ministry of Employment and Training (formerly the Ministry of Manpower) provides short courses for the unemployed. These courses target the unemployed—largely the graduates of industrial, commercial, and agricultural secondary schools according to preliminary statistics—but few studies exist to determine the courses' effectiveness. The ministry does estimate, however, that less than 5 percent of the unemployed apply for these programs. Another supplier of semiformal training intended to facilitate employment is the Ministry of Social Affairs. It has 56 major training centers and more than 1,000 small units in its Productive Family Program. Other ministries and parastatals also have their own training units.

Large and medium enterprises provide training (in-house or purchased from outside providers) for their employees. For example, Xerox offers courses on such subjects as "leadership through quality" for new and middle managers. Like most other countries, Egypt has no systematic information available on training in the private sector. Small firms dominate in some private sector industries, such as construction. Training in these firms is mainly through traditional apprenticeships rather than a formal program.

## The Demand for Skilled Labor

Table 15-3 shows the number of labor force entrants. More than 400,000 individuals who have attended training institutes or a university entered the labor force in 1989–90. Table 15-4 shows the sectoral distribution of workers by education level. The government sector and public enterprises,

TABLE 15-3
Labor Force Entrants, by Sex and Level of Education, 1989–90
(number of graduates adjusted by labor force participation rates)

| Level | Males | Females | Total |
|---|---|---|---|
| University | 67,000 | 36,000 | 103,000 |
| Technical institutes | 23,000 | 13,000 | 46,000 |
| Commercial secondary | 42,000 | 70,000 | 112,000 |
| Industrial secondary | 94,000 | 14,000 | 108,000 |
| Agricultural secondary | 24,000 | 5,000 | 29,000 |
| Training colleges | 8,000 | 12,000 | 20,000 |
| Total, excluding general secondary graduates | 258,000 | 150,000 | 408,000 |
| Dropouts reaching labor force age | — | — | 162,000 |

— Not available.
Source: Zytoun (1991).

TABLE 15-4
Distribution of Workers, by Sector and Education

| Sector | Below inter- mediate (percent) | Inter- mediate and above (percent) | University and above (percent) | Total employ- ment (millions) | Annual growth 1976– 86 |
|---|---|---|---|---|---|
| Government | 31.6 | 40.7 | 27.7 | 2.943 | 3.7 |
| Public enterprises | 53.3 | 30.4 | 16.3 | 1.322 | 2.2 |
| Private agriculture | 96.5 | 3.0 | 0.4 | 7.973 | −0.7 |
| Private nonagriculture | 80.5 | 12.6 | 6.9 | 4.925 | 3.3 |
| Urban | 73.3 | 16.5 | 10.2 | 2.957 | — |
| Rural | 91.3 | 6.9 | 1.8 | 1.968 | — |
| Other (e.g., joint ventures) | — | — | — | 0.145 | — |
| All sectors | 76.9 | 14.6 | 8.5 | 17.367 | 1.5 |

— Not available.
*Note:* Percentages are for 1990, employment figures are for 1988.
*Source:* World Bank (1994).

with total employment of about 4.5 million workers, have the greatest demand for educated workers. In the government sector the employment of
about 1.25 million workers with some secondary education and about 1.0
million workers with higher education is largely because of hiring policies,
which reflect social safety net functions rather than skill needs. In the public enterprise sector the actual demand for skilled workers is also probably
less than the 0.6 million workers employed who have at least some secondary education. For the purpose at hand, the relevant figures are those for
the private nonagricultural sector. Less than 20 percent of the 5 million
workers in this sector have secondary or higher education.

*Large Enterprises and Multinationals*

Large enterprises have begun demanding managers with a mix of management and technical skills ("technocrats"), supervisors, and maintenance
workers in greater numbers. Executives in large enterprises have expressed
concerns that the demand for maintenance workers has increased rapidly,
but they blame either training or "cultural norms" for the lack of an adequate supply. The demand for accountants, technicians, and office work-

ers appears to be largely met, although some employers have indicated the existence of unsatisfied demand for financial or corporate accountants.

The demand for skilled workers varies by sector. In manufacturing the demand for managers, administrators, and professionals is largely fulfilled, and marketing managers are the only specialty for which demand has been rising rapidly. Private entrepreneurs in manufacturing complain that as the demand for both foremen and engineers has begun to rise, the "high industrial" institutes have begun producing workers with neither engineering nor supervisory skills. In trade and finance, which entail more frequent contact with clients, specialists with good language skills are in great demand according to private entrepreneurs. In services, especially in tourism, demand for middle managers and workers with requisite language skills rose sharply. Demand for workers in services has eased since 1992.

## Small Enterprises and Microenterprises

Small firms and microenterprises (sometimes collectively referred to as the informal sector) dominate the economy. In 1986 the share of the informal sector in total employment was about 40 percent, but its share in private sector employment was more than 80 percent. In sectors such as construction, virtually all private sector employment is informal (tables 15-5, 15-6). Rizk (1991) cautions against assuming that the skill demands of small firms are negligible, but skills are probably developed primarily through informal mechanisms, such as traditional apprenticeships and learning by do-

TABLE 15-5
Informal Sector Employment, by Nonfarm Activity, 1986
(percent)

| | Informal sector employment | | |
|---|---|---|---|
| Activity | As a share of total employment | As a share of private employment | As a share of total informal |
| Industry | 38.8 | 73.3 | 22.6 |
| Construction | 81.0 | 97.2 | 24.6 |
| Services | 30.0 | 79.7 | 46.4 |
| All (nonfarm) | 39.7 | 82.7 | 100 |

Source: Shaban, Assaad, and Al-Qudsi (1993).

TABLE 15-6
Informal Sector Employment as a Percentage of Total Employment
and Private Sector Employment, 1974–88

| Year | Total | Private |
|------|-------|---------|
| 1974 | 44.9 | 91.9 |
| 1976 | 45.4 | 93.2 |
| 1978 | 42.8 | 91.0 |
| 1980 | 44.1 | 91.3 |
| 1982 | 46.3 | 92.1 |
| 1984 | 46.8 | 91.6 |
| 1986 | 42.9 | 90.8 |
| 1988 | 51.1 | 92.7 |

*Source:* Shaban, Assaad, and Al-Qudsi (1993).

ing. Employer federations representing small enterprises believe that the demand for semiskilled workers and technicians is increasing rapidly, but that trained technicians and otherwise competent workers are in short supply. In microenterprises the main constraints are credit availability and regulation. In the mid-1990s skill demands were small and relatively easily met (World Bank 1994b).

## Demand-Supply Imbalances

Some skill shortages are inevitable in an economy where formal sector wages are influenced through legislation and through public enterprise and civil service wage structures, and restrictions on importing skilled labor are in place. A World Bank (1994) survey of more than 200 enterprises highlights the importance of firm size as a correlate of skill shortages. Based on these results, occupational wage data, and other findings, table 15-7 summarizes the market for skills in the private sector.

Although there are exceptions to this simplified picture, the salient features are as follows:

• Microenterprises do not face a shortage of skills. The demand is mainly for semiskilled workers, and the Egyptian education and apprenticeship systems provide an adequate supply.

TABLE 15-7
Salient Features of the Market for Skills in the Private Sector

| Skill level | Firm size | | | |
| --- | --- | --- | --- | --- |
| | Micro | Small | Medium | Large |
| Administrative & managerial | Unimportant; owner does almost everything | Unimportant; owner/relatives/friends do almost everything | Unimportant; owner/relatives/friends do almost everything | Mismatch of demand and supply of skills |
| Technical | Unimportant; little or no demand | Acute scarcity of trained technicians | Entrants to work force hard to train | Entrants to work force hard to train |
| Vocational | Unimportant; little or no demand | Scarcity of trained workers | Adequate supply | Adequate supply |
| Semiskilled | Adequate supply | Adequate supply | Adequate supply | Adequate supply |

*Note:* Microenterprises, 1 to 4 employees; small firms, 5 to 9 employees (as many as 50 employees in some sectors, such as construction); medium-size firms, 10 to 100 employees; and large firms, more than 100 employees.

*Source:* Miller (1994); USAID (1994); World Bank (1994b).

• Small firms face shortages of technical workers and of workers with some vocational skills. Many of these firms rely on informal apprenticeship schemes and institution-based training to meet skill demands. Where the demand for skills is high, firms may face acute constraints.

• Medium-size enterprises do not seem to face shortages of skills, but because there are relatively few of these enterprises in Egypt, generalizations are difficult to make.

• Large enterprises can hire workers that are seemingly overqualified for the posts they fill, because they can usually pay higher wages and benefits than smaller firms. They encounter supply shortages for specialized managerial positions.

We describe next the main factors underlying these imbalances.

## Problems in Vocational and Technical Education

About 0.5 million students leave the Ministry of Education's commercial, industrial, and agricultural schools every year, either as graduates (0.4 million) or dropouts. From all accounts, the quality of education in government schools is poor. Some of the problems are the lack of teachers, inadequate or outdated equipment, and poorly motivated students. According to one estimate, only about 10 percent of these schools are well equipped and managed (World Bank 1989). Teacher shortages are particularly acute in theoretical subjects.

Although few studies evaluating the effectiveness of the Ministry of Education's vocational and technical schools are available, graduates—especially those from three-year programs—are believed to be ill suited for employment in the informal economy. Employers prefer the graduates of five-year programs and PVTD schools, believing that three-year-program graduates get neither a sound theoretical education nor a good practical education. Ministry of Education estimates of the theoretical content of curricula in three-year programs range from about 60 to 67 percent in the first and second years and 56 to 69 percent in the third year (World Bank 1989). The humanistic-scientific (as opposed to technical-vocational) content of education ranges from about 37 percent for three-year programs to about 52 percent for five-year programs. Because they demand workers with relatively general skills, employers may prefer graduates of five-year programs, but good three-year programs would be a far less expensive way of meeting this demand.

Reported unemployment rates are highest for those with an intermediate certificate (Fergany 1994a). This suggests either that the quality of secondary education is a problem or that the supply of vocational and technical skills is excessive relative to the demands of the economy. Assuming that the demand for workers with secondary education in the private nonagricultural sector doubles over the next 10 years because of growth and structural changes, fewer than 1 million additional workers would be in demand; however, the education sector would supply this in about two years. Even with no additional supply by the education sector, this demand could theoretically be met by drawing from the pool of unemployed workers with secondary degrees (25 percent of total unemployment in 1993).

### Imbalances in the Market for Engineers and First Technicians

The graduates of three-year industrial programs are called "technicians," and those of five-year programs are called "first technicians." The widespread employment of engineers as technicians and first technicians indicates an excess supply of engineers. In the past decade the educational quality of five-year industrial and commercial schools and two-year technical institutes has declined. Their graduates may in fact be regarded as technicians. Given the demand from a sluggish and largely informal economy, the absolute number of engineers supplied is excessive. Employers complain that while technical graduates usually have a reasonable theoretical base, they lack experimental and problem-solving skills. Zaytoun (1991) reports weekly private and public wages in skilled occupations; private sector salaries for mechanical engineers are about double those for engineers in government employment, but the private-public wage ratio is close to one for engineering technicians. Although there may be scattered shortages of well-qualified engineers, the supply of first technicians appears to be sufficient.

In the case of technicians and first technicians, the problem seems to stem more from poor quality of technical practice than from a shortage of instructors. Shortages of theoretical teachers were significantly greater than shortages of practical teachers at many levels of technical education. During the early 1990s about 70 percent of the required number of practical teachers were available; Ministry of Education schools and institutes operated with only 30 percent of required theory teachers (positions normally filled by engineers). This suggests that teachers' salaries are not high enough to attract unemployed engineers. In their review of vocational education and training projects, Middleton, Ziderman, and Adams (1993) found that the inability to pay competitive salaries adversely affected training quality in two-thirds of the countries studied.

## Mismatch of Managerial Skills

Egypt's transition from a public-sector-led closed economy to an open economy where the private sector is expected to take the lead has exposed the weaknesses of nontechnical higher education. To determine if unmet demand for management training existed, USAID (1994) sampled 60 private sector and 16 public sector enterprises in Alexandria and 12 suppliers of training nationwide. Its main findings were as follows:

• Private sector owners and top managers had little interest or financial resources for management training: only 27 of the 60 firms provided management training during the previous financial year. These firms spent less than LE 0.82 million—about LE 30,000 per firm or LE 8,300 per trainee. (One firm accounted for more than a third of all spending.)
• In contrast, 14 of the 16 public sector firms spent money on management training. It totaled about LE 4.09 million—that is, about LE 292,000 per company or LE 37,500 per trainee.
• Executives in the private sector were willing to send only close relatives for long-term training (for instance, MBA programs). The general, though limited, demand was for evening courses in quick-paying management training.
• There was no correlation between the size of the firm and its propensity to plan strategically and train its managers. Less than one-third of the 23 firms that had managers in training positions had strategic planning processes.
• Marketing and sales, financial management and cost reduction, strategic planning, and production management were the four areas of managerial skills most demanded by executives who expressed an interest in management training.

No more than one-third of the providers surveyed concentrated on any of these four areas. Institutions tend to concentrate on courses for general management, management systems (computers), total quality management, human resources management, and time management. These are areas of relatively low demand: only 25 percent or less of the 60 firms surveyed expressed an interest in these courses. Private-public wage differentials support these findings. In 1993 private-public wage ratios for financial and enterprise managers were higher than 300 percent, the highest among all occupations. While these results indicate a demand-supply mismatch in the market for management skills, the mismatch is likely to be self-correcting in a situation where such training is both privately demanded and (largely) supplied.

## Structural Problems

Some of the structural characteristics of Egyptian vocational and technical education can be traced to the economic assumptions of the 1950s. During this era sectoral ministries were responsible for significant portions of the economy: agriculture, manufacturing, services, and transport. As the economy liberalized and the role of the state in determining employment diminished, however, the role of sectoral ministries in determining training lessened. To be efficient, institutions require the latitude to shift their focus across sectors and fields of training. Efficient curricula increasingly are determined by local conditions. Agricultural institutions that used to train only for production now may need to include courses on agricultural services, credit, extension, health and safety, and nutrition. Permission to introduce a new course of study or to cease providing an old one may not need to be sought from central authorities, but depends on a budget constraint decided autonomously by the management of each institution. Segmentation by sector and central control over content are two legacies from the era of central planning that may require review; other problems are also apparent.

One of the problems is the proportion of the student population assigned to vocational and technical education programs. This proportion is established by an examination in upper secondary school. Students who do well on the examination are allowed to compete for places in higher education; students who do not are assigned to places in vocational and technical institutions. Many Organization for Economic Cooperation and Development (OECD) countries once assigned students in this fashion, but this practice has changed in the past two decades. It would be useful for Egyptian authorities to review the rationale for and results of these changes.

Modern economies now demand a wide variety of highly adaptable workers whose occupations may change repeatedly during a typical career. Training needs to be of a high quality and in a broad range of topics. Keyboarding, once considered a vocational skill, now is a requirement for everyone who completes compulsory education. Vocational students require much higher levels of general preparation, and postcompulsory education now includes training in a wide variety of vocational and technical professional skills. Distinctions between postcompulsory education and vocational and technical education have become less sharp over time. The opportunity to shift across subdisciplines in and out of vocational education has become commonplace. However, if all postcompulsory education requires selection, how is that selection made? Selection systems in Canada, France, Germany, the United Kingdom, and the United States differ, but they include common elements. For example, they all give students in compulsory education the opportunity to study a similarly broad spectrum of subjects, and they no longer track students into different career paths prior to selection for higher education.

The current problems of vocational and technical education in Egypt may stem in part from the extremely high proportion of students assigned to it after failing their examinations. Improvements to curricula, equipment, teachers, and pedagogy may not prove effective if students, against their better judgment, continue to be assigned to vocational institutions. Because modern selection systems now allow for the efficient allocation of large numbers of students simultaneously, and because of the blurring distinctions in content, it might be timely for the Egyptian authorities to rethink their assumptions behind who should attend vocational and technical institutions.[1]

One influence on the quality of vocational education is the extent to which it is used to ration higher education. Like all countries, Egypt faces a difficult tradeoff. It can expand higher education opportunities and maintain the current assumptions of public financing and public delivery if it is willing to make further sacrifices in quality. It can have higher quality and maintain current assumptions of financing and delivery if it lowers access. Or it can have higher access and higher quality if it is willing to diversify the sources of higher education financing and delivery. A choice among the three appears inevitable.

## Changing the Demand-Supply Balance

Even during an era of import-substitution, with the formal sector dominated by government, unpredictable input substitution by enterprises made it difficult for planners to forecast manpower needs. The substantial outmigration of skilled Egyptians in the 1970s and 1980s is ample testimony to labor market imbalances. However, falling output and employment growth rates in the public sector and slow growth in the formal private sector ensured that the supply of skills far exceeded the demand.

## The 1970s and 1980s

During the 1970s and 1980s, the main sources of supply of skills for private sector enterprises were public enterprises, the apprenticeship system, the education system, and returning migrants.

PUBLIC ENTERPRISES. For large and medium-size firms, the public sector was a major source of supply. The ratio of public to private earnings in Egypt fell from 1.5 in 1976 to about 0.9 in 1985. Because of these falling wage differentials in the public and private sectors, technicians, supervisors, and professionals trained abroad and with considerable work experience could be hired away from public enterprises. Over time, however, this source dried up for two main reasons. First, the declining quality of the formal education system has meant that the average quality of workers recruited into public enterprises has fallen. Second, public employment guarantees, combined with long waiting periods and deteriorating employment conditions in the public sector, have created an adverse selection problem: only the least qualified job seekers have been choosing to work in the public sector.[2]

THE APPRENTICESHIP SYSTEM. In an economy dominated by small and microenterprises, traditional apprenticeships have been the main supplier of skills. In 1991 more than 80 percent of skilled workers in the construction sector, for example, had been trained as apprentices (box 15-1). No concerted effort has been made to encourage skill acquisition through apprenticeships. Although Egyptian president Hosni Mubarak and German chancellor Helmut Kohl took an initiative in 1994 to promote enterprise-based training, it did not increase skill acquisition through apprenticeships.

THE EDUCATION SYSTEM. Until the 1970s, Egypt's formal education system provided the private sector with workers of moderately high quality. Since then, the quality of education seems to have declined. International equivalency tests indicate that the typical high school graduate is less numerate and literate than fifth graders in some other countries (Fergany 1994b). This problem has considerably diminished the trainability of workers in both the formal and informal sectors.

BOX 15-1
Demand-Supply Imbalances in Egypt's Construction Sector:
Formal Supply for a Largely Informal Sector

About 83 percent of craftspeople acquire skills through the traditional apprentice-ship system in Egypt's construction sector. This informal system dates back to the guilds that existed until the late nineteenth century. In addition to being taught the necessary skills, apprentices learn its values and behavioral patterns. Social net-works are often important for entry into the system: in 1991 more than 37 percent of craftspeople had relatives in construction when they entered the trade, while only 19 percent of common laborers did. Age of entry is also important: most craftspeople believe that it is extremely difficult to train a person older than 18.

The formal system consists of vocational training programs for construction offered by the Ministry of Housing and Reconstruction; vocational secondary schools run by the Ministry of Education; and schemes organized by public sector firms, local governments, the armed forces, and private organizations. The most ambi-tious is the Training Organization of the Ministry of Housing and Reconstruction (TOMOHAR). Between 1975 and 1991 it established 53 training centers, which turn out about 18,000 graduates annually, or about 45 to 80 percent of the entrants into the manual construction labor force. However, 1991 survey data indicate that only 5 percent of workers in construction had formal training, implying a high rate of attrition for TOMOHAR graduates. More than 50 percent of workers with formal training work for the government, compared with only 16 percent of all work-ers. Formally trained workers are thus more likely to end up in formal sector jobs, and those who cannot find such jobs probably drop out of the sector altogether.

The demand-supply imbalance for construction-related skills has both quality and quantity dimensions. Since a large fraction of construction jobs is informal, there is a mismatch between formal training and actual skill demands. Even more disconcerting is the fact that the rate of training in TOMOHAR accelerated in the early 1990s despite the severe recession in the industry. This suggests acute demand insensitivity in the formal training system.

*Source:* Assaad (1993).

RETURNING MIGRANTS. Migration to the Gulf and other countries less-ened the supply of skilled workers to both public and private sector enter-prises in the 1970s and 1980s; most migrants were secondary school graduates and college educated. After the Gulf War ended in 1991, about 0.7 million migrants returned to Egypt. Employers viewed them as a major source of skills. However, a large share of these workers chose to be self-employed in the informal sector; at current wage levels their skills are largely unavailable to firms (Shaban, Assaad, and Al-Qudsi 1993).

## The 1990s and the Future

With structural adjustment, the market for skilled workers has begun to change. Greater export orientation has already led to clearly identified demand in some areas. For example, the growing demand for graduates from Western universities and expatriates and the rapid rise in wages for trained workers in tourism-related services reflect the relative scarcity of workers fluent in English and endowed with attitudes of professional responsibility. While pockets of excess demand exist, the problem is mainly one of isolated demand-supply imbalances rather than a skill shortages. The demand for skills has been considerably overestimated in some areas, especially in the small-scale industrial sector.

Despite all these changes, informal small enterprises and microenterprises will continue to dominate the private sector in the foreseeable future. The skill needs of informal enterprises are best met informally; the best formal way to equip workers for productive careers in microenterprises is to ensure that they get good academic schooling (Fluitman 1994). As these firms formalize their operations, some will require workers with pre-employment training. For small firms it is often difficult to formally train workers on the job. The challenge in Egypt is to put in place institutions that will supply technical and vocational skills cost effectively and on demand.

We now discuss several potential sources and likely obstacles to the provision of an adequate skill supply for the private sector.

LINE MINISTRIES AND PUBLIC ENTERPRISES. During the period of transition from a formal economy led by public enterprises to one where the private sector takes the lead, public enterprises could continue to supply fledgling private firms with skills. Training institutions run by line ministries should be helped to reorient their programs so that they view the private sector as the primary client. Where this is not possible, the solution may be to close the programs and use the money to fund enterprise-based training in the private sector.

ENTERPRISE-BASED TRAINING IN THE PRIVATE SECTOR. Today the most important barrier to enterprise-based training in Egypt is uncertainty about the government's attitude toward private sector investment. Training is a long-term investment for both employers and workers, and the market for long-term investments in either human or physical capital is thin. Large private sector firms—which are most likely to train workers—also cite labor legislation as a deterrent. Union behavior, minimum wage legislation, and hiring and firing laws are the main reasons for hesitancy in hiring and in investing in upgrading workers' skills. The removal of administrative impediments to increased firm size will be accompanied by increases in the amount of firm-based training. The predominance of microenterprises and small enterprises, however, will continue to limit the amount of formal enterprise-based training.

THE TRADITIONAL APPRENTICESHIP SYSTEM. In the short to medium term, informal mechanisms will be the mainstay of postschool investments in human capital, especially in sectors, such as construction and manufacturing, where apprenticeship traditions are well entrenched. Although direct incentives to the informal sector are difficult to administer, a stable macroeconomic environment and well-designed regulatory framework are likely to rejuvenate traditional systems.

THE FORMAL EDUCATION SYSTEM. In any modernizing economy a robust education system is the key to ensuring that the work force is literate and trainable. In an economy dominated by microenterprises and small firms, the most relevant vocational skills are those provided by a good general education—especially arithmetic, language, and scientific skills—at the basic and secondary levels. Training in job-specific skills is best left for enterprises to design and deliver.

INSTITUTION-BASED TRAINING. Because small firms tend not to invest in formal training, institution-based vocational education and improved labor mobility can help fill skill gaps. However, overestimating or underestimating the skill demands of small firms is easy. A successful strategy for providing small firms in the formal sector with skilled workers includes a formal education system that equips students with general skills, and technical-vocational centers (run by the private sector or with its active participation) that specialize in relatively short courses that provide occupation-specific skills.

## The Cause of Demand-Supply Mismatches

Changing labor market demands, a supply-driven education system, and institutional weaknesses (such as poor labor mobility) have exposed deficiencies in the market for skills. If left uncorrected, these deficiencies may impede private sector development. The following paragraphs address the most important problems.

## The Declining Quality of Primary and General Secondary Education

While few systematic studies of the quality of basic and secondary education in Egypt are available, all investigations point to a declining quality of education (Heyneman 1997). Fergany (1994b) concluded that "measures to raise the quality of output of primary education, in terms of acquisition of basic literacy skills, with a major emphasis on mathematics, should be given top priority." Well-designed legislation will result in increases in the share of formal private employment over the long term, as the public sector shrinks in importance. The share of informal sector employment may well increase in the short term. The share of skilled labor in informal sector employment is far from negligible (Rizk 1991), but the process by which these skills are accumulated is generally informal. Improving educational quality may be the best way to help these firms meet their skill needs. Although basic literacy and numeracy skills are usually stressed as part of a poverty reduction strategy, they are important labor market skills in an economy dominated by self-employment and microenterprises. In Egypt's push to become competitive in a world economy, a literate population could provide not only a more stable socioeconomic environment but also a more trainable work force, one that provides foreign capital with complementary inputs at relatively low wages.

## The Misdirection of Vocational and Technical Education

Every year about 0.5 million persons graduate from or drop out of vocational and technical schools in Egypt. They are often unemployable in the jobs they are conditioned to expect. The problems seem to be fourfold.

First, there is an oversupply of technical and vocational skills to a sluggish economy. Even in technically demanding industries, such as machine tools, technicians make up only 5 to 6 percent of the total production work force (World Bank 1994). If it operated efficiently, the current system in Egypt could supply five to seven times the required number of skilled workers, according to conservative estimates.

Second, a fundamental mismatch exists between the needs of a largely informal economy and an education system that is designed to meet rela-

tively formal needs. The share of vocational enrollments in senior secondary education in Egypt is significantly higher than in countries that have
more formal economies.

Third, the quality of education in Egypt has deteriorated. Although the
graduates of three-year industrial programs are called technicians and those
of five-year programs are called first technicians, they are at best semiskilled
workers. The system conditions them to expect jobs that require technical
and practical skills they do not possess.

Fourth, technical and vocational education is used as a social safety net.
When Egypt's economy was centrally planned, it was assumed that the
lower 50 percent of the student population should be educated in vocational and technical skills and the upper 50 percent should be eligible for
selection to higher education. When employment could be more easily
guaranteed, this assumption was unquestioned, but now that employment
cannot be guaranteed, the rationale for attending vocational and technical
training has shifted from educational reasons to social reasons—that is, to
lower the likelihood of criminal behavior and social hostility.[3]

Although forecasting the likely demand for vocational-technical graduates is difficult, a rough idea can be garnered by examining the skill distribution of the work force and imputing the likely demand at alternative
employment growth rates. If employment in the private nonagricultural
sector were to grow at 10 percent from the level in the mid-1990s of 5
million workers—an optimistic scenario that assumes annual output growth
of about 20 percent—the employment of vocational-technical graduates
would grow by 60,000. If 1 in 30 workers were to retire every year, this
would imply a demand for 80,000 secondary school graduates. Even if all
of these positions were filled only from industrial and commercial schools
and technical institutes, this would imply a supply-to-demand ratio of more
than 400 percent. This does not take into account the roughly 2 million
secondary school graduates who are currently unemployed. At an annual
employment growth rate of 10 percent, simply absorbing existing job seekers would take 15 to 20 years. These numbers indicate a serious demand-
supply imbalance in vocational and technical skills for the private sector.

## Other Public Training Programs

Training institutions managed by sectoral ministries other than the Ministry of Education face an uncertain future because of the privatization or
the slow growth of public enterprises and the increased importance of the

private sector as an employer. These training centers were often unconcerned with placement, because this was traditionally guaranteed by client enterprises and agencies.[4] Some performed relatively well in ensuring that training remained demand oriented: the Ministry of Industry's PVTD centers are a case in point. However, most public training programs became supply driven and expanded capacity beyond expected demand. All these programs require an increased emphasis on placement and greater cost sharing with employers. In sectors that are dominated by informal enterprises, formal training programs, such as TOMOHAR for construction (Assaad 1993), are often irrelevant, but these programs can be useful for large and medium-size private enterprises that require relatively formalized technical and learning skills. Smaller, more focused programs can be cost effective if employers' participation is institutionalized.

## The Imbalance in High-Level Skills

This chapter has noted that management and professional skills may be in short supply. At least in management, there is little evidence of the need to create institutional capacity: existing institutions are capable of meeting the needs of small, medium, and large firms. In engineering, again there is little evidence that more institutional capacity is needed. At the high levels of specialization in professional skills, some mismatch between demand and supply is inevitable during transition. The challenge is to ensure that these gaps are closed quickly and cost effectively. While no additional institutional capacity to provide management training and engineering skills is required, efforts to encourage industry-academic links may be worthwhile. As the private sector replaces the public sector as the main employer, the role of administration and financing could shift from government agencies to business associations such as the Chamber of Commerce, the Alexandria Businessmen's Association, and the Federation of Egyptian Industries. In the meantime, public sector firms, which are likely to be overstaffed and on soft budgets, could continue training managers. In this way trained managers could be provided at relatively low (private) costs to small and medium-size private sector enterprises.

## Vocational Education and Training Reform

In this section we describe three aspects of the reform of Egypt's vocational education and training system: providing a suitable environment for private training, reorienting education enrollments and expenditures, and reforming initiatives in enterprise-based training.

## Providing a Suitable Environment for Private Training

Guaranteed public employment and narrow skill differentials in publicly administered wage systems distort the incentives to invest in skills development. For example, unskilled workers are paid higher than market wages in public enterprises, leading to general disincentives to acquire skills (Zaytoun 1991). Moving toward a market-driven system of wage determination would result in clearer signals of skill shortages. In the absence of broad regulatory reform, compensatory interventions, such as partial public subsidies or tax rebates for artificially high training costs, are sometimes advocated. However, such incentives need to be carefully monitored to prevent firms from repackaging already established training just to gain tax credits or subsidies: the current state of tax administration in Egypt may not be suitable for introducing such schemes. The government can encourage private provision of training by reducing barriers to entry, such as requiring the use of an official curriculum to obtain certification, and by allowing private and public institutions to set tuition levels freely. Private sector investments in skills can be encouraged by reducing distortions in incentives (for example, by ending the public employment guarantee and initiating public enterprise and civil service pay reform).

## Reorienting Education Enrollments and Expenditures

As noted earlier, accurately forecasting the demand for skills is impossible, but a rough idea can be obtained by examining the current skill distribution of the work force and estimating the likely demand for skills at alternative employment growth rates. Even under unrealistically optimistic scenarios, the numbers indicate a serious demand-supply imbalance in vocational and technical skills for the private sector.

This section provides some analysis using the Third Five-Year Plan expenditures on education (World Bank 1992) as the base. First, Egypt does not spend less on education as a share of its gross national product than do countries such as Chile and the Republic of Korea. However, the pattern of its spending differs dramatically. While Korea spends less than 10 percent of its education budget on higher education, Egypt spends about 45 percent on higher education. The inequity and costs of this policy are apparent when one considers that only 0.7 million students are enrolled in universities (compared with an enrollment of 12.5 million students in primary and secondary schools). Although 66 percent of nonuniversity spending goes to the more than 10 million students in basic education (primary and preparatory), 33 percent goes to the 2.5 million enrolled in secondary schools. Unit costs per student year are about LE 250 for general secondary schools and LE 500 for technical secondary schools. Estimates from Ministry of Education, PVTD, and private industrial schools in Cairo indicate that between LE 2,000 and LE 2,500 are needed to provide technical education of moderate quality, while the unit costs for general secondary education of reasonable quality are about LE 400 to LE 500. In other words, vocational-technical education is about five times costlier than humanistic-scientific education.

At the current spending levels for each subsector, the following strategies are feasible:

- Shift all secondary technical-vocational enrollment in schools run by the Ministry of Education into general education. This would not entail any additional expenses other than teacher training, but it would allow all students to obtain a secondary education of moderate quality.
- Shift one-third of technical-vocational enrollment into general secondary schools and give each student an employment voucher on successful completion of school that can be redeemed by employers on verification of employment. This scheme has economic benefits, such as providing direct incentives to private sector employment. It also has the obvious sociopolitical attractiveness of a highly visible attempt to address the problem of unemployment among young people. This option also does not add to costs.
- Combine the previous option with privatization of one-third of technical-vocational schools and use the freed-up resources to upgrade the quality of the remaining schools.

Combinations of these options can also yield beneficial results in terms of external and internal efficiency of secondary education. Ultimately, however, there are few ways to reform the education system without transferring resources from higher to primary education.

Introducing cost sharing in public higher education can significantly increase the ease with which the secondary education sector can respond to the demand for skills in the private sector. The potential for cost sharing in Egyptian higher education remains largely untapped. In 1994 the cost recovery rate in Egyptian higher education was just 4 percent of recurrent costs, compared with about 25 to 40 percent for Chile, Jordan, and Korea.

## Reform Initiatives in Enterprise-Based Training

In this section we discuss two initiatives that are particularly noteworthy: the high-profile Mubarak-Kohl training initiative and the Employment and Retraining Program of the Social Fund for Development.

THE MUBARAK-KOHL INITIATIVE. This initiative attempted to transform a traditional apprenticeship system to meet a modern economy's demands. Some policymakers believed that the German dual system could be adapted to revive a well-developed tradition of apprenticeships that was stifled in a command economy. However, the initiative encountered several obstacles.

The German dual system relies heavily on voluntary contributions from the private sector. In 1992 German industry spent about 87 billion deutschemarks on dual system trainees (Gill and Dar 1996). The Egyptian private sector seems less willing to make such investments, perhaps because of quality problems.

Locally, the initiative was viewed as part of the broader task of improving the quality of technical and vocational education in schools and institutes. This may contradict one of the lessons learned in other countries—namely, that a large share of instruction should be on the job.

Furthermore, on both the supply and the demand sides, expectations were unreasonable. Experts familiar with the effort believe that the government as well as the private sector grossly overestimated training needs, especially for technical workers. International experience suggests that technicians represent less than 10 percent of the work force in most manufacturing industries; the ratio is believed to be more than twice that among Egyptian government officials and businesspeople.

Vocational students are rigorously examined by employer associations in Germany, and successful completion of dual programs is no easy matter. In Egypt vocational education is reserved for those who cannot pass examinations that allow them to compete for university entry. Thus the pool of applicants has already been culled of the more gifted, and it is limited to those who may very well consider themselves as having failed. Creating a successful dual system in Egypt would be difficult unless the pool were expanded to include a far wider array of applicants.

The most important reason the private sector is hesitant to bear some of the financial burden may be that it does not expect immediate benefits. In Germany apprentices hired in the dual system can be paid wages lower than those mandated or collectively determined for entry-level workers, resulting in immediate benefits for employers as well as employees. In Egypt entry-level wages in the private sector are often close to subsistence, so apprenticeship schemes would result in no immediate benefit for employers in the form of lower wages.

THE SOCIAL FUND FOR DEVELOPMENT. The Employment and Retraining Program of the Social Fund for Development provides support for projects to help displaced public sector workers and unemployed workers who have more than a secondary education. The Employment and Retraining Program funded only 18 projects in 1993 (Government of Egypt 1994), and it has remained small. This may be because of the reluctance of public sector employees to enroll for training; they may fear that they will be marked for layoff if they are retrained. The training effort for unemployed graduates of universities and postsecondary institutes has also remained small. The Employment and Retraining Program compiles an inventory of institutions where training can be supplied. This is aimed at helping private contractors find suitable training facilities. The Enterprise Development Program also provides funds for training. Eight percent of the loan amount can be spent on training, and the funds do not have to be repaid.

The Employment and Retraining Program encourages training by the private sector. Its funds can be used to develop private sector initiatives in the provision of training and to help disadvantaged but educated job seekers. Those retrenched can be offered cash incentives rather than retraining. Funds for the training component of the Enterprise Development Program, where leakages are suspected, could be reduced.

## Conclusion

Reforms of the Egyptian economy should be accompanied by parallel reforms in vocational and technical education. The reforms that are needed, however, are not unique to Egypt. They are shared by the many countries shifting from a command to a market economy. Economic shifts require structural and organizational changes in training systems. Western European countries have had to review their assumptions about how training should be organized, and they all have had to confront similar facts: the rapid shift in career patterns, the blurring of distinctions between disciplines and professions, the open competition for comparative advantage, and the ineffectiveness of vocational education as a social safety net. These similarities have led many countries to institute similar reforms of training institutions and policies.

Egypt may need to change (a) the proportion of students assigned to vocational institutions; (b) the method by which it selects students for postcompulsory education; and (c) the tradition of delivering vocational and technical education through public institutions segmented by sectoral ministries, with central control over curricula. High-quality training and technical education can make an important contribution to growth. This chapter suggests, however, that the content and delivery of that education and the students who receive it will have to change for that contribution to be realized.

## Notes

1. The OECD countries use several types of selection mechanisms. Italy selects by attrition after entry to higher education, France has diversified the content of the baccalaureate and has assigned different weights to different subjects, and Japan and the United Kingdom have separated exit examinations from entry examinations.

2. Public sector pay fell by 30 percent in real terms between 1976 and 1985, and the waiting period was close to 10 years.

3. All OECD countries struggle with the same dilemma: what is to be done with young people who may not be qualified to enter university and who may pose a danger to the social order? And at one time or another all have attempted to use the vocational training system to delay labor market entry. Consensus now exists, however, that using the vocational system for this purpose is unwise. It lowers the value of vocational training, it exacerbates the disaffection of the young people for whom prospects of employment have not improved, and it wastes resources. Moreover, less expensive mechanisms are available to delay labor market entry that are socially more constructive (for instance, community service programs, work-study programs, and apprenticeships).

4. Vocational education institutions affiliated with state-owned enterprises pose a significant dilemma for all economies in transition (Heyneman 1994, 1996).

## References

Assaad, Ragui. 1993. "Structure of Egypt's Construction Labor Market and Its Development since the Mid-1970s." In Heba Handoussa and G. Potter, eds., *Employment and Structural Adjustment: Egypt in the 1990s*. Study prepared for the International Labour Office. Cairo: American University in Cairo Press.

Fergany, Nader. 1994a. "Labor Market Returns to Education and Poverty in Egypt: Rewards or Punishments?" Study prepared for United Nations Children's Fund, Cairo.

———. 1994b. "Survey of Access to Primary Education and Acquisition of Basic Literacy Skills in Three Governorates in Egypt." Study prepared for United Nations Children's Fund, Cairo.

Fluitman, Fred, ed. 1994. *Training for Work in the Informal Sector*. Geneva: International Labor Office, International Centre for Advanced Technical and Vocational Training.

Gill, Indermit S., and Amit Dar. 1996. "The German Dual System: Lessons for Low- and Middle-Income Countries." Working paper, Human Development Network. World Bank, Washington, D.C.

Government of Egypt. 1994. *Social Fund for Development*. Annual report for 1993. Cairo.

Heyneman, Stephen P. 1994. *Education in the Europe and Central Asia Region: Policies of Adjustment and Excellence*. Washington, D.C.: World Bank, Europe and Central Asia Region.

———. 1996. "Education and Economic Transformation." Paper presented at the Symposium on Economic Transformation and Social Sector Reform, September, National Academy of Sciences, Washington D.C.

———. 1997. "The Quality of Education in the Middle East and North Africa," *International Journal of Educational Development* 17(4): 449–66.

Middleton, John, Adrian Ziderman, and A. V. Adams. 1993. *Skills for Productivity*. New York: Oxford University Press.

Miller, Harry G. 1994. "Towards a Taxonomy of Microenterprises Training." Note for discussion at World Bank Resident Mission. American University, Cairo.

Ministry of Education. 1995. *Mubarak's National Project*. Cairo.

Rizk, Soad Kamel. 1991. "The Structure and Operation of the Informal Sector in Egypt." In Heba Handoussa and G. Potter, eds., *Employment and Structural Adjustment: Egypt in the 1990s*. Study prepared for the International Labour Office. Cairo: American University in Cairo Press.

Shaban, Radwan, Ragui Assaad, and S. Al-Qudsi. 1993. "Employment in the Middle East and North America: Trends and Policy Issues." Background paper for Social Summit, International Labor Office, Geneva.

USAID (U.S. Agency for International Development). 1994. *Management Training for Enterprise Development*. Project Study 263-0234. Cairo.

World Bank. 1989. *Arab Republic of Egypt: Study on Technical Education*. Report 7400-EGT. Middle East and North Africa Region. Washington, D.C.

————. 1994b. *Private Sector Development in Egypt. The Status and Challenges*. Prepared for the conference "Private Sector Development in Egypt: Investing in the Future," October 1994, Washington, D.C.

Zaytoun, Mohaya A. 1991. "Earnings and the Cost of Living: An Analysis of Recent Developments in the Egyptian Economy." In Heba Handoussa and G. Potter, eds., *Employment and Structural Adjustment: Egypt in the 1990s*. Study prepared for the International Labour Office. Cairo: American University in Cairo Press.

# 16 Jordan

ZAFIRIS TZANNATOS AND VICTOR BILLEH

JORDAN HAS FEW natural resources and a small domestic industrial basis. Its education and training system, however, is well developed. Workers have traditionally achieved high educational and skills levels and have proven to be the economy's most successful "export." In turn, less attractive jobs have been delegated to guest workers who are less qualified than Jordanians. These workers are paid wages that are closer to subsistence levels in their own countries and are typically lower than what Jordanians would accept.

Low wages for the relatively unskilled have increased Jordanians' willingness to get as much education as they can. These private considerations are greatly assisted by the government's deliberate policy to support basic education and training generously, while at the same time maintaining one of the highest cost-recovery ratios in postbasic education. The public-private interface has resulted in the commendable record of practically all Jordanians going through basic education, broadly defined as from Grade 1 to Grade 10 (that is, until the age of 16) and an initial enrollment in postsecondary education of 32 percent.

Past successes make future policies all the more challenging. When systems are well developed and have major fiscal implications, as is the case in Jordan, misguided, albeit well-intentioned, policies can have significant adverse effects. A multifaceted approach to human resources development is needed that will depart from the traditional view of the academic system and on-the-job training—namely, that it is the less able who tend to enter the vocational training stream. In addition, planners' reliance on

projections of past trends is unreliable, because of the uncertainties sur-
rounding the future sources of industrial growth given globalization, changes
in trading partners, and the political instability in the region. While investment in training can facilitate economic growth, growth prospects need to
be enhanced by macroeconomic and trade polices before human capital
investments can be induced (in the form of incentives) or afforded (in the
form of increased public budgets, which are stretched thin).

Jordan has anticipated the need for change and has redesigned its education and training system. Following an examination of the characteristics and trends of Jordan's labor market and the institutional setting for
human resource development, this chapter reviews the proposed and ongoing reforms. The main conclusion is that the structure of the education and training system is adequate, and what is required now is
consolidation and selective expansion, along with diversification and evaluation of the reforms.

## The Education and Training System

Jordan has an impressive record on education. Illiteracy rates were 68 percent in 1961, but the adult literacy rate in 1997 was well over 80 percent.
Thus its education policies have paid off: today enrollment in primary
education is universal with no gender differences, and the number of pupils, teachers, and schools has increased dramatically (table 16-1).

The Ministry of Education is responsible for providing public education at all levels and for monitoring private education. General education consists of 10 years of basic education (through age 16) and 2 years
of secondary education (Grades 11 and 12). Secondary education is divided into comprehensive secondary education and vocational education.
In the 1994–95 school year the number of students enrolled in Egypt's
education system were as follows: preschool, 57,734; basic education,
1,058,611; comprehensive secondary education, 100,834; public and
private universities, 64,830 (undergraduates); and public universities,
5,225 (postgraduates).

Three different organizations deliver vocational education and training
(VET). First, the Ministry of Education provides VET in its comprehensive, multipurpose, and specialized vocational schools. The ministry is the
main player in skills development at the secondary school level: 80 percent
of all vocational students were enrolled in the vocational streams of Ministry of Education schools in 1994–95.

TABLE 16-1

Number of Pupils, Teachers, and Schools (Grades 1 to 12),
Selected Years, 1960–61 to 1996–97

| Year | Pupils | Teachers | Schools |
|------|--------|----------|---------|
| 1960–61 | 278,496 | 7,947 | 1,200 |
| 1970–71 | 379,925 | 11,700 | 1,508 |
| 1980–81 | 720,759 | 27,151 | 2,593 |
| 1990–91 | 1,002,360 | 41,806 | 3,036 |
| 1996–97 | 1,251,023 | 60,219 | 3,517 |

*Source:* Calculated from data from the Ministry of Education and National Center for Human Resources Development.

Second, the Vocational Training Corporation (VTC), an autonomous entity governed by a board of directors and chaired by the minister of labor, provides applied vocational training in its centers. In 1995–96 most of the remaining 20 percent of vocational students were enrolled in its 35 public training centers that offered 215 programs. Ministry of Education schools provide comprehensive vocational education, while the VTC centers provide applied secondary education.

Third, at the postsecondary level, 45 community colleges under the Ministry of Education provided technical education and training. These centers were once run by the Ministry of Higher Education, which has since been abolished; its functions were passed on to the Ministry of Education. The United Nations Relief and Works Agency provides skills development at the two-year postsecondary level in two technical community colleges.

An interesting characteristic of Jordan's education system is the significant participation of the private sector. Table 16-2 shows enrollment by level of education and indicates that the private sector in 1995 had 11 percent of students even at the basic and secondary level. This ratio was 49 percent for community colleges and 37 percent for universities. Cost recovery within the public sector was minimal at lower levels of education, but reached 25 percent for postsecondary education. If one considers fees paid to public institutions plus the estimated expenses of private students, private expenditures accounted for some 11 percent of basic and secondary education and 40 to 50 percent of postsecondary education. These figures suggest that, on average, across the whole education system, the private sector contributed one Jordanian dinar (JD) for every four paid by the government.

Planners know virtually nothing about the activities of many private providers. This is one salient feature of Jordan's VET system. In 1995–96, 23,420 students were enrolled in 341 private "cultural" centers—an increase from 16,300 students in 256 cultural centers in 1992–93. Of the 45 community colleges in 1995–96, 19 were private and accounted for 40 percent of enrollment. Planners also are frequently unaware of training provided by employers. This lack of awareness of private training centers is largely a failure of the system to register, license, accredit, and generally monitor much of the national effort in this significant area of human capital development.

The Ministry of Education had the goal of increasing enrollment in vocational programs to 50 percent for males and 35 percent for females by 2000 (compared with 41 percent for males and 21 percent for females in 1996–97). This policy was inevitably associated with distortions. In addition, it had fiscal implications, since vocational education is usually more expensive than general education. Moreover, investment in vocational education, which produces narrow skills, is riskier than investment in general education. Ministry estimates suggest that the annual cost per student in vocational schools is JD 300 for business and commercial programs, JD 600 for agricultural training, and as much as JD 1,000 for training in hotel skills. The annual unit costs were JD 168 for basic education, JD 224 for secondary education, JD 337 for a community college education, and JD 1,020 for a university education (Ilon 1993; Ahlawat, Billeh, and Al-Dajeh 1995). Therefore, the decision to move to a 50-50 ratio of general to vocational secondary education could be costly. Vocational education does not have the income generating effect that general secondary education has, and those with a vocational education are more likely to be unemployed than are their counterparts who received a general secondary education (World Bank 1994b).

Distortions are evident among those who continue into postsecondary education. In 1995 the unemployment rate among women graduates of the largely vocational community colleges was 60 percent. Had these women pursued a general education, they might have entered nonvocational postsecondary education. Private universities have been allowed to operate only since 1990, but in 1995 they accounted for 40 percent of total university enrollment. General secondary education and university education have been constrained by government policies, the former because secondary

## TABLE 16-2
Financing of the Education System and Cost Recovery, 1995

| Education level | Number of students enrolled | | Public recurrent expenditures (JD) | | | Private expenditures |
|---|---|---|---|---|---|---|
| | Public (1) | Private (2) | Budget (3) | Fees (4) | Cost recovery (4)/(3 + 4) | as percent of total[a] |
| Basic & secondary | 1,054,592[b] | 130,191 | 190,947,419 | 3,021,345 | 2 | 11 |
| Vocational | 41,937 | 307 | 8,319,261 | 523,604 | 6 | 1 |
| Community colleges | 13,212 | 9,433 | 3,451,587 | 1,126,595 | 25 | 49 |
| Universities | 55,339 | 24,868 | 92,200,750 | 28,450,000 | 24 | 37 |

a. This is calculated as follows. First, obtain unit costs in public education by adding columns (3) and (4) and dividing the sum by column (1). Second, multiply public unit costs by column (2) to obtain private expenditures (assuming that costs are the same in the two sectors). Third, add column (4) to private expenditures and divide by total expenditures.

b. In 1995 the school system of the United Nations Relief and Works Agency had an enrollment of 147,039 students in the basic education cycle and 572 students in vocational education. These figures were added to the public category because these students do not pay fees. The total budget for the agency's basic education system was JD 29,452,000, and the total budget for vocational education was JD 1,239,000.

*Source:* Data from National Center for Human Resources Development.

school students are streamed into vocational education, and the latter because universities are restricted by legislation.[1]

The Ministry of Education has a good tradition of academic teaching
with broad-based education and tends to recruit more capable students
than in applied vocational training. It has a large network of institutions,
including comprehensive schools and multipurpose and specialized vocational training schools. Its programs cover a wide array of specializations,
including 32 in the industrial field alone. The ministry's institutions account for about 80 percent of all enrollments in VET. The centralized system of final examinations provides discipline for the studies and allows
some students to continue to higher education. Examination results provide a picture of the system's overall performance. Ministry institutions
have some credible vocational programs in selected areas, and many institutions benefit from committed staff and good buildings and equipment.

The Vocational Training Corporation's apprenticeship system and use
of modular training are unusual in the developing world. The VTC has a
solid organization dedicated to training with a 20-year tradition of industrial training. The VTC maintains extensive contacts with employers and
the labor market through training officers and student supervision. Most
of its programs are closely linked to jobs, and consequently VTC graduates
enjoy high rates of employment. The modular system of instruction provides for continuous assessment of student performance, reinforcement,
and progression to new levels of expertise. Students are trained at school
for three days per week, which allows for some training at the workplace
and is cheaper than center-based training for five full days a week. The
VTC has also developed flexible short-term and medium-term training
programs. It uses a system of training through production, which generates
some revenues and makes training more realistic. Follow-up (tracer) information, albeit sporadic, is available on graduates. In addition, the VTC has
developed capacity for instructor training and industrial extension.

By offering some practical subjects in short (two-year) programs, the
community college system helps alleviate pressures for enrollment in longer
and more expensive university programs, thereby saving public funds. Demand for those who complete technical courses in community colleges is
reportedly strong. The colleges offer a broad range of practical and academic subjects in some 95 specializations. There is a tradition of accreditation and comprehensive national examinations for graduates that can
enhance achievement of quality standards and provide information about
system performance. The existence of private community colleges offers

advantages in terms of (a) the relatively close attention they pay to labor market needs, the quality of training provided, and the incentives for efficient use of resources; and (b) the reduced burden on public finances.

The foregoing suggests that the basic elements of high-quality training are present. However, despite its strengths, the system does not appear to be efficient in using available staff or physical resources. Although informal coordination exists, the system's functions tend to overlap. Formal coordination, with the authority to direct the development of various parts of the system, is absent. Management tends to be overly centralized, and incentives for managers of individual institutions are limited. The articulation between the parts of the system is inadequate, and students lack opportunities for vertical and horizontal mobility. Equally important, the system lacks adequate information about employment demands, and partnerships with employers are lacking.

## The Labor Market

From the mid-1980s to the mid-1990s, aggregate economic growth remained robust, with GDP growth averaging 7 percent per year. However, this was disproportionately affected by the 16 percent growth achieved in 1992 and the continuing importance of construction activities. Because Jordan has a small economic base and a rapidly growing population, even high rates of growth may not be sufficient to absorb the continuing increase in the labor force. Table 16-3 indicates the economy's difficulties in generating new jobs. The number of applications for civil service positions illustrates that labor supply is greater than demand. In the early 1980s Jordanians showed little interest in public sector employment and the ratio of applicants to recruits was practically 1:1; in 1996 this ratio was almost 25:1 (table 16-4).

### Determinants of Labor Market Outcomes

The key determinants of labor market outcomes include the macroeconomy, fertility rates, and the public sector. Jordan is facing a crisis in terms of both macroeconomic growth and population growth. With regard to public sector employment, the labor market suffers from a "duality": in 1996 there were 165,000 civil servants and workers in parastatals in an employed labor force of just over 800,000, of whom only 640,000 were employees. This created fiscal implications at the macroeconomic level and a distorted incentive structure at the microeconomic level. With respect to the latter,

TABLE 16-3

Employment, Unemployment, and the Labor Force, 1985–96

| Year | Total number of employed | Number of Jordanians | Number of Jordanians employed | Unemployment rate (%) | Annual increase in employment | |
|---|---|---|---|---|---|---|
| | | | | | Number of workers | Percentage of workers |
| 1985 | — | 502,400 | 472,300 | 6.0 | 13,800 | 3.0 |
| 1986 | — | 535,400 | 492,500 | 8.0 | 20,200 | 4.3 |
| 1987 | — | 555,700 | 509,300 | 8.3 | 16,800 | 3.4 |
| 1988 | — | 572,166 | 521,815 | 8.8 | 12,515 | 2.5 |
| 1989 | 780,000 | 583,505 | 523,505 | 10.3 | 1,690 | 0.3 |
| 1990 | 794,000 | 630,070 | 524,197 | 16.8 | 692 | 0.1 |
| 1991 | 918,684 | 680,000 | 552,000 | 18.8 | 27,803 | 5.3 |
| 1992 | 932,000 | 839,000 | 691,700 | 17.6 | 139,700 | 25.3 |
| 1993 | 984,000 | 907,000 | 729,000 | 19.6 | 37,300 | 5.4 |
| 1994 | 1,038,000 | 963,000 | 811,000 | 15.8 | 82,000 | 11.2 |
| 1995 | 1,079,000 | 964,000 | 816,000 | 15.4 | 5,000 | 0.6 |
| 1996 | 1,070,000 | 950,000 | 826,000 | 13.1 | 10,000 | 1.2 |

— Not available.

*Note:* Figures for 1994 to 1996 are estimates.

*Source:* Data from Ministry of Labor and Department of Statistics.

TABLE 16-4

Civil Service Applications and Appointments, Selected Years, 1981–96

(number)

| Year | Applications | Appointments | Ratio |
|------|-------------|-------------|-------|
| 1981 | 7,175 | 6,188 | 1.2 |
| 1985 | 23,854 | 5,771 | 4.1 |
| 1990 | 47,555 | 2,346 | 20.2 |
| 1996 | 136,823 | 5,491 | 24.9 |

*Source:* Civil Service Commission data.

public sector wage and employment policies act unavoidably as a pace-maker for the entire labor market. On the labor demand side, private employers must compete with the large government sector on an uneven playing field: they cannot offer wages to workers that are significantly below those the public sector pays. Not only does pay in the private sector tend to be inferior to that in the public sector, but workers are unwilling to work for the private sector because it is deemed less prestigious, especially for women.

In 1960, 66 percent of the employed worked in the private sector, but this share decreased to 56 percent in 1979 (Al-Akel 1985) and to 50 percent by the mid-1990s. The private sector is shrinking in part because of past employment opportunities for Jordanians abroad: those who could not work for the government tended to emigrate instead of working in the private sector in Jordan. Government employment and emigration reduced the available supply of Jordanian workers at home and at the same time increased domestic wages. For a non-oil-producing country at the developmental stage of Jordan, the small size of the private sector is compatible with the claim that the sector has been repressed by high labor costs.

In addition to these domestic characteristics, regional aspects are important determinants of outcomes of the national labor market. Employment opportunities abroad have attracted many Jordanians. The number of Jordanian workers abroad increased from 265,000 in 1975 to 315,500 in 1983. However, their outflow has been considerably reduced since the mid-1980s. Before the Gulf War, the number of Jordanian workers in Kuwait and Saudi Arabia was 80,000 and 160,000, respectively (El-Khasawneh 1992). The regional total may have reached 275,000 and the world total 340,000. On the positive side, workers' remittances have contributed to Jordan's welfare, reaching 20 percent of GDP in the late 1980s, compared with less than 5 percent in Egypt and only 1.3 percent in Algeria. The volume of workers and the high salaries they have commanded explain the high figure for Jordan; however, emigration and workers' remittances have resulted in higher wages and segmentation in the national labor market. Emigration decreased the domestic labor supply while workers' remittances increased household incomes at home and pushed up the reservation wage of prospective workers. This income effect made domestic workers reluctant to accept work in certain jobs, sectors, or geographical areas. This opened up opportunities for foreign labor in jobs requiring fewer skills (El-Khasawneh 1992). In turn, behavioral reasons preclude less-qualified Jordanians from undertaking employment traditionally associated with immigrant laborers.

All these factors taken together have resulted in high labor costs. Labor is already priced out because the public sector has driven up the average wage and has increased the level of wages at which private employers can recruit. While one could argue that the consumption wage enables Jordanians to attain high living standards, the production wage in terms of labor costs, particularly for Jordanians, is above its market clearing level as evidenced by the high unemployment rates.[2]

## Unemployment

Unemployment levels vary somewhat with level of educational attainment, and the unemployment rates of the more educated have tended to decline over time (table 16-5). Yet these differences are not pronounced, and they seem to depend on the year of estimation. Unemployment has been, and still is, particularly acute among first-time job seekers who are relatively well educated (Lee 1989; World Bank 1994b).

Unemployment is a chronic condition in Jordan. The low growth of domestic employment opportunities acceptable to Jordanians has resulted in rising unemployment. In 1980 the unemployment rate was only 3.5 percent. Since then it has increased each year, passing the 10 percent level in 1989 and reaching 19 percent in 1991. The underlying demographic changes are important. During this period employment among Jordanians increased by nearly 3 percent per year, but the labor force grew by 4.5 percent per year. The unemployed tend to be young. In 1991, 75 percent of unemployed men were younger than 30. With respect to educational attainment, 60 percent of unemployed women are qualified at the postsecondary level, compared with 25 percent of men.

TABLE 16-5
Unemployment Rates, by Education Level, 1987 and 1996
(percent)

| Education level | 1987 | 1996 |
|---|---|---|
| Illiterate | 11 | 5 |
| Read and write | 13 | 10 |
| Primary | 16 | 13 |
| Preparatory | 15 | 13 |
| Secondary | 16 | 13 |
| Diploma (community college) | 22 | 20 |
| Bachelor's degree | 14 | 12 |
| Masters or doctorate | 9 | 6 |
| All (average) | 8 | 13 |

Source: Department of Statistics (1987).

One additional reason for unemployment is that production is charac-terized by capital bias. In the past two decades, while employment doubled, the capital stock tripled. Productivity growth was low, and output growth was achieved primarily through extensive growth—more inputs—rather than intensive growth—higher efficiency (World Bank 1994a, chap. 2). Cheap credit and low tariffs on capital goods favored the adoption of capi-tal-intensive production techniques in the more modern sectors while keep-ing wages for immigrant (guest) workers low in the traditional sectors.

## Education and Training Issues

Although the total supply of human capital is relatively abundant and Jor-dan "exports" workers to neighboring countries, each of the three main actors in VET face serious problems that affect the overall system in terms of relevance to market economy requirements, efficacy (the extent to which objectives are met), management effectiveness, quality of training, and effi-cient use of resources. The following paragraphs examine the role of each agency and its performance from a systemwide perspective.

### Ministry of Education

The Ministry of Education's VET schools tend not to be well linked to business, industry, and labor market demand. Some inertia is evident in adjusting teaching content to practices in enterprises. There are numerous examples. Computer courses teach programming, whereas the greatest demand is for training in software applications and databases. Television repair focuses on black and white televisions, whereas almost all of the sets delivered for repair are in color. Typing is taught on manual typewriters, whereas businesses are rapidly converting to word processing.

Moreover, schools provide students with little or no help with job counseling and placement. In addition, they do little systematic follow-up on graduates, and the lack of knowledge about what graduates do reduces the effectiveness of the ministry's activities. The directorate responsible for VET must report to a directorate general responsible for all academic matters. Thus VET managers operate in an environment where they are unable to impose trade training priorities in relation to the predominant position of academic education. The low esteem in which VET is held is reinforced by compelling about half of the students to enter vocational schooling, often against their wishes.

In terms of quality, students in Ministry of Education programs tend to receive little reinforcement of vocational content from academic programs. For example, mathematics is taught as a diluted version of academic mathematics; it is not applied to the occupations being taught. The quality of instruction in some industrial trades is poor, mainly because of instructors' lack of practical training and industrial work experience. The inability to maintain and replace equipment also affects the quality of instruction. Safety standards, while existing in theory, tend not to be employed in practice, resulting in hazardous working conditions in many workshops.

Finally, efficiency tends to be low. There are few incentives to coordinate the use of Ministry of Education facilities with those of the VTC. This results in duplication of facilities in some areas. Some of the costs could be reduced through the production and sale of goods or services by the institutions. The lack of interest in or ability to sell production arises partly because policies prevent the retention of earnings at the institution level. The high costs and lack of financing constrain the expansion of vocational instruction in needed areas.

## Vocational Training Corporation

The VTC has employer councils for each institution, but these rarely function as regularly or as effectively as intended. Problems that affect relevance are also apparent in several other areas. Students tend to specialize relatively quickly on entry into training centers. As a result, they lack broadly based general training. This contributes to some lack of flexibility among graduates. In addition, the VTC is constrained in increasing its intake of students by several factors, namely (a) the number of enterprises willing to accept apprentices (the small number is mainly because of the limited size of Jordanian industry), (b) the VTC's lack of sufficient staff to develop apprenticeship placement, and (c) parents' and students' low interest in vocational training. The VTC suffers from a lack of capacity to provide training for some target groups and in some areas of the country (for examples, for females and in the South).

Weak training standards in several industrial fields also affect the VTC's effectiveness. A good training ethos and environment is lacking. Another major factor is the instructors' lack of practical technical expertise. Undemanding, they are often satisfied with low levels of workmanship by students. In addition, there are localized problems: missing equipment, equipment that is inadequate for instructional purposes, or equipment in disrepair. All of these problems reduce the quality of instruction. Supervision of trainees in apprenticeship programs is also reportedly inadequate. The effectiveness of VTC programs could be compromised by a law on certification of workers and enterprises, which could overburden VTC management and staff resources.

Finally, efficiency is low as evidenced by the high dropout rates for apprentices (20 percent in the first year), which is largely traceable to low levels of student interest. This contributes to small class sizes and under-utilization of staff and workshop facilities. In general, the available facilities could handle many more trainees without incurring substantial additional costs.

## Community Colleges

Compared with the Ministry of Education and the VTC, community colleges, which tend not to have links with enterprises, suffer most from a lack of relevance of the courses offered. As a consequence, program content is sometimes not well related to employers' actual needs. Because of central financing and control, the community colleges are not particularly responsive to the needs and requirements of the communities in which they are located. Another reflection of their lack of flexibility is the narrow specializations (95 different specialties) and the rigid length of training (two years). Shorter programs would be more appropriate. The precipitous decline in enrollment suggests a shortage of jobs for graduates with this level of education, idle capacity, and unemployment of graduates in general fields.

An overriding issue is the community colleges' lack of a clear purpose and mandate, which has a definite impact on their effectiveness. Moreover, the community colleges do not have a suitable governance system. Central administrative control, particularly over private community colleges, tends to be excessive.

## Reform Priorities

Each part of the VET system (the Ministry of Education, the Vocational Training Corporation, and the community colleges) operates independently with little direction from economic development priorities. A capacity needs to be developed to analyze the human resource implications of overall economic strategies and convert these implications into guidelines for VET development. A prudent approach would be to take the system as a whole and examine the best way to improve it, starting with external efficiency (links with the world of work), internal efficiency (especially flexibility), and scope (coverage).

### Links and Feedback

The links between training suppliers, particularly the Ministry of Education, and employers are not well established and therefore the training programs are often unsuitable. The Ministry of Education vocational schools and the community colleges lack adequate knowledge about the employment performance of their graduates. Sporadic and incomplete efforts at tracer studies should be replaced with more efficient instruments and technical support.

A 1990 survey examined employers' views on factors affecting the productivity and profitability of their operations, the sources and methods of labor recruitment, the provision of on-the-job training, the use of outside skill development providers, and the VET system. Most firms (81 percent) indicated that they provided some sort of on-the-job training, and just over 50 percent indicated that they had difficulties finding new recruits with specific skills. Half of the respondents agreed with the following statement: "When hiring a new employee, I do not really want a worker who is already trained. Just give me people who are motivated and disciplined, and I will teach them what I want them to know." This reflects the fragmented nature of small Jordanian industries, which possess unstandardized equipment or production processes that require hands-on practice with internal supervision. Only 40 percent of respondents felt that the VTC could handle internal training, and only 6 percent of firms reported sending their employees to the VTC for outside training. Notwithstanding these responses, most firms seemed to be favorably disposed toward vocational training programs and rated them "rather good," and 60 percent rated vocational graduates "much better" than their other employees. Practically all firms (94 percent) agreed that the vocational system needed to have more contacts with employers.

### Flexibility

Rigidities appear in the supply response to labor market information. Programs almost invariably are of fixed length, and their content tends to become and remain out of date. The procedures currently in place mean that content updating is slow. Students sometimes specialize too early, thereby reducing their chances for occupational mobility, and few alternatives exist for continuing advanced skill training. In addition, students cannot move easily from a vocational track to an academic path that leads to postsecondary education.

### Coverage

Plans for expanding vocational education and training may go too far and waste resources. This includes the year 2000 goal of offering comprehensive or applied VET to 50 percent of male and 35 percent of female general-school graduates. Vocational training is expensive and should be limited to areas that offer immediate employment prospects. The provision of private VET needs to be encouraged.

Important areas of reform include improving the links between VET and employers, increasing the flexibility of the system, and deciding when and how to expand calls for better management practices to improve coordination, which is currently lacking. The various training suppliers lack incentives to adjust their offerings in relation to those of other suppliers. This results in high costs, failure to realize economies of scale, and lack of distinct mandates for the different parts of the system.

The lack of coordination reduces the scope for rationalization. One of the most important issues is the need to rationalize the provision of VET and eliminate wasteful duplication. There is a need to re-examine the rationale for maintaining two separate VET administrations. The current system fragments scarce management, staff, physical resources, and financial resources. Community colleges also need rationalization. Their purposes, functions, and mandate should be re-evaluated and made distinct from vocational training (Association of Canadian Community College 1996).

## Instructors

Arguably the factor contributing the most to the low or mediocre quality of instruction is workshop instructors' lack of work experience. Instructors frequently have not mastered the crafts they teach, and they lack role models with high standards. Training tends to be monopolized by academic teachers. Mechanisms to rectify the situation by means of instructor upgrading and on-the-job training are lacking at present.

## Materials and Equipment

Quality is also compromised by the lack of sufficient and updated materials and equipment. Pedagogical materials are in short supply. Serious, often localized, problems relate to equipment provision: too many machines are broken, have parts missing, or are inaccurate. This problem stems in part from incapable instructors, inadequately trained in the proper use and repair of equipment. The problem also is often attributable to overstretched public funding.

## The Training and Employment Support Fund

In 1998 the government, as part of its Social Productivity Program, introduced the Training and Employment Support Fund. Its focus is on short-term training for the unemployed. An addition to the system of vocational schools, training centers, and community colleges, the fund has the following objectives: to create an effective system of short-term training (training that lasts for less than six months and is relevant to the specific needs of employers) and to increase competition in the supply of skills (competition currently dominated by the public sector). The means to achieve these goals is competitive funding for "contract-based or output-based" training.

Training is envisioned as a continuation of education. Given the commendable educational attainment of Jordanians, training should play a complementary role. Since most workers are well educated, training can provide them with the necessary specific skills that would make them employable. The training fund has the potential to be used as a guide for long-run reforms.

The training fund is unlikely to provide a quick fix to the massive unemployment problem and the problems of underemployment and hidden unemployment. Neither will it address the main causes of unemployment: Jordan's rapidly growing population and small economic base. It can, however, contribute positively by reducing the supply price of youth to employers and increasing productivity. These changes in the supply curve and demand curve should increase employment.

Explicit estimates of the quantitative impact of a training fund on employment in the short run are lacking. (The impact may not be that much given the current underutilization of existing employees.) If it succeeds, the training fund could pave the way for the government to reduce the direct provision of training and increase the use of competitive funds for that purpose. At present, public providers of training have guaranteed allocations from the budget and are expanding. They have few incentives to adapt to the changing needs of employers despite the high unemployment rates among their graduates. If funding for training is awarded on a contract basis (that is, competitively and subject to achieving certain targets prescribed by the government that reflect the labor market), the relevance of publicly offered programs and courses will increase. If administration costs are kept under control, budgetary savings could result.

The proposed fund will last for three years. It is expected that this would be sufficient time to assess the desirability of such an intervention empirically through tracer surveys and impact evaluations. Although a training fund should not be seen as a short-term solution to the continuing problem of unemployment, it can contribute to reduction in unemployment among the groups it targets. Its greatest potential is to evolve into a comprehensive funding mechanism for training that can increase the effectiveness and efficiency of public social spending in this area of human resource development.

## Conclusions

Although Jordan has an adequate education and training system, what is now required is consolidation and selective expansion. The government's role is important, as the commendable record of Jordan's human resources development has shown. However, its role need not be in the form of direct provider. This chapter has emphasized publicly provided training because little is known about what is happening in the private sector. The extent of private sector involvement needs to be known not only to improve planning of public sector provision, but also to ensure that the private sector provides what it is supposed to deliver. The recent growth of private universities has been criticized on the grounds that they offer little and make money out of the ignorance of students and parents. To correct this, private institutions should be transparently licensed and accredited on a level playing field with public institutions. They also should not be crowded out by the public sector but encouraged to expand by providing financial incentives through credit and scholarship programs.

Within the public training sector, more effective management of VET should be sought through three principal means of policy coordination: rationalization of VET programs at the secondary level, decentralization, and improved resource management. In this respect, a VET policy council should be established with sufficient analytical capacity and authority to coordinate and direct the system toward priority areas and to avoid overlapping responsibilities. In addition, more authority and responsibility should be delegated to managers of training institutions. Managers should have the freedom to adjust training content to local requirements, and they should be able to retain and use earnings from their own activities and production.

Given the already high educational and skills attainment of Jordanians, the importance of short training programs (including, for example, one-year diploma programs in community colleges) cannot be understated. Such additional courses and qualifications should enable graduates of secondary education and second-level vocational training to enter postsecondary studies. VET system expansion should be guided by economic considerations to minimize the amount of money spent to train people who will be unable to find employment. The administrative streamlining of 16-year-olds into general or vocational tracks should be abandoned. Individual students and their families should be able to choose their course of study.

Self-employment in small business can play an important role in job creation, and the concepts and basic requirements of entrepreneurship should be introduced into VET programs. Programs on preparing business plans should be offered to returning VET trainees who have acquired work experience, and they should also have access to credit programs for business start-ups.

To adjust training supply to demand, it is helpful to know what happened to the graduates of VET institutions. The systematic collection of information about graduates' performance in the labor market should be a major responsibility of all training institutions, and the central authorities should provide technical guidance and simplified instruments for this purpose.

The quality of training instructors and their ability to teach modern curricula should be addressed as well. It is always tempting to argue that the government should spend more to bring these two aspects of training in line with the requirements of a fast-moving economy. However, the basic issue is how to accomplish this. One suggestion is to change the regulations to permit the hiring of part-time instructors from enterprises with the work experience needed to improve the standards of practical teaching. It also might be useful to reward public training institutions that achieve commonly agreed objectives and to make the system of remuneration more output based.

## Notes

1. In support of this argument, we note that 40,000 Jordanians in 1995 studied at universities abroad. Admission to public universities in Jordan is based only in part on academic achievement, and admissions are greatly affected by various quotas.

2. Note that Jordan has a high dependency ratio, as the low participation rate suggests. The average family of 7 members typically has no more than 1.5 workers.

## References

Ahlawat, K, V. Billeh, and H. Al-Dajeh. 1995. "Analysis of Budgets and Unit Costs of Public Universities, 1980–94." Paper prepared for the World Bank. Amman: National Center for Human Resources Development.

Al-Akel, M. 1985. "Manpower, Labour Markets, and Wage Development: The Case of Jordan." Ph.D. thesis, University of Sussex, United Kingdom.

Association of Canadian Community Colleges. 1996. "A Strategic Plan and Adult VET in Jordan." Economic Development through Technical Skills Project. Amman: National Center for Human Resources Development.

Department of Statistics. 1987. *Survey of Health, Nutrition, Manpower, and Poverty.* Amman.

El-Khasawneh, S. 1992. "Labour Migration in Jordan: Policies, Flows, Organization." Paper presented at the United Nations Development Programme/International Labour Office Seminar in Amman on Migration Policies in Arab Labour-Sending Countries.

Ilon, L. 1993. *Educational Finance in Jordan: Final Report.* Publication Series 32. Amman: National Center for Educational Research and Development.

Lee, Eddy. 1989. "Jordan: Issues in Employment Policy." International Labour Office, Geneva.

World Bank. 1994a. *Consolidating Economic Adjustment and Establishing the Base for Sustainable Growth."* Report 12645-JO. Middle East and Northern Africa Region, Country Department II, Human Resources Division, Washington, D.C.

———. 1994b. *Hashemite Kingdom of Jordan: Poverty Assessment,* 2 vols. Report 12675-JO. Middle East and Northern Africa Region, Country Department II, Human Resources Division, Washington, D.C.

———. 1996. *Jordan: Higher Education Development Study.* Report 15105-JO. Middle East and Northern Africa Region, Country Department II, Human Resources Division, Washington, D.C.

# 17 West Bank and Gaza Strip

Fred Fluitman

THE WEST BANK, including East Jerusalem, and the Gaza Strip are Palestinian territories that have been occupied by Israel since the Israeli-Arab War of 1967. Following the Middle East peace process in 1993, limited self-rule by a Palestinian Authority in West Bank and Gaza was agreed upon. The Palestinian Authority has, in accordance with what was agreed, assumed responsibility in the autonomous areas of the West Bank and the Gaza Strip, for labor and social welfare, health, education (including training) and culture, tourism, agriculture, energy, statistics, and taxation. Things are far from settled, however, and the future is extremely uncertain. Important spheres of jurisdiction have so far remained under Israeli control, notably external security, foreign affairs, and exports and imports. Opponents of the peace process have repeatedly succeeded in frustrating it by resorting to violence. As a result, punitive measures have been taken, which, in turn, have worsened the situation on the ground.

The economy of the occupied territories is essentially underdeveloped and fragile, vulnerable to unpredictable external shocks and subject to massive constraints. Agriculture (mostly small-scale, low-tech, and family-based) contributed between 25 and 35 percent of gross domestic product (GDP) in 1995, and it remains the major productive sector. However, agricultural development is hampered by problems of access to land, water, and markets. Manufacturing (around 8 percent of GDP) has remained based in small-scale enterprises: 90 percent of enterprises have fewer than 10 workers and 72 percent have fewer than 5 workers. The domestic construction sector (13 to 17 percent of GDP in 1995) depends largely on savings from income earned in Israel—most of it by construction workers. However, there has been a "building boom" in parts of the territories since the beginning of the peace process.

More than 85 percent of the territories' foreign trade is with Israel. A structural deficit on the balance of goods and a surplus on account of services, mostly wages earned in Israel, illustrate the dependence of the territories on the Israeli economy. Following a major drop in merchandise imports from Israel in 1988, at the start of the *intifada*, the value of such imports increased rapidly to reach US$1,340 million in 1995, according to the Bank of Israel. Exports of goods to Israel, in contrast, never recovered from their collapse in 1988–89; they were worth only US$205 million in 1995. Since Palestinians of the territories are increasingly prevented from working "across the green line," the ever-growing deficit on account of goods is no longer largely made up for by wages earned in Israel. Annual wage receipts by Palestinian workers in Israel plummeted from a record US$930 million in 1992 to US$252 million in 1995.

Data provided by the Israeli Bureau of Statistics suggest that economic growth in the territories has been low since 1987. Per capita gross national product reached almost US$2,500 in the West Bank (21 percent from work in Israel) and US$1,600 in Gaza (29 percent from work in Israel) in 1992. However, average incomes have collapsed since then. By 1995 the territories' gross national product had decreased by close to 10 percent per capita as a result of a 52 percent reduction in workers' remittances. Growth has not picked up substantially since.

## The Labor Market

There are no reliable census data about the population of the occupied territories. According to estimates made by the Palestinian Central Bureau of Statistics, the territories had a Palestinian population of almost 2.5 million by the end of 1995, 53 percent of them 15 years of age or older. By 1992 there were, in addition to those in the territories, around 1 million Palestinian refugees in Jordan and around 300,000 each in Syria and Lebanon. In total, an estimated 3.5 million Palestinians lived outside the West Bank and Gaza in 1995.

The first labor force survey undertaken by the Palestinian Central Bureau of Statistics suggests a 1995 labor force participation rate of 39 percent for the territories as a whole (PCBS 1996). With an estimated 1.3 million Palestinians 15 years of age and older, the size of the labor force was

TABLE 17-1
Labor Force Participation, by Gender, 1995
(percentage of the population age 15 and older)

| Location | Male | Female | Total |
|---|---|---|---|
| West Bank | 68.6 | 12.8 | 40.6 |
| Gaza Strip | 62.8 | 7.6 | 35.4 |
| Both territories | 66.9 | 11.2 | 39.0 |

*Source*: PCBS (1996).

around half a million. Labor force participation was found to be higher in the West Bank than in the Gaza Strip and significantly lower for women, particularly so in Gaza (table 17-1). Participation rates were particularly low (14 percent) for those without education and relatively high (63 percent) for those who had completed more than 12 years in school.

With a labor force growing at an annual rate of between 3 and 4 percent, 20,000 new job seekers (net) enter the market every year. If the government were to decide to do something for the tens of thousands of unemployed persons, it would have to identify, if not create, 30,000 or perhaps 40,000 new jobs year after year for years to come—a daunting challenge.

## Employment in the Occupied Territories and Israel

Less than half of the labor force are wage employees; the others are mostly self-employed in agriculture or in small shops. There are also sizable numbers of unpaid family workers and unemployed people. Many of the people who work for wages depend on jobs in Israel. While job growth within the territories has been remarkable in recent years, it could not entirely make up for a massive decline in employment of Palestinians in Israel.

The growth of employment within the territories after 1992 has certainly been significant, but it is unlikely to continue at current rates. Most of the new jobs were associated with the establishment of a Palestinian public service and with a building boom. In view of budget constraints facing the Palestinian Authority, doubts are justified about any further increase in the number of public servants, estimated in 1994 at around 65,000. Moreover, the construction sector is not expected to contribute to further large-scale job growth. New and lasting jobs created as a result of massive external investments (for example, in the much talked about industrial parks) have yet to materialize and may not unless a fundamental climate change occurs. Employment growth within the territories is most severely compromised by repeated and prolonged closures and other punitive measures restricting or preventing, at great expense, the movement of people and produce across and inside the green line. Imports of essential inputs, including flour and fuel, are frequently halted, and exports are prevented from leaving. As production falters, so does consumption, and incomes and jobs evaporate.

For more than 25 years, tens of thousands of Palestinians (at times more than 40 percent of the labor force, mainly construction workers and farm hands) have been working in Israel because there were no jobs for them within the occupied territories. In 1992, on normal days, almost 120,000 registered workers and—in spite of strict controls—an estimated 30,000 to 40,000 unregistered workers crossed the green line to earn a living. These days are over, or so it appears. For a long time there had been periods during which the borders were closed for all or some, usually but not always in the wake of terrorist activities. But closure became the rule rather than the exception in March 1993. Since that time the maximum numbers allowed back in have decreased. Consider the case in Gaza. Although an average of 43,000 daily workers came to work in Israel in 1992, this number had declined to below 12,000 by 1996. In order to make up for the many Palestinian workers prevented from coming to their jobs, Israeli employers have been steadily replacing them with foreigners. By the end of 1995, more than 70,000 foreign contract workers were legally employed in Israel, most of them construction workers from Rumania, Thailand, Turkey, and China.

## Unemployment in the Occupied Territories

Unemployment and underemployment have become serious problems. In 1993–94 unemployment varied between 17 and 33 percent in Gaza and between 11 and 30 percent in the West Bank, depending on whether workers had access to jobs in Israel (ILO 1995, p. 15). According to a September-October 1995 survey by the Palestinian Central Bureau of Statistics, 18 percent of the labor force of the occupied territories was unemployed— that is, 14 percent in the West Bank and 29 percent in the Gaza Strip (PCBS 1996). Results of the second round of the Labor Force Survey (April/ May 1996) suggest a dramatic surge in unemployment to 29 percent (24 percent in the West Bank and a record 39 percent in the Gaza Strip). These estimates imply that unemployment is now likely to affect more than 140,000 Palestinian workers and their families.

## The Education and Training System

In the West Bank compulsory basic schooling lasts ten years; after that students can opt for two years of secondary education, either general (with a scientific track and a literary track) or vocational. In Gaza compulsory education consists of six years of elementary schooling plus three years of preparatory schooling; secondary schools (general only) last three years. Since the Palestinian Authority assumed control of the education sector in 1994, steps have been taken to unify the system. The first secondary school examination (*Tawjihi*) under Palestinian supervision took place at the end of the 1994–95 school year. Well over half a million Palestinian children, 48 percent of them girls, received basic education in the territories in 1994–95 (table 17-2). There were 45,359 pupils (45 percent female) in secondary schools, including a small proportion in vocational secondary schools. Almost all of secondary education is provided by the authority.

Enrollments in vocational education are small compared with general education enrollments. The Palestinian Ministry of Education and Higher Education reports that there were 18 vocational schools in the West Bank and Gaza in 1995. These included vocational (or industrial) secondary schools following the Jordanian curriculum, all of them in the West Bank, as well as certain commercial, agricultural, and nursing schools. Ten of

TABLE 17-2

Enrollments in Basic and Secondary Education, 1994–95

| Level of education | West Bank | Gaza Strip | Total |
|---|---|---|---|
| Basic education | 355,269 | 217,260 | 572,529 |
| Government | 280,145 | 97,435 | 377,580 |
| UN Refugee Welfare Association | 43,969 | 117,363 | 161,332 |
| Private | 31,155 | 2,462 | 33,617 |
| Secondary education | 27,678 | 17,661 | 45,339 |
| Government | 24,091 | 17,026 | 41,117 |
| Private | 3,587 | 635 | 4,222 |

*Source:* PCBS (1995).

TABLE 17-3
Vocational Secondary School Enrollments, by Gender, 1995

| School type and specialization | Male | Female | Total |
|---|---|---|---|
| Vocational secondary schools | 1,233 | 235 | 1,468 |
| Commercial | 15 | 220 | 235 |
| Agricultural | 35 | — | 35 |
| Industrial | 1,162 | — | 1,162 |
| Nursing | 21 | 15 | 36 |

— Not available.
*Source:* PCBS (1995).

these schools were said to be governmental; the others included schools run by the Arab Development Society, the Salesian Brothers, and the Lutheran Church. According to the *Education Statistics Yearbook* (PCBS 1995), fewer than 1,300 students, mostly men, were enrolled in vocational secondary schools in 1995 (table 17-3); only 77 of these students went to such schools in Gaza. Upon completing the two-year program, about half of which is devoted to practical work, graduates may seek employment or pursue their education at the tertiary level in one of 17 community colleges that offer two-year technician-level courses. Graduates of general secondary schools may also enter these colleges.

Four of these community (or technical) colleges were administered by the Ministry of Education, 3 of them were with the United Nations Refugee Welfare Association, and 10 were private institutions. Together they enrolled 4,110 students, more than half women, and two out of three in the 19-to-21-year-old age bracket. Graduates of community colleges could, in principle, continue their education at a university.

In 1995 there were eight universities in the occupied territories: six in the West Bank (including an open university) and two in Gaza. Between 1992 and 1995, enrollments almost doubled to reach about 30,000 students; almost 45 percent of these students were women. A large share of the university students (27 percent) had opted to study education; other apparently attractive specializations were arts and letters (17 percent), science and technology (16 percent), economics and business (16 percent), and religious studies (12 percent).

In 1994, 21 vocational training centers (with an enrollment of 4,000) trained school leavers to become semiskilled or skilled workers. Since 1995

TABLE 17–4

Enrollments in the Training Centers of the Ministry of Labor,
by Gender, 1994

| Trade category | Male | Female | Total |
|---|---|---|---|
| Construction trades | 646 | 19 | 665 |
| Automotive repair | 438 | — | 438 |
| Metal trades | 339 | — | 339 |
| Woodwork | 127 | — | 127 |
| Electrical/refrigeration/radio/television | 208 | — | 208 |
| Tailoring | 43 | 592 | 635 |
| Hairdressing | — | 222 | 222 |
| Bookkeeping/word processing | 2 | 227 | 227 |
| Total | 1,801 | 1,060 | 2,861 |

— Not available.
*Source:* Ministry of Labor (1996).

the Palestinian Ministry of Labor has been responsible for 13 of these centers (namely, the ones set up and previously administered by Israeli authorities, primarily to prepare Palestinian workers for jobs available in Israel). These centers continue to offer short-term courses (5 to 12 months) in 24 occupations; around 75 percent of the time is devoted to practical work and 25 percent to theoretical training. Trainees must be at least 16 years of age and, depending on the course, have completed 6 to 10 years of basic education. In fact, many of the trainees are school dropouts. Fewer than 3,000 students were enrolled in the centers under the Ministry of Labor in 1994 (table 17-4).

Most of the women were enrolled in sewing classes; the remainder were in hairdressing or secretarial courses. Most of the men took courses related to either motor vehicle repair or the construction sector. The Ministry of Labor has taken steps to develop an "efficient, effective, and relevant national vocational training system" (Ministry of Labor 1996), including a review of these institutions. Its evaluation report alludes to a range of weaknesses with regard to coverage, curriculum, training methods, the qualifications of trainers, the state of facilities and equipment, and links with the world of work. The report points out that 63 percent of operating expenses in running these training centers was spent on salaries and 19 percent on trainee stipends. Thus less than 20 percent of operating expenses got spent on teaching and learning materials. Costs per course varied between US$500 and US$1,300 per student per year. Extra-budgetary resources, notably funds granted by external donor agencies, paid for special projects, including the "expert team on vocational training" that assists the directorate in formulating policy, in developing curricula, and in training staff.

In addition to the Ministry of Labor, the United Nations Refugee Welfare Association is providing vocational training in two large centers—one in Kalandia, just North of Jerusalem, and one in Gaza. In the mid-1990s the combined enrollment in both schools was about 1,100 students. The United Nations Refugee Welfare Association courses last two years; students begin them after completion of basic education. Additional vocational training is provided in six private centers with an estimated enrollment of around 500 trainees. Private centers are operated by the Al Bir Society, the Young Men's Christian Association, and the Near East Council of Churches; most of their courses last three years. Details concerning their operations and costs are unknown by the Ministry of Labor.

A fairly extensive informal network of nongovernmental organizations in the occupied territories offers additional opportunities for adults to acquire or improve certain skills. Such nonformal education and training was provided in 1994 to 13,898 students enrolled in 426 courses offered in 108 "cultural centers" (PCBS 1995). Two-thirds of the students were 19 years of age or older; almost half of the students were women. One-third of all courses were computer courses. Little information is known about the costs of training in these institutions.

The Palestinian training system is small. Presumably, most workers who need specific skills acquire them on the job—that is, by copying others or by trial and error—rather than as a result of structured learning. However, there is little data concerning organized training or skill upgrading by Palestinian employers for their employees. It may be assumed that private sector establishments in the territories do not provide much training either, given the nature and size distribution of enterprises and the fact, well-established elsewhere, that small enterprises do not usually train their workers.

## Reform of Vocational Education and Training

Soon after being established in the mid-1990s, the Ministry of Labor took an active interest in vocational training. The ministry explicitly recognized the weaknesses of the system it had inherited and "the importance of supporting and developing the system of vocational preparation . . . in particular the importance of defining clear objectives and establishing the necessary bodies." It stressed the urgent need for a "common vision of the priorities for developing the vocational training system" (Ministry of Labor 1996). It proposed (a) enhancing coordination among vocational education and training providers, (b) involving industry in the design of training policies, in the assessment of training needs, and in the provision of training, and (c) creating what is referred to as a "catalyst." This would be a body equipped to ensure the continuous adjustment and development of the training system by being aware of the labor market and of new training methods, and by training trainers and training managers.

To achieve its overall objective of developing an "efficient, effective, relevant, and sustainable" training system, the ministry decided to attach an expert team to its General Directorate for Vocational Training. It also set up the Advisory Council on Vocational Training, which has representatives of the ministries of Labor and Education and of the United Nations Refugee Welfare Association. There are additional seats for other ministries, for representatives of private training providers, for representatives of employers' and workers' organizations, and for the head of the expert team. The council advises the Ministry of Labor on training policies and on legislation or other forms of regulation. It coordinates all those involved in vocational training, and it directs and reviews the work of the expert team.

The technical arm of the Advisory Council, the expert team is a semiautonomous body based in the Ministry of Labor and financially supported by an external donor. Its objectives are to foster a flexible, demand-driven, and sustainable Palestinian training system, to become a platform for a continuous exchange of information and experience, and to develop the human and material resources for the new training system. The team is involved in data collection and policy analysis, curriculum development, and the training of trainers and training system managers.

In its efforts to develop a training policy framework, the team addressed numerous issues, such as the Palestinian economy and labor market, alternative modes of skill development, the division of training responsibilities, and the financing of training. A Palestinian training system, according to the team's recommendations, should

- Handle (in several years) up to 30 percent of the relevant age group
- Focus on the training needs of the local market
- Be as flexible as possible and modular in form

- Serve adults as well as youngsters
- Provide basic training as well as skills upgrading and retraining opportunities
- Lead to an occupational certificate and regained access to the general education system
- Ask those who can afford to pay for their training to do so.

At this stage the government should provide training in all fields, but particularly in strategic areas, and its role should move gradually toward policy formulation, curriculum development, training of trainers, and the setting of standards and certification. With regard to vocational training and vocational education, there is simply no one right system. It would be wrong to phase out completely any of the existing systems at this time. Establishing multipurpose training schools or centers might be an excellent way of experimenting with methods to find a harmonious combination (Ministry of Labor 1996).

The Ministry of Labor and its expert team have begun to implement a comprehensive plan of action to ensure the transition to a new Palestinian training system. The plan presents a series of distinct but related donor-funded projects covering the expansion of the system, administration, staff development, curriculum development, financial planning, the upgrading of certain facilities, and the improvement of links with industry.

## Constraints to Reform

Reforming training policy in the West Bank and Gaza Strip, because of their unique circumstances, is particularly difficult. Having decided that such constraints are no excuse for inaction, Palestinian authorities have embarked upon reforms that promise to be gradual but substantive and innovative. Success is likely to depend on the ability to obtain adequate information and to reach goals that are clearly stated and shared.

In 1995 no more than 5 percent of the relevant age group had ever been enrolled in formal VET programs. As stated above, the Ministry of Labor is striving for 30 percent. Whether the system will be able to attract significantly more students is another matter, especially given its current internal and external efficiency. Concerns about dilapidated facilities, outdated curricula, obsolete or unavailable equipment, and unqualified trainers are widespread. The Young Men's Christian Association conducted a tracer study of about 25 percent of the 1992 graduates of all West Bank VET institutions.

This study suggested that half of them found work in their field of study, 7 percent in related fields, 22 percent in unrelated occupations; 20 percent were unemployed. In Palestinian society more young people are enrolled in Palestinian universities than in VET programs. There is a clear preference for an academic education. Finally, and probably most importantly, the issue of financing a significant increase in VET enrollments has to be carefully studied. This will prove to be a daunting task particularly because of the lack of information on unit costs of training.

However small, the Palestinian training system is a "patchwork of formats and sponsors" (de Moura Castro 1994). Although the Advisory Council is intended to coordinate vocational education and training activities, numerous actors, including foreign donors, have entered the scene, each with its own view of what is to be done and how. There may be certain benefits in diversity, but it will be important for the Advisory Council to manage these often conflicting priorities.

A final issue to be considered concerns training providers' resistance to change in the occupied territories. Most of these providers have been doing an admirable job for years in difficult circumstances; now that the circumstances are supposed to get better, they should not be expected to unquestioningly abide by the directives of a new and largely inexperienced training authority. In other words, the willingness of certain key actors to play their part may be compromised either by their particular terms of reference or by their divergent views on the nature of change.

## References

de Moura Castro, Claudio. 1994. "Training in Palestine." In Mazen Hashweh, ed., *Training in Transition: Review of Issues and Options in Vocational Education and Training in Occupied Palestinian Territories.* Jerusalem.

ILO (International Labour Office). 1995. "Report of the Director General, Appendix." International Labour Conference, 82d Session, Geneva.

Ministry of Labor. 1995. *Towards an Efficient, Effective, and Relevant National Vocational Training System in Palestine.* Jerusalem: Society for Austro-Arab Relations.

———. 1996. *Meeting the Challenge—Vocational Training: Current Status and Future Perspective.* Jerusalem: Swiss Agency for Development and Cooperation.

PCBS (Palestinian Central Bureau of Statistics). 1995. *Education Statistics Yearbook, 1994–95,* No. 1. Ramallah: Ministry of Education and Higher Education.

———. 1996. "Labor Force Survey: Main Findings (September–October 1995 Round)." Ramallah.

PART

# IV  Two Special Studies

DURING THE PAST TWO decades Australia and Germany have strengthened their roles as international advocates of reform of vocational education and training (VET). Part IV examines how their experiences can provide useful lessons for low- and middle-income countries.

VET policies in Australia and Germany have increased the links between education and employment, a challenge preoccupying policymakers in all countries. In countries with rapidly growing economies, this preoccupation stems from the concern that demand for skilled workers will outstrip supply. In countries where economic growth is slow, the concern may arise because of growing unemployment among youth. In both cases the result may be the same: efforts by policymakers to vocationalize the curriculum, or involve employers in schooling decisions, or increase pre-employment training, or create incentives for employers to participate in apprenticeship training. These actions have been the hallmark of Australia's reforms and Germany's dual system in the past two decades.

Few countries have pursued reform of vocational education and training as persistently as Australia. After a decade of significant expansion of VET, Australian policymakers realized that expansion by itself was not a solution: the country needed to confront institutional issues that were inhibiting progress. Typically, countries seeking to reform vocational education and training have a VET tradition that is focused strongly on the public sector. Australia's experience shows that a public sector system, by itself, will eventually prove inadequate.

It is reasonable to ask what relevance the experience of a rich country like Australia can have for developing countries or countries in transition to a market economy. The answer is that the issues Australia faced were not unique, and its experience confirms that these problems are not easily resolved. The Australian experience highlights the importance of basing reform on sound institutions.

With the establishment of the Australian National Training Authority, the government sought to engage employers and the unions, not as advisors, but as integral parts of the management of the VET system. Countries that have depended on the public sector will find it difficult to adopt such an approach, but it is necessary if they are to get full value for their VET investments. Australia's experience also demonstrates how difficult it is to forge relevant links between the VET system and the labor market. The solution in Australia was the establishment of a single national ministry encompassing employment, education, and training. By joining all the players in one institution, Australia was able to resolve competing priorities more effectively.

For market forces to work, however, countries must do more than create an institutional framework that involves industry. Financial mechanisms that support the central role of employers must be put in place as well. The chapter on Germany provides more evidence in favor of this argument. In Germany the organization and control of vocational education and training are left to the body that pays for the instruction: state and local governments pay for and control relatively general skills that are acquired in school, and employers pay for and determine job-specific training acquired in the workplace. This is the so-called dual system.

It is unrealistic to expect a system that has matured in a highly industrialized country with strong workers' and employers' unions and well-developed regulatory and administrative mechanisms to be readily adaptable to countries lacking these attributes. However, such countries can learn general lessons from Germany's apprenticeship experience. The chapter on Germany summarizes the main features of the VET system, analyzes its institutional and financial prerequisites, and explains which aspects are applicable in low- and middle-income countries and which are likely to be prohibitively costly. Differences in the sectoral and size distribution of firms and high costs may pose insurmountable obstacles to developing countries eager to import the dual system, but its fundamental attributes are relevant across a broad socioeconomic spectrum.

Efforts by developing countries to adopt Germany's system are often characterized by governments, not employers, taking the lead in organizing and financing vocational training. Germany introduced the vocational education component of its VET system many years after the vocational training part had been formalized, a sequence that is often reversed in developing countries. Participation in the German dual system is voluntary; coercive measures, such as mandated minimum training requirements or levies, are inconsistent with the German model. Finally, the dual system is not cheap in any setting. It is likely that the dual system will be an expensive way to divert students in developing countries from pursuing higher education.

# 18 Australia

ALAN ABRAHART AND ZAFIRIS TZANNATOS

FEW COUNTRIES HAVE PURSUED the reform of vocational education and training (VET) as persistently as Australia. Change has been a constant theme for more than 20 years. A decade of significant expansion of VET did not yield the desired results. The country then confronted deep-rooted institutional issues that were inhibiting progress toward improved outcomes. As Australia's experience shows, no quick fixes are available. Reform must adapt as a country's economic, industrial, political, and social circumstances change. Understanding the institutional framework in which VET is set is vitally important. Institutional impediments need to be confronted no matter how difficult they are to overcome, if progress is to be made.

## Labor Market

By any measure Australia is wealthy. Earlier this century that wealth was based on agricultural products, especially the wool industry. The country has always had a reasonably significant manufacturing sector, which it built up during the 1950s and 1960s, largely behind tariff walls. Following the oil crisis in the mid-1970s, growth in the gross domestic product fell, and unemployment, which had rarely surpassed 2 percent, rose to more than 6 percent. This problem persisted. Unemployment rates in 1997 reached more than 8 percent.

Table 18-1 shows the growth of employment in industry between 1976 and 1994, and the Australian government's assessment in 1995 of its pros-

TABLE 18-1
Average Annual Growth of Industrial Employment,
Selected Years, 1976-2005
(percent)

| Industry | Actual 1976–86 | Actual 1987–94 | Projected 1995–2005 |
|---|---|---|---|
| Agriculture | 0.8 | –0.4 | 2.5 |
| Mining | 2.1 | –1.1 | 0.0 |
| Manufacturing | –1.2 | 0.2 | 0.1 |
| Electricity, gas, and water | 3.1 | –4.8 | –2.3 |
| Construction | 0.3 | 2.0 | 2.4 |
| Wholesale and retail | 2.0 | n.a. | n.a. |
|   Wholesale | n.a. | 1.7 | 4.0 |
|   Retail | n.a. | 2.4 | 3.2 |
| Transport and storage | 2.2 | –0.5 | –0.4 |
| Communication | 2.4 | –1.5 | 3.3 |
| Financial and business services | 4.5 | n.a. | n.a. |
|   Finance | n.a. | 0.4 | 3.7 |
|   Property | n.a. | 5.4 | 1.2 |
| Public administration | 1.7 | 1.1 | 2.7 |
| Community services | 3.7 | n.a. | n.a. |
|   Education | n.a. | 2.1 | 2.6 |
|   Health | n.a. | 3.1 | 2.7 |
| Recreation, personal, and other services | 2.2 | n.a. | n.a. |
|   Recreation | n.a. | 4.6 | 0.6 |
|   Personal services | n.a. | 3.2 | 2.9 |
|   Accommodation and restaurants | n.a. | 5.3 | 4.0 |
|    Total employment | 1.6 | 1.7 | 2.2 |

n.a. Not available.
*Source:* Actual: ABS (various issues); projections: Government of Australia (1995).

pects in the immediate future. Employment in agriculture, utilities (gas, electricity, water), transport, and storage declined, and this decline may well continue. Manufacturing employment remained more or less stable in absolute numbers, although its share declined given the overall increase in the level of employment. The changes have been associated with the decline in traditional job opportunities for male, blue-collar, full-time workers. New jobs have been created largely in the services sector.

AUSTRALIA   467

   The projected growth rate of the labor force suggests average growth of only 1.6 percent per year, compared with the previous rate of 2 percent (Government of Australia 1995). The decline will be the result of expected reductions in the rate of natural increase of the population, in the level of immigration, and in changes to the population's age structure. As has been the case for many years, newly created jobs will be more suitable for new entrants to the labor force (not only young people but mature women in particular) than for those who have been working for some time. Women are expected to increase their share in the labor force, increasing the trend toward part-time work and other flexible arrangements, with significant consequences for the composition of the labor force. Table 18-2 shows changes to the gender composition of the labor force and the incidence of full-time and part-time work. Note that an additional factor contributing to flexibility is the growth in self-employment. Between 1978 and 1995 the number of self-employed persons rose from 550,000 to 820,000, an increase of 50 percent

TABLE 18-2

Structure of the Labor Force, by Gender, Selected Years, 1978-2005

(percent)

| Gender of employee and duration of job | Actual | | | Projected 2005 |
|---|---|---|---|---|
| | 1978 | 1986 | 1994 | |
| *Women* | | | | |
| Full-time | 24 | 25 | 25 | 27 |
| Part-time | 12 | 15 | 17 | 19 |
| Total | 36 | 40 | 42 | 46 |
| *Men* | | | | |
| Full-time | 60 | 56 | 52 | 47 |
| Part-time | 3 | 4 | 6 | 7 |
| Total | 64 | 60 | 58 | 54 |
| *Employee of either gender* | | | | |
| Full-time | 84 | 81 | 76 | 74 |
| Part-time | 16 | 19 | 24 | 26 |
| Total | 100 | 100 | 100 | 100 |

*Note:* Figures subject to rounding.
*Source:* Actual: ABS (various issues); projections: Government of Australia (1995).

Changes in the demand for goods and services are also expected to affect future employment and future training needs. Growth is expected to be strongest in service sector industries such as finance, health, personal services, retail, and tourism. Employment in manufacturing is unlikely to grow much, or may even decline as the industry attempts to improve its international competitiveness through productivity gains and the resultant cutbacks in jobs. Other industrial sectors, such as electricity, gas, and water, will also attempt to increase their efficiency through reforms that will result in further adjustments in employment levels.

Whether Australia will be able to reduce the high level of unemployment that has persisted for over two decades depends on many factors. Perhaps the most important will be the economy's ability to make the necessary investment, trade, and financial links that would better integrate domestic opportunities of a relatively small economy with international economic conditions. The response of the VET system is also a critical factor. In the following sections we review this system and derive the main lessons of Australia's experience with reforms.

## The Institutional Context of VET

The VET system is firmly embedded in two institutional frameworks—the government framework and the industrial relations framework. Each had a profound effect on the way the system was established and developed, and each gives rise to issues that have dominated the reform process.

### The Government Framework

Australia is a federation of states. The constitutional responsibility for education and training is vested in state governments. The central element of VET has long been an apprenticeship system: state governments provide formal training in technical institutes, and employers provide on-the-job training. This arrangement typifies what has become widely known as a dual system, and it has been confined to traditional crafts (journeyman occupations) in sectors such as manufacturing, agriculture, and construction.

Despite its limited constitutional role, the federal government has managed to play a strong role in education and training for many years, particularly in higher education. This stemmed partly from its responsibility for providing income support (such as education allowances) and social security (pensions and benefits) for the general population, and partly from its responsibility as the collector of income taxes and the main collector of corporate taxes. As revenue collector, the federal government has always sought to influence state policies and programs, usually through income-sharing arrangements and through providing ad hoc funds to the states for what the government perceived to be national priorities. In the early 1970s, the federal government, in an expansionary frame of mind and with the agreement of the states, took over complete responsibility for financing and directly administering higher education. In doing so it abolished fees for higher education.

Until the mid-1970s, the federal government's influence in other education sectors had been limited. With little involvement by the federal government, states had managed both the school system and the vocational education system. When the federal government, in the same expansionary frame of mind, sought to influence the direction of VET, it encountered problems. The shift in federal and state responsibilities did not to prove to be as straightforward as it had been for higher education.

## The Industrial Relations Framework

The second dominating institutional factor that has shaped the history of VET is the industrial relations framework. While Australia's federal system of government may not be not unique, its industrial relations framework is. That framework is legalistic and adversarial. The federal government and all state governments maintain industrial courts intended to manage the complex, and often contentious, relationship between employers and trade unions. For example, the courts formalize industrial agreements between the parties through so-called industrial awards, setting wages and conditions for employment. The courts must ratify changes to awards, a process that, in the event of a dispute, frequently involves conciliation or arbitration.

The apprenticeship system was built into this legal framework from the outset. Education planners perceived it as a way to train young people, and adult apprenticeships were not permitted. Wage levels for apprentices were defined in awards just as they were for any other occupational group or level. Training standards were formalized in the same way. Proposed changes in training standards or age restrictions thus gave rise to changes in awards, something that then required ratification by the industrial courts, or conciliation or arbitration if the change was disputed.

Despite their interest in establishing adult apprenticeships, employers for decades were unable to influence the trade unions in this regard. Workers who developed their skills on the job, thereby effectively reaching skilled occupation status, were unable to convert this ability into a formal qualification, which might have considerably enhanced their marketability. Skill shortages were endemic in Australia for almost 30 years prior to the 1970s. Obtaining agreements about the duration of training, typically four years, proved difficult, even as technological advances changed the occupations covered by the apprenticeship system, and thereby the kind of training required.

As this chapter shows, some VET reforms introduced in the 1980s, particularly the traineeship system, have had to be accommodated within the same framework. This has affected both the speed and shape of reforms.

## Compulsory and Postcompulsory Vocational Education

Australia currently has no vocational schools. Until the 1960s, students interested in apprenticeships or less skilled occupations were usually directed toward what could be described as technical schools. The selection of students for various secondary school streams was based on academic achievement, with higher achievers being directed toward general secondary schools or, in some states, to more select government schools. During the 1960s, however, state education authorities abolished streaming and the distinctions between various secondary schools. Since then they have maintained a single system. School certificates are now obtained at the end of year 10, with higher school certificates awarded at the end of year 12.

With the continuing rise in unemployment among young people after 1974, many became concerned about school leavers' lack of work readiness. To overcome this problem, the federal and state governments implemented work experience schemes, introduced curriculum changes, and allowed some students to attend school and simultaneously participate in the postcompulsory vocational system. In each case the intent was to respond to industry criticisms of the basic lack of skills among many young people, especially among those who left school as soon as they were allowed to do so.

At the same time, however, the number of students who left school early began to decline dramatically. Between 1967 and 1982, retention of students to year 12 increased from about 25 percent to about 33 percent, which was low compared with other countries of the Organization for Economic Cooperation and Development (OECD). Three effects then combined to bring about substantial increases. First, the federal government embarked on a series of income-support reforms for young people still in school and older than 15. Eligibility for these benefits depended on parents' incomes. This reform reduced the cost of education for many young people who otherwise would have probably dropped out of school. Second, public awareness of the returns to education increased sharply. The public became aware that unemployment among young people was concentrated in early school leavers. Third, employers were able to lift their selection criteria for entry-level occupations, not only for apprenticeships, but for occupations (for instance, in the retail industry) that had become major sources of employment for school leavers. Increasingly, those with education beyond the school certificate took up apprenticeships.

The end result was a steady increase in school retention rates. By 1986 retention rates had risen to 50 percent, and by 1992 they were over 75 percent, more than doubling in less than a decade. This rise had a far greater impact on reducing the absolute levels of teenage unemployment than had concurrent labor market interventions on their behalf.

## Technical and Further Education Colleges

The major vehicle for postcompulsory vocational education is the system of technical and further education (TAFE) colleges. They rapidly expanded between 1975 and 1984 (table 18-3). The TAFE system has not been confined to training apprentices. It has provided training in technician-level occupations and paraprofessional fields; English language training for immigrants; and remedial education for secondary school dropouts, allowing them to obtain senior secondary school qualifications through the established examination system. TAFE colleges also offer adults numerous classes ranging from remedial courses to hobby courses. Note in table 18-3 the strong growth in the "other skilled" category, which reflects the increasing use of these colleges as a means of retraining the unemployed. TAFE colleges have always maintained a close association with industry, which in turn has meant an attachment to the industrial relations system. This attachment has also been forged through the strong unionization of the teaching profession, including in TAFE colleges.

With the dramatic economic changes of the mid-1970s, the federal government came to believe that industrial change was required and that it should take the initiative. TAFE became one of its starting points. As the

TABLE 18-3

Enrollments in Technical and Further Education Colleges, 1975–84

(thousands)

| Category | 1975 | 1976 | 1977 | 1978 | 1979 | 1980 | 1981 | 1982 | 1983 | 1984 |
|---|---|---|---|---|---|---|---|---|---|---|
| Professional | 3.5 | 4.8 | 5.7 | 2.4 | 2.5 | 2.8 | 2.9 | 2.8 | 3.1 | 3.2 |
| Paraprofessional | 149.5 | 156.0 | 160.4 | 165.3 | 176.6 | 192.6 | 191.3 | 195.7 | 214.7 | 221.8 |
| Trade | 133.0 | 131.4 | 142.3 | 145.0 | 152.1 | 159.5 | 160.4 | 162.4 | 164.9 | 158.8 |
| Other skilled | 117.5 | 140.0 | 150.2 | 166.5 | 173.4 | 207.8 | 212.9 | 208.5 | 230.2 | 239.4 |
| Preparatory | 96.5 | 102.1 | 108.3 | 117.5 | 123.8 | 127.7 | 151.8 | 139.7 | 164.9 | 174.7 |
| Total | 500.0 | 534.3 | 566.8 | 596.7 | 628.4 | 690.5 | 719.2 | 709.2 | 777.8 | 797.9 |

Source: Government of Australia (1995).

public sector component of the VET system, it was clearly amenable to direct action by the government. In 1974 the government instituted a review that concluded that TAFE was something of a poor cousin within the education system. The government chose to begin providing federal funds directly to the system for capital investment. The funding, however, remained the lesser part of all of the funding for TAFE, especially when recurrent costs are taken into account. Most funding continued to come from state governments.

## Labor Market Programs

As unemployment rose after the mid-1970s, particularly among the young, federal and state governments began spending on ad hoc programs to provide training courses for the young unemployed. This added yet more impetus to the expansion of TAFE. Many courses were short and in relatively new fields for TAFE, requiring a flexibility and responsiveness on the part of TAFE colleges. Their other activities did not ease, and they found themselves with growing responsibilities as well as growing budgets. The growth in the "other skilled" category in table 18-3 reflects growth in school-to-work transition programs as well as in retraining programs for the unemployed.

TAFE colleges were not the only institutions heavily involved in labor market programs. The federal government began financing other training providers, including ad hoc community groups, some local governments, and some voluntary organizations. The number of providers offering unaccredited, usually short-term, training for unemployed young people began to increase rapidly.

## Traineeships

The government's review of labor market programs had noted substantial spending on short-term programs for the unemployed, such as wage subsidies and public works schemes. The government then decided the emphasis should be shifted to training. Traineeships did not replace apprenticeships. Rather, they expanded the concept of a dual system of training into areas not covered by apprenticeships. The level of prerequisites and the degree of skill development for apprenticeships and for traineeships were not the same. Moreover, the duration of traineeships was much shorter than the four-year apprenticeships.

Traineeships were an extremely important initiative, and the reasons for the federal government's enthusiasm were clear. Many saw traineeships as a way to break down the inflexibility of the apprenticeship system. The industrial partners began to talk of training people according to the competencies required, not simply according to a time schedule. Large occupational and industrial groupings came within the purview of the system. In maintaining its historical roots, the apprenticeship system had largely failed to move into new fields, especially in the services sector, where employment growth for young people was concentrated. In 1985 the government committed itself to rapid and significant development of traineeships.

## Enterprise Training

Australian employers, in their own right, have always been heavily involved in training. Apprentices, for example, are trained mostly on the job. They typically are released by employers for formal training in technical and further education colleges for only one day a week, though under alternative arrangements they may be released for a few weeks at a time. Major employers are accredited to provide much of their own off-the-job as well as on-the-job training. Indeed, many employers train more than the number of crafts workers they actually need. Major companies did not cease this practice unless they began restructuring, a process that usually entailed substantial reductions in their overall staffing levels.

Employers who accept apprentices take on significant financial and legal commitments. Apprentices are usually indentured to employers for four years. Although apprenticeships impose obligations on both parties, they are probably stronger on employers, who are unable to break indentures without applying for a cancellation through a state-governed apprenticeship board. Because of the costs to employers, apprenticeship training is affected by economic cycles. During the 1982–83 recession, for example, the number of apprenticeship commencements declined by 27 percent, and the number of indentures canceled increased by 7 percent.

Employers are also involved in on-the-job-training and skill development in general. Studies around 1976 showed that employers sufficiently trained significant numbers of staff to undertake work in craft occupations. Nonetheless, these employees lacked credentials and hence were not formally qualified. This became most apparent in companies that began to retrench workers, including informally trained skilled crafts workers. State governments and the industrial partners agreed that ways would need to be found to provide qualifications for these workers and accredit this sort of training in the future.

Employers train in areas not covered by apprenticeships. For example, they train in entry-level occupations in the service industries. Industries such as banking and tourism have built up considerable expertise of their own. They are leaders in determining industry training requirements, and they push to meet those requirements, either on their own or through co-operation with training providers.

## Financing VET

Employers have traditionally borne most of the costs of training. For example, employers pay their apprentices full-time wages, including for periods of release to TAFE colleges, and they bear many other direct costs. As already noted, this direct cost to employers made training susceptible to employers' responses to economic cycles. The federal government's approach during the period of expansion of TAFE was to provide direct funding for apprentices. It gave employers wage subsidies and bounties for apprentice commencements, and it fostered group apprenticeship schemes. In addition, a large part of the administrative costs was picked up by the federal government. The government's objectives were to address two concerns: maintaining training at a reasonable level even during economic downturns, and dealing with the intransigent levels of unemployment among young people.

Many large employers undertook a great deal of training, but the government was concerned that many others were failing to make even minimum provisions for training their employees. It moved to correct this by introducing what it termed the training guarantee. With the exception of those small employers already exempt from payroll taxes, other employers were obliged, through their annual tax returns, to pay a levy equivalent to their shortfall in achieving a set minimum target for spending on training. The minimum was defined as equivalent to 2 percent of an employer's payroll (a figure based largely on OECD analyses of enterprise training). Employers who met the minimum paid no levy. The revenue collected was to be returned to employers (not to public sector training providers) in the form of training activities. Tripartite committees empowered to assess applications for funds would determine the training activities.

The guarantee was introduced in the early 1990s over a three-year period. It rose from an initial 1 percent in the first year to the full 2 percent in the third year. The guidelines for the scheme were debatable. For instance, employers could include administrative and accounting costs as eligible expenditures. Nevertheless, employers were able to demonstrate that they were bearing costs for training. Indeed, many of them were bearing considerable costs. In the three years of the scheme, the federal government collected virtually nothing, and thus set the minimum at zero in the third year. Although it did not abolish the scheme as such, it effectively reversed its earlier policy.

## Major VET Issues

Despite the expansion of the VET system until the mid-1980s, it remained subject to criticism. Critics charged that the system was too inflexible to respond quickly to skill shortages or to adjust to new demands in the labor market. VET procedures and standards, they said, were out of date and no longer cost effective. The period of expansion of government provision of vocational education and training led to a reconsideration of institutional issues and financial issues. Those VET reforms continued after 1985.

### Institutional Issues

The federal government addressed institutional issues relating to government structures, industrial relations, and accreditation.

REFORMS TO GOVERNMENT STRUCTURES. From 1975 to 1985 the federal government increasingly intervened in the labor market. In particular, it introduced major changes in the relationship between the ministries of Employment and Education. The different approaches of these two ministries can be observed in many countries, and Australia is no exception. Focused increasingly on economic objectives, the government gave the Ministry of Employment growing responsibilities. To develop traineeships, the ministry became involved in negotiations with employers and unions to assess needs and determine the type of training required. It also implemented programs for the unemployed, which led to a significant increase in the number of non-TAFE training providers, both profit and nonprofit based. Nevertheless, TAFE, which formed part of state education ministries, remained the country's major vehicle for the VET system's formal training component. The engagement between employment and education portfolios at the state and federal levels reached new heights.

At the federal level the government found itself unwilling to tolerate the division between the Education and Employment ministries and combined them. Since its role in education was mainly as a financier rather than as an administrator, the federal government was able to take major initiatives in setting policy. It decided to do this to bring about an even closer relationship between the vocational education system and the labor market. Its approach was not confined to TAFE but spilled over into the higher education system, where increasing costs had led the government to conclude that higher education institutions had to be more efficient. In particular, they needed to carry greater teaching loads and relate their courses to the needs of the economy. Eventually, some states followed the federal government and brought their labor and education portfolios under one umbrella.

THE AUSTRALIAN NATIONAL TRAINING AUTHORITY. The second major reform was the establishment of the Australian National Training Authority (ANTA) by the federal and state governments. ANTA was required to work on behalf of all the governments acting in unity. This was particularly important since the constitutional responsibilities of the two layers of government remained unchanged. ANTA was established as a company; the federal and state governments were equal shareholders. The authority was set up in one of the state capitals supported by its own secretariat.

All governments recognized that their role in developing vocational education and training could not be paramount to the role of employers and trade unions. Even though the formal structures of industrial courts had changed somewhat and industrial legislation had been amended, the industrial roots of the VET system were intact. All developments in vocational training still depended on industrial agreements being reached. As a result, employers and unions were incorporated into ANTA, thereby making it a tripartite authority.

Through ANTA, governments and the industrial partners embarked on an ambitious plan to develop new accreditation procedures, to encourage new training providers, and to develop a nationwide system of assessment and certification. The most important task, however, was to develop new competency standards on an industry-by-industry basis. The approach to this task was based on the understanding that the major responsibilities should not be vested in government bureaucracies. The central intent was to pass control from the suppliers of a skilled work force, hitherto mainly government organizations, to those who gave rise to the demand in the first place, that is, industry.

ACCREDITATION. Accreditation procedures across the states were inconsistent. One state did not necessarily recognize courses of study and diplomas offered in another state, skills learned on the job were not readily recognized, and no formal method was available to distinguish between the courses offered by public and private institutions. The development of competency-based training and the subsequent adoption of a set of national competency standards helped to overcome some of these problems.

The move to achieve competency-based training is largely industry driven. The skills in demand in the economy and the standards to be achieved in those skills are being set by industry. The public VET system, essentially TAFE, is being required to adhere to those standards and to issue certificates that attest to that fact. So too are major enterprises, such as those in the motor vehicle industry. They have long conducted both on-the-job and off-the-job training, the latter in formal classroom settings that are as well established as any public institution. Such industry courses are being accredited through the same process as the TAFE courses.

The burgeoning private sector training providers may subscribe to the same accreditation processes if they choose to do so. Long-established private providers have well-earned reputations that suggest that there is no great need or urgency for them to subscribe. Indeed, they are likely to be more instrumental in setting the standards than in following them.

One major advantage of training standards is that they allow participants maximum flexibility in moving between education systems—from secondary school to VET and from VET to higher education. As important as anything else in the system is the notion that development paths, especially for the young, should not be closed off. Figure 18-1 is a schematic representation of the system. Level I Certificates from the VET system are regarded as educationally equivalent to Senior Certificates from secondary schools. Diplomas and advanced diplomas may be issued by the VET system or by higher education institutes. Depending on the courses of study, credits may be allowed as participants choose to move between the three sectors. Note that some VET certificates may be issued to persons with little or no formal training (for example, to enterprise workers who have obtained their skills over a number of years on the job).

## Financing

While some people might think that the financing of VET is not as big an issue in a country like Australia as it is in developing countries, it clearly is.

FIGURE 18-1
The Scope of VET in Australia

| Secondary school | VET sector | Higher education |
|---|---|---|
| Senior certificate | Certificate I | |
| | Certificate II | |
| | Certificate III | |
| | Certificate IV | |
| | Diploma | Diploma |
| | Advanced diploma | Advanced diploma |
| | | Bachelor's degree |
| | | Graduate certificate |
| | | Graduate diploma |
| | | Master's degree |
| | | Doctorate |

Employers, of necessity, are concerned with containing their own costs and continue to look critically at the cost of training. States, as the major financiers for TAFE, have always wanted to make sure their money was being spent effectively and efficiently. The federal government, as the main agent for policy initiatives, has also grown increasingly interested in a more cost-effective system. Trainees and students, however, have probably been less concerned about costs. When the reforms began, they bore few direct costs for any of the training they received. As we will explain in the following sections, the federal and state governments acted in a number of different ways to bring about a new distribution of costs between themselves and users.

STUDENT CHARGES. By the mid-1980s the federal government, with its sole management responsibilities for higher education, was finding that the decision it had taken a decade earlier to abolish higher education fees was difficult to sustain. Consequently, it introduced the higher education contribution, which initially covered roughly 20 percent of the actual cost of higher education. Students were given the option of paying the charge up front at a discount, or of paying from their subsequent earnings through income tax. Charges accumulated over the duration of a course were accumulated as a future taxation debt. Naturally, charges could not be recouped through income tax during those times when former students had no income, either because they were unemployed or out of the labor force.

However, the federal government took no action concerning student charges or fees for TAFE. This was left to the states, given their continuing administrative and financial responsibilities for TAFE. In their turn, the states did not consider the wholesale introduction of student charges, since the states viewed most TAFE courses as alternatives to senior secondary schooling. However, they scrutinized such courses as hobby courses, adult courses, and repeat courses, and in most cases subjected them to substantial, or even full, cost recovery. In addition, the states restricted their provision of funds to TAFE to what they regarded as core activities.

TRAINEE WAGES. Traineeships had opened up the question of trainee wages. The wages paid to young people generally had been a contentious issue for at least a decade before the review. In the early 1970s, before the economic shocks, unions pushed for reducing the age at which adult wages were paid to 18 years. For instance, the wage for a first-year apprentice fitter was increased from 33 percent of a qualified fitter's wage to 42 percent. Traineeships offered an opportunity to reconsider the wages paid to young people.

It was not until 1996 that the government announced new measures designed to realign the cost sharing of training for apprentices and other trainees by introducing a training wage. It proposed that the training wage be calculated to recompense trainees for their productive work, but not for the time they spent on training, which was unproductive from an employer's point of view. Calculating the balance between training and productive work will be the responsibility of an agency established for that purpose. Trainees will be asked to bear a far greater share of the cost of training. However, in anticipation of the possibility that the training wage might fall below an acceptable standard, the government proposed topping up the wage to bring it to an agreed minimum.

The proposal to introduce trainee wages represents the most important development in VET so far. It shifts a large part of the cost away from employers—in the main to trainees but to some extent to the government. How the balance of cost sharing will evolve through this new system remains to be seen.

ADOPTION OF A MARKET SYSTEM. The federal government and state governments have both wanted to improve the efficiency and effectiveness of the TAFE system. The states have negotiated new employment conditions affecting teachers' workloads (for example, with regard to teaching hours and the structure of the teaching year). These reforms were not easy to achieve. The most important moves for the long-term future of vocational education and training have come about through the governments' introduction of market elements in an attempt to shift the VET system from a supplier's to a buyer's market.

The federal Ministry of Employment received funds for retraining the unemployed, for restructuring industry, for setting up group training schemes, and for promoting industry involvement in training. The ministry introduced competitive bidding among training providers. Training courses were put out for bids, and although TAFE colleges maintained their position as the major supplier, others began entering the field. The community-based training network that the ministry was financing separately was allowed to submit bids, as were private providers. The number of small providers increased greatly as a result of this initiative.

The governments also debated the question of who should be receiving the direct financial support: the suppliers or the buyers. They concluded that employers should be allowed to use nongovernment training providers, including for apprenticeship training, even though in many cases such providers did not yet exist. Employers would be supported to buy training from whatever supplier seemed to them to be the most appropriate, rather than having funds go automatically to TAFE or other government-funded providers.

In 1996 the federal and state governments moved to implement their conclusions, a process completed by 1998. Employers are now able to negotiate with training providers of their own choosing. Many choose to remain with TAFE colleges, however. Training must be in accordance with standards agreed to by the industrial partners. The governments will provide the financing for the negotiated agreements up to a given maximum; beyond that employers must bear the cost themselves.

## Lessons Learned

Are the experiences of a country like Australia applicable to developing countries or to countries in transition to market economies? This is a relevant question to ask. After all, Australia is developed—not only economically but also institutionally. It is in the area of institutional change that the Australian experience offers the most pointers for others.

Countries seeking to reform vocational education and training usually have a tradition that is focused strongly, if not entirely, on the public sector. Countries in transition, for example, have virtually no private sector tradition at all, either among business enterprises or within the VET sector. Developing countries also tend to be driven by the public sector, if only because of the strong role that governments and their agencies usually play in guiding national affairs. As far as VET is concerned, Australia shows that a public sector system, by itself, will eventually prove inadequate to handle the entire task.

### Expanding VET without Institutional Change Rarely Works

Often the first object of reform in developing countries, and perhaps even more so in transitional economies, is to expand public sector VET by investing in new or substantially upgraded facilities, equipment, and training materials. Investments also frequently provide for curriculum development and teacher training or for improved employment conditions for those already in the system. All this is usually done in anticipation of a growing demand for skills even when the projected growth may be quite distant in time or extremely uncertain. Countries assume that once they have made the investments, good returns will follow. However, case studies have demonstrated that such investments should not be made without greater certainty about future labor market demand.

Australia's experience reflects the same reality, but it also underscores the importance of basing reform on sound institutions. Indeed, without this investments are likely to be counterproductive and turn bad systems into expensive bad systems. One particular problem concerns the relationships among the industrial partners, employers, and unions and between each of them and the VET system. In this respect, a great deal depends on the broader relationship between the industrial partners and the government. Australia can regard itself as fortunate in having strong industrial partners, but this is not enough. With the establishment of ANTA, the government sought to engage the employers and unions, not as advisors, but as integral parts of the executive management of the VET system.

Such an approach is extremely difficult to adopt in countries that have depended on the public sector for their development. Countries encouraged to follow the same approach often come to regard it as too difficult and end up making little or no effort to bring about change. In the end, however, employers must become involved in VET for countries to realize the full value of their investments.

### Links with the Labor Market Must Be Predominant

Australia's experience demonstrates the difficulty of keeping the link between the VET system and the labor market secure and relevant. A great deal of work is required to maintain this link. If the connection with the labor market is weak, the system will fail. Part of the answer lies in forging effective ties with industry as partners in the executive management of VET. The government also should look closely at its own internal structures and operations.

In many countries a tension exists between achieving educational objectives and achieving labor market objectives. Resolving these tensions is not easy, even in industrial countries, and solutions change as the relative strengths of different government organizations ebb and flow. Countries with well-entrenched public sectors where interagency discussions are often weak have an even more difficult task. The solution in Australia was to amalgamate the players into a single entity—the Australian National Training Authority. With the establishment of a single national ministry encompassing employment, education, and training, competing priorities were resolved closer to the operating level and had far less chance to create conflict among trainers and confusion among students.

### VET Financing Should Support Market Forces

Allowing market forces to work does not depend only on an institutional framework that involves industry in determining its own training needs. With the establishment of ANTA, Australia has gone farther than most in doing this. Financial mechanisms that will support market directions also are needed. This can be achieved to some extent by ensuring that costs are shared. Too often, however, training levies are seen as a way to expand and strengthen the public sector system. Unfortunately, extracting training levies without any regard to the labor market is too easy.

Costs are best apportioned in a way that enables the buyer to exercise judgment. Competition among suppliers is essential. This again implies a shift in control and management away from the public sector toward employers and VET participants. Industry, in particular, should become the main force behind the development of training standards, assessment procedures, and accreditation. However, in the end, industry needs must be determined pragmatically. Accreditation, for example, is important to most employers only in so far as it genuinely provides them with information they would not otherwise have about the type and quality of training being offered. It should not be used as a means of enforcing de facto licensing on training providers, a move that protects public sector providers more than consumers. In short, VET should benefit buyers more than suppliers.

## References

ABS (Australian Bureau of Statistics). various issues. *The Labour Force.* Report 6203.0. Sydney.

Government of Australia, Department of Employment, Education, and Training, Economic Policy Analysis Division. 1995. *Australia's Work Force 2005: Jobs in the Future.* Canberra: Australian Government Publishing House.

# 19 Germany

## INDERMIT S. GILL AND AMIT DAR

GERMANY'S APPROACH to vocational education and training (VET)—the so-called dual system introduced in 1969—strengthens the links between education and employment. The system is "dual" because vocational education and occupational training are provided simultaneously (that is, during a single program of work and study) to participants by schools and employers respectively. The system is believed to be an effective strategy for keeping youth unemployment low and ensuring an adequate supply of skilled workers.

For these reasons the dual system is an alluring alternative for other countries, some of which have sought German technical assistance in transforming their VET systems to resemble Germany's. Concerned that its supply of technicians was not keeping pace with the demands of a rapidly expanding economy, the Republic of Korea experimented with cooperative training and a master technician training college in the 1980s; German training experts actively assisted in this effort. In the early 1990s President Hosni Mubarak, faced with high unemployment among Egyptian youth, asked German chancellor Helmut Kohl for his country's assistance in reforming Egypt's VET system. More recently, Indonesia, in dealing with youth unemployment and perceived skills shortages, attempted—with German help—to introduce the dual system.[1]

Imbalances between the demand and supply of skilled workers have been experienced at various times by all countries, and they have been addressed in different ways depending upon the countries' education-related and labor-related institutions. Japan, for example, has eschewed vocational education in favor of formal, lifelong in-service training. The United States has

485

resisted vocationalizing secondary education. Instead, it has relied largely on a process of matching jobs with job-seekers through job changes and subsequent informal on-the-job training of workers with relatively high education levels. Like Germany, Japan and the United States have maintained relatively low unemployment rates among youth and have ensured a steady supply of skilled workers. Germany, with well-defined relations between central and state governments and a labor market with powerful unions, has taken a different approach.

This chapter reviews the main features of vocational education and training in Germany and analyzes the institutional and financial prerequisites for an effective dual system. Some aspects of the dual system are applicable in low- and middle-income countries, and others are likely to be prohibitively costly. Before we examine the dual system in more depth, we will briefly discuss how other industrialized countries have tried to ensure strong linkages between the education system and the workplace.

## Country Comparisons

France, Japan, and the United States have adopted quite different approaches to VET under varying institutional and labor market conditions (table 19-1). The comparisons made in this section between these countries and Germany may help to underscore the conditions under which the dual system operates.

### Education

As the table shows, the education levels of workers in 1990 were higher in the United States than in Germany and Japan. Almost 37 percent of the U.S. population had more than a secondary education in the United States. Japanese workers—one-fifth of whom had more than secondary schooling—fell in the middle between the United States and Germany. In most low-income countries, educational levels are considerably lower. Education levels in middle-income countries and countries making a transition to a market economy may be closer to West European levels.

### Labor Force

Labor force growth between 1965 and 1995 was highest in the United States (1.7 percent) and lowest in Germany (0.5 percent). The labor force

TABLE 19-1

Skill Formation Mechanisms, Selected Countries of the Organization for Economic Cooperation and Development

(percent)

| Characteristic | Germany | United States | Japan | France |
|---|---|---|---|---|
| *Education level in 1990* | | | | |
| Percentage of population with more than a secondary school education | 7.2 | 36.9 | 19.5 | — |
| *Enrollment ratio in 1990* | | | | |
| Upper secondary school | 88.6 | 90.2 | — | — |
| Tertiary-level school | 28.7 | 65.9 | — | — |
| *Labor force growth* | | | | |
| Annual average (1965–95) | 0.52 | 1.70 | 0.83 | 0.95 |
| *Unemployment* | | | | |
| Average rate (1982–94) | 7.9 | 7.0 | 2.5 | 9.9 |
| Youth rate divided by average rate (1973–89) | 1.25 | 2.75 | — | 3.25 |
| *Vocational education* | | | | |
| What level? | Secondary | Postsecondary | None | Secondary |
| Where? | School (theoretical education); firm (practical education) | Community colleges | None | Vocational schools |
| Who pays? | Government and firm | Government and worker | — | Government |

(Table continues on the following page.)

TABLE 19-1 (continued)

| Characteristic | Germany | United States | Japan | France |
|---|---|---|---|---|
| *On-the-job training* | | | | |
| Structure | Formal | Informal | Mainly formal | Mainly informal |
| Formal for new hires | 71.5 | 10.2 | 67.1 | 23.6 |
| Who pays? | Firm | Worker and firm | Firm | Firm |
| *Training institutes* | | | | |
| Technical/commercial | Commercial | Both | Commercial | Both |
| Public/private | Both | Private | Private | Public |
| *Skill certification* | | | | |
| Central body | Tripartite | None | None | Government |
| Local bodies | Employers and unions | None | Firm-level | Government |
| *Labor contracts* | | | | |
| Union influence | Strong | Weak | Weak | Strong |
| Turnover | Low | High | Low | Low |
| Average tenure (years) | 10.4 | 6.7 | 10.9 | 10.1 |

— Not available

*Source:* Federal Ministry of Education (1995); OECD (1993).

grew by less than 1 percent annually in Japan and France. It is worth keeping in mind that annual labor force growth in low-income countries exceeds 2 percent, while it is closer to 1 percent in most transitional economies and other middle-income countries.

## Unemployment

Unemployment rates averaged about 7 percent in Germany and the United States during the 1980s and early 1990s, lower than the 10 percent average for France but considerably higher than unemployment rates in Japan. In the mid-1990s unemployment rates in Germany and France were much higher (about 12 and 15 percent respectively) than those in the United States and Japan (about 6 and 3 percent respectively). Germany's unemployment rates have remained below the average levels in Europe.

It is difficult to compare unemployment rates in countries in the Organization for Economic Cooperation and Development with rates in developing countries, which generally do not have formal unemployment compensation systems. In transition countries, where such systems do exist, open unemployment rates resemble those in Western Europe. Youth unemployment rates, relative to average rates, are strikingly low in Germany: youth are likely to experience higher unemployment rates than others, but this differential is far higher in the United States and France.

## Labor Relations

Labor unions in Germany and France help ensure that the turnover of workers is low. In Japan, which had implicit lifetime contracts in large firms until recently, the same result was obtained even though unions are relatively weak. The United States' labor market is characterized by lower average tenure on the job. Tenure is about 30 percent shorter in the United States than in Japan, Germany, and France.

## School-to-Work Transitions

When tenure statistics are adjusted for the high turnover that characterizes the U.S. labor market for new entrants, the intercountry differences become much smaller (Hall 1978). Japan, Germany, and the United States take different approaches to matching the skills of labor force entrants to jobs. In Japan more than two-thirds of new hires—who have reasonably high levels of general education—are formally trained by employers. In the United States informal on-the-job training is relied upon to impart job-specific skills to new hires, a large number of whom have some postsecondary education. In Germany, until recently, relatively few labor force entrants had received a postsecondary education. But nearly three-fourths of all new hires in Germany get formal training, mainly through firm-sponsored apprenticeships in conjunction with vocational education provided by the state. This approach has strong intuitive appeal. Employers provide occupation-specific skills to workers, sharing those costs with them through lower wages during the apprenticeship period, and taxpayers finance more general—but still work-relevant—vocational education. It is hardly surprising that many developing nations want such a system.

## Experiments in Korea, Indonesia, and Egypt

During the past decade or so, countries at varying levels of development have sought to import the dual system. German training experts can be found in countries as diverse as China, the Czech Republic, Egypt, Eritrea, the former Soviet Union, Indonesia, the Republic of Korea, Laos, Lebanon, Malaysia, Tunisia, and the West Bank and Gaza. We do not attempt an evaluation of efforts to adapt the dual system to the special circumstances in developing and transition countries. But in Korea, Egypt, and Indonesia information on German-assisted experiments with the dual system is available, and we have found their experiences useful.

### Korea's Cooperative Training and Industrial Master's College

Since the early 1970s, Germany has provided financial and consulting aid for establishing public vocational training institutes in South Korea. Jeong (1995) has informally evaluated two initiatives to introduce the German dual system in Korea: the cooperative training program and the Changwon Industrial Master's College. The aim of the comparative training program was to provide industrial workers with adaptable skills. Public vocational training institutes provide theoretical and basic practical training, while firms provide applied and specialized training. The Changwon Industrial Master's College was set up to improve the skills, earnings, and social status of persons in the intermediate managerial category (similar to the German "meister" class). Between 1982 and 1991 the college had more than 3,000 graduates, including about 600 master craftsmen.

The operative training program failed to generate the multiple and highly adaptable skills envisioned. No training was conducted within firms: the apprentices were instead used as low-wage workers. Managers of machine tool firms stated that there were no significant differences between the skills of graduates of comparative training and the skills of graduates of other training institutions. Interviews with personnel managers at machine tool firms confirm that "master craftsman" is just a nominal title; graduates of the Changwon Industrial Master's College do not perform the functions of workers in an intermediate managerial category. The prestige envisioned for Changwon Industrial Master's College graduates did not materialize because of a strong societal preference for higher education (Jeong 1995).

## Indonesia's "System Ganda"

Indonesia's "System Ganda" is a pilot program begun in 1994 that targets the "best" 250 government vocational and technical schools. About 6,000 small and medium companies were expected to participate. Apprentices attend school and are placed in jobs for three or four years. The length of programs is chosen to keep approximate parity with senior secondary education. The government bears the cost of in-school vocational education; in-firm training expenses are borne by the companies. The annual unit cost of System Ganda is about US$2,000, which is almost four times the cost of senior secondary education and about three times the per capita gross national product (GNP).

A 1995 survey found that participation in the system was negligible despite active encouragement by the government. Other surveys point to the usual reasons apprenticeship programs in low-income countries falter: students prefer general education to vocational streams, and companies are not keen to offer apprenticeships because they consider them to be unprofitable. Moreover, a vibrant private training sector in Indonesia has been effective in providing school leavers with skills required for quick placement in jobs (World Bank 1995).

## Egypt's Mubarak-Kohl Initiative

This high-profile effort sought to use German experience to revive the tradition of apprenticeships in Egypt that had been stifled in a command economy. Egyptian policymakers believed that the German dual system could be adapted in a way that would transform the apprenticeship system into one that would meet the needs of a modern economy. They planned six high-level training centers like those in Germany. The centers would be fully funded by the Germans. Practical training would be with local manufacturing firms. Two centers near Cairo were inaugurated in 1995 (Ministry of Education 1995).

The German dual system is unlikely to be implemented on a wide scale in Egypt because of the predominance there of small and microenterprises. Such firms often do not participate in the dual system in Germany. Small Egyptian firms may be hesitant to bear the costs because they do not expect immediate benefits from participating in formalized apprenticeship programs. In Germany apprentices hired in the dual system are paid wages lower than those mandated or collectively determined for entry-level workers, resulting in immediate benefits for small employers. And a system that is planned and supervised largely by the Ministry of Education is unlikely to elicit the enthusiasm of large employers. The Egyptian government and private sector representatives may overestimate training demands, especially for technical workers. Although international experience suggests that technicians are less than 10 percent of the work force in most manufacturing firms, Egyptian officials are aiming for twice this ratio.

## Germany's Dual System

It may seem unrealistic to expect a system that has matured in Germany—a rich country that is highly industrialized, has strong workers' and employers' unions, and well-developed local, state and federal government regulatory and administrative mechanisms—to be readily adapted to low- and middle-income countries that do not share any of these attributes, but it is our belief that these countries *can* learn from the German apprenticeship experience. Although the dual system cannot be transplanted as a whole or even in parts, all countries can learn valuable lessons by carefully examining the principles on which the system is based (table 19-2 and box 19-1).

### Organization and Institutional Framework

The German apprenticeship is a joint undertaking between the public and private sectors. Theoretical aspects of training are provided in publicly run and financed vocational secondary schools, and practical aspects in firms

TABLE 19-2

Organization, Regulation, and Financing of Germany's Dual System

| Feature | Vocational education | Training |
|---------|---------------------|----------|
| Venue | School | Firm |
| Duration | One year full time or 1 to 2 days a week for 3 or 3.5 years or more | Two years, full time or 3 to 4 days per week for 3 or 3.5 years |
| Curriculum | General education; job-related theory | Occupation-specific training |
| Legal framework | State school laws | Federal training laws; industry rules and regulations |
| Teacher | Theory teacher (university degree plus practical training); practical teacher (secondary degree, master craftsman title or technical diploma, plus work experience) | Vocational trainers (master craftsman or equivalent) |
| Costs | Staff, material, and plant | Trainee compensation; staff, material, and plant |
| Funding | State and municipal tax revenues | Employers |
| Responsibility | State ministries of education and culture | Employers, with federal regulations and union monitoring |

*Source:* Adapted from Dicke, Glismann, and Siemben (1994).

that provide and finance apprenticeships. The program usually lasts about three years for commercial trades—longer for technical occupations. Apprentices spend one or two days each week in vocational schools, and the remainder in the firm. In small firms, apprentices acquire skills through learning by doing; in large firms training is often in specialized centers (Bosch 1993). In the early 1990s about 600,000 firms, 700 interfirm training centers (organized by firms that cannot provide in-plant training), and 1,800 schools participated in the dual system (Soskice 1994).

BOX 19-1
Salient Features of Germany's Dual System of Training

- The dual system in Germany has evolved from the medieval tradition of guild training. Employers, unions, government, and research institutions all play important roles.
- Students over the age of 15 are prepared for higher education in *gymnasia*, or the dual system prepares them for work. Many of those who complete education in *gymnasia* also go through dual system programs.
- Most of the recognized training companies are small enterprises, but many small firms do not provide training. All large companies provide training places.
- *Berufsschulen*—postsecondary technical and vocational colleges—work with companies to administer three-year programs of vocational education and training.
- Public and private investment in VET is high. The cost of dual system training is high (because of training allowances, the costs of professional trainers, the administrative costs of examinations, and the costs of enforcing standards). The Federal Institute for Vocational Training (BIBB) estimates the gross costs to be about DM30,000 per student per year.
- The costs net of trainee productivity are estimated at DM 18,000. Nonetheless, it is believed that "overall the employment of trainees brings a positive balance to the employer."

*Source:* Adapted from Schmidt and Alex (1995).

## The Role of the Federal Government

After the end of World War II, the *länder*—state governments—were given responsibility for vocational education and training. The Vocational Training Act of 1969 formalized this control. But the Vocational Training Law (*Berufsbildungsgesetz*) governs only enterprise-based training and not school-based education, the other component of the dual system of VET. A formal agreement between the federal government and the state ministries of education and cultural affairs lays out the procedures for coordinating education and training. The Federal Institute for Vocational Training (BIBB) can establish or reform training regulations. It draws up the rules to implement changes in training laws, standards, or curricula after they have been deliberated upon by the employers' associations, unions, and the state governments. It also monitors training costs and effectiveness through periodic nationwide surveys, and it finances federal government initiatives to increase vocational training.[2]

## The Role of State and Local Governments

Vocational schooling can be either full-time or cooperative; both types of schooling are run by state ministries of education and culture. The state ministries of education develop draft curricula for vocational schools. The curricula are supposed to reflect the opinions of employers, but in practice curriculum development in vocational schools is done without the active participation of employers. Vocational schools are financed by municipalities or district governments, which provide equipment and material costs, and the states, which provide personnel costs. The state minister of economics and other "competent" ministers (such as agriculture, justice, and industry) play a more important role than the minister of education in regulating in-firm vocational training. These ministers have some influence in selecting members of the "competent body," which oversees in-firm training in each state.

## The Role of Employers' Associations and Labor Unions

After World War II a pluralist system ensured nongovernment forces a strong influence in important areas of government policy, including VET. Control of vocational training is decentralized among 480 regional chambers. Responsibility for supervision lies with these chambers (employers' associations). Within them vocational training committees are formed. These bodies are passively regulated by the relevant state ministers. Vocational training committees include labor union representatives and vocational education teachers (who only have an advisory role). These committees determine the suitability of firms to provide training, monitor (through training counselors) the quality of training provided by member firms, and take punitive action if necessary (nullify or refuse training contracts). The main conflict in vocational training committees is over training quality. Labor union representatives generally demand more training and, since training counselors are paid by employers, they try to ensure that counselors are even-handed in assessing training activities.[3] Chambers also set up exam committees—consisting of employers, employees, and instructors—for each occupation.

## Reform and Change

Since the early 1960s, debate about the organization and legal framework of VET has become less important, and structural reform and new subject matter have become the dominant concerns due to rapid technological change. The establishment or reform of training regulations can be initiated by labor unions, employers' associations, or by BIBB. The state or local government representative acts only as a notary during the discussion of these reforms. After successful talks, the state minister issues an order to the BIBB to draw up the rules to govern the implementation of these changes, especially regarding the coordination between the federal and state governments. The state ministry develops curricula for vocational schools. BIBB develops a "draft training regulation" for workplace training in cooperation with experts from employers' associations and unions. Employers' associations aim largely to keep workplace training standards reasonable. Unions aim to ensure that wage growth reflects occupational upgrading. Often the only role of the federal government lies in helping forge a compromise, since unanimous consent is required for changes to become law. Syllabi for vocational schools are slow to change; for some subjects, it can take two decades to change the curriculum (*The Economist* 1994). Schools are sluggish in responding to changing technology, but companies—which are half responsible for drafting the curriculum—are also accused of being indifferent to the content of vocational school instruction.

## Profile of Dual System Participants

The ages and education of participants in the dual system vary. The average age of beginners is 18 years. The number of participants in the dual system decreased from 1985 to 1990 and then increased markedly (table 19-3). Germany's demographic trends indicate a sharp fall between 1983 and 1990 in the cohort ages 15 to 19, the age group of most of the participants.

The ratio of participants to the size of this cohort has risen steadily from less than 30 percent in 1975 to more than 40 percent in 1990. It should be kept in mind, though, that youth ages 20 to 24 are increasingly participating in the dual system.

TABLE 19-3
Participation in the Dual System, Selected Years, 1975–92
(millions)

| Year | Number of participants | Population 15–19 years | Participants as a percentage of the 15–19 population |
|------|------------------------|------------------------|------------------------------------------------------|
| 1975 | 1.33 | 4.45 | 29.8 |
| 1977 | 1.40 | 4.81 | 29.1 |
| 1979 | 1.64 | 5.12 | 32.1 |
| 1981 | 1.68 | 5.23 | 32.0 |
| 1983 | 1.72 | 5.19 | 33.2 |
| 1985 | 1.83 | 4.94 | 37.1 |
| 1987 | 1.74 | 4.39 | 39.6 |
| 1988 | 1.66 | 4.12 | 40.4 |
| 1989 | 1.55 | 3.84 | 40.4 |
| 1990 | 1.48 | 3.57 | 41.3 |
| 1991 | — | — | — |
| 1992 | 3.33 | — | — |

— Not available.

*Source:* Bosch (1993); Federal Ministry of Education (1995); ILO (various issues).

In 1970, 80 percent of participants came directly from lower secondary schools (*hauptschule*) and the remainder mostly from short-term vocational secondary schools (*realschule*). By 1989, 34 percent each came from *hauptschule* and *realschule*, while 16 percent each came after finishing general secondary school (*abitur*) and university diploma programs or *fachhochschulreife* (Maurice 1993). Thus the average education level of entrants to the dual system increased by about 15 percent—from 10 years of schooling in 1970 to 11.5 years in 1989. Since then the average education level is believed to have increased even more. In the past two decades, therefore, the average education level (and the age) of participants in the dual system have increased by about two years.

Apprentices in the *handwerk* sector—comprised largely of small artisans—are less well educated than those chosen by *industrie*—defined as large-scale manufacturing and services. Although about 60 percent of *handwerk* apprentices had no more than a lower secondary education in 1989, this ratio was less than 30 percent in the *industrie* sector (table 19-4).

TABLE 19-4

Education Levels of Participants in the Dual System, by Sector, 1989

| Level | Handwerk sector | Industrie sector |
|---|---|---|
| No school-leaving certificate | 5.4 | 0.8 |
| *Hauptschule* certificate | 55.0 | 27.9 |
| *Realschule* certificate | 18.6 | 35.3 |
| *Abitur* | 5.3 | 19.2 |
| Higher education | n.a. | n.a. |

n.a. Not applicable.
*Source:* Soskice (1994).

The increase in the average education level of dual system trainees may be attributed in part to the growing importance of large-scale services.

In 1989 the most common apprenticeships for men were in these fields: auto mechanic, electrician, joiner, clerical worker in trade, and banking. Together they accounted for about a quarter of all male apprenticeships. The most common apprenticeships for women were as hairdressers, clerical workers, and medical assistants. These occupations accounted for a third of all female apprentices. It should be noted that in 1989 there were more than 300 occupational categories for dual system trainees.

### Size Distribution of Participating Firms

Large firms predominate among corporate training institutions. Only about a third of all dual system trainees are in the handwerk sector, which is comprised of small firms. Large companies form the mainstay of the dual system. Soskice (1994) illustrates this well: while almost all firms with more than 500 employees offer apprenticeships, this ratio is close to one-third for firms with fewer than 10 employees (table 19-5). Postapprenticeship retention rates are higher for large firms, which can be rationalized either by differences in the company-specificity of training or because handwerk firms may be more likely to view apprentices as cheap temporary labor than potential long-term employees.[4]

### Sectoral Distribution of Participating Firms

It has been difficult to obtain the distribution of dual system participants by sector, as defined according to international norms. German data report

TABLE 19-5
Employer Participation and Trainee Retention, by Size of Firm, 1985
(percent)

| Number of workers in firm | Firms with apprentices | Post-training retention rate |
|---|---|---|
| 5–9 | 35.0 | 56 |
| 10–49 | 59.0 | 64 |
| 50–99 | 78.0 | 69 |
| 100–499 | 91.0 | 73 |
| 500–1,000 | 99.5 | 82 |
| More than 1,000 | 99.6 | 87 |

*Source:* Soskice (1994).

distributions by categories that are a composite of occupation, company size, and sector. For example, Steedman (1993) reports that in 1990 the shares were as follows: 46 percent in *industrie*, 40 percent in *handwerk*, 3 percent in the public sector, 7 percent in professions, and 3 percent in other sectors. "Craft" training (for example, for garage mechanics, bakers, painters, plumbers, hairdressers) is done in small, *handwerk* firms. Such training is apt to be at a lower level and cost than training in *industrie*, which is generally professional or technical in nature (for example, for bank clerks, machine operators, and nurses).[5]

*Costs*

Detailed cost information is available (although usually in German documents) for company-based training of dual system participants. The BIBB conducted three extensive surveys in 1972, 1980, and 1991, and employer organizations also periodically gather this information. The costs of vocational education have proved much harder to come by, and we report only the most rudimentary statistics here.

COSTS OF COMPANY-BASED INSTRUCTION. Gross costs of company-based instruction include staff, materials, and investment costs (65 percent), and compensation for trainees (35 percent), according to Timmermann (1993). Gross annual costs per apprentice for firms with more than 500 workers were about 30 percent higher than those for firms with fewer than 10 employees in 1991. It is likely that this is because of sectoral-occupational

TABLE 19-6
Costs per Apprentice of Workplace Training in the Dual System,
by Company Size, 1991
(1990 U.S. dollars)

| Number of workers | Gross | Apprentice productivity | Net | Net cost as a percentage of gross cost |
|---|---|---|---|---|
| 1–9 | 16,392 | 7,292 | 9,100 | 56 |
| 10–49 | 16,811 | 6,841 | 9,971 | 59 |
| 50–499 | 18,105 | 7,219 | 10,886 | 60 |
| More than 500 | 21,296 | 6,152 | 15,144 | 71 |
| All firms | 17,645 | 6,987 | 10,657 | 60 |

*Source:* Harhoff and Kane (1996).

differences in training type rather than company size differences per se. BIBB has also estimated costs net of trainee productivity: net per apprentice costs for firms with more than 500 workers were about 66 percent higher than those for firms with fewer than 10 employees in 1991. Note, however, that *absolute* apprentice productivity levels do not differ significantly by company size (table 19-6).

Harhoff and Kane (1996), using BIBB data, report that the costs of workplace training are highest in public service, but this accounts for less than 5 percent of trainees. Among the more important groups, gross training costs in *industrie* (industry and commerce) are about 35 percent higher than those for the *handwerk* sector (crafts). Sectoral-occupational differences in net costs are much more pronounced: in 1980 net costs of training in public service were more than six times the net cost of agricultural apprenticeships. For the two main categories, net costs of training in *industrie* were 57 percent higher than those for the *handwerk* sector. Interestingly, gross and net costs of workplace training more than doubled in real terms between 1972 and 1991, but average net costs remained about 60 percent of gross costs (table 19-7).

COSTS OF SCHOOL-BASED INSTRUCTION. In 1991 the costs of school-based instruction amounted to almost DM8 billion. With almost 2 million apprentices, the treasury costs per student were DM4,000 per year, implying a full-time equivalent of about DM13,000, or about US$8,000:

TABLE 19-7
Costs per Apprentice of Workplace Training in the Dual System,
by Sector, 1972, 1980, 1991
(1990 U.S. dollars)

| Sector | 1972 | | 1980 | | 1991 | |
|---|---|---|---|---|---|---|
| | Gross | Net | Gross | Net | Gross | Net |
| Industry and commerce | 9,971 | 6,123 | 14,654 | 9,381 | 18,988 | 12,237 |
| Crafts | 6,233 | 3,071 | 10,939 | 5,991 | 14,850 | 7,370 |
| Consultancy | 7,869 | 1,890 | 13,199 | 8,499 | — | — |
| Public service | — | — | 17,855 | 17,041 | — | — |
| Agriculture | 6,360 | 453 | 10,420 | 2,746 | — | — |
| Health | 6,299 | 102 | — | — | — | — |
| All sectors | 7,774 | 4,255 | 12,845 | 7,755 | 17,645 | 10657 |

— Not available.
*Source:* Harhoff and Kane (1996).

1.6 times the cost of public university education. Information for school-based instruction is difficult to find, since it is not a federal responsibility.

NET COSTS OF DUAL SYSTEM INSTRUCTION. For every dollar spent by the government, firms spend two dollars as gross costs and about US$1.25 as net costs. If government finances both school-based instruction and workplace instruction for participants in the dual system, the total (gross and net) costs are considerably higher.

## Factors Influencing Applicability in Developing Countries

From the preceding analysis we have identified five of the most striking features of Germany's dual system of training. First, firms pay for and control the content and delivery of vocational training, and the government (taxpayer) pays for and controls the content and delivery of vocational education. Second, small firms tend not to participate in dual system vocational training. Third, the unit costs of school-based vocational education are high, even when compared with university education. The state and local governments meet all of the costs of school-based instruction. Fourth, workplace training is not cheap either, and its costs have risen steeply over the past two decades. Finally, the federal and state governments and German firms appear to respect each other's domains. Federal and state governments set only broad guidelines for the content and delivery standards of workplace training, which firms provide and fund. Firms appear to accept the content and delivery of school-based vocational education, which is provided by the government at taxpayers' expense.

From the perspective of low- and middle-income countries, these features are critical for determining the suitability of the German dual system as an instrument for improving the relevance and efficiency of VET systems. These features suggest three questions that policymakers should consider before attempting to adopt the German dual system in its entirety or any of its components. First, will firms willingly organize and pay for workplace training of apprentices? Second, if they are willing, is the government prepared to relinquish control of vocational training beyond providing oversight and broad guidance? Third, if they are not willing, can the government finance both training and vocational education components? We will examine these questions in turn, contrasting—for illustrative purposes—conditions in Egypt, Indonesia, and Korea with those in Germany.

## Will Firms Organize and Pay for the Training Component?

In this section we explore the implications of structural differences between Germany and other countries interested in importing the system.

DIFFERENCES IN SECTORAL DISTRIBUTION. The dual system is not a small scheme for training labor force entrants. It is "the single biggest (apprenticeship) scheme of all" (*The Economist* 1996). It is pertinent, therefore, to ask whether the employment structure of countries that are seeking to import the system is similar to Germany's. The sectors in which most apprentices are trained—manufacturing and services—have almost 90 percent of employment in Germany compared with 45 percent, 48 percent, and 75 percent respectively in Indonesia, Egypt, and Korea (table 19-8). Only Korea would probably "qualify" for large-scale implementation of the dual system using this criterion. In Egypt and Indonesia a significant share of employment is in subsistence and small-scale agriculture, and the likelihood that an ambitious apprenticeship program would succeed is little.

DIFFERENCES IN SIZE DISTRIBUTION OF FIRMS. Even in the relatively modern manufacturing and services sector in Egypt, Indonesia, and Korea, employment is concentrated in microenterprises and small-scale enterprises

TABLE 19-8

Sectoral Composition of Employment in Germany and Selected
Developing Countries, Selected Years, 1986–90

(percent)

| | Share of employment | | | |
|---|---|---|---|---|
| Sector | Germany 1990 | Rep. of Korea 1991 | Indonesia 1990 | Egypt 1986 |
| Agriculture | 3.6 | 16.7 | 49.9 | 32.7 |
| Mining | 0.8 | 0.4 | 1.0 | 0.4 |
| Manufacturing | 31.6 | 26.6 | 11.4 | 11.2 |
| Construction | 6.6 | 8.3 | 4.1 | 6.2 |
| Services | 57.4 | 48.0 | 33.7 | 37.1 |
| Transport | 5.7 | 5.3 | 3.7 | 4.9 |
| Other | 0.0 | 0.0 | 1.0 | 0.0 |
| Total | 100 | 100 | 100 | 100 |

*Source:* ILO (various years).

(table 19-9). The German experience with the dual system since 1969 clearly shows that very small firms (fewer than 10 employees) usually do not provide apprenticeships, and when they do, they usually do not retain trainees upon completion of the program (Soskice 1994). In Germany employers' associations that oversee vocational training often do not burden their smallest members with the responsibility of accommodating apprentices. In developing countries where even the regulated, formal private sector is dominated by small firms, following this principle would imply marginal participation in the dual system. Even for large firms the threat that if they do not accept apprentices, the government will train job-seekers with funds gathered from taxes on employers may be less credible in settings where tax collection mechanisms are weak.

DIFFERENCES IN REGULATION AND UNION COVERAGE. Firms in developing countries are more likely than German firms to be unregulated and to have weak union representation. (Even in transitional countries, the private sector may be both nascent and largely informal.) Thus it may be difficult for the government or unions to ensure that employers conduct apprenticeships in conformity with established standards and regulations.

TABLE 19-9
Size Distribution of Firms, Selected Countries and Years

| Country | Percentage in small firms | Explanation | Year |
|---|---|---|---|
| Germany | 10.9 | Share of employment in firms with fewer than 10 workers out of all firms registered with the Hanover Chamber of Commerce and Industry. | 1996 |
| Indonesia | 67.3 | Share of manufacturing employment in firms that are classified as home industries and small and medium firms. | 1986 |
| Egypt | 78.0 | Share of construction employment in firms that have fewer than 10 workers | 1984 |
|  | 59.4 | Share of manufacturing employment in private small-scale enterprises | 1984 |

*Source:* Germany: personal communications; Indonesia: Nachrowi, Dwiantini, and Dwiswati (1995); Egypt: Assad (1991), Handoussa and Potter (1991).

In the German *handwerk* sector, where conditions most resemble those in manufacturing and services in developing countries, many German firms use trainees as cheap and flexible labor (Abraham and Houseman 1993). This helps explain the moderate retention rates of trainees among the small firms (table 19-5). In most developing countries, however, minimum wage legislation is either nonexistent or not enforced, which reduces the incentive for firms to take advantage of apprenticeship wage laws to avoid hiring untested workers at high entry wages.

In Germany dismissal of workers is difficult or costly, so participation in a large-scale apprenticeship program may be viewed as a blessing. This may not be the case for small firms in developing countries, where dismissal regulations and mandated severance benefits are not enforced strictly (for instance, in Egypt), or not strictly enough (for example, in Indonesia or Korea).[6] Even where such regulations are strict and binding, the absence of strong unions for workers may result in training of poor quality. This training can be monitored mainly at the place of delivery. Employers have been coerced (or artificially induced through incentives) into providing it. Apprentice training in Germany conforms most with regulations in those sectors or occupations where powerful nationwide labor unions represent workers (Bosch 1993; Harhoff and Kane 1996).

## Are Governments Ready to Let Industry Take Control of Training?

Unlike the federal and state governments in Germany, governments in most low- and middle-income countries are reluctant to give up control of vocational training. In Bahrain, Indonesia, Tanzania, and Tunisia, public training institutes are funded at least in part by special levies on employers. The case of Korea perhaps best illustrates how difficult it is for policymakers to relinquish control of vocational training to firms or private sector providers. Korea has had a "training promotion levy" for two decades. Its goal has been to induce employers to provide in-service training of specified type and duration to stipulated numbers of employees. The levy was introduced because of the government's belief that the private sector, left to itself, would not invest adequately in training. Even when it became apparent that the government's efforts had not succeeded in increasing training, or had done so at unsustainably high costs, the levy was not repealed. This is partly because public training institutions rely upon the levy for financing. The Korean government, known for hard-nosed evaluation of its own policies, decided to phase out the levy after more than 25 years of experimentation. It may prove difficult for other countries to do the same.

## Can Governments Finance both Vocational Education and Vocational Training?

If the government is not ready to give up control of vocational training, employers may be reluctant to provide and pay for it. This has been the experience of countries such as Egypt and Korea. Under these circumstances, the government will have to bear the costs of both components of the dual system: vocational education and vocational training.

METHODOLOGY. To determine the costs of both parts of the dual system in low- and middle-income countries, we adopt the following four-step methodology. First, we determine the (gross) cost of each component in Germany. In 1993 the unit costs of vocational training were US$17,700, and those of vocational education were US$3,300. Second, we calculate the ratio of these costs to the costs of (a) public secondary education and (b) public university education in Germany. For example, the ratio of secondary education costs to apprenticeship costs was about 1:7. Third, using these ratios and the actual costs of, alternatively, secondary and university education in selected low- and middle-income countries, we impute two sets of costs of the vocational training and education components. For example, we find that, using secondary education costs as the numeraire, the unit costs of vocational training in Korea in 1993 were US$15,300, and those of vocational education were US$2,900. The corresponding numbers for Indonesia were US$1,400 and US$300 respectively. Finally, we calculate the average of costs using secondary and university costs as the numeraire, and we impute the total costs for the dual system. In Egypt the total imputed cost for putting one trainee through a year of the dual system was about US$2,800.

COSTS OF VOCATIONAL TRAINING COMPONENT. Calculated using this methodology, the imputed costs of the vocational training component—which is borne by employers in Germany—is between US$13,700 and $US15,300 in Korea, between US$1,400 and US$2,400 in Indonesia, and between US$1,200 and US$3,500 in Egypt (table 19-10). Note that we have used gross costs of vocational training in Germany to impute the cost of this component in other countries. We do so to show the costs that governments must bear if employers are unwilling to shoulder the costs of apprenticeships, and because we are skeptical whether the methodology used by BIBB to value the net productivity of apprentices is reliable (or even feasible).

COSTS OF THE VOCATIONAL EDUCATION COMPONENT. The imputed cost of the vocational education component—which is borne by the state governments in Germany—falls between US$2,500 and US$2,900 in Korea, between US$300 and US$400 in Indonesia, and between US$200 and US$600 in Egypt. Since these costs are based on unit costs of vocational education in the German dual system where trainees usually attend school for one day each week, they are not full-time equivalent costs (which would be more than three times higher).

TOTAL COSTS OF THE DUAL SYSTEM. Averages of the vocational training and vocational education costs (estimates using secondary and university costs as numeraires) are summed to get the imputed unit cost of implementing the dual system in each of these countries. The averages are US$17,200 in Korea, US$2,300 in Indonesia, and US$2,800 in Egypt.

TABLE 19-10
Annual Unit Costs of Dual System Components, 1990–91
(thousands of U.S. dollars)

| Country | Training cost | | Vocational education cost | | Public cost of | | Dual system | GNP/ capita |
| | $I$ costs[b] | $II$ (1993) | $I$ | $II$ | Public secondary education | Public university education | | |
| --- | --- | --- | --- | --- | --- | --- | --- | --- |
| Germany | 17.7 | 17.7 | 3.3 | 3.3 | 2.26 | 6.00 | 21.0 | 23.56 |
| Korea[a] | 15.3 | 13.7 | 2.9 | 2.5 | 1.96 | 4.57 | 17.2 | 7.66 |
| Indonesia[a] | 1.4 | 2.4 | 0.3 | 0.4 | 0.18 | 0.80 | 2.3 | 0.74 |
| Egypt[a] | 1.2 | 3.5 | 0.2 | 0.6 | 0.15 | 1.15 | 2.8 | 0.66 |

a. Costs are imputed using German estimates of ratios of training and vocational education component costs to, alternatively: (I) secondary education costs, (II) public university costs.

b. Dual system unit costs are computed by adding up the average (of methods I and II) costs of training and vocational education.

*Source:* Egypt and Indonesia: World Bank data; Korea: KEDI (1994); Germany: Dicke, Glismann, and Siemben (1994), Harhoff and Kane (1996).

Assuming that the average dual program lasts a little more than three years, we impute the cost of putting an Indonesian trainee through the dual system at about US$7,000, which is identical to the cost of System Ganda reported in independent surveys (World Bank 1995). The annual unit cost of the dual system in Germany is roughly the same as Germany's per capita GNP, but this ratio is greater than two in Korea, three in Indonesia, and four in Egypt. The poorer the country, the greater will be the real burden of implementing a German-style dual system.

It is unlikely that the dual system can be imported by low- and middle-income countries, even with some adaptation and on a much less ambitious scale than in Germany, where two-thirds of labor force entrants come through the dual system. A critical look at the dual system, however, does reveal lessons that these countries can learn from Germany.

## Lessons for Other Countries

Developing countries often attribute Germany's low unemployment of youth and adequate supply of skilled workers to its dual system and are eager to replicate it. These countries frequently have a public vocational education system that is expensive, or irrelevant, or both. To improve the relevance of their vocational education, or to reduce public expenditures on it, they try to increase employers' involvement in the planning, financing, and delivery of vocational training. Adding a vocational training component based on the workplace while reducing the school-based vocational education segment is viewed as the obvious solution. Observing (correctly) that Germany has a system that combines vocational education with workplace training for almost two-thirds of its secondary school students, developing-country governments ask for German assistance in reforming their training systems to resemble the dual system. But it will be unsustainably expensive for these governments to transplant the dual system wholesale. The main reason is that their industrial structures and governmental attitudes are far different than Germany's.

In their preoccupation with importing the dual system, many developing countries may overlook its relevance to *any* system of vocational training. Two of the German dual system's fundamental attributes deserve special mention. First, government-financed, school-based instruction is not the centerpiece of the German dual system. In fact, it is a relatively recent addition to Germany's formal training mechanisms. Second, employer-financed training based in the workplace, nurtured but not dictated by government, is the mainstay of the German dual system. This is the product of both a longstanding tradition in the German *handwerk* sector and of current industrial labor relations.

### School-Based Vocational Education Is Important, but Not the Central Component

The foundations of the dual system lie not in school-based education but in apprenticeships that evolved over several centuries. School-based instruction is a relatively recent addition to the dual system: the growing sophistication in production technology required work-relevant but general skills. Initially, school-based instruction was informal, sometimes the extension of Sunday school. It was formalized by the Vocational Training Act of 1969, only a generation ago. In-school instruction remains the less important part of the dual system. It accounts for only about 25 percent of instruction time and expenses.

The Vocational Training Act recognized that because the aim was to provide general skills to future workers, vocational education should be financed by the taxpayer and not by individual employers. Although an elaborate set of rules stipulates that employers participate in reforming the subject matter of vocational school instruction, employers, in practice, are often indifferent to curriculum issues. This should not be surprising since the subject matter, although relevant to work, is in fact quite general.

The organization and control of vocational education are best left to the body that pays for the instruction. This is one of the most important lessons from Germany's experience. In the case of relatively general skills that are acquired in school, the paying entity would be the state and local governments. Another lesson relates to the sequence in which dual system components are introduced. In Germany the formal vocational education component came many years after the vocational training part had been formalized. Many countries trying to adopt the dual system reverse this sequence. For example, in Egypt, a formal apprenticeship system is being tacked on to a public vocational education program through the Mubarak-Kohl Initiative. Such efforts may yet bear fruit, but it would be naive to think that German trainers have any more expertise than others in successfully adding workplace training to a school-based vocational education system.

### Employers Control the Central Component: Vocational Training in the Workplace

The mainstay of the dual system is workplace training, and it is controlled by employers. This component has matured over a long period in Germany, and it continues to change as the industrial structure changes. Its importance may have lessened somewhat since the "dualization" of the German training system in the 1960s, but it still accounts for 75 percent of instruction time and resources. Today adaptability rather than mastery of specific skills is increasingly valued in workers. Despite the pressure this change has brought to bear on vocational training, it remains the critical component of the dual system.

Although the government provides a broad regulatory framework within which dual system trainees and employers interact, individual employers pay for and decide which skills are taught, and employers' associations (regional chambers) decide how skills are tested and certified. The legal system gives labor unions a voice in training matters, and the government provides some advice, but employers decide the details, and whether to offer apprenticeships in the first place. In Germany 10 percent of all firms in the industry and commerce sector and 45 percent in the trade and crafts sector do not offer apprenticeship opportunities at all. Neither these firms nor the ones that do offer apprenticeships are coerced into offering training. When firms and students voluntarily decide to sign an apprenticeship agreement, training advisors paid by the regional chamber of business (*industrie* or *handwerk*) of which the firm is a member—not the government—determine whether the firm is capable of delivering training of a sufficiently high standard. Again, the government does not determine apprenticeship wages, which are occupation specific.

Perhaps the most important lesson is that job-specific training is financed and organized by employers who have a vested interest in ensuring that relevant skills are taught and taught cost effectively. This training is usually provided in the workplace, either in formal training sessions or on the job. If a firm chooses to offer an apprenticeship, it is examined to determine if it has the facilities needed to train the apprentice effectively. This examination, however, is by employers' associations and not by the government. In their efforts to adopt the German dual system, developing countries have violated this principle. Governments, not employers, appear to take the lead in organizing and financing vocational training. Another important feature in Germany is the complete absence of coercion. Participation in the system is voluntary. Even some firms that are "qualified" to offer apprenticeships do not do so. And employers are under no obligation to retain trainees upon completion of the dual program. In fact, fewer than half do. Developing-country governments that are trying to adopt the dual system on the one hand and using coercive measures (such as minimum training requirements or levies) on the other should be warned that this is inconsistent with the German dual system.

Vocational tracking is no less expensive than higher education, and it is not used by governments to divert students from higher education. The annual unit cost of dual system training is roughly equal to Germany's per capita GNP (close to US$25,000). Our simulations indicate that while the absolute unit cost would be lower than this in developing countries, it would be higher as a proportion of per capita GNP. For a middle-income country such as Korea, this ratio could be higher than two. For a low-income country such as Egypt, it may be as high as four. Another yardstick is the share of GNP spent on the dual system: the total cost of the dual system was over DM67 billion in 1993, or more than 2 percent of GNP. In developing countries the entire education budget is generally 4 percent of GNP. It is also noteworthy that costs of in-firm training increased much faster than education costs in Germany between 1972 and 1993, and this may in part be the reason for the system coming under stress in recent years.

The dual system is not an instrument to keep students out of higher education, which is almost entirely at taxpayers' expense. While a large share of dual system graduates enter the labor force, many go on for higher education either immediately or after working a few years. A growing number of junior secondary school graduates choose the academic track and head for college. In the 1950s, only 5 percent of a graduating high school class obtained the necessary academic diploma (*Abitur*); the predicted percentage for 2000 was 40 percent. Recent reforms have made it even easier for graduates of the dual system to go on to university. Conversely, higher education does not rule out subsequent participation in dual system training. In 1995 more than 5 percent of dual system participants had a university diploma.

Not cheap in any setting, the dual system is likely to be the most expensive in the poorest countries. The social costs of effective dual system training are higher than for university education. Vocational tracking could be effective in keeping high school graduates from pursuing costly higher education, but this is certainly not the case in Germany, where there is no significant difference in costs. Participation in the dual system does not preclude a person from going on for higher studies, and as the economy has become more complex and technological change has escalated, the general education level of dual system entrants has risen significantly. Germany's experience clearly shows that when the mix between general education and job-specific training is determined by employers and workers (who presumably care the most about the costs and returns to these investments), the importance of general education increases.

## Notes

1. Countries as diverse as Kazakhstan, Lebanon, Tanzania, and the United States have seriously considered adopting this system. See chapters 5 and 13 in this volume and Lynch (1994).

2. The Federal Labor Office—through its state and local bureaus—provides information on training and job opportunities, helps mediate training demand and supply, provides financial support for training special groups (such as girls, foreigners, and dropouts), and carries out research. It also finances special efforts such as the "Qualifications Offensive," which was launched in 1986 in response to

increased unemployment of youth. The Federal Labor Office exhorted employers to offer more training.

3. Works counselors and shop stewards supervise vocational training at the firm level. In 1990 about 75 percent of works counselors were members of unions affiliated with the German Federation of Trade Unions. This supervision is usually limited to large firms. There is no such coordination at the company level in small enterprises.

4. For this reason, the attractiveness of the dual system was probably weakened by the reform of the labor laws in 1986. The reform allowed firms to hire workers on fixed-term contracts for up to 18 months and to fire them during this period without the usual (high) dismissal costs (Harhoff and Kane 1996).

5. Soskice (1994) reports that the annual net costs in the *handwerk* sector are about DM7,250 per trainee, about half the cost of training in *industrie* sector firms with more than 1,000 employees.

6. Dicke, Glismann, and Siemben (1994) attribute the equilibrium of the German dual system largely to the highly regulated labor markets. Regulations and collectively bargained work contracts help explain wage differentials between unskilled and skilled labor and the uniform relative changes of these wages over time.

## References

Abraham, K., and S. Houseman. 1993. "Job Security in America: Lessons from Germany." Working paper. Washington, D.C.: The Brookings Institution Press.

Assad, Ragui. 1991. "Structure of Egypt's Construction Labor Market and its Development since the Mid-1970s." In Heba Handoussa and Gillian Potter, eds., *Employment and Structural Adjustment: Egypt in the 1990s.* Study prepared for the International Labour Office. Cairo: American University Press.

Bosch, Gerhard. 1993. "Vocational Training and Changes in Patterns of Labor Relations in Germany." In Gilles Laflamme, ed., *Vocational Training: International Perspectives.* Geneva: International Labour Office, Training Department.

Dicke, Hugo, Hans Glismann, and Sönke Siemben. 1994. "Vocational Training in Germany." Working Paper 622. Kiel, Germany: Kiel Institute of World Economics.

*The Economist.* 1994. "Education in Germany: The Next Generation." August 20, p. 44.

————. 1996. "Training and Jobs: What Works?" April 6, pp.19–21.

Federal Ministry of Education. 1995. *Basic and Structural Data, 1994/95.* Bonn.

Hall, Robert E. 1978. "The Importance of Lifetime Jobs in the United States Economy." *American Economic Review* 72:716–24.

Handoussa, Heba, and Gillian Potter. 1991. *Employment and Structural Adjustment: Egypt in the 1990s.* Study prepared for the International Labour Office. Cairo: American University Press.

Harhoff, Dietmar, and Thomas Kane. 1996. "Is the German Apprenticeship System a Panacea for the U.S. Labor Market?" Working Paper 1311. London: Center for Economic Policy Research.

ILO (International Labour Office). various years. *Yearbook of Labor Statistics*. Geneva.

Jeong, Jooyeon. 1995. "The Failure of Recent State Vocational Training Policies in Korea from a Comparative Perspective." *British Journal of Industrial Relations* 33(2): 237–52.

KEDI (Korean Educational Development Institute). 1994. *Educational Indicators in Korea.* Seoul.

Laflamme, Gilles. 1993. *Vocational Training: International Perspectives.* Geneva: International Labour Office, Training Department.

Lynch, Lisa, ed. 1994. *Training and the Private Sector: International Comparisons.* Chicago: University of Chicago Press.

Maurice, Marc. 1993. "The Link between the Firm and the Educational System in Vocational Training: The Cases of France, Germany, and Japan." In Gilles Laflamme, ed., *Vocational Training: International Perspectives.* Geneva: International Labour Office, Training Department.

Ministry of Education (Egypt). 1995. *Mubarak's National Project: Educational Achievements in Four Years.* Cairo.

Nachrowi, D., J. Dwiantini, and C. Bea Dwiswati. 1995. "Labor Market Issues in Indonesia: An Analysis in a Globalization Context." *Journal of Population* 1(1). Published by the Demographic Institute, Faculty of Economics, University of Indonesia.

OECD (Organization for Economic Cooperation and Development). 1993. *Employment Outlook.* Paris.

Schmidt, Hermann, and Laszlo Alex. 1995. "The Dual System of Vocational Education and Training in Germany." Briefing Note 3. National Council on Education, Paul Hamlyn Foundation.

Soskice, David. 1994. "Reconciling Markets and Institutions: The German Apprenticeship System." In Lisa Lynch, ed., *Training and the Private Sector: International Comparisons.* Chicago: The University of Chicago Press.

Steedman, Hilary. 1993. "The Economics of Youth Training in Germany." *Economic Journal* 103:1279–91.

Timmermann, Dieter. 1993. "Costs and Financing Dual Training in Germany: Is There any Lesson for Other Countries?" Paper submitted to the International Symposium on the Economics of Education, May 18-21, Manchester, United Kingdom.

World Bank. 1995. "Training and the Labor Market in Indonesia: Policies for Productivity Gains and Employment Growth." Report 14413-IND. Washington, D.C.

# Contributors

Alan Abrahart, a consultant to the World Bank, has helped develop and implement vocational education and training strategies in the former Soviet Union, the Middle East, East Asia, and Bosnia and Herzegovina. As a senior executive with the Australian government, he formulated employment, education, and training policies. His experience covers many areas of public sector reform, among them industrial relations.

Arvil Van Adams is a sector manager for human development in the Africa Region of the World Bank. He is a former professor of economics and education policy at the George Washington University in Washington, D.C. His areas of specialization include education, training, and employment policy. He is currently studying African labor markets with a focus on real wage movements and household labor adjustments to economic shocks.

Wim Alberts joined the World Bank in 1992 and since then has prepared the vocational education and training components of the Bank's education portfolio in Angola, Eritrea, Ghana, Liberia, Malawi, Mozambique, Sierra Leone, and Zambia. The main focus of these assignments has been to make vocational education and training systems more responsive to labor markets. He holds degrees in social-economic history from the University of Utrecht and development economics from the Free University in Amsterdam.

Victor Billeh is the director of UNESCO's regional office in Beirut. He was the president of the National Center for Human Resources Development in Jordan. He holds a Ph.D. in science education from the University of Wisconsin. He has taught at the American University of Beirut, Lebanon, and served as director of the Education Department and the dean of arts and sciences at Yarmouk University, Jordan. He was also a general educator at the World Bank in the East Asia Education Division, and the dean of graduate studies and research at Yarmouk University.

Amit Dar is currently an economist in the Social Protection Unit of the Human Development Network at the World Bank. He has worked extensively on issues related to labor markets and vocational education and training in Brazil, Egypt, Indonesia, Jamaica, Laos, Nigeria, Tanzania, and Zambia. He has a Ph.D. in economics from Brown University.

Alejandra Cox Edwards is a professor of economics at California State University, Long Beach. She has written books and journal articles on a wide range of issues in labor economics. Her contribution to this book was made when she was a senior economist at the World Bank. She completed her undergraduate education in Santiago, Chile, and has a Ph.D. in economics from the University of Chicago.

Peter Fallon is currently principal economist in the Economic Policy Group of the Poverty Reduction and Economic Management Network at the World Bank. After receiving his Ph.D. in economics from the London School of Economics, he taught economics at the University of Sussex from 1976 until 1988. He then joined the World Bank's Southern Africa Department where he served as country economist for Lesotho, Swaziland, and later South Africa. A specialist in labor economics, he has worked in many countries including India, China, Sudan, Zimbabwe, Malawi, Mozambique, Tanzania, Angola, and Ukraine. In addition to making numerous contributions on labor issues within the Bank, he has co-authored a book on labor economics and written several articles in journals and books of readings.

Fred Fluitman is an economist who joined the International Labour Office in 1972. He worked in Zambia and Ethiopia before being assigned to ILO headquarters in Geneva in 1976. Since February 1999 he has been on secondment to the ILO's International Training Centre in Turin, Italy, where he is in charge of the employment and skills development program.

Indermit Gill is currently the lead economist for human development in the World Bank's Latin America and Caribbean Region. This book was written while he was a labor economist in the Poverty and Social Policy Department of the World Bank, during which time he worked in Malaysia, Egypt, Bahrain, West Bank and Gaza, Ethiopia, Eritrea, Argentina, and Chile. He has since served as a country economist in the Brazil Country Management Unit based in Brasilia. Before joining the World Bank in 1993, he taught at the State University of New York at Buffalo and the University of Chicago. He has a Ph.D. in economics from the University of Chicago.

Martin Godfrey is a consultant who specializes in issues related to labor markets, education, and training. He has advised a variety of international and bilateral organizations.

Peter Grootings, a social scientist from the Netherlands, is an expert on Central and Eastern Europe. As a freelance education and labor market analyst since the beginning of the 1990s, he has assisted governments in the design, implementation, and evaluation of vocational education and training reforms. He also has advised many international organizations and published widely. Since 1994 he has lived in Poland.

Stephen Heyneman is currently vice president at International Management and Development and was previously at the World Bank. He is an expert on issues related to education and vocational education and training, and he has published extensively in these fields. He has also provided technical advice to governments on these issues in many countries around the world.

Gordon Hunting is a consultant who has worked extensively on issues related to vocational education and training in different regions of the world.

Chon Sun Ihm is currently a professor and dean of humanities at Sejong University in Korea. He has worked extensively on analyzing VET systems in developing and industrialized nations and has served as consultant to the OECD, World Bank, UNESCO, and other international organizations. Before joining the faculty at Sejong University, he served in the Korean Educational Development Institute. He studied economics and education as an undergraduate and graduate student at the University of California at Berkeley and Harvard University. He also visited as a fellow at the Institute of Education, London University.

Richard Johanson is an education and training specialist. During his 18 years at the World Bank from 1969 to 1987, he was chief of the education divisions for the Asia and Latin America and the Caribbean regions as well as senior adviser for education on the operations policy staff. From 1988 to 1992 he was chief of vocational training for the International Labour Organisation in Geneva, where he later served as senior adviser on human resources. As a private consultant he developed the Management and Financial Training Project for the World Bank in Russia in 1994 and the Higher Education Reform Program in Hungary in 1997. Since then he has analyzed vocational training and higher education for the World Bank in Bangladesh and for the Asian Development Bank in the Philippines.

Mari Minowa is a labor economist for the World Bank in the Human Development Department, Latin America and the Caribbean Region. She has managed vocational education and training projects in several Latin American countries. Her current work focuses on public works programs.

Haneen Sayed is an adviser to the executive director for the Middle East Region at the World Bank. She was formerly in the East Asia Region at the Bank where she worked extensively on education and training issues. She is a graduate of Stanford University and Columbia University. Before joining the World Bank, she taught at Barnard College and Fordham University.

Hong W. Tan is the principal economist in the Business Environment Unit of the World Bank's Private Sector Development Department. He has specialized in worker training and industrial development, primarily in East Asia and Latin America. His current research interests are training policy, social safety nets and labor market adjustment, technological change, and skills development.

Zafiris Tzannatos is the manager for social protection in the Middle East and North Africa Region of the World Bank. He also is the leader of the Bank's program on child labor. For more than 15 years he taught in Britain, where he is an honorary research fellow at a number of universities. He has advised numerous international organizations and been widely published.

Adrian Ziderman, formerly a senior economist at the World Bank, is professor of economics and education at Bar-Ilan University in Israel. He also is the editor of the *International Journal of Manpower*. He is a specialist in labor market economics and the economics of education. His current research interests lie in three main areas: the economics and evaluation of vocational education and training; university finance (including student loan schemes); and labor market participation of female workers and the effects of participation gaps.

# Index

Note: *b* indicates boxes; *f* indicates figures; and *t* indicates tables.

private VET providers in, 26
public expenditures on primary/
secondary education, 81*t*
retraining programs in, 19*b*
school enrollment at different
education levels, 78*t*
school leavers' labor market status after leaving school, 76*t*
stakeholders in VET, 90–91
VET and the labor market,
81–82
VET and other education types,
80–81
VET assessment and certification, 83–84
VET costs and financing, 83
VET curricula and delivery
reforms, 88–90
VET issues and reforms, 85–93
VET management/funding
reforms, 87–88
VET organization/management,
82–83
VET reforms in, 92*b*
VET structural/organizational
reforms, 86
VET system in, 77–85
vocational education in, 80–84
wages and salaries in, 74–75
Poverty Survey, South Africa, 342
Pre-employment training
management of, 14*b*
successful financing models of,
33
Preliminary Examination for College
Entrance, Korea, 272
Presidential Commission on Educa-
tional Reform, Korea, 274, 278,
283–84, 285–88
Presidential Decree against
Privatization of Educational Estab-
lishments, Russian Federation, 131
Private providers, VET, 22, 26–29

balanced funding formulas for,
26, 28
relevant employment growth
and, 28
successful models of, 34
transparent laws for, 26, 27*b*
universal accreditation and, 28
unplanned public provision and,
28–29
Private sector employment, high open
unemployment and, 10, 12
Productive Family Program, Egypt,
406
Productivity and Vocational Training
Department (PVTD), Egypt's
Ministry of Industry, 405, 411,
422, 424
Providers, VET. *See also* Private
providers
competition among, 24–25
private, 22, 26–29
Public Administration College,
Hungary, 59
Public Education Act (1993),
Hungary, 46
Public Employment Service, Czech
Republic, 102–3
Public training program controls,
Czech model for, 108
Pulay, Gyula, 54
Pusat Giat MARA, Malaysia, 222

Qualifications Act (1995), South
Africa, 356–57
Qualifications Authority, South Africa,
357

Reform issues, 22–32
dual VET systems, 23, 29–32
political will and, 34–35
VET organization, 22, 23–26
VET private providers, 22,
26–29